Iberian Moorings

THE MIDDLE AGES SERIES

Ruth Mazo Karras, Series Editor

Edward Peters, Founding Editor

A complete list of books in the series
is available from the publisher.

IBERIAN MOORINGS

Al-Andalus, Sefarad, and the Tropes of Exceptionalism

Ross Brann

PENN

UNIVERSITY OF PENNSYLVANIA PRESS

PHILADELPHIA

Published by
University of Pennsylvania Press
Philadelphia, Pennsylvania 19104-4112
www.upenn.edu/pennpress

Printed in the United States of America on acid-free paper
1 3 5 7 9 10 8 6 4 2

A Cataloging-in-Publication record is available from the Library of Congress
ISBN 978-0-8122-5288-0

For EMY, my one and only

Contents

Preface

Although I did not know it at the time, my research for this book began in the years leading up to 1992, which marked the quincentenary of the end of al-Andalus, the expulsion of the Jews of Sefarad, and Christopher Columbus's first voyage to the so-called New World. I began receiving flyers, notices, and invitations to numerous academic and public conferences, colloquia, symposia, and exhibitions in the United States, Spain, Morocco, Israel, Iran, and Pakistan. I participated in a select few of these proceedings and published a comparative study of paradigmatic Andalusi Arabic and Hebrew laments. In the process, I created a substantial archival file to preserve all the materials that had found their way to me in the lead-up to and execution of the celebratory and critical commemorations taking place and the publications, catalogs, and films that appeared in 1992. Then I moved on to other projects.

In the ensuing years, I read some of the major publications produced during the quincentenary. I soon came to realize that the meanings ascribed to the events of 1492 and 1992 were informed by cultural tropes going back to tenth-century Córdoba and that these tropes left lasting imprints on Islamic, Jewish, and Spanish culture. As far as its significance for the history of the Mediterranean is concerned, 1992 might have come and gone with less notice than it received without the enduring sense that al-Andalus, Sefarad, and Spain were different, distinctive, and exceptional. The origin, early history, trajectory, and agency of that exigent trope are the subject of this book.

Acknowledgments

I have many people and institutions to thank for assisting me in countless ways in the research, writing, and now, at long last, publication of this book. First among them all is Jerome Singerman, Senior Humanities Editor of the University of Pennsylvania Press. I am deeply indebted to Jerry, a prince among senior editors and a boon companion in humanistic and practical wisdom, for supporting this project and patiently guiding me throughout its long incubation. Lily Palladino and Noreen O'Connor-Abel, expert managing editors at the Press, and Janice Meyerson, my manuscript's skilled copyeditor, were instrumental in improving the book. My sincere thanks to Melissa Hyde, who skillfully prepared the index. Each of these individuals set a standard for professionalism. It was a pleasure to work with them.

I am deeply appreciative of the Frankel Center for Advanced Judaic Studies at the University of Michigan, Ann Arbor, for providing me the opportunity to participate among the fellows assembled during the 2018–2019 academic year to interrogate "Sefardic Identities." In particular, I thank Ryan Szpiech, who served as the intellectually dynamic organizer and lead fellow of our research group, and the vibrant director of the Frankel Center, Jeffrey Veidlinger, along with the center's uncommonly gracious staff. My daily and weekly interactions with Ehud Krinis, Moshe Yagur, and Sarah Pearce among the center's fellows were immensely beneficial. Among the fellows Marc Herman and Martin Jacobs, in particular, provided me with new leads and references.

Although I completed the research and writing for this book at the University of Michigan, I am indebted to various people at Cornell University. My academic home in the Department of Near Eastern Studies provides me with interdisciplinary intellectual stimulation regarding virtually every facet of Near/Middle Eastern studies from well before the historical record through the modern period; and the NES department's dedicated office staff is simply without peer in supporting my advising, teaching, and research endeavors.

For this project my colleague Munther Younes stood out as an invaluable resource on account of his encyclopedic knowledge of the Arabic language through its history. Ziad Fahmy, my department chair, also answered a query about an odd Egyptian Arabic term in a modern bibliographical reference. So too, I thank my graduate students Rama Alhabian (now Dr. Alhabian) and Kiley Foster for their penetrating questions and comments in seminars and during office hours and through their own lucid research and writing. Cornell University Olin librarians Ali Houissa and Patrick Stevens are incomparable magicians when it comes to finding the textual resources I needed. Finally, the Department of Near Eastern Studies, Cornell University, subsidized the University of Pennsylvania Press's publication of this book.

Among the many colleagues, some former students, who advised or assisted me on various matters I thank Esperanza Alfonso, Mercedes García-Arenal, Peter Cole, Jonathan Decter, Susan Einbinder, Rachid El Hour, Sharon Kinoshita, Joseph Lowry, David Nirenberg, Tova Rosen, Jessica Streit, and Kenneth Wolf, each of whom graciously answered the call with my questions and requests. I also gratefully acknowledge the Press's two blind readers for their initial comments. I am indebted to the reviewer that read the completed manuscript and offered an especially valuable critique that I endeavored to follow as best I could.

Talks from the book in progress at various academic institutions including Ben-Gurion University of the Negev, Consejo Superior de Investigaciones Científicas, CUNY, Emory University, Johns Hopkins University, Kings College London, NEH Summer Institute (The Mediterranean Seminar, Barcelona), NYU Abu-Dhabi, Princeton, UC Berkeley, University of Colorado, University of Connecticut, the University of Minnesota, University of Toronto, University of Washington, University of Wisconsin-Madison, and Yale, assisted me in framing and refining my thoughts. A precis of the project, "Andalusi Exceptionalism," appeared in *A Sea of Languages: Rethinking the Arabic Role in Medieval Literary History*, edited by Suzanne Conklin Akbari and Karla Mallette (Toronto: University of Toronto Press, 2013), 119–134. Parts of Chapter 2 and Chapter 4 appeared in preliminary form in "Competing Tropes of Eleventh Century Andalusi Jewish Culture," in *Ot LeTova: Essays in Honor of Professor Tova Rosen*, edited by Eli Yassif, Haviva Ishay, and Uriah Kfir [*Mikan 11/El Prezente 6*] (Be'er Sheba: Heksherim Research Center and the Department of Hebrew Literature, Ben-Gurion University and the Gaon Center for Ladino Culture, 2012), 7–26.

After I had completed writing this book and delivered it to the Press, two of my senior academic mentors sadly passed away. Frank Peters of NYU broke the mold for irrepressible wit and brilliance; Isaac Kramnick of Cornell inspired me with his incomparable intellect, educational vision, and humanity. I miss their wisdom, their humor, their friendship.

My immediate family, Eileen, Amir, Allon, Leah, and Talia, are sources of endless inspiration for me. In particular, Talia's scintillating intellectual curiosity and luminosity are wondrous to behold. I dedicate this labor of devotion for al-Andalus and Sefarad to my one and only love and partner for life, Eileen Yagoda, whose tolerant embrace of my eccentricities and idiosyncrasies is legendary.

Introduction

Andalusi and Sefardi Exceptionalism as Tropes of Islamic and Jewish Culture

> The Andalusis are found to have a sharpness of intellect, a nimbleness of body, and a receptivity for instruction such as no one else has.
>
> —Ibn Khaldūn (d. 1406)

> His land [Sefarad] is the "Garden of God."
>
> —Judah al-Ḥarizi (d. 1225)

> But then Spain, as everyone knows, is a peculiar place.
>
> —Yosef Hayyim Yerushalmi

Al-Andalus, conventionally called "Islamic Spain" or "Muslim Spain,"[1] is regularly identified by scholars and celebrated in popular culture as the site of an extraordinary period of dynamic social interaction, cultural ferment, creativity, and transfer among the Muslims, Christians, and Jews of the medieval Iberian Peninsula. And Sefarad, the Hebrew name for Iberia since late antiquity, is likewise widely remembered in scholarship and in public discourse for its acclaimed "Golden Age" of Jewish culture. Modern scholars and writers were, however, not the first to cast the medieval Iberian Peninsula in an uncommonly positive light. European historians of "medieval Spain," early modern Sefardi Ottoman intellectuals, Ashkenazi Jewish *maskilim*, German Jewish historians of the *Wissenschaft des Judentums* school, and Turkish and Arab historians enchanted by the glories of al-Andalus past or the "Golden Age of the Jews of Spain," all signed on to early versions of this cultural project. They designated al-Andalus or Sefarad as a place where exceptional social and religious tolerance prevailed and produced far-reaching intellectual and cultural achievement. Subsequent historians, critical theorists, intellectual and literary historians, and literary and cinematic artists have been inspired by the singular social, intellectual, or artistic merits of Hispania, Sefarad, and al-Andalus.[2] Al-Andalus and Sefarad have long since metabolized and come to constitute tropes of culture with histories of their own, fertilized and constructed by the interface of memory and the history constructed from it, the literary imagination, and geographical desire.[3]

The tropes persisted as powerful and comforting, if nostalgic, signs of Andalusi-ness and Sefardi-ness, even when al-Andalus and Sefarad were no more. Two illustrations should suffice. An early sixteenth-century Morisco collection of apocryphal hadiths celebrates the "virtues of al-Andalus" for that beleaguered community.[4] As for Sefarad following the expulsion of the Jews from Spain, the great courtier, communal leader, biblical exegete, and philosopher Isaac Abravanel (1437–1508) rendered his former land and its people at the center of Jewish history. For Abravanel, the recurrent cycle of domicile and exile that is the stuff of Jewish history led from Jerusalem directly to Sefarad: "For the portion of God is His people . . . and that was the exile of Jerusalem in Spain while it dwells in the land of its abode. . . . This [is] what the Holy One had in His world. . . . From where the sun rises to where it sets, from north to south, the likes of it never was before, a people treasured for praise, renown, and glory in its beauty and graciousness, and after it there will be no other like it."[5] The royal charter of expulsion was dated March 31, 1492, but not issued until the very end of April.[6] Small wonder, then, that in a potent gesture to Sefardi "exceptionalism," tradition followed Abravanel and dated the exile not to July 31, in accordance with the edict, but to August 2, coinciding with the Ninth of Av in the Jewish liturgical calendar.[7] That was the very day rabbinic tradition assigned to the destruction of the Temple in Jerusalem by the Babylonians in the early sixth century BCE and the Romans' leveling of the Second Temple in the first century CE and the exiles associated with these events.

What with the tropes' temporal staying power and geographic diffusion and numerous modern enthusiasts and critics, it is essential to consider how Andalusi Muslims and Jews originally conceived of, depicted, and subsequently remembered the place and evoked their cultures. Indeed, the tropes of Andalusi and Sefardi exceptionalism familiar from historiography, literature, and popular culture are not modern inventions at all but a reassertion and recalibration of Islamic and Jewish traditions going back to the tenth century.

Spain by Any Other Name

As much as Hispania, al-Andalus, and Sefarad were assuredly the names of a place, the names given to the Iberian Peninsula by Christians, Muslims, and Jews, respectively, they also were constituted as ideas. Like all ideas, they have a history of their own in which the toponyms were and remain overlapping, interrelated, and competing signs. As places as well as ideas, al-Andalus and Sefarad followed similar, if not entirely shared, historical trajectories. From the mid-tenth through the early thirteenth centuries, al-Andalus and its polity and Sefarad and its community were integral players in the western Mediterranean. Over the course of those centuries, al-Andalus and Sefarad concurrently experienced social maturation and political development and produced outstanding cultural achievements. Disruption and transformation followed, in each case. By contrast, the toponym España does not appear until the thirteenth century, under King Alfonso el Sabio of Castile. But "Spain," in the early modern geopolitical but not yet fully national sense, would not come into existence until 1469, when Ferdinand and Isabella consolidated power by unifying the kingdoms of Aragon and Castile. Subsequently, they conquered Naṣrid Granada in 1492, the last remnant of an Islamic polity on the Iberian Peninsula.[8]

Nevertheless, Spanish historiography, informed by modern nationalism, especially in its most conservative configurations, has long projected the idea of "Spain" retroactively to incorporate Roman and Visigothic Hispania at the beginning of an unbroken national history going back to late antiquity. From this perspective, it is as though five centuries of Islamic rule over the better part of the peninsula, eight hundred years of an Islamic presence there, and extensive rivalry and division between the monarchies of León, Navarre, Castile, and Aragon were historical imaginaries detracting from the eternal essence that was and is Spain.[9] In so doing, nationalist historians frequently deployed the striking tribute to the land authored by Isidore of Seville (d. 636) in the prologue to his *History of the Kings of the Goths*. The earliest statement of Hispania's exceptionalism, it established the genre of *Laudes*

Hispanae ("In Praise of Spain") that would inspire other writers down to the Renaissance:

> Of all lands from the west to the Indies, you, Spain, O sacred and always fortunate mother of princes and peoples, are the most beautiful. Rightly are you now queen of all provinces, from which not only the west but also the east borrows its shining lights. You are the pride and the ornament of the world, the more illustrious part of the earth, in which the Getic people are gloriously prolific, rejoicing much and flourishing greatly.
>
> Indulgent nature has deservedly enriched you with an abundance of everything fruitful. You are rich in olives, overflowing with grapes, fertile with harvests. You are dressed in grain,[10] you are shaded by olive trees, you are covered with the vine. Your fields are full of flowers, your mountains full of trees, and your shores full of fish. You are located in the most favourable region in the world; neither are you parched by the summer heat of the sun, nor do you languish under icy cold, but girded by a temperate band of sky, you are nourished by fertile west winds. You bring forth the fruits of the fields, the wealth of the mines, and beautiful and useful plants and animals. Nor are you to be held inferior in rivers, which the brilliant fame of your fair flocks ennobles.[11]

By contrast, the so-called *Mozarabic Chronicle of 754*, the earliest extant Latin account focusing on Iberia and the events of 711, accentuates the country's lavish affluence in the form of its luxury commodities rather than the lushness and abundance of the land. The *Chronicle*'s urban perspective identifies Córdoba as "always the most opulent of cities."[12]

Isidore posits a continuous narrative of life on a land uniquely favored by God, connecting Roman Hispania to the Visigothic kingdom of his era. His admiring readers would later extend this uninterrupted narrative to Christian resistance to Islamic power in the form of the "Reconquista" (beginning in Toledo, 1085) and subsequently to the ascendancy of the "Catholic Monarchs" Ferdinand and Isabella in the late fifteenth century down to the modern period. In any case, the cultural historian is obliged to eschew the still-common anachronism of "medieval Spain." Otherwise, we would be forced to speak of the Jews or Muslims "of Spain"—the name of the modern nation-state—when referring to these other religious communities and earlier periods in peninsular history when Islamic sovereignty prevailed in al-Andalus and the Jews of al-Andalus were integrated into the dominant Islamic society and fully acculturated into its Arabic milieu.

What's in a Name, and How Did It Get There?

The Muslims and Jews had their own names in their own languages for Iberia and developed their own constructions of their place in that land. What, exactly, is in a name? A great deal, it turns out. Al-Andalus and Sefarad were customarily the names by which Muslims and Jews of the Iberian Peninsula referred to their homeland.[13] But as signifiers, these toponyms also could serve its inhabitants' sense of provincialism, chauvinism, or outsiders' notion of its otherness. For example, in a paper on the Coptic origins of the toponym "al-Andalus," Federico Corriente observed that "in the old times nothing good was expected in the East from the western lands and people, as only the East and its people played the leading roles in history and culture, and were held in high esteem. This could possibly only stem from an old dislike and even enmity felt by Egyptians towards a part of the world whence they never expected or received anything good, to the point of placing Hades there."[14] This ancient and late antique prejudice toward the West was transmitted to and absorbed by residents of the Islamic East, as we will discover in the sources discussed in Chapter 1.

Naturally, inhabitants of the western Mediterranean did not share the easterners' view of their domain. Like people of other places and times and their coreligionists in other lands, Andalusi Muslims and Jews displayed attachment to and pride in their native country, regardless of, or as a consequence of, how outsiders represented it and portrayed them. One finds abundant occasional expressions of pride in *waṭan* (Ar., "homeland") related to Andalusi and Sefardi origins, customs, traditions, and scientific and cultural production. For example, as a rabbinic scholar and jurist in Egypt, Moses Maimonides (1138–1204) occasionally expresses his admiration for and indebtedness to his Andalusi Jewish teachers. He famously utilized the phrase *ʿindanā fī l-andalus* or *ʿindanā fī l-maghrib* (lit., "at our place in al-Andalus" or "at our place in the West"; but more idiomatically, "back home in al-Andalus" or "back home in the West") to identify religious practices and rabbinic interpretations specific to the Andalusi Jewish traditions in which he was reared and which he zealously embraced his entire life.[15] Maimonides also singled out for approval Andalusi Jewish religious thinkers and Andalusi Muslim mathematicians and scientists, respectively, in *Guide of the Perplexed*, his theological and philosophical masterpiece: "As for the Andalusians among our nation, all of them cling to the affirmations of the philosophers and incline to their opinions, insofar as these do not ruin the foundation of the Law. You will not find them in any way taking the paths of the Mutakallimūn."[16] . . . "Then came latter-day groups of people in Andalusia who became very proficient in mathematics and explained, conforming to Ptolemy's premises, that Venus and Mercury were above the sun. In fact, Ibn Aflaḥ of Sevilla, whose son I have met, has written a celebrated book about this. Thereupon the excellent philosopher Abū Bakr ibn al-Ṣa'igh, under the guidance of one of his pupils, I have read texts reflected on this notion."[17] The second quotation lends credence to S. D. Goitein's observation that attachment to *waṭan* in classical Islamdom could transcend the boundaries of religious community.[18]

Anna Akasoy views Maimonides' attachment to his homeland and devotion to its intellectual traditions as comparable with that of the great Sufi master Ibn al-ʿArabī (1165–1240) from Murcia, who commented on the sharp differences he observed between Sufis in the Islamic West and East: "He recounts how on his arrival in the East he met a group of Ṣūfīs who lived in a lofty building and wore ostentatious clothes instead of leading simple lives. They claimed that the Ṣūfīs of the West were the people of the truth [*ḥaqīqa*], whereas they were people of the method or path [*ṭarīqa*]. Ibn ʿArabī dismissed such talk as nonsense since truth required method, and he criticized them for their ignorance and their vanity—something which could not be found among their Western brothers."[19] For his part, Ibn Rushd (d. 1198), the great Andalusi Islamic jurist and philosopher, sketches with evident satisfaction the traits of the inhabitants of "this peninsula" in his commentary on Aristotle's *Meteorology*.[20] Such expressions of regional pride or affirmation of one's countrymen's correct opinions appear to be especially prominent among Andalusi travelers away from home. Whether, like Ibn al-ʿArabī, they sought spiritual refreshment or, like Maimonides, were refugees, they were sensitive to social and cultural differences that they encountered in other lands.[21]

Yet al-Andalus and Sefarad were neither simply toponyms nor only the subjects of conventional expressions of attachment to and pride in homeland of the universal sort displayed in other Islamic lands and their Jewish communities. As signs with histories of their own, the toponyms al-Andalus and Sefarad also absorbed and conveyed cultural meaning that was constructed, transmitted, recalled, and re-envisioned. This study traces that process of investing the place names with cultural significance. It also observes how the dynamic nature of history disrupted the stability of the terms and ideas of al-Andalus and Sefarad, whose singularity and indispensability were recalibrated to suit social and political changes engulfing their respective communities. Leading Muslim and Jewish figures and intellectuals infused the ideas of al-Andalus and Sefarad with programmatic, ideologically minded entitlements conferring legitimacy, privilege, and authority upon their inhabitants and bestowing various forms of exceptionality upon them. If we consider Islamic al-Andalus and Jewish Sefarad within the realm of ideas and as signifiers, we can draw useful distinctions "between the *lived* on the one hand and the *perceived* and the *conceived* on the other" as Henri Lefebvre theorizes it.[22] Cultural tropes such as ours originate in the latter sphere and infiltrate the former.

What, exactly, were the major themes that Muslim and Jewish political, communal, religious, and literary elites conceived in representing al-Andalus and Sefarad as unique and extraordinary, the material that constituted the trope and defined the significance of these toponyms? During late classical Islam, the Andalusi Muslims' and Jews' claims to exceptionalism—their assertion of religious, political (for the Jews, within their imagined political community), intellectual, and aesthetic authority—rested foremost on the following themes, which were elaborated in various cultural discourses and practices:

1. Al-Andalus and Sefarad were beneficiaries of the providential blessing of their terrain and environment, which produced agricultural plenty and abundant wealth, just as Isidore maintained for Hispania.
2. Andalusi Muslims and Sefardi Jews merited privileged leadership predicated on their noble ancestry, going back to the classical ages of their respective religious traditions. The Umayyad dynasty hailed from the lineage of the Prophet Muḥammad's Qurayshī clan. Select Andalusi religious scholars were entitled to favored rank on account of their pedigree as *tābi'ūn* (the "Successors"), that is, members of the second or third generation of the Prophet's companions who settled in al-Andalus. The Jews of Sefarad were self-described descendants of the ancient Jerusalemite aristocracy of biblical Israel.

3. Al-Andalus and Sefarad deserved their status as chosen stations within Islamdom and its Jewish communities (as well as in other Mediterranean lands) because they were bastions of religious orthodoxy and tradition. Sefardi rabbinic authorities and their academies, in the case of the Jews, and the supremacy of Mālikī scholars, scholarship, and institutions for Andalusi Muslims served as signs of their privilege.
4. Andalusi Muslim and Jewish elites constructed and promoted the image of al-Andalus and Sefarad as exemplary sites where literary and religious intellectuals embodied and elevated the social and intellectual practice of Arabic and Hebrew and Judeo-Arabic *adab*.[23] *Adab* signified refined manners, a finely tuned aesthetic sensibility, and cultural sophistication in the form of surpassing knowledge of the arts and sciences, and control of the discourses reflecting and conveying such etiquette. We can also think of Andalusi *adab* as the regimen and performance of Arabo-Islamic humanism in its Andalusi setting.[24]

Note that these motifs and the representational practices shaping them perform each of three configurations of capital that Pierre Bourdieu identified—economic, social, and cultural—in orchestrating the ideas of Andalusi and Sefardi exceptionalism as instruments of power.[25]

For its producers and consumers, the particulars of our trope—the richness of the land, its people's noble lineage and commitment to religious orthodoxy, and erudition and love of learning, cultural sophistication, all inscribed in the social, intellectual, and literary history of al-Andalus and Sefarad—defined "Andalusi-ness" and "Sefardi-ness."[26] Accordingly, the trope marked an idealized and transcendent al-Andalus and Sefarad with respect to their complex association with the Maghrib, in terms of their political, religious, and cultural competition with and dependence upon the Islamic East and, for Andalusi Muslims, their struggle against the Christian Iberian north from the late eleventh century onward.

The Trope in History and Comparative Perspective

How, why, when, and for which purposes did the tropes of Andalusi and Sefardi exceptionalism develop? What accounts for the tropes' subsequent trajectories, temporal longevity, and geographic diffusion? In what ways did the tropes of al-Andalus and Sefarad differ, considering the fundamentally asymmetrical psychosocial circumstances of religious and literary intellectuals of the Andalusi Muslim majority and the Jewish minority communities? *Iberian Moorings* examines the construction, iteration, and function of the geographical, social, religious, and political ideas of Sefarad and al-Andalus as cultural signifiers during the period in which they overlapped, from the first literary evidence of the formulation of the idea of their exceptionalism in the mid-tenth century until the early thirteenth century.

This historical, cultural, and critical inquiry is the first work to address these questions and scrutinize the tropes of Andalusi and Sefardi exceptionalism diachronically, comparatively, and with a focus on their social agency in Andalusi Islamic and Jewish culture. The study investigates the various stable and unstable elements in literary, geographical, and historical representations of Andalusi and Sefardi exceptionalism. It pinpoints the tropes' etiology and traces and analyzes the tropes' history by examining their shifting contours and contingencies, significance, and social capital for the architects and producers of Andalusi Islamic and Jewish culture and subsequently for the guardians of these legacies beyond its borders. The following chapters delve into paradigmatic texts and, occasionally, practices as case studies, relying on ways of reading texts critically, uncovering what they represented for various audiences and, in the process, exposing hidden patterns, connections, and discrepancies in the discourse of exceptionalism. In the course of these readings, this study illuminates the complexity of larger social, historical, and political processes, transactions, and transformations captured in the signs of al-Andalus and Sefarad.

This book charts the diachronic dimension of the processes by which Andalusi Muslim and Jewish elites created, asserted, refined, and adapted to new circumstances their respective claims of Andalusi and Sefardi singularity. The historical starting point for this inquiry—the mid-tenth century—is established by the textual evidence that has come down to us. The endpoint of this study's historical parameters is occasioned by social, religious, and political upheaval, collective trauma, and their jarring effects on cultural memory. For the Jews of Sefarad, the mid-twelfth century witnessed disruption within Andalusi Jewish society and transformation of its traditions. It saw the dispersal of most of the Jews of al-Andalus to the Iberian Christian kingdoms, to Provence, and to North Africa, where Andalusi Jewish exiles found refuge and Andalusi Jewish cultural production was relaunched in modified forms. For Andalusi Muslims, the Almohad military defeat at Las Navas de Tolosa in 1212, known in Arabic historiography as the monumental Battle of al-ʿIqāb, and the Almohads' ensuing withdrawal from Andalusi territory signaled the end of the classical age of al-Andalus. Within a generation, Córdoba and Seville fell to Castilian control, leaving the Naṣrid kingdom of Granada—all that was left of al-Andalus—as the sole remaining outpost of an Islamic polity and society on Iberian soil down to 1492.

Why adopt a comparative perspective to research the subject? As ideas as well as places occupying the same territory, al-Andalus and Sefarad followed a similar trajectory. Andalusi Muslims and Jews developed a strong sense of attachment to the land that they inhabited. They also negotiated long-standing economic, cultural, and intellectual ties to and rivalries with Islamic and Jewish regional centers in North Africa, the Levant, and the Islamic East, along with fundamental devotional orientations and connections to their respective holy places in the Hijāz and Palestine. Both Andalusi Islamic and Jewish religious communities sought and achieved stature as sites of social, political, and religious importance and centers of significant cultural production at exactly the same time and in the same place: Umayyad Córdoba was the incubator for the ideas of Andalusi and Sefardi exceptionalism. Indeed, the emergence of Sefarad as an influential Jewish community was completely dependent upon the maturation of al-Andalus as a formidable Islamic society in the mid-tenth century. In this respect, we can say that without al-Andalus, there would have been no Sefarad.

The Jews' acculturation to Arabic, their accommodation to Andalusi society, and adaptation of the idea that they, too, were exceptional, alongside their Muslim counterparts, calls for a comparative, integrative approach to the study of the tropes. So, too, for both religious communities, a "golden age" was followed by social and political upheaval, fragmentation, and eventual dispersion, typically attributed to the supposed religious failings of their communities and leaders. With the disintegration of central Andalusi authority and then the dwindling of the territory under Islamic control, and for the diminished community of Andalusi Jews, the breakdown of their society and institutions through exile and migration, Andalusi and Sefardi traditions, including the idea of their exceptionalism, were transmitted and transformed by their heirs, diasporas, and admirers.

A related literary, rather than sociohistorical, consideration also warrants comparative study of the trope. Muslim and Jewish literary intellectuals shared a discursive tradition for inscribing their reflections on al-Andalus in Arabic and on Sefarad in its Hebrew and Judeo-Arabic subcultural literary adaptations. That is, majority and minority communities textualized their spatial desire and their attachment to the country, viewed its landscape, and defined its heritage in similar ways, at the same time, and in closely related discourses. While Andalusi Muslims and Jews remained profoundly indebted to Eastern centers of learning and always intimately connected to their coreligionists in North Africa, they took pains to chart an autonomous or virtually independent course in diverse endeavors, in counterpoint to the traditional Islamic and Jewish centers of authority and learning in the East. Yet, notwithstanding the tropes' thematic correspondence, convergence in history, and commensurate impact on the literary imagination, there are important asymmetries in its arcs for the Muslim majority and Jewish minority communities.

To understand how political, religious, and psychosocial cultural capital works for its architects and audiences, *Iberian Moorings* investigates the intersection of the trope's spatial, temporal, and conceptual modalities and its varied incarnations in different literary discourses and forms and through their diverse rhetorical formulas, keeping in mind questions of historical periodization. Because a trope is a form of representation, as Derek Gregory observes, it "draws attention to the different ways in which the world is made present, represented, discursively constructed . . . working through grids of power."[27] Accordingly, we are obliged to inquire under what circumstances, in what forms, and for which purposes Muslim political and Jewish communal leaders and literary and religious intellectuals constructed, developed, promoted, and transmitted the notion of Andalusi and Sefardi exceptionalism as tropes of Islamic and Jewish culture.

Recent scholarship investigates tenth-century gestures and discourses in considerable detail and typically attributes the origins of Andalusi uniqueness to the Umayyad quest for Islamic legitimacy. However, the Umayyad pursuit of legitimacy does not fully account for the notion of Andalusi exceptionalism its various restatements, or its longevity as a trope. The Andalusis' expressions of their perceived otherness and their concern for Islamic legitimacy outlasted the Umayyad caliphate. Indeed, religious, political, and cultural anxiety were channeled assiduously into the idea of exceptionalism, which became a defining and empowering marker of Andalusi-ness. For that matter, the Umayyad quest for Islamic authenticity does not explain why Andalusi Jewish elites, with no genuine political authority at stake, would monitor and emulate their Muslim counterparts and develop the corresponding idea and practice of Sefardi exceptionalism.

Research typically ascribes the trope's persistence, following the fall of the unitary state, to nostalgia for a paradise lost. Various Andalusi Muslim and Jewish literati and religious scholars certainly expressed in stylized form and conventional terms grief and longing for the restoration of the immediate or more distant and imagined past. That nostalgia is said to be the principal posture of post-Umayyad Arabic texts for Andalusi Muslims and post-Almohad Hebrew and Judeo-Arabic texts for Sefardi Jews. However, nostalgia can also be viewed as a discursive position where it is inherently programmatic, aesthetic, and ideological; performative function and social agency are inscribed in this poetic voice just as in any other form of discourse.[28] Accordingly, nostalgia is historically contingent and variable, and it necessarily serves particular social, political, and artistic purposes. The nostalgia expressed by politically and religiously minded literati and cognoscenti during the eleventh century in the immediate aftermath of the collapse of the Umayyad caliphate and unitary state necessarily differs from that of their counterparts in the twelfth and thirteenth centuries. During this later period, Andalusis were preoccupied with fending off or accommodating themselves to incursions from the north and south—the military-political threat posed by Castile and its advance upon Andalusi territory and by the successive incorporations of al-Andalus into the Almoravid and Almohad Maghrib-based kingdoms. Beyond its legitimacy-granting and nostalgic dimensions, Andalusi Muslims' and Sefardi Jews' traditions of their exceptionalism laid claim to privilege and cultural authority that never expired. Andalusi and Sefardi self-fashionings were constituted and reconstituted through their evolution at the intersection of social, political, cultural, and religious authority-delivering agency.

Iberian Moorings: The Book's Plan

This study is structured chronologically, according to the conventional periodization of Andalusi sociopolitical history: it identifies the origins and analyzes the Islamic and Jewish inflections of the trope's evolving contours from the tenth century to the early thirteenth century. Chapter 1 traces the early stages of the idea of Andalusi exceptionalism and its derivation from the singular political geography of al-Andalus in Islamdom, on the one hand,

and the Umayyad quest for Islamic legitimacy, on the other. It discusses how the tenth-century Umayyad caliphs employed various textual, material, and performative tools for grounding their authority in the language of Islamic legitimacy. *Iberian Moorings* identifies the pre-tenth-century genesis of Andalusi exceptionalism with the peculiar ninth-century impression of Andalusi geographical and temporal alterity. This image persisted in the religious imagination throughout the classical age of Islam while the singularity of Andalusi otherness morphed and was reshaped into the notion of Andalusi exceptionalism during the Umayyad caliphal age. Specifically, religious intellectuals and historically minded tradents developed a set of traditions regarding al-Andalus's unique role in an envisaged eschatological future. Al-Andalus's image as inhabiting a distant place at the westernmost edge of Islamdom, far from its geographic center, along with the uncommon temporal space that al-Andalus occupies between the legendary past and the end of history, as well as between the here and now and the apocalyptic age, thus functioned dialectically to situate al-Andalus and Andalusis at the epicenter of an unconventional rendering of Islamic history.

Chapter 2 examines the complex process of how, why, and for what purpose tenth-century Andalusi Jewish elites alighted on the idea of their own exceptionalism and advanced ambitions on behalf of their community at precisely the same time and in the same place that Andalusi Muslim elites were formulating theirs. In the case of the Andalusi Jews, a religious community without a polity, their leaders' and scholars' concern over authority and legitimacy such as animated their Muslim counterparts was necessarily different in kind, even if it was expressed in remarkably similar terms. The Jews' relatively secure position in Andalusi society and their economic prosperity certainly provided them with the opportunity to assert and trumpet their sense of privilege. In this study, I primarily understand the genesis of Sefardi exceptionalism as an important sign of the social and cultural agenda that Andalusi Jewish elites absorbed through their deep acculturation and multilayered integration within Andalusi society and then constructed for their own purposes. That is, the Andalusi Jews mirrored the Andalusi Muslim elites' claim to dignity and distinction and adapted the majority's rhetorical strategies and idioms to their own minority circumstance.[29]

The next three chapters turn to the eleventh and twelfth centuries in what were politically fractured yet culturally productive periods for Muslims and Jews alike. Chapter 3 begins by analyzing Andalusi Muslim nostalgia for the imagined wholeness of Islamic society under the unitary state in its most frequently observed manifestation: elegies for Andalusi cities from the eleventh to sixteenth centuries. The laments' conceptual framework and register of images of what was lost—and, more important, what survived—informed the ways in which Andalusi Muslim literary intellectuals employed their elite practice of Arabic *adab* to compensate for the loss of a unified polity and, by the end of the eleventh century, the forfeiture of Andalusi territory to the Christian kingdoms. That is, Andalusi literary intellectuals effected a lasting cultural turn in the articulation of the trope, and they continued to represent Andalusis as much as al-Andalus as distinctive and exceptional in Islamdom, in counterpoint to their significantly diminished political circumstance.

Chapter 4 charts and interrogates Andalusi Jewish expressions of, and claims to, a position of communal, religious, and cultural privilege among the Jewish communities of Mediterranean lands in the post-Umayyad age. Ironically, the proliferation of Andalusi courts on a smaller scale than Umayyad Córdoba created new opportunities for outstanding Jewish figures to fulfill political, communal, intellectual, and aesthetic ambitions far beyond what their tenth-century predecessors imagined. During the eleventh century, their assertion of religious and cultural authority and empowerment found ample expression in the trope of Sefardi exceptionalism. Following the social and political disruptions of the early to mid-twelfth century, Andalusi Jewish literary and religious intellectuals endeavored to consolidate their traditions and proceeded to direct the discourse of exceptionalism to their heirs, exiles, and enthusiasts.

Chapter 5 is devoted to reading literary products composed by three paradigmatic author-travelers from al-Andalus and Sefarad to the Islamic East. Their respective "cognitive and imaginative maps" and literary geographies incorporating the sociopolitical, religious, and cultural glories of al-Andalus and Sefarad feed the rhetoric of cultural otherness that they deploy toward the Muslims and Jews of the Islamic East, whose own successes and failures serve to recall for the audience what was exceptional about al-Andalus and Sefarad.

The Conclusion reviews and offers reflections on how historiography, art, literary and intellectual history, and imaginative literature and cinema addressed and utilized the tropes of Andalusi and Sefardi exceptionalism. Modern social, literary, religious, and art historians variously observe, endorse and celebrate, or repudiate and debunk the self-fashioned identity-relating Andalusi and Sefardi traditions of exceptionalism, often with a minimum of critical reflection or sense of the trope's complex, evolving expression in history, or the complex agency of its cultural capital. Deeply contested visions of al-Andalus and Sefarad (as well as "medieval Spain") clearly invite a critical and analytic inquiry into the source, arc, and significance of the ideas of Andalusi and Sefardi exceptionalism that are the subject of this study.

The Toponyms' Etymologies

Before we turn to the genesis of Andalusi and Sefardi exceptionalism, it is worth reviewing the linguistic details of the history of the toponyms themselves, the containers into which cultural meaning was dispensed. The origins of the Arabic toponym *al-Andalus* are hazy, if not downright mythical. But unlike Sefarad, the toponym lacks any sort of implicit or expressed genealogical, communal-political, or cultural authority based on an ancient prooftext from Scripture and its interpretation in religious tradition.[30] "Al-Andalus" is first attested as the Arabic equivalent of Hispania on a bilingual (Latin and Arabic) dinar dated 715/716—merely five years after Muslims and Islam arrived in Iberia and instituted an Islamic polity there.[31] For many modern scholars who rely on the testimony of Arabic geographers and historiographers, for want of other sources or explanations, "al-Andalus" is supposedly derived from "Vandalicia," the name that the Vandal (Ar., *al-Andalūsh* or *al-Andalīsh*) invaders of the early fifth century gave to the Roman province of Baetica. Werner Vycichl posited the origins of "al-Andalus" from a hypothetical Berber "land of the Vandals."[32] Paul Wexler explains this possible origin by noting that "Berber speakers could have dropped *v*- that they interpreted as the Berber genitive maker 'of' in the expression 'land of the Vandals.'"[33] Heinz Helm, however, dissects the historical and philological problems with the received scholarly explanations for this assumed origin and derivation of al-Andalus. Reviewing all the scholarly literature, Helm posits a Gothic origin (*landahlauts* = "allotted territory") for the Arabized term.[34] George Bossong disputed the Gothic source on phonetic, morphosyntactic, and historical grounds. Instead, he identifies the toponym al-Andalus as "the original name of the Punta Marroqui near Tarifa" that was then "generalized to designate the whole Peninsula."[35] An alternate but highly problematic explanation suggests an origin from an Arabization of the legendary island of Atlantis, presumably from the Greek place name.[36]

Federico Corriente, the peerless authority on Andalusi Arabic, originally accepted the Greek etymon, for want of other satisfactory explanations.[37] Corriente subsequently deduced that "al-Andalus" was derived from the Coptic *amenti*, signifying "Hades; the West." He surmised that "in the epoch of the Islamic conquest of Egypt, the local population must have called the Southwest **emender/lēs*, which the Arabs would hear as *am+andalīs, and most of them being of Yemenite extraction, they would metanalyze */am+/* as their own dialectical shape of the definite article, instead of /al+/, thus producing a standard /al+andalīs."[38] Recently, José Ramírez del Río traced the probable origins of the toponym al-Andalus by lexeme and image to the Greek "Anadolis-Hesperus" or "Anatolé" which later evolved to "Anadolu" and, ultimately, to al-Andalus.[39]

What do the Arabic sources relate about the origins and meaning of the toponym? Aḥmad b. Muḥammad al-Rāzī (d. 955), the first significant Muslim historian of al-Andalus, whose work survives in partial form as transmitted by later writers, establishes the etiology of the Arabic place name for Islamic historiographical tradition: "The first people who inhabited al-Andalus after the Great Flood were, according to the non-Arab scholars of that land, a people called al-Andalush, with *shīn*. The land was named after them and then was Arabized."[40] Al-Rāzī and his contemporary from the Islamic East, the tenth-century Eastern geographer Abū Iṣḥāq al-Iṣṭakhrī, who drew one of the earliest maps of al-Andalus,[41] employ the term al-Andalus as a geographical marker for the entire peninsula (*jazīrat al-andalus*), without regard for considerations of polity. This convention is reflected in the Arabic sources up to the seventeenth century and, in some quarters, by Muslims of other lands ever since. Al-Maqqarī (b. Telemcen; c. 1577–1632), the supreme Maghribi authority of Andalusi history and tradition, cites the conventional etymologies presented by the scholars Ibn Sa'īd al-Maghribī (thirteenth century) and Ibn Khaldūn (fourteenth century).[42]

Speaking strictly historically, al-Andalus served as both a political and a geographical signifier, depending on the context of the source in which it is employed. In the latter sense, it is simply shorthand for the aforementioned Arabic name for the peninsula, *jazīrat al-andalus*. In the former sense, al-Andalus is the name applied to the territory of the Iberian Peninsula under Islamic rule at any given time. Between 711 and 1492, the period during which Islam maintained a sovereign presence in the peninsula, the western frontier between Islamdom and Christendom in Iberia was a shifting border. From the eighth through the eleventh centuries, most of the Iberian Peninsula was under Islamic control. But the territorial map of al-Andalus receded radically in the mid-thirteenth century, when Córdoba (1236), Seville (1248), and their surrounding lands fell into Castilian hands. From this point on, the polity of al-Andalus was confined geographically 250 years to the Naṣrid state of Granada, until its own demise at the end of the fifteenth century. Al-Andalus thus supposedly faded into memory, myth, and the stuff of nostalgia, the subject of exceptionally vivid social and literary imaginations. As with Sefarad, the origins and historical trajectory of the Andalusi quest for political and socioreligious authority and cultural significance in Islamdom are the subject of this study.

The toponym Sefarad, like the Arabic al-Andalus, is a fluctuating sign. *Sefarad* is a *hapax legomenon* (i.e., attested only once in the Hebrew Bible) appearing in the minor prophetic book Obadiah (1:20): "the exiles of Jerusalem that are in Sefarad they shall possess the towns of the Negev." Modern scholarship understands this biblical toponym as referring to the Persian satrap *Sparda*, identified with Sardis in Asia Minor on account of its attestation in an Aramaic inscription and array of other ancient Mediterranean and Near Eastern languages.[43] However, the earliest Jewish textual evidence for the appropriation-interpretation of the biblical verse to signify Iberia dates to late antiquity in the form of Targum Jonathan (probably edited in the fourth century from an earlier source). Its gloss on Obadiah already identified the biblical place name Sefarad with *Ispamia*, that is, Roman Hispania ("'And the exile of Jerusalem that is in Sefarad'—and the exile of Jerusalem that is in Spain").[44] The authoritative eleventh-century Hebrew lexicographer and grammarian Jonah ibn Janāḥ refers in his *Book of [Hebrew] Roots* (*Kitāb al-uṣūl*) to Obadiah, verse 20, by noting "'that is in Sefarad' is translated by the Targum as 'which is in Hispania,' and it is well known that Hispania is Sefarad."[45]

The sociolinguist Paul Wexler, among others, studies the etymological mechanism by which a biblical toponym for a site in Asia Minor became identified with Iberia. He allows for the possibility proposed by J. Brutzkus that biblical "Sefarad" was suggested (for Hispania) by its similarity to the Gothic *swarts* or *svard*, the word for "black" that the Goths are said to have applied to the indigenous people of Iberia.[46] Ultimately, Wexler seems to prefer to view the derivation as the Jews' identification of a biblical place name with another similar-sounding non-Hebrew phrase such as the Punic *i sephanim* (isle of rabbits),[47] the probable origin of "Hispania," as Solà-Solé observed previously. Wexler understands it in the sense "northern island," derived from the Semitic root *s-f-n* / *ṣ-f-n*.[48] Mariona Vernet Pons offers a new, ingenious explanation on why translators of antiquity associated Sefarad with Hispania. She suggests that Targum Jonathan "might have had in mind the Greek loanword *Hesperides*, the nymphs who tend a garden in a far western place of the known world, not least because of the phonological closeness between this word and Sepharad."[49] Cyril Aslanov proposes yet another Byzantine-era extralinguistic "etymology" for Sefarad, based on a trans-linguistic pun involving Hebrew, Aramaic, and Greek and "more related with the signified than with the signifier."[50] Finally, José Ramírez del Río identifies the Hebrew *Sefarad* as a transcription of the Greek (He)speria, Venus as the evening star, a term that was important for the Christians of the Iberian Peninsula from the sixth century.[51] In any case, the traditional identification, whether a gloss or an interpretative translation or dictated by a similar-sounding phrase in another language, is ancient, perhaps nearly as old as Jewish residence in Roman Iberia. Indeed, the *Peshiṭta*, the Syriac Christian translation of the Hebrew Bible dating to the second century, also translates Sefarad as *Ispania*.[52]

What do medieval Jewish sources besides Ibn Janāḥ report? The tradition (Sefarad = al-Andalus) appears in Saʿadia Gaon's *Commentary on Lamentations* ("'the exile of Jerusalem that is in Sefarad' is from the time of Hadrian and no one was exiled to al-Andalus before that"),[53] the late geonic-era chronicle *Seder ʿolam zuṭa* ("Vespasianus came and destroyed the Temple and exiled Israel and many families from the House of David and Judah to Espamya, which is Sefarad),"[54] and in *Midrash ʿeser galuyot*.[55] Subsequent Andalusi Jewish scholars of the eleventh and twelfth centuries disagreed about whether the Obadiah prooftext refers to the Babylonian exile of 586 BCE (the position taken by eleventh-century authorities Samuel the Nagid and Moses ibn Giqaṭilla) or the Roman exile of 70 CE (the view of twelfth-century intellectuals Abraham ibn Ezra and Abraham ibn Daud, following Saʿadia). This dispute is secondary for our purposes, even if the earlier dating affords greater longevity to the idea and history of Sefarad.[56] As we shall read in detail in Chapters 2 and 4, the traditional, late antique linkage of Sefarad and Jerusalem encoded Sefardi exceptionalism genealogically and served to transmit various forms of Jewish religious, political, and cultural authority to its leaders, scholars, and their community.

For the Jews living under Islamic rule from the tenth century till the mid-thirteenth (and in Naṣrid Granada through the fifteenth), Sefarad applied in the restricted sense as the Hebrew equivalent of the Arabic al-Andalus. The eleventh-century biblical commentator Judah ibn Bil'am (*Commentary on Obadiah* 1:20) glosses the Obadiah prooftext as follows: "The opinion that Sefarad is al-Andalus has spread among our people; its name of yore was 'Espamya.'"[57] That is, Sefarad originated as a spatial-political signifier and only later in the mid-twelfth century began to morph into a portable cultural signifier. Rabbinic literature from geonic circles in the Islamic East clearly differentiated the Jewish communities living in the Islamic and Christian domains of the Iberian Peninsula. Before he became gaon (in 968), the illustrious R. Sherira (ca. 906–1006) dispatched a Hebrew letter to the Jewish communities of North Africa and Iberia, appealing for funds in support of geonic institutions in Iraq: it refers to both "al-Andalus" and "Aspāmya."[58] This geonic perspective was thus in accord with the Andalusi Jewish view differentiating the two Iberian domains of Islamdom and Christendom. Ḥasdai ibn Shaprūṭ, a court physician, adviser, and diplomat for the tenth-century Umayyad caliphs 'Abd al-Raḥmān III al-Nāṣir and al-Ḥakam II al-Mustanṣir, identified his community in correspondence with a foreign dignitary as follows: "The name of our land in which we dwell is Sefarad in the holy tongue, but in the language of the Arabs, the inhabitants of the land, al-Andalus."[59] The eleventh–twelfth-century literary intellectual Moses ibn Ezra recapitulates these traditions in *Kitāb al-muḥāḍara wa-l-mudhākara* while also incorporating elements of Islamic lore:

> These aforementioned populations . . . and the other exile to the lands of Rome and to al-Andalus, as Scripture testifies: "And that exiled force of Israelites [shall possess] what belongs to the Phoenicians as far as Zarephath, while the Jerusalemite exile community of Sepharad shall possess the towns of the Negeb" (Obad. 1:20). Our religious community received the tradition that Zarephath is the land of the Franks and Sepharad is al-Andalus in the language of the Arabs, associated with a person called Andalusān from the period of al-Izdihāq, the ancient king; and in the Romance language, Ishfāniyya, also derived from a ruler in the Roman country prior to the Goths, whose name was Ishfān, and whose capital was Ishbīliyya (Seville), on his account was it named, among the earliest (settlers) Isfamyā.[60]

Finally, Abraham ibn Daud's (d. ca. 1180) *Chronicles of Rome* reports: "In [Honorious's] day, the Uzides, who are the Goths, entered Spain in three groups: the Vandals, the Alans and the Suevi. After the Vandals, Sepharad [Spain] was called Andalusia, and they conquered all of Spain from a nation called *Espan*."[61]

After 1150, the Jewish communal presence in al-Andalus diminished significantly under Almohad rule. Andalusi Jewish exiles such as Abraham ibn Daud transferred the notion of Sefarad with its revered cultural baggage and claims of privilege to the new centers of Jewish life in the Christian kingdoms of northern Iberia. There, Andalusi Judeo-Arabic cultural traditions and practices were relished, preserved, and redeveloped in conversation with Romance elements, especially in Toledo. Jewish literary and religious intellectuals of the Christian kingdoms thus viewed themselves as the natural heirs of Andalusi Jewish tradition and referred to the new lands in which they lived as Sefarad, even as they remembered Sefarad in its original Andalusi setting. In the new sociopolitical and religious environment, Sefarad accordingly came to serve as the Jewish marker for all the Iberian Peninsula (except for Catalonia, on occasion).

Concerning this period of cultural transfer, Yom Tov Assis observes: "What came to be identified as Sefarad was essentially the meeting of Judeo-Arabic culture of al-Andalus with Romance civilization which was then in its embryonic form."[62] Jonathan Ray speaks of the Jews of Christian Iberia "attaching themselves to this already established concept of Sepharad" and its "proud cultural legacy."[63] Jonathan Decter calls attention to an obvious yet critical feature of the toponym: "Sefarad never had a political reality; it existed only in the minds of Jews." His observations resemble Assis's "definitions," but Decter articulates it differently: "With time, especially as Jews moved from Islamic to Christian territories within the Iberian Peninsula, the borders of Sefarad were reimagined to include the new communities. Only after centuries did the whole of the Iberian Peninsula come to be identified with Sefarad."[64] The history of the unstable term "Sefarad" thus complicates how we refer to the Jews of al-Andalus and the Jews of all Iberia. Ultimately, "Sefarad" functioned broadly as a trope—a cultural, rather than a purely geographical, signifier—and it was imbued with unambiguous authority like its Islamic counterpart, al-Andalus, to whose origins and significance we now turn in Chapter 1.

Chapter 1

Geography and Destiny

The Genesis of Andalusi Exceptionalism in the Umayyad Caliphal Age

> The land of al-Andalus is the western extreme of the fourth clime. In the opinion of the knowledgeable, it is a land abundant in lowlands with good soil, fertile agricultural settlements, flowing with plentiful rivers and abundant fresh springs.
>
> —Al-Rāzī

Al-Andalus was situated on an unfamiliar continent at the westernmost frontier of Islamdom and surrounded by the sea on three sides. The peninsula was widely considered as altogether remote, different, and even dangerous, at the very limits of Islamdom and civilization. Obviously, designations of place, ways of seeing the Islamic world, and explaining it were inseparable from the prevailing structures of power in which the East inhabited the center and al-Andalus the marginal edge. Andalusi elites thus were acutely sensitive to the power dynamic implicit in the notions of center and periphery and their assignment to the outer reaches of the latter realm. In the tenth century, they devised ways to challenge this order.

On account of its geographical remove, al-Andalus operated as a virtually autonomous province from the moment Muslim troops entered the peninsula in 711, trounced King Roderick and commenced overthrowing Christian Visigothic Hispania. Until the middle of the eighth century, many of al-Andalus's first twenty-one governors only nominally answered to the regional governor of the Maghrib. Stationed in Qayrawān, even that authority represented Damascus only in theory.[1] The administrators of al-Andalus attempted, with little success, to consolidate centralized control over the country and bring a semblance of order to the new Islamic domain. 'Abd al-Raḥmān ibn Mu'āwiyya, a refugee from the Abbasid overthrow of the Syrian-based Umayyad dynasty and slaughter of its members in 750, famously arrived in al-Andalus in 756. He is said to have gathered enough of a following of Berbers, *mawālī* (clients of Arab tribes), and Syrian Umayyad loyalists to become emir (r. 756–788). Soon after his accession to power, 'Abd al-Raḥmān I banned the conventional recitation of the Abbasid caliph's name during Friday communal prayers, signaling that al-Andalus was a self-governing Islamic realm independent from Baghdad and Abbasid authority.[2]

One hundred and fifty years of political instability followed the establishment of the Umayyad emirate in al-Andalus. This long period was marked by widespread disorder frequently directed against Umayyad authority of the Córdoba-based Andalusi state and its efforts to centralize power and extend it over the provinces. Incessant factionalism, interethnic struggles, tribalism, and revolts gripped Arabs, their *mawālī*, Berbers, and Muslim converts of Roman or Visigothic origin.[3] An official proclamation of the ultimate expression of Andalusi Umayyad dominion came in 929. The eighth Umayyad emir of al-Andalus, the politically ambitious and adept 'Abd al-Raḥmān III al-Nāṣir (r. 912–961),[4] eventually succeeded in subduing the insurrections and bringing relative order to al-Andalus. A resplendent Córdoba served as its Baghdad-inspired imperial capital. Indeed, he implemented various Abbasid-style practices and reforms, including with the army, upon which the consolidation of Umayyad power rested. Taking advantage of military successes against both the Christian kingdoms and rebels against the state, 'Abd al-Raḥmān III strategically assumed the designation of caliph as "Commander of the Faithful" (*amīr al-mu'minīn*), thereby claiming symbolic or titular authority over the entire *umma* of Muslims. This maneuver gestured primarily in opposition to the rival Fāṭimid (Ismā'īlī Shī'a) caliphate centered in Ifrīqiya (est. 909, central North Africa) and secondarily to the remote and progressively weak Abbasid caliphate in the Islamic East.[5] The Umayyads increasingly allied themselves with anti-Fāṭimid forces in the westernmost part of North Africa, in resistance to Fāṭimid propaganda circulating in al-Andalus and the threat that the Fāṭimids supposedly posed to them. By the time the Fāṭimids moved their capital from Ifrīqiya to Cairo in 973, al-Ḥakam II al-Mustanṣir (r. 961–976), 'Abd al-Raḥmān III's son and successor, was engaged in his own anti-Fāṭimid political activity, undertaking building projects in North Africa such as the construction of the minaret of the iconic Qarawiyyin mosque in Fez expressly to connect al-Andalus and the Maghrib.[6]

Andalusi society was uncommonly complex, with its mix of Arabs of diverse ancestral tribal affiliations who arrived in al-Andalus at different moments, "old," long-settled, and "new" Berbers, likewise of different tribal backgrounds who entered Andalusi society earlier or later, neo-Muslims mostly of peninsular Christian origins, *ṣaqāliba* (slave-soldiers imported from Christendom), Mozarabic Christians, and Jews. Yet little is known with any degree of certainty about the demographic situation leading up to declaration of the Umayyad caliphate in the tenth century that would have informed the social, political, and religious developments of this critical turning point in Andalusi history. Richard Bulliet's influential work on the history of conversion to Islam and the "conversion curve" of the first few earliest Islamic centuries has provided the method and framework for inquiry regarding the rates by which Christians, Zoroastrians, Jews, and others became Muslims in the geographically contiguous central and eastern territories of early and classical Islam. Based on careful analysis of names in biographical dictionaries, al-Andalus represents something of a special case of individual social conversions, according to Bulliet's scheme. His demographic research—inexact, to be sure—also suggests that the community of Muslims became the majority in Andalusi society by the mid-tenth century.[7]

The rapidly growing Islamic community of al-Andalus thus was constituted through dynamic historical and social processes—immigration from North Africa and the Islamic East and, most notably, conversion to Islam. The impulse to differentiate Islam strictly from Christianity and to distinguish Muslims clearly from Christians was especially imperative while Christians outnumbered Muslims in al-Andalus. It remained significant even when Muslims finally constituted the demographic majority. Since al-Andalus was located at the far western reaches of Islamdom bordering Christendom, its unique geographical position also reinforced the urge to implement and maintain boundary-making traditions and practices. This sense of unusual place, the traditions and practices encoding it, and the Andalusis' hyperawareness of al-Andalus's otherness, from the patronizing perspective of the Islamic East, became permanent drivers and markers of Andalusi "self-fashioning," cultural politics, and collective memory.[8] Of course, construction of a distinct Andalusi identity required a political foil—namely, Fāṭimid Egypt and the Abbasid East, against which Andalusi authority could be measured and "Andalusi-ness" defined.

Social historians offer conflicting interpretations of the politico-religious significance of 'Abd al-Raḥmān III's declaration of an Umayyad Andalusi caliphate in the tenth century. David Wasserstein discounts the "universal" implications of the caliphal proclamation and views its adoption in al-Andalus as "a local Iberian variant of the title emir."[9] By contrast, Janina Safran draws attention to the Umayyads' domestic and foreign political agendas, especially as applied to their ambitions in North Africa and their competition with the Fāṭimids, a rivalry that Maribel Fierro, among others, also views as pivotal to Andalusi Umayyad ideology, statecraft, and practice.[10] Whatever the complex intention behind this change in political posture, social and cultural historians agree that the tenth-century Umayyad caliphs successfully sought to transcend the unremittingly troublesome ethnic tensions and internecine conflicts of the eighth and ninth centuries by constructing a distinctively "Andalusi Islamic identity,"[11] just as the aforementioned demographic, political, and historical developments converged.

Al-Andalus's moment of self-discovery also coincided with and represents an example of an emergent sense of regionalism and localism across Islamdom. An awareness of place and sensitivity to its difference was partly predicated on the deep political and religious divisions between rival caliphates and the complex history informing these ruptures (between the Umayyads, Fāṭimids, and Abbasids; Sunnis and Shī'is). The newfound attachment to the particularities of homeland (*waṭan*) and the Arabic literary forms in which it was voiced (various *mafākhir* and *faḍā'il* traditions appearing in dedicated literary genres and motifs *al-ḥanīn ilā l-awṭān* and *kutub al-ghurabā'*)[12] arose as expressions and markers of regional and local difference. These emblems stood in dialectical relationship with the universalist ideal of the Islamic *umma*'s oneness, an ideal represented in the freedom of movement across the political borders within Islamdom that informed the experience of pilgrimage to Mecca and the Islamic institution of travel for knowledge.[13] Because of its abiding reputation for "otherness," the Andalusi investment in regionalism became an especially prominent component of "Andalusi-ness" in the political and religious sense and a major theme of cultural production.[14]

However one reads the religious and political aspirations of tenth-century Umayyad al-Andalus, we can trace the origins of the idea of al-Andalus as a legitimate and ambitious Islamic state with a culturally vibrant society to this historical moment in which a distinctive Andalusi-ness was conceived, articulated, and promulgated in the service of the country. As Maribel Fierro keenly observes: "Along with belonging to a universal religious community, they [Andalusi elites] had a distinct, but not static, Andalusi identity that separated them from other Muslims. . . . This Andalusi identity is generally considered to have been promoted especially by the Córdoban Umayyad caliphs, beginning with 'Abd al-Raḥmān al-Nāṣir, as it helped them strengthen their rule."[15]

What, exactly, are the origins and the earliest incarnation of the trope of Andalusi exceptionalism? What animated political leaders and religious authorities utilizing different administrative, social, and religious practices and religious and literary intellectuals writing in various literary genres and employing different discourses to situate al-Andalus at the very center of Islamic history and culture, if not Islamdom? Fierro and Safran, among others, have meticulously deciphered the discourses and practices that the Andalusi Umayyad caliphs applied and exercised to assert their political and religious legitimacy and articulate their power. However, the trope of Andalusi exceptionalism represents a previously unrecognized, encoded dimension of these authority-conferring discourses and practices: it was derived from the dynamic confluence of an idiosyncratically Andalusi sense of place and the difference that it imparted and the Umayyad quest for Islamic legitimacy.

The ground for the construction, articulation, and dissemination of the trope of Andalusi exceptionalism was laid in the tenth century, based on an Islamicized version of Isidore of Seville's depiction of the land's divinely ordained bounty, the Umayyads' appeal to Islamic genealogy, and al-Andalus's steadfast adherence to the Mālikī legal rite. However, to appreciate the fullness of the trope's history and evolution, we must consider its original manifestation, which took the peculiar form of a sense of radical Andalusi otherness. The origin of this defining myth of Andalusi cultural politics predates the tenth century, when the Umayyad caliphs began to convert it from a deleterious to a constructive effect.[16] The trope's genesis was rooted, I believe, in the Andalusis' uneasy grappling and coming to terms with, internalizing, and subsequently transforming an Islamic identity, which geography and Islamic history provided for them, as viewed and narrated from afar in the Islamic East. Their socially constructed geographic identity was defined by the notion of the "island of al-Andalus" (*jazīrat al-andalus*) and its unique position as a remote outpost on the westernmost edge of Islamdom and the very limits of civilization. The reputation of the place and its peculiar geographic identity naturally informed the Andalusis' mental map of their standing and station in Islam and Islamdom, a map that identified the Islamic East as the center and placed them on the extreme periphery—in effect, marginalizing their place in Islamdom.[17]

Andalusis were well aware of the pointed opinions of Eastern geographers, travelers, observers, and authors during the classical age of Islam. Following ancient and late antique traditions rooted in pre-Islamic Egypt (noted in the Introduction) residents of the Islamic East frequently viewed al-Andalus as a marginal or perilous place. Easterners could regard Andalusis with disdain and derision, denigrating their courage and martial fortitude, or disparaging and dismissing the creativity of their cultural production.[18] From the tenth through thirteenth centuries, the Andalusis' sense of their otherness thus was defined by the geographical position of their remote "island," as Islamic cartography represented the peninsula.[19] It was compounded by their supposed isolation and the demographic peculiarities of residing in a distant backwater of Islamdom. Their sense of uniqueness or strangeness was exacerbated by awareness that, of all the lands that Muslims ruled, al-Andalus alone enjoyed no territorial contiguity with the rest of Islamdom—yet another sense in which al-Andalus was an island. Piotr Michalowski defines the impact of human and physical geography on human cognition: "Geography is a human problem that involves both universals, which purportedly stem from the physical reality of mankind, as well as culturally independent variables. Certain conceptions of space . . . appear to differ little across societies. There do exist strong cultural variations, however, and one of the problems . . . is the question of mental or cognitive maps, that is, the ideas of space and its relative seriations that men and women carry in their heads, so to speak. These mental maps include notions of preference, as well as vague ideas and value judgments about places that speakers or authors have never seen."[20] Michalowski's critical observation explains how Andalusis could not help but internalize the sense of their place as outsiders viewed it, and it explains why their intellectuals would confront this construction discursively.

An indirect early Andalusi response to their geographic "condition" in Islamdom recognized al-Andalus as the essential site of events in Islamic (Sunni) eschatology.[21] In Islamic lore, the End of Days drama typically plays out in the East, where Andalusi warriors make an appearance in an apocalyptic battle against the Byzantines in Palestine.[22] 'Abd al-Malik ibn Ḥabīb (ca. 790–852) was an early Andalusi hadith tradent and an important jurist, credited by some traditions (although not history) with establishing the

Mālikī rite in al-Andalus. Like many pious Andalusis, Ibn Ḥabīb journeyed east in quest of Islamic learning, where, ironically, he gleaned information on the history of al-Andalus available in Egypt. Returning home amid great sociopolitical turbulence in al-Andalus that he associated with the Last Judgment,[23] Ibn Ḥabīb authored *Kitāb al-Ta'rīkh*—a brief universal "history" and richly imaginative work related in the distinctive voice of (Sunni) Islamic piety.[24] In Ibn Ḥabīb's ninth-century mythic and prophetic telling, al-Andalus is already a place of great treasure and abundance, as would be observed and proclaimed during the tenth century by the various architects of Andalusi exceptionalism as an unmistakable sign of divine favor. Ibn Ḥabīb's devotional-apocalyptic sensibility, however, inverts the significance of the gifts that God bestowed on the land and its people. Instead of serving as a divine blessing to its inhabitants, the natural wealth of al-Andalus seduces them into the greedy excesses of materialism, completely contrary to the dictates of Islam. Accordingly, four factors turn al-Andalus into the ideal locus for the imminent End of Days (Day of Judgment) in Ibn Ḥabīb's Islamic apocalyptic eschatology: its geographical position at world's end; the supposedly debased ethical habits of Andalusi rulers and society; apprehension about al-Andalus's hazardous proximity to Christendom; and the significant Andalusi Christian population in their midst, which still outnumbered the Muslims.[25]

Justin Stearns identifies the apocalyptic-eschatological motif as one of three interconnected themes by which Andalusi and Maghribi authors effectively integrated al-Andalus into more general Islamic historiography,[26] a project of considerable urgency, given the peripheral place in Islamdom that it was assigned by Eastern authors: al-Andalus was conceived as the site of eschatological events; as a "land of jihad" (*wa-l-andalus dāru jihād*[in]);[27] and as a place of *'ajā'ib* (wonders or marvels). *'Ajā'ib* literature, the Islamic incarnation of the antique genre of paradoxography that destabilizes and entertains, took two distinct thematic forms:[28] religious intellectuals favored reports devoted to invoking the wonders of God's creation (*makhlūqāt*) as a source of religious awe; and literary intellectuals and geographers were drawn to accounts of the fantastic and abnormal. *'Ajā'ib* in the sense of "wonders" fits into Todorov's discussion of the fantastic in the category of the "uncanny": the traditions discussed here involve accepted elements of mythic and sacred history and therefore do not exactly trespass the realm of the natural. They are "readily accounted for by the laws of reason but . . . are, in one way or another, incredible, extraordinary, shocking, singular, disturbing or unexpected."[29]

For our purposes, the frequently interrelated themes of jihad and *'ajā'ib* in the sources accentuate al-Andalus's distinctive role in the Andalusi inflection of the Islamic religious and historical imagination. They stake al-Andalus's claim to an unusual yet central position in the geography of the ultimate chapter of Islamic history in what I think of as a potent synthesis of "end times" and "end place." The traditions of the geographers and the chroniclers describe al-Andalus as a locus of *'ajā'ib* from the outset of sacred and mythic history. For example, it was the site of the legendary "Tree of Life,"[30] the "City of Copper" (Ar., *Madīnat al-nuḥās*),[31] and the famed "Solomon's Table" (*Mā'idat Sulaymān b. Dāwūd*), an artifact from the Jerusalem Temple "discovered" in Toledo.[32] These traditions dialectically placed al-Andalus outside of and inside at the center of a normative Islamic historical and geographical framework. Apart from sacred history, Andalusi interest in and references to legendary figures and sites from Greek late antiquity served the same purpose. The "Pillars of Hercules" were identified with the Strait of Gibraltar. Legends of *Dhū l-qarnayn* (identified with Alexander the Great) told of his exploits and regime in ancient "al-Andalus" along with his close association with Mérida, Saragossa, and Toledo.[33] This mythic al-Andalus, like Ibn Ḥabīb's, uniquely inhabits the spatial limit of Islamdom and the temporal end of Islamic history, conferring upon al-Andalus a singular and exclusive Islamic identity.[34]

The appeal, longevity, and agency of Ibn Ḥabīb's discursive strategy centering the events of Islamic eschatology in the West and attributing political turmoil to the rulers' corruption and depravity—itself a prominent trope in Andalusi and Maghribi historiography from the eleventh century onward—is attested in the work of the thirteenth-century Andalusi pietist Abū 'Abd Allāh Muḥammad ibn Aḥmad, known as al-Qurṭubī. Writing after the Almohads ceded his native Córdoba to Castile in 1236 and Seville in 1248 as well as relinquishing Fez to the Marīnids (also in 1248), al-Qurṭubī endeavors to give the impression that he simply collects and transmits a random selection of received Islamic apocalyptic traditions. In fact, however, his own politically tumultuous age was perfectly suited to the renewed urgency of Andalusi apocalyptic thinking: al-Qurṭubī's original scheme casts the Maghribis and Andalusis in the critical role of the Mahdī's earliest ardent followers.[35] In the retelling, this eschatological figure will first appear in the Islamic West, where he will organize the Muslims into a fighting contingent and then lead them east to engage the Byzantine forces.[36] The Andalusi eschatological tradition retained its deeply meaningful psychological agency in cultural politics into the Naṣrid era. Jurists such as the Málagan Abū Bakr Muḥammad al-Fakhkhār (d. 1323) tapped into this traditional reservoir of the Islamic religious-historical imagination as a means of confronting and surmounting the sense of Islamic weakness, the shame of Granada's paying annual tribute to Christian Castile, the Muslims' fears of the Christians' physical immediacy, and the constant threat of their encroaching power.[37]

By contrast with Andalusi-centered Islamic traditions, some of which originated in Egypt, Muslim geographers of the Islamic East, such as al-Muqaddasī (b. 954), construed al-Andalus as a land at the periphery of Islamdom and of civilization per se, as a typically remote, beguiling, and ominous place of marvels and dangers, a curious place to which the imagination is drawn but that is best avoided in person.[38] Such conventional views found voice in unexpected places. Even the man of letters and otherwise Andalusi chauvinist Ibn Bassām al-Shantarīnī (1084–1147) gestures firmly in this direction. The introduction to his *adab* compilation, *Al-Dhakhīra fī maḥāsin ahl al-jazīra* (The Treasury of the Excellent Qualities of the People of the Peninsula) declares: "On account of their location in this clime, close to Christians in a land which is at the extremity of those conquered by Islam and quite removed from the influence of Arabic traditions, surrounded by the vast sea, by the Christians and the Goths—they [the people of al-Andalus] reap nothing but perdition and drink of a torrential sea."[39]

To summarize: the image of al-Andalus as an island or a triangle (*wa-balad al-andalus muthallathu l-shakl*),[40] surrounded on three sides by the uncertainties and perils of the "encircling ocean,"[41] inhabiting a distant place at the westernmost edge of Islamdom far from its eastern geographic center, and as an Islamic polity threatened by Christendom, endured. Al-Andalus was also portrayed as occupying an uncommon temporal space between the legendary past and the end of history, as well as between the here and now and the apocalyptic age. These elements of Andalusi-ness all functioned dialectically to situate al-Andalus at the epicenter of an unconventional rendering of Islamic history. The peculiar ninth-century representation of Andalusi geographical and temporal alterity clearly endured in the religious imagination throughout the classical age of Islam while the singularity of Andalusi otherness was reshaped during the tenth and eleventh centuries into the notion of Andalusi exceptionalism, to which we turn below and in Chapter 3. In other words, any residual sense of Andalusi provincialism was turned to constructive effect and served as an articulation of Andalusi power and ambition during the Umayyad caliphal period. For Andalusi political elites and religious and literary intellectuals of the classical age of Islam, geography dictated, but did not determine, destiny until they interfered with its conventional expression.

Al-Andalus: The Blessed Fertility of the Land

The abundant fertility and agricultural productivity of the land of al-Andalus and the wealth that it conferred on the Umayyad state and its inhabitants were construed first and foremost as signs of God's blessing and divine favor. This notion and the resultant image of the country go back to Isidore, as noted above, but its iteration in Andalusi Islam specifically signaled a crucial element of Andalusi exceptionalism. Prevailing astro-climatic theory reinforced the idea, since it situated al-Andalus in the temperate and desirable fourth region and the most moderate of seven habitable climatic zones (*aqālīm*). This medieval form of environmental determinism followed Hellenistic thinking going back to Ptolemy's *Megale Syntaxis*, as mediated by its late eighth-century Arabic translation.[42] Here is how the famous Andalusi historian Abū Bakr Aḥmad al-Rāzī (d. 955), most of whose work has been lost although significant parts were apparently preserved by his successors, put it (*apud* al-Maqqarī): "The land of al-Andalus is the western extreme of the fourth clime. In the opinion of the knowledgeable it is a land abundant in lowlands with good soil, fertile agricultural settlements, flowing with plentiful rivers and abundant fresh springs. Venomous beasts are rare. It is temperate in climate, weather and breezes. Its spring, fall, winter, and summer are relatively temperate and well-balanced such that no season generates excess. . . . Its fruits are ripe, at most times not wanting."[43] Al-Muqaddasī's nearly contemporaneous depiction of the Maghrib, including al-Andalus, a land he never visited, affirms al-Rāzī but concludes on a different, decidedly Mashriqī, note:

> This is a splendid region, extensive and distinguished. It is possessed of many towns and villages, remarkable in its resources and abundance. It has important border towns with many fortresses; here too are delightful gardens. Here, also is a number of separated tracts—islands as it were—as Andalusia, distinguished and marvelous. . . . The cities of this region are concealed from

> view by olive trees, the ground covered with fig trees and vineyards; streams make their way through it, trees fill the lowland valleys. However, some of its areas are remote, much of it is desert, the roads are difficult and dangers many. Situated in a remote corner of the realm of Islam, part of it is intercepted from the rest by the sea. No one wants to go there, no one goes there, no one enquires of it, and no one speaks well of it. It has produced no scholar of renown, no celebrated ascetic, except, perhaps for a very few.[44]

The tenth-century Eastern geographer Ibn Ḥawqal, who actually visited al-Andalus as a Fāṭimid agent during ʿAbd al-Raḥmān III's reign, likewise commented positively on the agricultural richness of the land and its significance for the country's prosperity. Nevertheless, he was even more blunt and graphic than al-Muqaddasī, offering a view of the serious ethical, martial, and intellectual shortcomings of al-Andalus's residents: "Among the extraordinary things in this Peninsula is that it still remains in the hands of its ruler, because its inhabitants are simpleminded, stupid, and low-spirited. They are far from such qualities as fortitude, courage, chivalry, and intrepidity and seldom do they encounter men of distinction and strength and brave soldiers."[45] Yet Ibn Ḥawqal also observed that Córdoba "has no equal in the Maghrib, or in the Jazīra, or Syria, or Egypt, to approximate the size of its population, the extent of its territory, area of its markets, cleanliness of its inhabitants, construction of its mosques, and number of its baths and hostelries."[46]

Representations of al-Andalus's agricultural bounty and the religious and political legitimacy that it conferred were especially pronounced from the time of the Umayyad caliphate. During this period, advanced irrigation methods and importation of new plants and techniques of cultivation from the East called *filāḥa hindiyya* (Indian agriculture) contributed significantly to the abundance, affluence, and stability of the country.[47] The thriving urban merchant middle class residing in Córdoba, in particular, supported this successful agricultural and trade-based political economy.[48] Regardless of the extent to which the caliph and the caliphate and its extensive central bureaucracy were responsible for these developments, the nexus between virtuous state administration and abundant agricultural yield, of a well-ordered landscape and justly ordered Islamic society, was reinforced by current notions in Islamic political philosophy connecting a general prosperity based upon successful agricultural cultivation with just governance and good statecraft.[49] Ibn Qutayba's (d. 889) "Kitāb al-sulṭān," in *'Uyūn al-akhbār*, for example, communicates the idea in the following maxim: "There is no rule except through men, and men do not subsist except through property, and no property except through cultivation and no cultivation except through justice and good policy" (*Lā sulṭāna illā bi-rijāl wa-lā rijāla illā bi-māl wa-lā māla illā bi-'imāra wa-lā 'imārata illa bi-'adl wa-ḥusn siyāsa*).[50]

This nexus of agronomy, political economy, and administration was inscribed in the celebrated "Calendar of Córdoba" (*Kitāb al-anwā'*; The Book of Lunar Mansions), an agriculturally oriented meteorological almanac attributed to the polymath 'Arīb ibn Sa'd al-Kātib al-Qurṭubī (d. ca. 980), commissioned by 'Abd al-Raḥmān III and dedicated to his son and successor al-Ḥakam II.[51] The image of a uniquely verdant and fertile al-Andalus and the ensuing traditions about it established the framework for descriptions of al-Andalus by later Muslim geographers and Andalusi historians. The Naṣrid court historian Ibn al-Khaṭīb (d. 1374), for example, amplifies the picture of a marvelously fertile landscape and depicts a divinely blessed country whose people's material prosperity, cultural productivity, and intellectual character set them apart and above: "God, may He be exalted, has endowed the country of al-Andalus with fertile land and abundant irrigation, sweet foods and swift animals, bountiful fruits, plentiful waters, extensive dwellings, clothing of excellent quality, fine utensils; plenty of weapons and pure air. He has endowed its people with whiteness in complexion, superior intellect, an aptitude for crafts, verve for the sciences, penetrating discernment, cultural refinement mostly lacking in other lands."[52]

Ibn Khaldūn noted the Andalusis' eagerness to take advantage of the land's agricultural bounty: "As we know, the [people of al-Andalus], of all civilized people, are the ones most devoted to agriculture. It rarely happens among them that a man in authority or an ordinary person has no tract of land or field or does not do some farming."[53] According to art historian Francisco Prado-Vilar, the Andalusi preoccupation with agriculture was so pervasive that it had a broader social upshot and aesthetic effect manifested in Andalusi material and literary culture: "This identification of vegetation and fertility as blessings from God was especially prominent in the minds of the people of al-Andalus who used this argument to demonstrate the superiority of their country in comparison with the rest of the Islamic world and its status as the chosen land of God."[54] Prado-Vilar's assertion readily applies to the eleventh and twelfth centuries, when Abū l-Walīd al-Ḥimyarī (d. ca. 1048) compiled an anthology of Andalusi nature poetry, *Al-Badīʿ fī waṣf al-rabīʿ*, as evidence of a superior Andalusi cultural product and Abū Iṣḥāq ibn Khafāja (1058–1138/1139) famously composed Andalusi *nawriyyāt* (floral poetry).[55]

Genealogy, Election, and Providential History in Umayyad al-Andalus

Besides the divinely endowed aura of al-Andalus's agricultural abundance, the nucleus of what would become the trope of Andalusi exceptionalism was also inscribed in various Andalusi assertions of their political leaders' and religious scholars' Islamic nobility, authenticity, and legitimacy: they traced their political and religious lineage back to the first century of Islam.[56] Avid interest in genealogy, its religious and political instrumentality in Islamic society, and its status as a branch of learning were not unique to al-Andalus.[57] At the same time, the significance of what authority genealogy rightly confers was highly contested in classical Islam, with its opposing emphasis on piety as the sole arbiter of religious and political legitimacy going back to the Quran (49:13) itself ("Indeed, the most noble of you in the sight of Allah is the most righteous of you"). Yet the Quran (23:101) also appears to concede that genealogy's social function of will not vanish until the Day of Judgment ("For when the Trumpet is blown, that day there shall be no kinship any more between them, neither will they question one another").

Specifically, the Andalusi Umayyad dynasty traced its ancestry back to a related clan of the Prophet Muḥammad's Qurayshī tribe as well as to their assassinated forebear, the third Caliph ʿUthmān b. ʿAffān, the Caliph Muʿāwiyya, and their ancestors of the ill-fated Damascus-based caliphate.[58] For example, the historical *urjūza* authored by the Umayyad court poet Ibn ʿAbd Rabbihi chronicles poetically the divinely favored pious exploits of ʿAbd al-Raḥmān III. The epic poem introduces Ibn ʿAbd Rabbihi's religiously charmed patron ʿAbd al-Raḥmān III as "the most eminent of the Banū Marwān" (i.e., the Umayyads) (line 15) and the "Caliph of God whom He chose and elected over all creation" (line 26).[59] It should be noted that, as a rule, the Umayyads promoted the genealogical connection to Muḥammad with utmost caution because of stronger Fāṭimid and Abbasid claims of closer proximity to and direct descent from the Prophet's inner family.[60] In any case, the overdetermined religious language and themes of Ibn ʿAbd Rabbihi's *urjūza* assert the Umayyad caliph's sacred charisma and divine guidance: the frequency of the title imam over the worldly political titles *malik*, emir, sayyid, and sultan, and even more than *khalīfa*, in the poem emphasizes ʿAbd al-Raḥmān III's religious merit and the transcendent nature and legitimacy of his authority, which he employs for "restoration of the divine order over al-Andalus."[61]

Andalusi and Maghribi chronicles, such as the anonymous *Fatḥ al-andalus* (completed after 1087, the last year it chronicles), amplify the association of the Andalusi Umayyads with the Prophet Muḥammad.[62] The similarly anonymous compilation *Akhbār majmuʿa* (ca. the eleventh century, probably containing earlier materials) extols the Umayyad emirs whose virtues prefigure ʿAbd al-Raḥmān III's, especially the founder of the dynasty ʿAbd al-Raḥmān I.[63] These sources narrate episodes of the heroic adventures of ʿAbd al-Raḥmān I (d. 788), the orphaned grandson of the Umayyad caliph Hishām. This first emir of Umayyad al-Andalus is famously identified as the "Falcon of Quraysh" (*ṣaqr Quraysh*) in a tale involving the Abbasid caliph al-Manṣūr.[64] Such hagiographical accounts of ʿAbd al-Raḥmān I follow his exploits traversing Syria and North Africa en route to al-Andalus. Typically, he encounters jealous rivals and is pursued by enemies and Abbasid agents. Eventually, the young man picks up support among Berbers, to whom he was related on his mother's side, along with garnering the backing of Umayyad *mawālī* (clients) and Syrian Umayyad loyalists already present in al-Andalus. Notably, neither Ibn Ḥabīb in the ninth century nor Ibn al-Qūṭiyya (d. 977; author of *Taʾrīkh iftitāḥ al-andalus*)[65] in the tenth century narrates heroic traditions about ʿAbd al-Raḥmān I. Such traditions appear to have been the product of the eleventh century, although, as noted, some of them are likely based on earlier, perhaps orally transmitted, tales of his adventures.

In these striking, imaginatively constructed, episodic accounts, ʿAbd al-Raḥmān I's grandfather and others, typically outsiders such as Jews, recognize him as destined by God for greatness. Many such tales involve the narrative deployment of dramatic scenes of "recognition" (anagnorisis), wherein the Umayyad refugee is identified as destined to rule. Some narrative anecdotes are suggested by typological episodes in the *Sīra* of the Prophet Muḥammad. Yarns also are vested with intertextual authority derived from other ancient Near Eastern religious narratives regarding figures of great significance in Islam—notably, Moses.[66] They portray the orphaned Umayyad exile ʿAbd al-Raḥmān I by association to Muḥammad and Moses as a larger-than-life epic figure in Islam.[67] For example, *Akhbār majmūʿa* tells the well-known *Sīra*-inspired story of the governor of Ifrīqiya chancing upon a Jew who informs him: "A man from the royal line will take over al-Andalus; he is called 'Abd al-Raḥmān, and his hair is in two braids" (*dhū al-ẓafīratayn*). Eager to fulfill this prophecy himself by imitating 'Abd al-Raḥmān's sartorial style or by killing him, the governor is cautioned by the Jew: "You are not from the royal line."[68]

Islamic traditions regarding the preordained Islamization of al-Andalus complement the topos of 'Abd al-Raḥmān I's providential chosenness. Such traditions developed around the figures of Ṭāriq ibn Ziyād, the ostensibly Berber commander of the Muslim troops in 711, and his apparent rival (according to later sources) Mūsā ibn Nuṣayr, the governor of Ifrīqiya who arrived on the scene to direct the final stages of the conquest of the peninsula and administer the new Islamic polity. Ibn Ḥabīb, for instance, relates that Ṭāriq came across an old man in Tlemcen who predicted the conquest of al-Andalus.[69] Like the typological motifs found in the traditional biography of the Prophet and recast for 'Abd al-Raḥmān I, stories concerning Ṭāriq display parallels to elements in the *Sīra*. Just as the monk Baḥīra is said to have identified the Prophet Muḥammad by a distinguishing birthmark on his skin, Ṭāriq is reported to have encountered an old woman with the foreknowledge that the peninsula's conqueror would have a mole (like his) on his left shoulder.[70] Ibn Ḥabīb also relates a vignette about the legendary "House of Locks," located in Toledo, in which the last Visigothic king, Roderick, uncovered a prophecy of the imminent Islamic conquest. Subsequently, Ṭāriq enters the peninsula and, in due course, locates the marvelous house.[71] The Umayyad loyalist Ibn al-Qūṭiyya relates the tale as well in his *Ta'rīkh*, albeit with considerably different details.[72] The passage in Ibn al-Qūṭiyya is followed by another anecdote in which Ṭāriq, en route to the peninsula aboard a ship with his troops, has a dream in which the Prophet Muḥammad appears to reassure him of the successful outcome of the Muslims' impending invasion of the Visigothic kingdom.[73]

In the same way that sources sympathetic to the Umayyads affirmed the dynasty's Islamic credentials via genealogy, typology, prediction, foretellings, and prophecy—that is, through myths and symbols—Andalusi religious authorities endeavored to identify themselves as recipients of Islamic traditions from the prestigious *tābi'ūn* ("successors" or "followers of the Prophet's companions").[74] These pious warriors, members of the early Islamic aristocracy—the second or third generation of the Prophet Muḥammad's immediate followers—were supposedly among the earliest Muslims to settle in al-Andalus, as already noted by Ibn Ḥabīb in the ninth century. They are said to have died in battle as martyrs, with all the accompanying religious legitimacy that that status conveys.[75] Ibn al-Faraḍī's (d. 1013) biographical dictionary of Andalusi religious scholars, *Ta'rīkh 'ulamā' l-andalus*, identifies five such "successors" from its various sources.[76]

The importance that Andalusi tradition assigned the *tābi'ūn* who arrived in the peninsula appears to have grown over time, effectively amplifying the religious stature of al-Andalus within Islamdom. Writing in the seventeenth century, al-Maqqarī recognizes twenty-eight such individuals through his many different sources.[77] Modern historians consider the number of *tābi'ūn* who actually landed in the peninsula to be few in number, but they certainly included the redoubtable Mūsā ibn Nuṣayr, an Umayyad "client" (*mawlā*) and governor of Qayrawān, who joined the campaign and assumed leadership of the effort to take over al-Andalus, and Mu'āwiya b. Ṣāliḥ (d. ca. 774), who was imagined by later tradition as having been the first scholar to introduce hadith to al-Andalus.[78] Finally, the supposedly indiscriminate Andalusi practice of adopting the *nisba* "al-Anṣārī" after the legendary Medinese "defenders," devoted and devout followers of the Prophet Muḥammad, provided many Andalusis with a distinguished and pious Islamic genealogy. The practice was so deeply rooted in Andalusi society and culture that it continued into the Naṣrid period.[79]

Al-Andalus: Bastion of Islamic "Orthodoxy"[80]

The pursuit, study, cultivation, production, transmission, and dissemination of knowledge (in its religious, scientific, philosophical, and aesthetic forms and in the power it conferred) stood at the center of classical Islamic civilization and its Jewish subcultural adaptation.[81] For Muslims and Jews, religious knowledge, its highest manifestation, originated in the East in the form of their revelation-scriptures, interpretive traditions, and resultant systems of holy law. Accordingly, the Islamic West found itself intellectually and spiritually dependent on the Eastern sources where the earliest figures in religious, scientific, and literary scholarship appeared and where the major institutions of Islamic (and Jewish) learning were first founded.

The spread of Islam from the Hijāz to the Levant and North Africa during the seventh century and subsequently to al-Andalus shortly after the turn of the eighth stoked interest in and demand for the sacred knowledge of Islam (*'ilm*) from its Eastern sources, authorities, and teachers. Córdoba did not begin to become a center for the study of the Islamic disciplines in its own right until the mid-ninth century. Few visitors arrived from the East during its first two centuries; so as an Islamic polity, al-Andalus relied on religious pilgrimage and travel for study. Andalusi seekers of knowledge (*ahl al-riḥla*; *al-riḥla fī ṭalab al-ʿilm*), intellectually and spiritually ambitious individuals, sought out teachers and established conduits of transmission with centers of Islamic scholarship in the East.[82] Indeed, as Houari Touati puts it in his seminal study on the subject: "Muslim men of letters of the Middle Ages were mad for travel."[83] Numerous Andalusi scholars, accordingly, traveled east in quest of knowledge, for study, and pilgrimage.[84] They returned to their homes in the West, laden with books and bearing learning, eager to enlighten Andalusi students and scholars with their erudition, scholarship, and connections.[85] Extensive commercial activity across Islamdom reinforced the East–West channel, transmitting knowledge of sacred law and lore, scientific wisdom, and the texts dedicated to these spheres of inquiry.[86]

The corpus of Islamic religious knowledge and the intellectual regimen and methods of study required to appreciate and make use of it eventually were transferred through the movement of population from the Islamic East to the Islamic West during the ninth and tenth centuries, apparently catalyzed by pervasive climate change, resultant food shortages, ensuing economic decline, and political instability, among other factors.[87] Furthermore, the waning of Eastern political hegemony, a complex process that also involved religious-political tensions internal to Islamic society, occasioned the rise of regional urban centers throughout Islamdom, each requiring its own religious elites. The calamitous developments in the ecological and political economy of the Islamic East coincided with the successful application of the aforementioned new irrigation techniques that brought greater agricultural bounty to al-Andalus in the westernmost Mediterranean.[88]

Umayyad Córdoba thus began to draw an increased number of visitors from the Islamic East, including religious scholars, although none were regarded among the most accomplished. This latter development did not go unnoticed. The "chapters" of Ibn al-Faraḍī's biographical dictionary of religious scholars in al-Andalus are arranged alphabetically, according to first names. They conclude with an addendum providing information on *ghurabāʾ* ("foreigners"), that is, nonnative newcomers to the Andalusi intellectual scene. By the early tenth century, Córdoba also had become a magnet for aspiring religious scholars from other Andalusi cities and for Mālikī *ʿulamāʾ*

from Ifrīqiya, some apparently fleeing Fāṭimid persecution or authority, such as the renowned Ḥārith al-Khushanī (d. 971), who entered the circle of scholars and literati sponsored by al-Ḥakam II.[89]

The Islamic "genealogy" of shapers and transmitters of religious knowledge and the legitimacy that it conferred figured prominently in the formation of Andalusi religious self-identification. Al-Andalus's self-image and station as a bastion of Islamic religious probity and orthopraxy was predicated on the nearly exclusive and continuous supremacy of its Mālikī scholars, scholarship, and institutions, down to the demise of the last Andalusi polity at the turn of the sixteenth century.[90] Mālikī legal practice seems to have been established as the preferred rite in al-Andalus during the mid-ninth century emirate of al-Ḥakam I and the formation in Córdoba of a circle of Andalusi Mālikī religious intellectuals.[91] During the tenth century, the Umayyad caliphs formally adopted the Mālikī *madhhab* as the official legal tradition and practice in al-Andalus. Mālikism enjoyed implicit and explicit lines of Islamic continuity, going back to the time of the Prophet Muḥammad in Medina and subsequently through the Medinese authority and thinker Mālik ibn Anās (d. 796).

The predominance of Mālikī scholars, scholarship, and law in al-Andalus served as a reassuring and effective marker of the Andalusi Sunni religious character. Mālikism's firm embrace was textualized in the prominent and peculiarly Andalusi literary custom of recording, transmitting, and updating in biographical dictionaries the uninterrupted centuries-long chain of Andalusi Mālikī religious scholars. This literary convention reflected the significance attached to anchoring Andalusi religious tradition and Mālikī practice in historical continuity. Thus, Maribel Fierro notes: "Al-Andalus stands out in the Islamic world as the region that produced an uninterrupted chain of such compilations," a practice that manages "to create the impression of an unbroken pedagogical process ensuring the correct transmission of doctrines and practices . . . whether explicitly in their teachings or implicitly with their biographies what the Andalusi *'ulamā'* were claiming was that they had been able to preserved intact the truest understanding of both Revelation and the example of the Prophet Muhammad."[92]

As late as the Naṣrid period, Andalusi scholars such as Shams al-Dīn Muḥammad al-Rā'ī (b. 1380) continued to hew to Mālikī tradition. More significant, they asserted its observance as a critical sign of Andalusi Islamic authenticity. Al-Rā'ī's *Intiṣār*'s tribute to Mālik and the merits of his followers includes the following passage on "Why the People of the West Follow Mālik":

> You should know that when the Maghribis and the 'ulamā' of al-Andalus wanted to seek knowledge, they would head for the City of the Messenger of Allah. . . . There they found Mālik, who was the most knowledgeable of the people of his time with regard to the Book, the Sunna, the opinions of the Companions, *qiyās*, understanding words and their meanings, and knowing those matters on which there was a consensus and those about which there was difference of opinion. . . . So they took from him the knowledge and *'amal* [practice] of the people of Madina and returned to their country, where they ousted all of the *madhhab*s of the people of Iraq and any others.[93]

The Andalusi reputation for adhering strictly and chauvinistically to Mālikī doctrine rapidly reached the Islamic East.[94] For example, the geographer al-Muqaddasī famously cites conversations with "some Andalusi shaykhs" visiting the East who reported to him regarding the universal, absolute, exclusive, and unyieldingly strict Andalusi adherence to Mālikī law. The account clearly presents an embellished and hyperbolic depiction of Andalusi religiosity, although it is impossible to discern whether it exaggerates Andalusi practice, inflates the sources, or reflects the reporter's imagination: "if they learn of any Ḥanafī or Shāfi'ī, they expel him, and if they detect any Mu'tazilī or Shī'ī or the like, they often kill them."[95] Indeed, the predominance of Mālikism in tenth-century al-Andalus meant that its society managed to avoid the religious discord and division that plagued the Islamic East at that time.[96]

Recall al-Andalus' high-standing reputation for its interconfessional tolerance among many modern social, religious, and cultural historians. The famous account of the late tenth-century Andalusi scholar Abū 'Umar ibn Muḥammad ibn Sa'dī, who journeyed East in quest of learning, paints a different picture in which the conduct of interreligious discussion in the East eclipses the Islamic West in its religious elites' willingness to negotiate difference. The report, originally preserved in al-Ḥumaydī's (b. ca. 1029) biographical dictionary, relates how the pious visitor to Baghdad is said to have consulted with a prominent Andalusi scholar whom he encountered on his journey and to have related his experiences to another in

Qayrawān on his return trip. Ibn Saʿdī supposedly was horrified to witness representatives of various religions, denominations, theological, and intellectual orientations engaged in disputations with Muslims on an equal footing in which only rational arguments were permitted.[97] This critical sensibility—that Andalusis did not always appreciate enlightened social practices that they discovered in the Islamic East—carried over into the Almohad period, as evident in Ibn Jubayr's (b. 1145) over-the-top blanket critique of the Islam that he encountered in the Mashriq: "There is no Islam except in the land of the West" (*lā islāma illā bi-bilādi l-maghrib*).[98] Such regional differences—real, emphatically exaggerated, or imagined—served the purposes and self-image of Andalusi political, religious, and literary elites.[99]

Although it recognized the sway of the Mālikī *ʿulamāʾ* and their knowledge-based social and religious power, the Umayyad state was not content to leave it to scholars and jurists alone to secure Islamic legitimacy for the polity of al-Andalus. Mālikī exclusivism was the perfect vehicle for expressing Andalusi difference in Islamdom as rigorously orthopraxic. Politically speaking, the Umayyads' strict support of Mālikī law was one of the bases for how they portrayed their military activity and political struggle against the Ismāʿīlī Shīʿa Fāṭimids and their opposition to the supposedly Ḥanafī-inclined Abbasids. Their resolute investment in Mālikism also explains the impulse behind the Umayyads' offensive directed against certain Islamic esoteric circles in al-Andalus.[100]

At the intersection of Islamic history and material culture, a dizzying array of Umayyad traditions, gestures, projects, and practices was designed to reinforce the aura of the dynasty's Islamic legitimacy before the Andalusi public and to onlookers abroad. Consider the following roster of expressive acts in the form of the testimony of material culture. Around the time of the declaration of the caliphate in 929, the Umayyad state commenced minting gold dinar, a more than symbolic prerogative of their righteous authority to rule.[101] So, too, the legendary bloodstained ʿUthmānic Quranic codex (*muṣḥaf*) found its way to al-Andalus by "miraculous journey." It was stored in the Great Mosque of Córdoba, whose new ornate *miḥrāb-maqṣūra* complex during the caliphate is thought to have functioned as the "architectural reliquary" for the artifact.[102] This congregational mosque was originally completed in 786–787, enlarged during the second quarter of the ninth century, and then three times during the tenth century, in order to accommodate the ever-growing community of Andalusi Muslims. Its imposing dimensions were so grand that al-Rāzī (*apud* al-Maqqarī) described it as "the largest in the world."[103] The mosque was rededicated in 965 under al-Ḥakam II as a testament to the Umayyads' triumph and served as "an iconographic image" of the layout of the Prophet's mosque in Medina.[104] Furthermore, the new movable *minbar* in Córdoba's congregational mosque was specifically designed to evoke the Prophet Muḥammad's own pulpit in Medina.[105] Finally, the Umayyad caliphs' use of specific symbolic prophetic colors—green and red—for their building and decorations, military tents, and flags were calculated to conjure the figure of Muḥammad and their association with him.[106] These many performances, maneuvers, practices, and procedures—"resorting to every means at their disposal," in the words of Maribel Fierro—represent a deliberate and concerted effort to link Córdoba and the Umayyads with Medina and the Prophet Muḥammad: they served related ideological and legitimizing functions as visible signs of the Islamic rightfulness of the Umayyads' restoration for the entire community and visitors to gaze upon and for others to hear about via oral and written testimony.[107]

The vocabulary of Islamic legitimacy predicted on "the sanctity of immemorial tradition" and religious and political charismatic leadership in the senses introduced by Weber was also inscribed in Umayyad court poetry, such as Ibn 'Abd Rabbihi's aforementioned historical epic poem;[108] in the production of ceremonial panegyrics addressed to the Umayyad caliphs;[109] in the decoration and calligraphy on ivory caskets and other luxury commodities commissioned at court;[110] in public gestures and protocols such as 'Īd celebrations and the performance of rituals of allegiance to the caliph al-Ḥakam II as head of the community of Muslims, recorded in detail by official historiographers 'Isā al-Rāzī and Ibn Ḥayyān (as preserved by al-Maqqarī);[111] in the Umayyads' architectural patronage of suburban villa-estates (Ar., *munya*; pl., *munan* or *munyāt*) and inclusion of them as sites for civic processions;[112] in the Umayyads' extensive patronage of scientific and Islamic religious scholarship, including biographical dictionaries of Mālikī religious scholars and their practice of extending of invitations to scholars from the Islamic East such as the eminent Arabic grammarian and philologist Abū 'Alī Ismā'īl al-Qālī (d. 967) to come from Baghdad to Córdoba, where he taught al-Zubaydī, the famous Andalusi scholar from Seville;[113] in the framing as jihad of 'Abd al-Raḥmān III's campaigns against the Christian kingdoms to the north and his expansionist ambitions in North Africa to the south, for which he earned the *laqab* (sobriquet) al-Nāṣir li-dīn allāh (Defender of the [True] Religion of God); in the Umayyads' monumental building projects, especially the expansion of the aforementioned Friday Great

Mosque and construction of the caliphal palace city Madīnat al-Zahrā' on the outskirts of Córdoba (construction beginning in 936);[114] and in al-Ḥakam II's establishment of the fabled imperial caliphal library on a previously unheard-of scale. This legitimacy-striving caliph earned the reputation as an uncommonly intellectual ruler: al-Khushanī reported that al-Ḥakam II "conceived the excellent plan of initiating the study of history [and] the knowledge of genealogies, and he wished for the merits of the ancestors to be published."[115]

All the highlighted practices and gestures signal the Umayyads' ambitious purpose to identify al-Andalus as a political, religious, and cultural center of Islam, notwithstanding its location on the western frontier of Islamdom. Here is how Fierro keenly puts it: "If al-Andalus was on the periphery of the Islamic world and its caliph did not rule over the Holy Places of Islam (Mecca and Medina), these shortcomings were compensated for by the fact that al-Andalus safeguarded the Medinese legal practice that represented orthodoxy. Given that the Umayyads were the legitimate inheritors of the Messenger of God, it was as if the Prophet himself ruled over al-Andalus."[116]

Islamic Legitimacy and the Trope of Andalusi Exceptionalism

For two centuries before 'Abd al-Raḥmān III declared it a caliphate, the Andalusi Umayyad emirate persevered as an outlying Islamic polity on the western edge of Islamdom, far removed from the central Islamic lands. By necessity and design, the Umayyad emirs charted a pseudo-independent course for al-Andalus: it was politically disconnected from the Abbasid caliphate while economically and culturally integrated with the rest of Islamdom through trans-Mediterranean trade networks and by language and religion. At the same time, paradoxically, al-Andalus would appear to its inhabitants and to outsiders as somewhat apart and seemingly different, largely on account of its geographical position, its supposed isolation, its peculiar history and society, and its proximity to Christendom. Andalusi religious scholars relied upon authorities in Qayrawān, Cairo, and the Hijāz for acquiring Islamic knowledge and obtaining books. Their need to turn to outsiders for such purposes reinforced the hierarchical order that the political geography of Islam imposed, in which the East inhabited the center and al-Andalus the periphery of Islamdom, Islamic history, and Islamic society. Andalusi dependence on Eastern centers of learning and their sages meant that Andalusi religious intellectuals accepted the authority implied by Eastern control of knowledge and of Islamic cultural and symbolic capital.[117]

Acquisition of sacred knowledge, with its incommensurate Islamic value, brought implicit Andalusi recognition of the power of those from whom it was obtained. Those who originally produced, possessed, and transmitted it—the *'ulamā'* from the eastern lands of Islamdom—functioned as the authentic religious heirs of the Prophet and genuine guardians of his legacy in the knowledge and piety-based "genealogy" of Sunni Islam. This powerful intersection of the politics of geography and of knowledge production loomed large and was absorbed into the consciousness of Andalusi political, religious, and literary elites. Tenth-century Umayyad ideology and propaganda and the supremacy, if not exclusivity, enjoyed by Mālikī *'ulamā'* in Andalusi Islam represented first responses to cope with and transcend the anomalous sociohistorical and sociocultural condition of Andalusi otherness.

The ideas, ideology, practices, performances, and productions sketched in this chapter are conventionally understood as expressly designed to confer incontestable Islamic legitimacy on the Umayyad Andalusi caliphs, their realm, and the unassailable Islamic authority of Andalusi Mālikī religious scholars. They were indeed legitimacy-seeking, constructing, conferring, and affirming myths, symbols, and signs in the political-religious sense shared by every Islamic polity.[118] However, the vocabulary of Islamic legitimacy was uniquely exigent for Andalusi political, religious, literary, and scientific elites. These players were also always concerned with and anxious about the legitimacy specific to al-Andalus—not only in complex counterpoint to the Fāṭimids and Abbasids, as commonly thought, but regarding the authenticity of Islam in al-Andalus, the legitimacy of al-Andalus itself as an Islamic polity, and the value of the Andalusis' intellectual achievements and literary artistry.

The Umayyads responded to the Andalusi condition dictated by geography and history by asserting the Islamic legitimacy of their own religious and political aspirations. They developed an intricate system of defensive discursive and symbolic efforts of resistance to the conventional Islamic geographic paradigm, inverting its representation and overturning the dominant political hierarchy. In so doing, the Umayyad used precisely the same conceptual, discursive, and performative tools—genealogy, orthopraxy, and symbolic gestures to providential Islamic history—on behalf of the "normative" model of Islam and Islamdom viewed from the East.[119] They increasingly took the literary form of representing al-Andalus as a place of significance in Islam rather than a place defined by its imagined isolation, difference, and supposed marginality. Accordingly, we can trace the textual origins of the idea of al-Andalus as a culturally distinct, ambitious, and legitimately essential and central place in Islamdom to that historical moment in which an idiosyncratic Andalusi religious and political self-image was constructed and promulgated and its power articulated. It would evolve into the full-fledged trope of Andalusi exceptionalism during the eleventh century, when Andalusi religious and literary intellectuals would build upon the Umayyad legacy. The history of the trope signals how Andalusi self-consciousness of religious, political, and cultural otherness was inverted to become a carefully crafted expression of Andalusi self-esteem and exceptionalism.

Chapter 2

Without al-Andalus, There Would Be No Sefarad

The Origins of Sefardi Exceptionalism

> Sefarad is al-Andalus in the Arabs' language.
>
> —Moses ibn Ezra

> Every king trembles
> and descends from his throne and dispatches tributes
> to him in Sefarad.
>
> —Dūnash ben Labrāṭ

Judaism and the Jews, whose very names are determined etymologically by ties of memory to a particular place (Judea), embraced the concept of diaspora out of political, religious, and historical necessity. Following the exile of Judean elites to Babylonia in 587–586 BCE, the idea of diaspora became enmeshed in a complex bundle of remembered and imagined experiences, along with decidedly ahistorical aspirations such as redemption and return. Scattering, dispersal (Ezek. 36:19: "I scattered them among the nations, and they were dispersed through the countries"), and recuperation (Ezek. 36:24: "I will take you from among the nations and gather you from all the countries, and I will bring you back to your own land") were already inscribed as tropes in biblical literature of the First Exile. Diaspora thus became a critical feature of the dialectic of Jewish history in that it described the current state of the Jews' dispersion and sense of rupture with a past "pristine age" yet reinforced their expectation and hope that it was destined to come to an end with the "ingathering of the exiles." Jews of very different literary, intellectual, and spiritual orientations produced what Esther Benbassa calls a "liturgization of suffering" and treated exile/diaspora as the pivotal trope of Jewish experience.[1] Needless to say, the Jews' notion of diaspora represented a fundamentally different conceptualization of space and place from the Muslims' "Dār al-Islām" (Islamdom). How, exactly, did Jewish social, religious, and literary elites of tenth-century al-Andalus negotiate this complex theme of Jewish life, history, and thought, even as they grappled with the sense that, like their Andalusi Muslim neighbors, they inhabited the periphery while the Jews of the Islamic East occupied the center?

It is not an accident that the place the Jews called "Sefarad," in Hebrew, came of age as an independent-minded, significant site of Jewish society and culture at the same historical moment as Islamic al-Andalus.[2] Although it was neither urgent nor even necessary since, unlike as with the Umayyads, no political legitimacy was at stake, Jewish elites took advantage of the favorable conditions created by the consolidation of Umayyad authority and the relative security of their place in the dynamic political economy and society of tenth-century al-Andalus. It is a sign of the fullness of their social and cultural integration in Islamic al-Andalus that they began to think of and assert themselves as inhabitants of something far greater than a provincial center, just as the power of the ecumenical rabbinic authorities in Baghdad showed signs of declining.

As observed in Chapter 1, the tenth century brought substantial changes to the demography and political economy of al-Andalus. Its small but decidedly urbanized Jewish community never amounted to a numerically significant percentage of the overall population but was demographically concentrated in major cities and larger towns.[3] Freedom of movement from al-Andalus to the Maghrib, Ifrīqiya, and the Islamic East and the economic prosperity of the Umayyad state and society were factors in the formation of an ambitious, influential, and interrelated class of Andalusi Jewish courtiers, Mediterranean traders, and religious and literary intellectual elites.[4] They famously conjured and evinced communal and personal aspirations without parallel in Jewish history; and they established new institutions and traditions, pursued original cultural ventures, and produced innovative forms of expression, all of which left a lasting impression of their unique place in Jewish history.

Construction of a distinct Andalusi Jewishness also required a foil—namely, the Jewish communities of Eastern lands, against which Andalusi Jewish society, culture, and authority could be measured and defined, although not nearly to the extent of their Andalusi Muslim counterparts' struggle to achieve recognition in relation to the Islamic East. In the tenth century, Umayyad al-Andalus, Islamic and Jewish, found itself in a sufficiently independent position to imagine itself in competition or on an equal par with the East in terms of political-communal significance, religious stature, and, eventually, cultural standing. Let us first sketch the cultural history of the Jews of Hispania and al-Andalus up to the Umayyad caliphal age and then scrutinize the origins of the Andalusi Jews' emergent sense of Sefardi exceptionalism in the tenth century. Then we will turn to probing the sociopolitical work that this discursive trope accomplished for them.

Archaeological evidence of Jewish life in Roman Hispania dates to late antiquity in the form of inscriptions (a few trilingual in Greek, Latin, and Hebrew) on artifacts such as troughs and tombstones and considerable literary testimony from Latin sources regarding the Jews of Visigothic Hispania. Yet very little is known with any degree of reliability regarding the supposedly well-established community of the Jews of the Iberian Peninsula prior to tenth-century al-Andalus.[5] For our purposes, it is simply uncertain and arguably unlikely whether the Jews of Roman or Visigothic Hispania maintained any informal contact with the Palestinian rabbinical academy (yeshiva) that served as the authoritative center in matters of sacred law and custom for Jews of Roman-Byzantine lands from late antiquity into the early Middle Ages.[6]

Rabbinic tradition identified the extension of Eastern geonic authority over the Jews of al-Andalus with the spread of Islamic rule over most of the Iberian Peninsula in the eighth century.[7] Specifically, the arrival from Iraq (ca. 722) of the exilarch (*nasi*) Naṭrūnai bar Ḥaninai (or Ḥavivai) is said to mark a turning point: Naṭrūnai fled to the Maghrib after he was deposed in a dispute with the gaon of the Pumbedita academy.[8] According to a slightly later Sefardi legend-cum-tradition transmitted by Judah ben Barzillai al-Bargeloni, Naṭrūnai is said to have introduced the authoritative Babylonian Talmud and its study to the Jews of al-Andalus: "and he is the one who wrote the Talmud for the Sefardi Jews, from memory, not from a written text."[9] Thanks to Naṭrūnai's scribal and pedagogical efforts, the Jews of al-Andalus are said to have shifted their primary allegiance from the Palestinian geonim to the Iraqi Jewish rabbinic authorities. As evident in ninth-century correspondence from the Cairo Geniza, the Jews of al-Andalus would henceforth follow the traditions taught and circulated by the two rabbinical academies and their leaders in Baghdad. Theoretically, they would defer to Eastern geonic authority in matters of Jewish law, tradition, and culture.[10]

Abraham ibn Daud, the mid-twelfth-century Andalusi Jewish intellectual who relocated to Castilian Toledo, was instrumental in shaping the way in which Sefarad would be viewed as the successor to the traditional centers of Jewish life and lore in the East.[11] *Sefer ha-qabbalah* (The Book of Tradition) implicitly regards Sefarad and its Jews as central to the unfolding drama of Jewish history, going all the way back to the first century: "when Titus empowered Jerusalem, his lieutenant in charge of Spain request of him to send him some nobles of Jerusalem."[12] Then there is *Sefer ha-qabbalah*'s quizzical assertion that, after the destruction of the Second Temple, "the mastery of the Talmud now rested [exclusively] in Spain."[13] Modern Jewish historiography followed *Sefer ha-qabbalah* and linked the emergence of Jewish elites in al-Andalus to the decline of the East and interpreted the rise of North Africa and al-Andalus as autonomous regional centers of Jewish life as a break with the fading centralized geonic authority in the East.[14] Drawing on newly discovered documentary and literary material from the Cairo Geniza, Menahem Ben-Sasson noted problems with the conclusions espoused by Salo Baron and Gerson Cohen, among others, and painted a more complex picture of intercommunal developments between the Eastern centers in Palestine and Iraq and the farthest-flung Jewish diaspora communities. It seems likely that the Jewish communities of the Islamic West were never bound by absolute fidelity to Eastern geonic authority partly because they lay outside the confines of the four traditional realms divided among the Babylonian and Palestinian academies and the exilarch. Rather, the Jews of the Maghrib and al-Andalus sought engagement with or expressed allegiance to Jewish ecumenical and rabbinic leaders and institutions in the East for their own purposes and, conversely, were courted for their allegiance and financial support.[15] Indeed, the Qayrawānī rabbis' relationship with the Eastern geonim was complex and decidedly ambiguous at times. While the North Africans were highly deferential in their correspondence with the geonim, in practice they were selective in their actual application of geonic rulings, preferring to consult on legal principles and on textual issues in the Babylonian Talmud while diverging from geonic epistemology. After dissemination of the Talmud in written form, the Qayrawānī rabbis increasingly derived applied law on their own from its text and their traditions.[16]

Information yielded by the documents of the Cairo Geniza indicates that the Jewish communities of the Maghrib and, presumably, al-Andalus maintained a formal affiliation with the Iraqi rabbinical academies and their leaders. Yet the Westerners still cultivated a secondary, informal relationship with the geographically more proximate Palestinian academy, partly on account of Maghribi synagogues in Egypt and Palestine that fell within the orbit of the yeshiva and geonim there.[17] So, too, economic opportunity and commercial activity across the Islamic Mediterranean and Levant in what has been called a "closely knit trading area" created a network of business and social relationships involving Jews from West and East and including representatives from each of the tripartite (Babylonian, Palestinian, Karaite) congregations, especially in Fāṭimid Cairo.[18] The fluidity of this commercial network was further reinforced by the movement of population from east to west and from west to east, whereby Andalusis and Maghribis, including Jews, could be found in virtually every urban center of classical Islamdom. In any case, the primary intercommunal affiliation with the historically ascendant Iraqi academies had profound consequences for religious and literary scholarship and the cultural life of the Jews of al-Andalus.

Like Umayyad al-Andalus and its Andalusi Muslim religious and literary intellectuals who depended upon Eastern sources of knowledge, the transformative cultural developments of mid-tenth-century Jewish al-Andalus that accompanied and justified the first inkling of Andalusi Jewish exceptionalism were preceded by, and would scarcely have been possible without, the vibrant intellectual activity among the Jews of ninth- and early tenth-century Iraq. From Moritz Steinschneider to Salo Baron, Eliyahu Ashtor and S. D. Goitein, scholars of Jewish history have long recognized the multifaceted communal, religious, and literary activities of Saʿadia Gaon, a native of Egypt drawn to the centers of rabbinic scholarship in Baghdad at the turn of the tenth century, as setting the stage and laying the intellectual foundation for the blossoming and thriving of Judeo-Arabic culture, in general, and for subsequent developments in Golden Age Jewish al-Andalus, in particular.[19] For instance, scholars cite the twelfth-century polymath Abraham ibn Ezra's (b. ca. 1089–d. ca. 1167) homage to his predecessors in Hebrew grammatical studies. He famously appreciated Saʿadia using a Talmudic designation as "the foremost speaker in every area" or alternatively understood as "foremost speculative theologian" in loan translation from the Arabic *mutakallim* [*ro'sh ha-m^edabbrim b^e-khol maqom*].[20] Nevertheless, Andalusi Jewish sources themselves do not fully credit Saʿadia for their cultural awakening in general, but rather they acknowledge his specific insights, traditions, and accomplishments.

Sa'adia was indeed a seminal and innovating Rabbanite figure who explored the latest Arabo-Islamic modes of inquiry and tested the entire range of new literary genres, including biblical Hebrew grammar and philology, linguistic-literary and stylistically sensitive biblical translation, rational exegesis and linear commentary, communal polemic, halakhic monographs, Hebrew poetics, and systematic speculative theology that Jewish literary intellectuals absorbed from Arabo-Islamic culture.[21] His rabbinic authority as head of the Sura academy and his unimpeachable religious credentials were undeniably critical in transforming Jewish intellectual and cultural life under Islam. However, Sa'adia had predecessors, partners, and competitors in each of these ventures. Until relatively recently, the conventional historical narrative tended to neglect or downplay the significant, even essential, contribution of Karaite thinkers and scholars in shaping the new Jewish intellectual agenda. For example, a generation before Sa'adia, the idiosyncratic and presumed Karaite Dāwūd ibn Marwān al-Muqammaṣ, author of *'Ishrūn maqāla* (Twenty Chapters), appears to have been the first to compose a work of Jewish theology.[22] The ninth-century Karaite thinker, biblical exegete, and communal leader Daniel al-Qūmisī, who wrote in Hebrew and added Arabic glosses, followed shortly after Muqammaṣ, by most accounts.[23]

Aside from their critical role in establishing the new disciplines of dialectical theology and biblical exegesis and initiating the literary genres associated with these discourses, tenth- and eleventh-century Karaite religious intellectuals centered in Jerusalem, such as Abū Ya'qūb Yūsuf ibn Nūḥ and his student Abū l-Faraj Hārūn ibn al-Faraj, contributed mightily to the new field of Hebrew philological research.[24] Their importance was such that the latter is apparently mentioned favorably, although not identified, by the aforementioned Andalusi Rabbanite grammarian, exegete, scientist, and poet Abraham ibn Ezra.[25] In sum, the intellectual and cultural history of the Jews of classical Islam currently draws ever closer attention to the critical role that Karaite Jewish religious intellectuals played in the Islamic East before, alongside, and in competition with Sa'adia Gaon in stimulating the development of Arabic-inspired literary models in a new Jewish literary system and in placing systematic inquiry into the linguistic, stylistic, aesthetic, and theological facets of the Hebrew Bible at the center of Jewish culture in the lands of Islam.[26]

Typically, the perspective of Jewish social and literary history on the intellectual life of this period moves rapidly from early tenth-century Baghdad to the Andalusi awakening in mid-tenth-century Córdoba; a cursory nod is given to the Maghrib as the natural geographical intermediary in the process.[27] Indeed, Andalusi Jewish tradition and its projection of exceptionalism encouraged such a view. Abraham ibn Daud's report of the exilarch Ḥezekiah ben David's two sons "who fled to Sefarad" in the eleventh century (because of internecine political intrigue in which their father was deposed from office) signals the symbolic relocation of religious and communal-political authority from Iraq to al-Andalus.[28] However, this prevailing traditional narrative of Jewish intellectual history insufficiently appreciates and overlooks, if not erases, the critically significant role that North Africa played in the transmission of Eastern cultural models, values, forms, and genres to al-Andalus as well as the deep socioreligious and cultural association between the Maghrib and al-Andalus throughout the classical age of Islam. The persistent narrative thereby follows and reinforces the notion of eastern center and western periphery that pervades scholarship on the relationship between the Islamic East and the Islamic West for Muslims and Jews alike. In so doing, this still-conventional paradigm diminishes the independent cultural creativity charted and often shared by the Maghrib and al-Andalus for minority as well as majority religious communities.

Independent Jewish literary and religious intellectual activity appeared in North Africa in the form of "the sages of Qayrawān" two generations before it emerged in al-Andalus. Qayrawān obligingly continued to give the impression of remaining within the formal orbit of the Iraqi academies and the authority of their territorial heads and ecumenical religious-intellectual leaders, as attested in a Judeo-Arabic text (among other sources) written apparently for a tenth-century Maghribi audience. Attributed to Nathan the Babylonian, the famous "report" narrates an idealized picture of the domain and authority of the figure of the exilarch in Iraq.[29] At the same time, early tenth-century figures such as Isaac Israeli (Isḥāq ibn Sulaymān; b. ca. 855), a thinker originally from Egypt and Fāṭimid court physician in Qayrawān who corresponded with Saʿadia Gaon on philosophical matters,[30] along with Isaac's student Dūnash ibn Tamīm (fl. turn of the tenth century), a physician, scientist, jurist, and philologist, charted a relatively independent course in devoting themselves to the new systematic religious thinking. Ibn Tamīm, who shared his teacher's Neoplatonism, authored a linguistic-philosophical commentary on the mystical treatise *Sefer yᵉṣirah* (Book of Creation).[31] Saʿadia had appropriated Muʿtazilite *kalām* (scholastic theology), with its emphasis on God's oneness, justice, and human free will, for Jewish purposes. He followed that school's approach to the problems common to monotheistic theology of reconciling the canons of reason and revelation and defining divine attributes in accordance with God's absolute oneness.[32] In any case, Israeli and Ibn Tamīm's activities established North Africa as a conduit for transmitting religious thinking from the Islamic East to al-Andalus. The nexus is evidenced in the works of the first Andalusi Jewish thinker, the poet Solomon ibn Gabirol (b. ca. 1021), and subsequently the rabbinic scholar, poet, and philosopher Joseph ibn Ṣaddīq (d. 1149), among others.[33]

Because of the importance that Muslims attached to Arabic, and Jews to Hebrew, as the revered language of their divine revelations, the discipline of philology became a critical enterprise for religious and literary intellectuals. Their research in this study became central to rational biblical hermeneutics, legal studies, rational theology, and poetics. On the philological front, Judah ibn Quraysh (fl. early tenth century), a native of Sijilmassa, lived in Tāhert (present-day Algeria) and subsequently Fez. Ibn Quraysh wrote the first systematic work of comparative Hebrew, Aramaic, and Arabic grammar in the form of an epistle to the Jews of Fez.[34] David ben Abraham al-Fāsī, a Karaite who apparently resided or worked in Fez and eventually Jerusalem, compiled the first Hebrew-Arabic lexicon of the Hebrew Bible, *Jāmiʿ l-alfāẓ*.[35] The evolution of Hebrew philological research conducted in Arabic and the specific comparative issues that it dealt with and debated need not concern us here.[36] What matters is the critical role that Maghribi Jewish scholars played as intermediaries between the Islamic East and West and as innovators in their own right. They paved the way for their successors in al-Andalus to develop a full program of Arabic-inspired philological activity applied to the study of biblical Hebrew.

It is doubtlessly significant that two of the earliest important literary intellectuals of tenth-century al-Andalus, the poet and philologist Dūnash ben Labrāṭ (ca. 920–990) and the grammarian Judah Ḥayyūj (d. before 1013), were natives of Fez.[37] Dūnash arrived in Córdoba by way of Baghdad, where he had the opportunity to absorb and reflect upon the literary and religious significance that Saʿadia Gaon attributed to the notions of *al-ʿarabiyya*, the singular literary-stylistic properties of classical Arabic, and *faṣāḥa*, elegant linguistic clarity (Heb., *ṣaḥot*), applying them to biblical Hebrew with what were deemed its own unique, sacred, and divine aesthetic-literary qualities.[38] Historical scholarship credits Dūnash with two major literary innovations: devising a scheme for adapting the complex system of classical Arabic prosody and its quantitative meters to biblical Hebrew (concerning which, Sa'adia is said to have exclaimed: "nothing like it has ever been seen in Israel"),[39] along with introducing the Arabic-style *qaṣīda* themes to Hebrew verse, including social motifs aside from the panegyric attested in al-Andalus before him. Following Ibn Quraysh's example, Dūnash was also drawn to recognizing the similarities between Arabic and Hebrew and to applying this knowledge to biblical Hebrew philology, with significant implications for biblical exegesis. This effort, composed in the form of critical responses to entries in the Hebrew-Hebrew biblical lexicon (*Sefer ha-pitronim*, known commonly as *Maḥberet m^enaḥem*) of his rival Menaḥem ibn Sarūq,[40] stimulated vigorous debate in al-Andalus about the value of comparative philology for the proper understanding of the Hebrew Bible.[41]

Nevertheless, Andalusi tradition barely acknowledges Dūnash as a transformative figure of such historical significance. The second generation of poets pays Dūnash his historical due,[42] but later authors who addressed aspects of the cultural history of the Jews of al-Andalus, Moses ibn Ezra and Judah al-Ḥarizi, assign Dūnash a relatively minor, rather than groundbreaking, role in the making of Andalusi Jewish culture.[43] Abraham ibn Daud's sketch of Andalusi Hebrew poets in *Sefer ha-qabbalah* does not even mention Dūnash at all, as it famously reports that "in the days of R. Ḥasdai the Nasi the poets began to chirp."[44]

Dūnash's rival Menaḥem ibn Sarūq, along with his followers such as Isaac ibn Qapron and Isaac ibn Giqaṭilla, left a literary record of contemporary responses to Dūnash's philological and poetic innovations. They read his writings on comparative Semitic philology, his Arabic-style Hebrew prosody, and novel Arabic-style Hebrew social verse as edgy, baleful rejections of the proud state (in their view) of Andalusi Jewish culture prior to his arrival from the East. That is, they construed Dūnash's innovations as a frontal assault on their social and intellectual standing. Accordingly, they vociferously denounced him in lengthy obloquies:

> Do not think it is on account of Menaḥem and his [*Book of*] *Interpretations* I have spoken so far. Rather it is on account of the wickedness in your heart and the foolishness of your writings and because of your haughty heart and your blurting mouth, imagining that the sages and savants of Sefarad are mindless and devoid of wisdom, your acting as though they did not even exist, paying them no attention and saying that "there are none among them

> who can understand my words and respond to me," and comparing them to the Philistines who "saw that their champion was dead and fled," thinking that in slaying Menaḥem the standards of the rest of the scholars of Sefarad would be reduced to waste, and they would flee and hide. Thus I have filled myself with words, for you have stirred the spirit within me to nullify your thoughts so that you realize that there are in Sefarad those who have attained wisdom and men of intellect.[45]

Indeed, Dūnash seems to have thought of al-Andalus as a cultural backwater prior to his appearance on the scene. In "Lᵉ-doresh ha-ḥakhamot," the second of two introductory poems to Dūnash's detailed critique of Menaḥem's biblical lexicon, the poet ridicules the "sages of Sefarad," namely, Menaḥem's disciples, whom he will set straight and enlighten with his more informed discourse:

> Therefore must I
> send him my words,
>   my poems and discourses
>   instead of gifts
> In verse and prose
> like the fallen dew
>   on the heart of the "sages" of Sefarad
> for all generations.
> With an open refutation
> inflamed to its core
>   against one who brought ruin
>   to the hearts of humanity.[46]

There is a double irony involved in Dūnash's decidedly unenthusiastic impression of the Andalusi Jewish culture as Menaḥem practiced it, Dūnash's pioneering work in Hebrew philology, prosody and poetry, and the negative local reception of it. Social and literary history, if not tradition, would claim him as a founding figure of Andalusi Hebrew culture; and the forward-looking, Arabic-inspired innovations that Dūnash introduced in the Islamic West were never welcomed and adopted quite as fully when they were exported back to the Jews of the Islamic East. There, by comparison, Jewish society remained faithfully conservative in its approach to Hebrew philological research, to Hebrew poetics, and, especially, in its literary tastes, which strongly preferred liturgical over social compositions.[47]

In a gesture toward the enduring trope of Andalusi exceptionalism in modern scholarship, Aron Dotan attributes Dūnash's resourceful and bold application of Arabic philology (and, one should add, poetics) to the specifically Andalusi milieu: "This could happen in tenth- and eleventh-century Spain, where Islam and Judaism, and consequently Arabic and Hebrew cultures, managed a peaceful coexistence, and the prevailing Moslem superiority was not felt as a threat. In the East this was not so. But in Spain, with its atmosphere of reconciliation, it was possible."[48] By contrast, Jonathan Ray follows Gerson Cohen in reading this formative period in the social history of the Jews of al-Andalus as defined by a series of political struggles between native Andalusis and outsiders.[49] In this interpretation of the story of Ḥasdai ibn Shaprūṭ and his competing circles of literary and religious intellectuals—what Ray dubs the "nativist party"—Menaḥem ibn Sarūq and his disciples and Joseph ibn Abītūr (b. ca. 939–d. after 1012) from Mérida, a candidate to head the rabbinic academy of Córdoba following the death of R. Moses, are deeply resentful of the encroachment of "foreigners" on the prerogatives and position of the Andalusi Jewish community's own notables and scholars. Regarding these episodes, Ray keenly observes: "What has not been emphasized is that these intellectual ties to eastern institutions also have important sociopolitical corollaries."[50] In other words, the substantive philosophical debates over the merits of comparative philology and legitimacy of Arabic-style Hebrew verse and poetics were also transactional struggles over cultural capital with winners and losers in the politics of an emergent elite Andalusi Jewish society.

Ironically, the quintessential leader of the Andalusi Jewish community during the Umayyad age, Ḥasdai, appears to have sided uniformly with the so-called outsiders' party against his fellow Andalusis, perhaps on account of his admiration for, and his reputedly close relationship with, Saʿadia Gaon, memorialized in Dūnash's panegyrics.[51] In circumstances that remain unclear, Ḥasdai dismissed Ibn Sarūq from his service in favor of Dūnash, and he single-handedly championed the Italian Rabbi Moses ben Ḥanokh's appointment to head the new Andalusi Jewish school of advanced rabbinic studies.[52] Those who opposed Ḥasdai in luring, recruiting, and welcoming talent from abroad were, in effect, resisting his determined program to turn Córdoba and Jewish al-Andalus into an independent center of Jewish life on a plane with, or as rival to, the traditional rabbinic centers in the Islamic

East, in similar fashion to what ʻAbd al-Raḥmān III and al-Ḥakam II did for Islamic al-Andalus. Ray attributes the Andalusi Jewish oligarchy's defiance of Ḥasdai as mirroring the Andalusi Muslims' own provincial sensibilities and as an indication of the extent of their common Andalusi moorings. By contrast, leaders of each religious community understood that to set al-Andalus and Sefarad on a truly autonomous footing and enhance their status in Islamdom and among the disparate Jewish communities west to east, respectively, required ambitious plans, grand plays, and bold displays.

Judah Ḥayyūj, who introduced to al-Andalus the practice of writing in Arabic about biblical Hebrew pioneered by Saʻadia and Ibn Quraysh, also came to be viewed by scholars as a founding figure of Golden Age culture—in this case, of the Andalusi school of Hebrew philological research.[53] In his aforementioned roster of important Hebrew grammarians, Abraham ibn Ezra lavishes high praise for Judah's preeminent place in their ranks (*rav ʻal kol ḥoshvei maḥshavot*).[54] Ḥayyūj drew upon a deep knowledge of recent developments in Arabic philological and grammatical studies (such as the works of Sībawayhī and al-Khalīl) to advance the notion of the Hebrew trilateral root that inexplicably had gone unnoticed (or, more likely, unexplored or uncommented upon) by previous comparatists.[55] Ḥayyūj's work also supplied the necessary Arabic grammatical terminology that would henceforth be used to describe the behavior of biblical Hebrew.

Before the end of the century, Isaac ibn Khalfūn, an early and important professional poet, was either drawn to al-Andalus from North Africa or born in al-Andalus to a recent immigrant from the Maghrib.[56] The first truly itinerant Hebrew poet,[57] Ibn Khalfūn, subsequently departed al-Andalus for North Africa. Most Andalusi Jewish religious and literary intellectuals remained in close contact with their counterparts in North Africa, as evidenced by letters and lyrics by Samuel the Nagid and Judah Halevi, among others (discussed in Chapter 4).[58] In North Africa and in the Islamic East, literary works by Andalusi Jews were disseminated, preserved, and imitated even though the poetic tastes of their Jewish societies reflect a more conservative social and religious posture. Andalusi-inspired Arabic-style Hebrew lyrics—especially panegyrics and eulogies for celebrated communal figures, scholars, and merchants—were cultivated, along with an abundance of religious poetry for recitation in the synagogue.[59] Hayya Gaon (commonly referred to as Hai in secondary literature), for instance, the last of the great ecumenical rabbinic authorities in Baghdad (d. 1038), was among the first Eastern poets to try his hand at Dūnash's Arabicizing Hebrew prosody.[60] However, as a halakhic authority, he ruled that poetry was religiously permitted or prohibited according to its content rather than its form or language. Among the forbidden genres were "songs pertaining to the love of a person for another, praising a beautiful person on account of his beauty, lauding a warrior on account of his valor and the like, such as the Arabic poems called 'love poems' [*ash'ār al-ghazal*]."[61]

Corresponding to the uncontested prominence in intellectual life that Muslims granted the Islamic sciences (study of Arabic language, the Quran and its exegesis, hadith and *fiqh*), rabbinic scholarship was unquestionably the most important and prestigious intellectual venture in a culture and society defined by the individual's religious affiliation and by state-recognized autonomous religious communities. In this sphere, North Africa was just as productive and influential in determining the course of Jewish legal research and halakhic practice in al-Andalus as it was in catalyzing philological and philosophical inquiry. By the end of the tenth century, the rabbinic academy of Qayrawān was universally regarded as the preeminent Jewish institution in North Africa, as evidenced by the formal respect with which Sherira Gaon's *Epistle* addresses its head, Jacob ibn Shāhīn (*marrana wa-rabbana ya'aqov*; "our master and teacher Jacob").[62] Within a generation, Jacob's son, Nissim ibn Shāhīn (d. 1062), author of an important Talmudic commentary and other works of rabbinic tradition, was regarded as an independent authority and virtual peer of the last Iraqi geonim.[63] Finally, the migration from Qayrawān of the elderly Isaac ben Jacob al-Fāsī (b. ca. 1013) in 1078 or 1088 to become the head of the rabbinic academy of Lucena, following the death of Isaac ibn Ghiyāth (b. 1038), formally cemented the relationship between the Maghrib and al-Andalus in rabbinic scholarship. Al-Fāsī produced discrete topical Talmudic and post-Talmudic rabbinic digests on practical, applicable law (*Sefer ha-halakhot*; *halakhot qᵉṭanot*). Works such as these set in motion a process that granted wider public access to the sources and decisions of rabbinic law and arguably culminated in Moses Maimonides' reorganized and complete code of Jewish law, the *Mishneh Torah*.[64] Like the tenth-century North African literary intellectuals Dūnash ben Labrāṭ and Judah Ḥayyūj, al-Fāsī became revered as an "adopted" Andalusi rabbinic master for the major figures whom he taught, such as Judah Halevi and Joseph ibn Migash, as well as those he influenced, such as Maimonides.[65] To put it another way, North African émigrés were critical in the invention and production of the Hebrew poetry, linguistic research on biblical Hebrew, and rabbinic studies in al-Andalus, the very literary and literary-religious endeavors that, along with philosophy and speculative theology, would characterize the Golden Age of Andalusi Jewish culture.

The close relationship between North Africa and al-Andalus in Jewish religious and intellectual life is evident in the documents of the Cairo Geniza.[66] Indeed, the Geniza amplifies our sense of the depth of this proximate relationship by providing a detailed picture of the socioeconomic ties between the communities of the western and central Mediterranean. Although Geniza documents originating in al-Andalus are relatively scarce, mention of Andalusi merchants and scholars operating in the Maghrib, Egypt, and the Islamic East indicates that they were active and prominent participants in S. D. Goitein's "Mediterranean society," including the international trade from al-Andalus to India by way of Qayrawān, Cairo, and Aden. Goitein noted that most of the Jewish India traders came from the lands of the western Mediterranean: despite the incredible distances, many Indian merchants hailed from al-Andalus, Morocco, Tunisia, and Sicily.[67] Viewed through the Geniza's lens, the Islamic West, including al-Andalus, was hardly on the periphery of the Jewish world under the orbit of Islam. Rather, the Jews of al-Andalus participated in a recentering of the Jewish world in Islamdom in the tenth through twelfth centuries. The cultural and economic unity of the southern and eastern Mediterranean—the Islamic world west of the Iranian plateau—reflected in the Geniza documents contributed to the virtual unity of the Jewish communities of the Arabic-speaking world. They also inform us about the merchant-scholars' support of Jewish communal institutions and advanced research and the ways in which economically based travel with pilgrimage was a conduit for cultural transmission, including ideas about Sefardi exceptionalism.

Constructing Sefardi Exceptionalism

As noted, Andalusi Jews seized the opportunity to make themselves central players in Mediterranean Jewish life precisely when the Umayyad emir-turned-caliph ʿAbd al-Raḥmān III elevated and formalized al-Andalus's previously de facto political independence in the mid-tenth century. The resultant centralizing program expanded the Córdoba-based Umayyad state bureaucracy, a meritocracy of sorts in which Andalusi Jews could rise to prominent office. However, Jewish courtiers, many of whom were physicians, were found in other countries of classical and late classical Islam, especially

Zīrid Ifrīqiya, Marīnid Morocco, Fāṭimid and Ayyūbid Egypt, and the Abbasid East.[68] Since Egypt, the Levant, and the East were lands with large and important Christian minorities as well as relatively small Jewish communities, along with Zoroastrians in Iraq and Iran, the religiously diverse Andalusi society in its classical age does not appear to be all that different from other Islamic societies during the period, save Ifrīqiya and the Maghrib.

The first of a succession of Andalusi Jewish courtiers was the aforementioned physician, scientist, secretary, diplomat, and communal leader Ḥasdai ibn Shaprūṭ (d. ca. 975), whom tradition and historiography credited with initiating or enabling many of the religious, intellectual, literary, and social developments that would come to characterize the Golden Age of Andalusi Jewish culture and society.[69] Ḥasdai was the prototypical Jewish physician in the age of classical Islam who attained a position in the state chancery. He served first as a customs official and, in due course, became a counselor in the Umayyad caliphal court under both ʿAbd al-Raḥmān III and al-Ḥakam II. Ḥasdai was credited with undertaking diplomatic missions on behalf of the Andalusi state,[70] especially in negotiations with Christian powers such as the kingdoms of Navarre and Byzantium. As a scientist-physician, Ḥasdai was recognized for participating in translating Dioscoridies' text *De Materia Medica* from Greek into Arabic and was credited with the rediscovery of the medicinal compound theriac.

These singular accomplishments and responsibilities even drew the attention of Muslim biographers, historians of medicine, and historiographers who otherwise paid scant attention to Jews and Christians, except as required by issues of direct and immediate concern to Muslims and Islam. Ibn Abī Uṣaybiʿa, the canonical biographer of physicians in Islamdom, even recognized Ḥasdai as an expert in Jewish law (*wa-kāna ḥasday bin isḥāq min aḥbār al-yahūd mutaqaddim*[an] *fī ʿilm sharīʿatihim*), although there is no evidence for it in any Jewish source.[71] Ḥasdai's usefulness, stature, and influence with the Umayyads also appear to have conferred upon him recognition as leader of the Jews of al-Andalus, or *nasi*. Accordingly, literary sources represent him as the embodiment of Jewish ideals of political—that is, communal—leadership.[72] Ḥasdai's supposed status as *nasi*, the recognized political head of the entire Andalusi Jewish community, while accepted in virtually all of the secondary literature, is historically problematic insofar as it is based on Abraham in Daud, a single, mid-twelfth-century Jewish source.[73] It is unclear whether the designation of Ḥasdai as *nasi* was intended to signal an honorific title or an actual office or institution; in the Islamic East, such a title typically was reserved for a scion of the House of David, of which Ḥasdai assuredly was not.[74]

In any case, we can say with greater confidence that Ḥasdai, like Jewish courtiers in Abbasid Baghdad and Fāṭimid Cairo, seems to have utilized his connections to protect his minority religious community and represent its interests to the Islamic authorities.[75] Furthermore, Ḥasdai engaged in correspondence with other Jewish communities and their leaders around the Mediterranean basin that sought his assistance, financial support, or garnered his attention and concern, including in North Africa, Provence, Sicily, Byzantium, and, notably, the Khazar kingdom.[76] What set Ḥasdai apart from Jewish courtiers in other countries? Texts authored in his circle document a grandly ambitious program to elevate the outlier, peripheral status of the Andalusi Jewish community to prominence among the Jews of Mediterranean lands. In effect, Ḥasdai was cast as the visionary architect and original enabler of the idea, ideology, and program of Sefardi exceptionalism.

The Jews shared an idyllic construction of the Andalusi landscape with their Muslim (and Christian) neighbors, as evident in a mid-tenth-century Hebrew letter that was nearly contemporary with the Andalusi Muslim geographer al-Rāzī.[77] Commissioned by Ḥasdai ibn Shaprūṭ, his court secretary Menaḥem ibn Sarūq composed the well-known missive, initiating the Andalusi Jew's famous correspondence with the Turkic monarch Joseph of the Eurasian Jewish Khazar kingdom:

> I, Ḥasdai, son of Isaac, may his memory be blessed, son of Ezra, may his memory be blessed, *belonging to the exiled Jews of Jerusalem, in Spain*. . . . We, indeed, who are of the remnant of the captive Israelites, servants of my lord the King, are dwelling peacefully in the land of our sojourning, for our God has not forsaken us, nor has His shadow departed from us.
>
> The name of our land in which we dwell is called in the sacred tongue Sefarad, but in the language of the Arabs, the indwellers of the land, al-Andalus. . . . The land is rich, abounding in rivers, springs, and aqueducts; a land of corn, oil, and wine, of fruits and all manner of delicacies; it has pleasure-gardens and orchards, fruitful trees of every kind, including the leaves of the tree upon which the silkworm feeds, of which we have great abundance. In the mountains and woods of our country, cochineal is gathered in great quantity. There are also found among us

> mountains covered by crocus and with veins of silver, gold, copper, iron, tin, lead sulfur, porphyry, marble, and crystal. Merchants congregate in it, and traffickers from the ends of the earth, from Egypt and adjacent countries, bringing spices, precious stones, splendid wares for kings and princes, and all the desirable things of Egypt. Our king has collected very large treasures of silver, gold, precious things and valuables such as no king has ever collected.[78]

Ḥasdai ibn Shaprūṭ *apud* Ibn Sarūq echoes al-Rāzī and Isidore regarding the lushness and fertility of the land. But he links its agricultural bounty, abundance of natural resources, and commercial prosperity to his principal concern: the status and sociopolitical security of its community of Jews ("We, indeed . . . are dwelling peacefully in the land of our sojourning"), thanks to the protection of the Umayyad caliph.[79] Furthermore, the communiqué strikes many of the notes that we observed in the Umayyad and Mālikī representations of the Andalusi state and Andalusi Islam. It emphasizes the aristocratic, Jerusalemite origins of the Andalusi Jewish community and the role that Providence plays in safeguarding its well-being and assigning it agency. Later figures (discussed in Chapter 4)—notably, the twelfth-century literary and religious intellectual Moses ibn Ezra—explicitly connected the motifs of land, genealogical nobility, and divine guidance to the matter of the Andalusi Jews' mastery of Hebrew and their extraordinarily rich cultural production.

How did Ḥasdai advertise his prominence to the wider audience of Jews in Mediterranean lands and establish his place of honor in the constellation of Jewish grandees? How did he represent the Jewish community of al-Andalus as privileged and accomplished in the process? Consider "De'eh libbi ḥokhmah," one of Dūnash ben Labrāṭ's Hebrew panegyrics for his benefactor. The lyric employs conventional hyperbolic and aggrandizing images derived from Arabic verse to fancy the poet's patron Ḥasdai as the consummate counselor among counselors (with intertextual references to the prototypical biblical courtiers Joseph and Mordechai serving in foreign lands) for all the Christian and Muslim regents of the world. Ḥasdai presides in Sefarad and, in effect, designates it as the center of the Jewish world:

> Every king trembles
>   and descends from his throne
>   and dispatches tributes

to him in Sefarad. . . .
East and West
his renown is grand and great
Christendom and Islamdom
seek his unstinting counsel.
He seeks his people's good/and expels their foes.[80]

The poem projects Ḥasdai's communal leadership, depicts his sway beyond the country's geographical borders, and portrays his power as Christian and Muslim regents seek his valuable guidance, as if Ḥasdai were actually the commanding leader of a real, rather than an imagined, polity. From everything we know about Ḥasdai, his exercise of "dominion" beyond the Andalusi Jewish community is virtual, not real. His agency is imagined and grounded solely in the poets' rhetoric. Yet Ḥasdai's (here *apud* Dūnash) representation of Sefarad with himself at its head is the socioreligious context in which he conducted correspondence with the Khazar king Joseph (authored by his erstwhile court poet Menaḥem ibn Sarūq).[81] The introductory letter paints an idyllic picture of the Andalusi Jews' material abundance and sociopolitical security amid a detailed depiction of the richness of al-Andalus in general (*anu p^{e}liṭat yisra'el 'avdei adoni ha-melekh sh^{e}ruyim b^{e}-shalwah b^{e}-ereṣ m^{e}gurenu*, "we dwell peacefully in the land of our sojourn").[82] By contrast with this entirely rosy portrait of Andalusi Jewish life, the panegyric that Ḥasdai commissioned from Ibn Sarūq portrays catholic Israel (*k^{e}nesset yisra'el*) as subjugated, that is, still in exile and awaiting the messianic age.[83] This lyric, one of two poems accompanying the epistle to the Khazar king, cast the Jewish Khazars as "a tribe of rulers" (*sheveṭ moshlim* [from Isa. 14:5]) with a genuine monarch, kingdom, and victorious army.[84]

Ḥasdai's letter to the Khazar king represents the earliest extant text of Andalusi provenance to associate the Jews of al-Andalus with the exiles from Jerusalem.[85] The eleventh-century biblical exegete, Hebrew philologist, and grammarian from Toledo Judah ibn Bil'am already seems to sense the constructedness of the tradition. In his commentary on Obadiah (v. 20), Ibn Bil'am observes: "The opinion that Sefarad is al-Andalus has spread among our people; its name in olden days was Espamya."[86] In due course and notwithstanding Ibn Bil'am's uncertainty about the tradition's origin or reliability, the identification of Sefarad with the Jerusalemite elite became a touchstone for the Jews of al-Andalus. Jonah ibn Janāḥ (tenth–eleventh century), Moses ibn Ezra (eleventh–twelfth century), Abraham ibn Daud (twelfth century), and David Qimḥi (twelfth century), among others, cited the tradition because it gave prophetic corroboration to their claims regarding the Andalusi Jews' noble lineage, their possession of authoritative Jewish learning and lore, their preeminent expert knowledge of biblical Hebrew, and their uniquely endowed flair for producing aesthetically marvelous and elegant Hebrew poetry.[87]

How, exactly, does Ḥasdai's correspondence with the Khazar monarch signify the sense of mission and the Sefardi exceptionalism empowering it? Ḥasdai's various activities were neither discrete nor isolated but interconnected components of an apparent scheme to put Jewish al-Andalus, that is, Sefarad, on the map, as if he and Sefarad were bent on serving as a prominent model community for Jews of other realms or, as seems far less plausible, assuming an ecumenical role of Jewish leadership by wresting it from the Islamic East, as Gerson Cohen thought. David Wasserstein designates the historical circumstances authorizing Ḥasdai's correspondence with the Khazar king as "special," that is, exceptional:

> It was the special character of this Islamic world that made it all possible. It was the special character of Islamic Spain, al-Andalus, as an Islamic state, and as an Islamic state that was not part of the Abbasid Islamic state, that propelled Ḥasdai, a Jew, to what looks to have been a position of some importance. It was the special character of the Mediterranean basin as a largely Islamic lake that made it possible for Jews both to travel widely—as they had more or less ceased to do before the rise of Islam—and to make contact with Jews in other places; it was the special nature of relations between Córdoba, in Islamic Spain, and Constantinople that encouraged in Ḥasdai the idea that he could make contact with the Khazars. All of this would have been wholly impossible before the rise of Islam.[88]

The discourse of Ḥasdai's first letter to Joseph, the Khazar king (composed by Menaḥem ibn Sarūq), accentuates his community's economic prosperity, sociopolitical standing, and his wide-ranging efforts at amassing books to enable Andalusi Jewish religious scholars to conduct their research independently and productively. While the first two achievements were undoubtedly necessary for the third undertaking, it is the last that truly marks the Andalusi Jewish assertion of privilege on account of the primacy of rabbinic studies in the advanced Jewish curriculum. Fundamental to the claims, legitimacy, and reputation of the Jewish community of al-Andalus was their elites' cultivation of advanced rabbinic studies, akin to the Andalusi Muslims' embrace of Mālikī orthodoxy, with its emphasis on an uninterrupted line of tradents going back to the Prophet's city, Medina, and the beginning of Islam in history. Furthermore, the Jewish religious intellectuals' capacity to engage in recognizably advanced rabbinic scholarship was vital to the Andalusis' success in advancing all the other intellectual and artistic activities and production that came to characterize their culture, standing, and self-image. When did the Andalusi Jews establish their own independent center for the advanced study, training of scholars, and dissemination of their holy law? Their turn toward virtual autonomy from the Iraqi and Palestinian rabbinical academy dates to the mid-tenth century.

As previously observed, the Jews of al-Andalus and the Iraqi academies and their religious leaders maintained strong ties dating back as far as the end of the eighth century. Through their centralizing program and systematizing efforts, the Eastern ecumenical heads sought to preside over a unified Jewish community and regulate Jewish religious practice in Islamdom. Diaspora communities were connected to the Iraqi center through their contributions, legal queries, and dispatch of promising or accomplished scholars to engage in higher rabbinic studies at the academies. This matrix of relationships was made possible by the economic and cultural unity of the Islamic world, a unity that withstood political and religious divisions and from which the Jewish minority benefited immensely.

The growing and increasingly prosperous Jewish communities of North Africa, in general, and Qayrawān, in particular, served as intermediaries between the Andalusis and the rabbinic centers of the Islamic East. The city was a center for copying Babylonian manuscripts and communications and transmitting them to other Jewish communities of the Maghrib and al-Andalus. So, too, Qayrawān served as the way station for the collection and remittance of funds raised in the West to support the operation of the Eastern academies.[89] Sherira Gaon's famous Aramaic epistle (dated 986) relates the literary history of rabbinical scholarship and its assertion of an antique chain of unbroken transmission. It was arguably occasioned by the emphasis that Islam placed on the authority of uninterrupted history of religious tradition (*tawātur*) as well by as the struggle between Rabbanite and Karaite Judaism. Addressed to Jacob ben Nissim ibn Shāhīn on behalf of the elders of Qayrawān, the epistle is indicative of the close relations between the Iraqi rabbinic academy and the North African and Andalusi communities. Furthermore, the epistle reports that the exilarch Naṭrūnai was deposed from office and "went to the West."[90] This tradition was remembered and appears to have become significant in al-Andalus. Recall that Judah ben Barzillai al-Bargeloni (twelfth century), who also asserts that "Sefarad has been a place of abundant Torah study since the time of the First [Temple], the exile of Jerusalem, until today," reported that Naṭrūnai wrote the Babylonian Talmud for the Andalusis "from memory, not from a written text."[91]

At the turn of the ninth century, a polemical letter to the Jews of North Africa and al-Andalus from Pirqoi ben Baboi on behalf of the Iraqi academies was occasioned by internecine Jewish rivalry of another sort. The highly partisan communication proclaims the supremacy of Babylonian rabbinic traditions and the preeminence of its geonic authority over their rival Palestinian Rabbanite counterparts.[92] A mid-tenth-century report authored by the otherwise unknown figure Nathan the Babylonian, who emigrated to Qayrawān, also champions the authority of the Iraqi community (again, as opposed to the Palestinian), along with his view of the supremacy of the Sura rabbinic academy over Pumbedita (both relocated in the ninth century to Baghdad, where they retained their distinct identity and traditions). Nathan the Babylonian paints a picture of the numerous political conflicts within the Iraqi Jewish religious and communal establishment. The Judeo-Arabic original of this narrative survives only in fragments and in a late medieval Hebrew translation, marred by problems of historicity and significant inconsistencies with contemporaneous sources.[93] It includes a report of one of the many political struggles among the Babylonian Jewish elite. In this instance, the fallout involves another unseated exilarch, 'Uqba, who, like Naṭrūnai, turns up in North Africa as an exile.[94]

It is worth recalling the tradition that in 883, a mysterious character from Yemen or Ethiopia named Eldad ha-Dani supposedly turned up in Qayrawān.[95] Speaking only Hebrew, Eldad announced that he belonged to the Danites (one of the Ten Lost Tribes of ancient Israel), who lived in a distant land "beyond the rivers of Ethiopia" under the aegis of a powerful and wealthy Jewish king. I draw attention to a significant motif attributed to Eldad—the classification of his Lost Tribe (or Tribes) with Jewish warriors: "We have a received tradition that we, the sons of Dan, were once tent-dwellers in the Land of Israel, and there were no, among all the tribes of Israel, men of war and mighty of valor like us."[96] The Jewish communities of the Maghrib are said to have welcomed Eldad in excitement but also with uncertainty. Perhaps they even invented him. His mystifying appearance, enigmatic manners, and cryptic declarations were treated cautiously but with genuine interest by a contemporary rabbinic authority in Baghdad to whom the Qayrawānī religious leaders turned for guidance.[97] In any case, Eldad's phantasm and fantastic tales of a Jewish king, a Jewish kingdom, and a Jewish army, the first of their kind in medieval Jewish literature, fueled the Maghribis' and Andalusis' geographical, religious, and political imaginations. Subsequently, he disappeared into legend, much as the Ten Lost Tribes from whence he supposedly came.

What was the Andalusi Jewish reception of the far-fetched Eldad accounts? The Andalusi Jewish elite's cultural politics, beginning with Ḥasdai's diplomatic correspondence with the Eurasian Jewish king of the Khazars, twelfth-century literary references to this sovereign figure,[98] and the manuscript history of the Eldad traditions all testify to the lasting appeal of real or imagined spectacles of Jewish political and military empowerment. Andalusi and, subsequently, Christian Iberian Jews hoped to negotiate a place for themselves in history or, alternatively, to escape their social and political predicament of living lives between Islamdom and Christendom, through indulging in signs of messianic fantasies.

For example, Ḥasdai ibn Shaprūṭ refers to the Eldad episode-myth in his epistle to the Khazar king:[99] "In the time of our father there was among us a certain Israelite, an intelligent man, who belonged to the tribe of Dan. Who traced his descent back to Dan, the son of Jacob. He spoke elegantly and gave everything its name in the holy language. Nor was he at a loss for any expression. When he expounded the Law he was accustomed to say, 'Thus has Othniel, son of Kenaz, handed down tradition from the mouth of Joshua, and he from the mouth of Moses, who was inspired by the Almighty.'" Immediately after conveying this notice, the letter turns to a matter of utmost importance: it inquires about what information the king may possess regarding "the final Redemption," thereby intimating a direct connection between the appearance of Eldad, Ḥasdai's glorious Sefarad, the news of the Khazar Jewish kingdom, and hopes for the advent of the messianic age: "We have been cast down from our glory, so that we have nothing to reply when they say daily unto us, 'Every other people has its kingdom, but of yours there is no memorial on the earth.' Hearing, therefore, of the fame of my lord the King, as well as the power of his dominions, and the multitude of his forces we were amazed, we lifted up our head, our spirit revived and our hands were strengthened."

To return to the geonim of the East and their ties to the Maghribis and Andalusis: a few generations after Eldad's ostensible appearance in Qayrawān, 'Amram ben Sheshna Gaon authored the first comprehensive rabbinic prayer book.[100] According to a *responsum*-letter he dispatched in the mid-ninth century to Isaac b. Simon, apparently a leader of a local community in the Iberian Peninsula, the text was occasioned by Isaac's many questions regarding the details of rabbinic prayer throughout the liturgical year.[101] Until the tenth century, then, the Jews of Iberia clearly relied for religious guidance upon the venerable rabbinical academies in the East. At the same time, another item of correspondence from Sherira Gaon to the Maghrib (mentioned in the Introduction) is indicative of a reverse dependence of the Eastern academies on the diaspora communities like al-Andalus, the Maghrib, and Ifrīqiya for financial support. Sherira pleads for financial support for the academies in the East. The letter bitterly implies that the Jewish communities of the West had relinquished their historical ties to the Iraqi yeshivot and become content with the new regional rabbinic academies in their own realm.[102]

The center of the Islamic world remained in the East; but from the ninth century on, political disorder in Baghdad brought economic and social consequences that encouraged substantial westward migration. In the ninth and tenth centuries, resettlement strengthened and transformed the North African Jewish communities.[103] That mutually dependent relationship of western periphery to eastern center is also apparent in the documents of the Cairo Geniza because of the role played by Jewish members of the Mediterranean merchant class, many of whom had close ties to religious scholars or were religious intellectuals themselves. Immigrants from the Islamic East further reinforced existing links to the rabbinic academies and also stimulated the new regional centers' significant economic growth. While Easterners brought religious and literary traditions, knowledge, and connections, their arrival laid the foundation for independent scholarly endeavors in theology, sacred law, and biblical Hebrew lexicography and grammar.[104] Such intellectual and institutional developments afforded Maghribi and Andalusi thinkers the opportunity to begin to fill the vacuum created by the waning of Iraqi authority.

Against the background of these socioeconomic transitions, the aforementioned Rabbi Moses ben Ḥanokh arrived in Córdoba (in 972) and, with Ḥasdai's blessing, support, and largesse, established and served as head of a new Andalusi rabbinical academy.[105] Ḥasdai's efforts to reduce Andalusi Jewish dependence upon the Eastern academies even caught the attention of Muslim intellectuals such as Ṣāʿid al-Andalusi, in his universal history of science:

> Among those who studied medicine was Ḥasdāy b. Isḥāq the servant of al-Ḥakam b. ʿAbd al-Raḥmān al-Nāṣir li-Dīn Allāh. He was skilled in the practice of medicine, very learned in the legal science of the Jews, and he was the first to open up for those of them who were in al-Andalus their legal and historical and other sciences. Before that they had to have recourse to the Jews of Baghdad in matters connected to the law of their religion and the years of their era and the dates of their feasts; they would get from them the calculation of a number of years, and in accordance with that they would know the start of their [calendrical] cycles and the beginnings of their years. And when Ḥasdāy became connected to al-Ḥakam, and received the highest honor from him on account of his talent and his great skill and his culture, and managed thanks to him to obtain access to the Jewish writings that he wanted from the East, then the Jews of al-Andalus came to know what they had been ignorant of before, and were able to do without what had caused them a lot of bother.[106]

In the next generation, Hayya Gaon, the leading and last great rabbinical figure in Baghdad, registered a complaint with Jacob ben Nissim ibn Shāhīn, the rabbinic authority and geonic ally in Qayrawān: Ḥanokh ben Moses, son and successor of the founder of the Andalusi academy, deigned to disregard messages sent to him by Hayya's illustrious father, Sherira Gaon.[107] For that matter, there is additional evidence of tensions between the Iraqi authorities and the Maghribis. Both Sherira and Hayya Gaon confronted Qayrawānī correspondents with what they deemed a grave epistemological error by privileging the text of the Talmud over rabbinic interpretative tradition, of which the geonim were stewards.[108]

Significantly, Ḥasdai's enterprise established a pattern unique to Jewish al-Andalus that would continue after him: he committed his own resources to sponsor a rabbinic, scientific, and humanistic cultural program that mirrored, on a much smaller scale, the cultural and ideological agenda of Andalusi Muslim literary and religious intellectuals and their Umayyad patrons.[109] That is, Ḥasdai sought to emulate the social manners and behaviors of Muslim elites—their *adab*—assembling his own circle of scholars and literati and serving as their patron. His own master, the intellectually minded Umayyad caliph al-Ḥakam II, was arguably an exemplary figure in this respect.[110] Ḥasdai's entourage of literary-religious intellectuals included the aforementioned poets Dūnash ben Labrāṭ and his predecessor as Ḥasdai's court secretary-poet, Menaḥem ibn Sarūq. Ḥasdai thus introduced courtly activities, manners, and values with lasting consequences for the Jewish society of al-Andalus and later, in somewhat different form, for Jewish society and culture in still-Arabaphone Christian Toledo. Andalusi Jewish culture became noteworthy for its cultivation of social poetry in classical Hebrew, for rational inquiry, philosophical study, advanced rabbinic studies, and a finely developed sense of aesthetics, along with a deep appreciation for literary pleasure and elegance in all its manifestations—in particular, beauty of the linguistic kind. Ben Labrāṭ and Ibn Sarūq's factions would carry on their masters' debate over the legitimacy of comparative linguistics and the place of Arabic prosody, poetics, and learning in Jewish artistic and intellectual life. Yet Ḥasdai's efforts to promote Judeo-Arabic and Hebrew *adab* (Arabic for *paideia*) would have come to naught without the establishment in Córdoba of a first-rate, self-sufficient rabbinic academy. To that end, Ḥasdai designated Moses ben Ḥanokh, the established and respected Italian scholar who had come to al-Andalus, to serve as head of the newly established Andalusi yeshiva.[111]

Let us briefly return to the tenth-century poet Dūnash ben Labrāṭ and a prominent motif in his famous poem "Wᵉ-omer al tishan."[112] Shulamit Elizur's recent Geniza discovery (textual corrections and eleven additional lines) identifies the lyric as a *qaṣīda* in honor of Ḥasdai, of which the famous "wine song" is but the lyrical introduction for the encomium.[113] This is not the place to reconsider the lyric and rehearse literary discussions of what was previously thought of this poem before Elizur's finding, including my own reading of it as textualizing Andalusi Jewish cultural ambiguity.[114] Rather, I draw our attention back to the text because there is an obscured and implicit source of tension embedded in the lyrical introduction that has yet to be unpacked. The poem famously opens with a voice issuing a conventional Arabic-style invitation to a wine soirée, set in a lush, alluring Andalusi garden:

There came a voice: "Awake!"
Drink wine at morning's break.
'Mid rose and camphor make
A feast of all your hours.

A second voice, explicitly identified with the poet's persona, appears in the last quarter of the poem's introduction to deliver a stern historical-religious rebuke to his would-be drinking companion:

I chided him: Be Still!
How can you drink your fill
When lost is Zion hill.

What is the overlooked ideological contest concealed in the poem to which I referred? Dūnash ben Labrāṭ was an arrival from the Islamic East and the circle around Sa'adia Gaon. He would certainly have understood that the Andalusi social and cultural moment that was described in the poem's extended introduction and that he himself introduced to Hebrew verse—wine and song—might appear to compromise the Rabbanite position in its struggle against Karaite Judaism.[115] By the mid-tenth century, exactly when Dūnash was drawn to Umayyad al-Andalus as a maturing center of Jewish culture and society, Karaite intellectuals in the East were vigorously challenging their community's diaspora to come settle in Jerusalem. Wherever we turn in Karaite literature, the reader encounters historical reports, homilies, ritual prescriptions, and scriptural interpretations reinforcing emphatically the singular significance of earthly Jerusalem as the center of Jewish life as well as the focus of spiritual devotion. By contrast, Rabbanite Jews can be said to channel their geographical desire, deferring and projecting restoration to the Land of Israel into the apocalyptic future or in engaging fantasies of the sort suggested by the figure of Eldad and the Khazar king. In another poem, Dūnash reiterates the classical biblical and later rabbinic hope-appeal for God to intervene on behalf of Jerusalem and catholic Israel:

Build the City of our joy,
    Madmannah and Sansannah [of the far end of Judea]
And the stone the builders rejected
    turn into the chief [Temple] cornerstone.
May the Lord's ransomed return
    And reach Zion in glee.[116]

Three major Karaite biblical exegetes took up residence in Jerusalem during the tenth century: Yefet ben 'Alī from Basra, David ben Abraham of Fez, and Salman ben Yeruḥim, whose place of origin is uncertain. In his Arabic commentary on Psalm 69, Salman ben Yeruḥim surveys the activist Karaite enterprise: "People appeared from the east and the west who intensified their devotion and the study and knowledge [of the Law]. They made it their intention to settle in Jerusalem. So they have abandoned their possessions and their homes and renounced worldly pleasures. They are now residing in the Holy City and await the arrival of the Remnant. . . . They are the Shoshanim."[117]

Salman further reads Psalm 137 (v. 4: "How can we sing the Lord's song in a foreign land?") as a biblical prooftext forbidding the composition and performance of sacred Hebrew song on "alien soil," that is, outside the Land of Israel.[118] Levi b. Yefet (Yefet b. 'Alī's son) positions two psalms (Ar., *mazāmir al-quds*) pertaining to the destruction of the Temple in Jerusalem (Psalm 74, "Why have you rejected us forever, O God!" and Psalm 79, "O God, the nations have invaded Your inheritance") at the beginning of the recitation of Psalms in the synagogue service. Such texts received a double reading: as historical references to ancient Israel and as prophetic allusions to the Jews' socioreligious situation in the tenth century. Their prominent liturgical placement is a sign of the urgency and imminence of Israel's redemption in the Karaite religious imagination and of the Karaite belief in the obligation to overturn exile and diaspora through human agency.

To further underscore the intra-Jewish cultural sensitivity buried in Dūnash's Hebrew panegyric introduced by a wine song, a poem revolutionary in style, form, and content, it is worth citing a few passages from "The Epistle to the Diaspora." The text is a pointed and passionate appeal for Karaite settlement in Jerusalem attributed to Daniel al-Qūmisī, the leading Karaite intellectual and founder of the important Karaite community and center in the Holy City at the turn of the tenth century: "Know that the scoundrels who are among Israel say one to another, 'It is not our duty to go to Jerusalem until He shall gather us together, just as it was He who cast us abroad.' These are the words of those who would draw the wrath of the Lord and who are bereft of sense. Therefore it is incumbent upon you who fear the Lord to come to Jerusalem and to dwell in it, in order to hold vigils before the Lord until the day when Jerusalem shall be restored, as it is written: And do you not give him rest" (Isa. 62:7).[119] The *Epistle*'s most biting summons refers to the performance of Christian and Muslim pilgrimage to Jerusalem, indicating that the question of geographical desire was not only a point of sensitivity in an internecine Jewish contest: "Do not nations other than Israel come from the four corners of the earth to Jerusalem every month and every year in the awe of God? What, then, is the matter with you, our brethren in Israel, that you are not doing even as much as is the custom of the Gentiles in coming to Jerusalem and praying there?"

Apart from the *Epistle*'s rhetorical power and ideological program, it correctly contends that Jerusalem became the renewed focus of piety within each of the three monotheistic religious communities during the latter part of the ninth and into the tenth century. A monk named Bernard, a Christian pilgrim in Jerusalem around 870 who left a narrative of his itinerary,[120] attests to Charlemagne's interest and stake in Jerusalem. That two Egyptian governors ('Isā b. Muḥammad al-Nusharī, d. 909, and Muḥammad b. Tughī, founder of Ikhshidids, d. 964) were buried in Jerusalem suggests that revived religious interest in Jerusalem among Muslims was also stirring in the tenth century.[121] The Andalusi literary anthologist Ibn 'Abd Rabbihi (d. 940) already devotes a chapter of *al-'Iqd al-farīd* to the theme.[122] Writing about his native Jerusalem around 985, al-Muqaddasī observes: "Her streets are never empty of strangers"; but he notes with some annoyance: "Everywhere the Christians and Jews have the upper hand."[123] Finally, the genesis of full-fledged treatises on *faḍā'il al-quds / faḍā'il bayt al-maqdis / faḍā'il bayt al-muqaddas* ("the [religious] merits of Jerusalem") dates to al-Wāsiṭī no later than 1019–1020.[124]

To return to the Jews: in addition to encouraging pilgrimage and advocating collective resettlement in Jerusalem, the "Mourners of Zion" and Karaites in general were known for their ascetic regimen and liturgical predisposition to lamentation as a fundamental register of Hebrew prayer.[125] In the aforementioned epistle attributed to Daniel al-Qūmisī, we find a powerful critique of those Jews who are too busy, distracted, and preoccupied with material considerations to return to God's presence in the Land: "Now you, our brethren in Israel, do not act this way. Hearken to the Lord, arise and come to Jerusalem, so that we may return to the Lord. Or, if you will not come because you are running about in tumult and haste after your merchandise, then send at least five men from each city in the Dispersion." The voice of conventional piety that we hear in Dūnash ben Labrāṭ's lyrical introduction thus seems keenly attuned to three principal Karaite concerns articulated by al-Qūmisī and espoused by the Mourners of Zion: a sense of urgency to the Jews' temporal predicament; a tendency toward expressions of sorrow and ascetic practice; and a heightened awareness of and sensitivity to the Jewish religious investment in Palestine, on the one hand, and the Jews' psychosocial angst regarding the political irrelevance of this stake, on the other. A famous Hebrew lament, "Weep, my people," is preserved in the Romanian *maḥzor* among laments for the fast day of the Ninth of Av. A Geniza manuscript gives the acrostic signature Adonim ha-Levi b. Nissim Ḥazaq, and the poem bears a striking resemblance to the introduction of Dūnash's poem:

I will not drink wine with song
    nor raise my eyes to the sky
While the enemy is girded with weapons
    within my home and my wall.
He glories in his gods
    and bows down before idols
He swears by graven images
    made in his own likeness and in my form.
Through the courtyards they carry
    the impurity of corpses and graves
The adulterer's eye as well as strange women
    are within my sequestered Temple.[126]

In the mid-tenth century, then, three social, religious, and political issues appear to converge around a contest over territorial orientation and fidelity to place and its memory. Andalusi Jewish elites were beginning to assert themselves as occupying a deserved position of privilege in the diaspora; the compass of Islamic, Christian, and Jewish devotion was increasingly pointed toward Jerusalem; and Jerusalem-centered Karaite Jews were embroiled in a contest with Rabbanites for advantage in claiming to represent the authoritative voice in defining Judaism. I thus believe that the aforementioned topos in Dūnash's poem served the purpose of establishing the "identity" of the Jews of al-Andalus as suspended, so to speak, between meta-historical religious longing for Jerusalem and historical rootedness in and spatial attachment to al-Andalus, that is, to Sefarad. In the chapters to follow, we will see the extent to which these issues left further traces in Andalusi Jewish culture and how the idea of Sefardi exceptionalism evolved from its tenth-century origins as a subcultural adaptation of Andalusi (Islamic) exceptionalism.

Chapter 3

The Cultural Turn

Andalusi Exceptionalism Through Arabic *Adab*, Following the Collapse of the Unitary State

Weep for Córdoba the beautiful; for the evil eye has befallen her.

—Ibn 'Idhārī

In four things, Córdoba transcends the [other] capital cities: they are the bridge [over] the river, and its mosque; these are the first two. The third is [Madīnat] al-Zahrā'. And knowledge is the greatest thing, and that is its fourth.

—Al-Maqqarī

What became of the notion of Andalusi exceptionalism after the abrupt downfall of the 'Āmirid regime (in 1009) ruling on behalf of the nominal Umayyad caliph Hishām II?[1] What forms of the trope's vocabulary remained deployed, and what new inflections and emphases emerged in the eleventh century? And what survived of the trope's social agency under the new political conditions, which effectively marked the end of the Umayyad state? Insofar as the Umayyad quest for religious and political legitimacy generated the trope to begin with and Andalusi intellectuals' pride in their country originally depended upon the power, self-definition, and image of the unitary state, we might expect the end of Umayyad rule to render irrelevant the idea of Andalusi exceptionalism. The swift disintegration of the Andalusi polity and the additional uncertainty of al-Andalus's place in Islamdom surely undermined the trope's original purpose and cultural armature. To make matters worse, by century's end the security of al-Andalus, situated at the edge of civilization and Islamdom in the farthest west, also was endangered from the Christian Iberian north. Political disorder, the absence of salutary Islamic rule, inherent difference, and now external threat informed the problematic geographic dimensions of the Andalusi cognitive map and entailed a shift in the ideology of Andalusi exceptionalism. Andalusi literary intellectuals adapted to the new circumstances and henceforth endeavored to immortalize Umayyad rule as prosperous and socially just, a bulwark of orthodox piety and sponsor of every manner of scientific scholarship and the arts—in sum, as an idealized model Islamic polity and society, deserving of remembrance, emulation, and perpetuation.[2]

Al-Andalus in general and Córdoba in particular dissolved into what was deemed *fitna*—political discord and civil strife. It is an Arabic term with powerful Quranic resonances that Islamic tradition took as warnings for future generations to ponder and avoid at all cost. To that end, religious tradition stipulated that it was incumbent upon all Muslims to preserve Islamic unity and avoid dissension and sedition.[3] Conflict spread between people of various political allegiances, initially between the ʿĀmirid party and supporters of the Umayyads, and between people of various social classes and ethnicities. The resulting chaos witnessed the siege of the capital by Berber mercenaries, failed attempts to reinstate the caliphate and install an Umayyad as ruler, the appearance of caliphal pretenders, and ongoing conflict between the populace and notables of Córdoba and Berber contingents new to al-Andalus.[4] In the process, the once-powerful centralized Islamic state was torn asunder. Al-Andalus disintegrated into competing Andalusi "party-kingdoms" (1031–1086) led variously by rulers (*mulūk al-ṭawāʾif*) of Andalusi Arab, Berber, and "Slav" (*ṣaqāliba*) dynasties in a politically turbulent period nevertheless renowned for its rich cultural production.[5]

These rival mini-polities contracted incrementally: they lost control of critical Andalusi territory beginning with Alfonso VI of Castile's pivotal conquest of Islamic Toledo (1085) in the virtual center of the peninsula. Thereafter, the party-kingdoms also ceded sovereignty over what remained of al-Andalus to successive Maghribi Berber dynasties representing different tribal confederations—the Almoravids and Almohads—Islamic revivalist movements–turned North African kingdoms that were summoned to assist the Andalusis in turning back the Christian advance on Andalusi territory.[6] Following their success against the Castilians in the famous Battle of Zallāqa (Sagrajas) in 1086, the Almoravids, led by Yūsuf ibn Tāshufīn and supposedly encouraged by prominent Mālikī jurists such as the distinguished authority Abū l-Walīd ibn Bājī (d. 1081), reluctantly assumed power over al-Andalus (1091 until 1147). In turn, the Almohads displaced them in the Maghrib and subsequently began to take control over al-Andalus in 1148 under 'Abd al-Mu'min.

Within three generations, the legendary Battle of 'Iqāb (Las Navas de Tolosa, 1211) signaled the weakening of Almohad authority in al-Andalus.[7] The political instability and vacuum between the Battle of 'Iqāb and the Almohad departure from the peninsula in 1228, a period referred to as the "Third Taifas,"[8] briefly empowered the anti-Almohad figure Abū 'Abd Allāh Muḥammad b. Hūd al-Mutawakkil. The stage was set for the fall of Córdoba in 1236 and, in 1248, Seville—the erstwhile Almohad capital in al-Andalus—to a coalition of Christian kingdoms led by Ferdinand II of Castile. This defining historical moment effectively marked the completion of the key phase of the collapse of al-Andalus as a major Islamic polity on the Iberian Peninsula.[9] Subsequently, the Castilian-Aragonese capture of the Naṣrid state of Granada in 1492 was the culmination of five centuries of loss upon humiliating loss and the passing of al-Andalus from history into memory.

The cumulative effect of these events even as they unfolded and the impression created by the spiraling downward trajectory of al-Andalus represented unprecedented historical traumas for intellectual and literary elites of the once-important and dominant Islamic polity in Western Islamdom. We might even say that these episodes and the sense of things falling apart in al-Andalus seemed exceptional in Islamic history, save for the parallel with formerly Islamic Sicily when Palermo fell to Norman forces in 1072 after nearly two centuries of Islamic rule. The catastrophic events of the eleventh through mid-thirteenth centuries also reinforced or, rather, aggravated the sense of al-Andalus's uniquely exposed, vulnerable, and outlying position in Islamdom that we observed in Chapter 1 as a central theme of Andalusi historiography and Islamic geography. The experience of overwhelming loss and uncertainty about the future left a lasting imprint on Andalusi memory and thus on post-Umayyad expressions of the cultural trope of Andalusi exceptionalism.

How did Andalusi intellectuals react to this string of sociopolitical upheavals, misfortunes, and calamities? From a psychosocial perspective, the aforementioned historical events bundled with memories of Umayyad dignity, glory, and power intensified the pressure on Andalusi literary intellectuals to recover their bearings and reconsider the significance of what exactly was left of a fractured al-Andalus. The anxiety wrought by political and religious turmoil and, by century's end, military defeat and loss of territory, paved the way for eleventh- and twelfth-century Andalusis to associate themselves and their self-image with the might and grandeur of a previously intact al-Andalus, despite their detachment from its formerly unified polity. If the caliphal age and its formidable political and religious legitimacy could not be restored anytime soon, if ever, literary intellectuals would champion "Andalusi-ness" and market the idea of the distinctiveness of al-Andalus and Andalusis for their own purposes. They found willing partners and sponsors in the "party-kings" who aspired to conduct and represent themselves through courtly administrative and cultural practices, as though they were worthy and legitimate replacements for Umayyad rule.

Ironically, the extent of robust Andalusi cultural activity in the eleventh century was partly a consequence of the new fragmented political situation. The *ṭā'ifa* courts' pervasive competition in patronizing the arts and sciences and cultivating administrative savoir faire, and their circuitous attempts to identify themselves with and reconstruct, on a slighter scale, the exalted position of Umayyad Córdoba marked the period as culturally ambitious and uncommonly productive.[10] The *ṭā'ifa* rulers' prestige and thus their political legitimacy increasingly relied upon the work of propagandists: the court poets. In Seville, the 'Abbādids are said to have established a body called *dīwān al-munādama* ("Register of Confidants"), or *dīwān al-shi'r* ("The Bureau of Poetry"), responsible for vetting and authorizing aspiring candidates to compose on behalf of the dynasty.[11] The literary intellectuals' construction of an increasingly "virtual al-Andalus" and their sense of Andalusi exceptionalism as an ideology came to be authorized by their claim to be custodians of the heritage and practiced connoisseurs of outstanding, refined Andalusi cultural production in the Islamic sciences, natural sciences, and humanistic-aesthetic endeavors. As during the Umayyad age, the Andalusis' noble genealogy and habitation in the climatic zone most favorable for civilization served as critical enduring touchstones for their self-image. Along with their learning and cultural production, these elements were not dependent on the Andalusi polity or the lapse of righteous Islamic authority.

Before we examine paradigmatic signs of this unmistakably cultural turn in which new affirmations of Andalusi exceptionalism were inscribed during the eleventh through thirteenth centuries, let us review the closely related, more conventional, literary trope: expressions of nostalgia for Córdoba and other important cities and, eventually, for an al-Andalus lost. The nostalgia that Andalusi elites expressed for the Umayyad caliphal age and its grandeur is the most often observed, discussed, and analyzed idiom of Andalusi exceptionalism. Textual evocations of nostalgia were, however, by no means the Andalusis' sole answer to the unprecedented historical circumstances in which they unexpectedly found themselves in the early eleventh century. For that matter, nostalgia denotes a literary mood and discursive position. It was constructed, unstable, and of variable meaning, spanning the lengthy period from the eleventh century to the turn of the sixteenth and thereafter, when al-Andalus was no more.

Svetlana Boym provides the reader with critical tools for grappling with the range of textual evocations of nostalgia. Boym addresses the nexus of loss, memory, and place, declaring that "two kinds of nostalgia characterize one's relationship to the past, to the imagined community, to home, to one's own self-perception: restorative and reflective. . . . Two kinds of nostalgia are not absolute types, but rather tendencies, ways of giving shape and meaning to longing. Restorative nostalgia puts emphasis on *nostos* and proposes to rebuild the lost home and patch up memory gaps. Reflective nostalgia dwells in *algia*, in longing and loss, the imperfect process of remembrance."[12] This conceptual differentiation and the space between the two is useful in reading Andalusi lyrics. They explicitly call for the political resurrection of al-Andalus via external intercession, and, alternately, they associate the present cultural ambiance and its production with the legacy and accomplishments of the idyllic past with its power to inspire the present.

The elegiac-nostalgic paradigm of literary response to calamity originated in the eleventh century, when fresh memories of Umayyad power, splendor, and its still-visible wreckage in the ruins of imperial Córdoba aggravated the immediacy of loss. Subsequently, two and a half centuries of interrelated sociopolitical turbulence, fragmentation, and historical shocks catalyzed genuine anxiety among Andalusi Muslim religious and literary intellectuals and political elites that found expression in their nostalgia for the wholeness of a past remembered and then increasingly imagined. Under these circumstances, highly stylized Arabic literary forms rooted in the classical and neoclassical poetic motif *al-ḥanīn ilā al-awṭān* ("pining for one's homeland"), the *ubi sunt* topos, and the poetic genre *rithā' l-mudun* ("city elegies") served as evocative, if stylized and conventional, literary vehicles for giving expression to the Andalusis' melancholic longing for the supposed unity and majesty of what once had been.[13]

The "city elegies," a traditional Arabic literary rejoinder to loss and catastrophe with rich ancient Near Eastern antecedents,[14] served alternately as a personal or communal-political poetic response to traumatic historical experience, inscribing memories of displacement, hope for collective recuperation, desperate pleas for assistance and intervention addressed to the Maghribi and Ottoman leaders, and, more specifically, subjective representations of home, homelessness, and homesickness. Here we can draw a distinction between lyrics addressing the collective sense of loss and longing from the occasional highly personal poems that Andalusi Arabic and Hebrew poets composed. Ibn 'Ammār, al-Mu'tamid ibn 'Abbād, and Moses ibn Ezra, for example, each produced haunting lyrical complaints on the theme relating to their individual experiences of exile from their homeland.[15] Both types of lyrics, individual and collective, draw freely upon the traditional Arabic theme *shakwā 'alā l-zamān* ("complaint against Time") that has been described as "a poetry of setback and impotence."[16]

In approximate chronological order of composition, illustrious aristocratic poets such as Ibn Shuhayd (992–1035),[17] Ibn Ḥazm (994–1064),[18] and the preeminent poet Ibn Zaydūn (1003–1070), likewise from the patrician class, composed the earliest and best known of these Andalusi Arabic city elegies as literary responses to the collapse of Umayyad Córdoba.[19] Established reading of lyrics such as Ibn Shuhayd's classic lament are thought to represent the poet's genuine yearning for restoration of Umayyad glory. Cynthia Robinson challenges such readings by historicizing the text. She demonstrates the unstable, evolving significance of the elegiac motifs in verse and historical anecdotes conditioned by the sociopolitical moment of their production.[20] As analyzed by Alexander Elinson, Ibn Shuhayd's lament for Umayyad Córdoba relies upon conventional—that is, Eastern—Arabic poetic images and ideals to evoke "a certain cultural milieu that was lost with its destruction," an "ideal cultural space" recalling al-Khuraymī's lament for Basra and Ibn al-Rūmī's for Baghdad.[21]

Immediately following the collapse of the unitary state, the ruins of Madīnat al-Zahrā', the resplendent Umayyad palace city constructed by 'Abd al-Raḥmān III as a suburb of Córdoba, became a conventional symbol of the past and the site of poetic meditation and grief for eleventh-century Andalusi poets. To cite a prominent illustration: the eleventh-century poet al-Sumaysīr's occasional lament (*waqaftu bi-l-zahrā'i musta'bir*[an]) over the demolished monument to Andalusi Umayyad greatness and acclaim provides a keen illustration of the way in which the Arabic poetic tradition that conventionally inclines toward a wistful, nostalgic mood appropriates images of communal destruction to deepen the sense of personal loss:

I stopped at al-Zahrā' weeping, considering it,
 I lament its broken fragments.
And I said, "O Zahrā', come back!"
 And she answered: "Can someone return from the dead?"
I did not cease crying, crying there,
 But, oh, how the tears were of no use, none at all.
They were like the traces of tears shed by professional
 mourners of the dead.[22]

Al-Sumaysīr projects meaning onto the ruined site as the physical embodiment of the disintegration of Umayyad Córdoba and, metonymically, al-Andalus itself. Recasting a conventional trope of classical and neoclassical Arabic poetry, the disconsolate poet visits the site and its wreckage and addresses Madīnat al-Zahrā' as though it were his lost beloved whose traces were left behind at an abandoned encampment. He manages to recapture a degree of intimacy with his beloved al-Zahrā' through their "conversation": she speaks to him but only to remind him of the quiet finality of her death. Ironically, the poet-lover's copious tears are transformed into the mere vestiges of the formulaic, manufactured tears that professional mourners left on the site. His own tears are thus twice removed, substituting the collective and ritualized for the personal sobbing voice, as if depriving the poet of his own emotional display before his cherished al-Zahrā'.

Thereafter, Arabic city elegies increasingly were constructed to recall the demise of Andalusi cities and towns apart from Córdoba, and they turn transparently political in accordance with the imaginative modality of "restorative" nostalgia:[23] Ibn al-Labbāna (d. 1113) bemoans the Almoravid conquest of Seville.[24] Ibn 'Abdūn (d. 1134) composed an ode on the fall of Afṭasid Badajoz to the Almoravids and subsequently regarding the territories lost to the Christian kingdoms.[25] Elegies were authored by Ibn Khafāja (1058–1139) on the loss of Valencia (another of Ibn Khafāja's lyrics on the city's temporary recovery is discussed below)[26] and by the Almohad secretary Abū l-Muṭarrif ibn 'Amīra ('Umayra) al-Makhzūmī (d. 1258).[27] Abū 'Abd Allāh ibn al-'Abbār (1199–1260) and Ḥāzim al-Qarṭājannī (1211–1285) crafted poetic appeals to the Ḥafṣids of Tunisia to come to the defense of al-Andalus.[28] A dirge on the fall of Seville to Castile in 1248 is attributed to Abū Mūsā b. Hārūn.[29] The

Naṣrid king Yūsuf III (d. 1411) penned a lament on the loss of Antequera to Castile.[30] An anonymous elegy bewails the downfall of Naṣrid Granada at the end of the fifteenth century.[31] And the irreplaceable seventeenth-century Maghribi scholar of Andalusi history and culture, al-Maqqarī, brings to a close the introduction to his monumental composition *Nafḥ al-ṭīb* by reenacting this poetic tradition with a 103-line lament. It is replete with numerous clusters of anaphoric *ubi sunt* gestures sandwiched around the following verse: "She [al-Andalus] was the Garden of this world, which brought to mind the Eternal Abode" (line 61, p. 10).[32]

The definitive communally oriented elegy addressing the loss of al-Andalus practically in its entirety was composed by Abū l-Baqā' l-Rundī (d. 1285). It speaks despairingly of the demise of al-Andalus—the poem's collective, as opposed to personal, voice—and recalls the sensibility of outstanding Arabic laments from previous centuries: an elegy by the Zīrid court poet and literary critic Ibn Rashīq al-Qayrawānī (1000–1063 or 1071) over the fall of Qayrawān to the Banū Hilāl;[33] and Ibn Ḥamdīs' (1056–1113) dirge over the loss to the Normans of his native Islamic Sicily from which he fled to al-Andalus and became al-Muʿtamid of Seville's boon companion and court poet.[34] Dated by some readers to 1267 and thus not an eyewitness poetic response to events, al-Rundī's poem represents a lyric meditation on the experience of displacement, defeat, and exile, apparently reacting to the fall to Castile-León of the former Almohad capital Seville in 1248.[35] That momentous event all but completed the process that Spanish historiography designated as the "Reconquista" that was said to be initiated two hundred years earlier when Islamic Toledo, epicenter of the peninsula, fell to Castile (1085). Within 160 years, the hierarchy in power relations between Islamic and Christian polities across the peninsula was completely overturned and reversed, the political map redrawn, and the religious, cultural, and mental landscape of al-Andalus and the Christian kingdoms reshaped correspondingly.

Al-Rundī's elegy comprises forty-two lines of monorhymed verse. In contrast to poems wherein the personal point of view mediated by poetic tradition is channeled into the collective perspective, there is no hint of an individual voice throughout the ode-like lyric. Rather, the audience-reader encounters an implied speaker who serves as a mouthpiece for the communal values of the surviving Andalusi *umma*. The sorrowful tone and mournful subject of the poem require that its expression be direct. Accordingly, the text is nearly free of manneristic artifice, a sign of how far the discourse is removed from the stylized and ornate Andalusi Arabic courtly poetry of the period.

For our purposes, I have divided the poem into four units in order to discuss the text's thematic elements, which unfold according to a conventional anticipation-resolution conceptual model:[36] introduction, presenting the general problem of history's merciless disregard for past glories (lines 1–13); a transition verse (line 14); depiction of the definitive cataclysm—the tragic ruin of al-Andalus, a loss that far exceeds the historical examples drawn from the Eastern central lands of Islamdom enumerated in the introduction (lines 15–24); and poetic resolution in the form of an appeal for external military invention from North Africa (lines 25–42). The lament begins on a note of conventional wisdom, as though it were the incipit for a meditative poem addressing the universal themes of the brevity of life and the ephemeral, even illusory, nature of earthly pleasure (*dhamm al-dunyā*) (line 1):

> Everything declines after reaching perfection,
> therefore let no man be beguiled by the sweetness of a pleasant life.

Here al-Rundī's lyric is reminiscent of the manner in which renowned Abbasid poets Ibn al-Rūmī (836–ca. 896) and al-Mutanabbī (915–965) evoke a sense of profound loss and strike a melancholic mood by referring to the desolation of pre-Islamic Sassanian relics.[37] The poem's first unit (lines 1–13) laments the fleeting accomplishments of the great and legendary kings and empires of the distant Eastern past—pre-Islamic Arabian figures such as Shaddād and the Sassanian dynasty of Persia, as well as the even more ancient Achaemenid Persian king Darius and the Israelite king (and Islamic prophet) Solomon—each of whom has been swept aside along with their accomplishments by the "irrevocable decree of fate."

Line 14 marks the transition to the poet's subjective complaint. At this juncture, the poem moves from the despondent mood occasioned by the universal human lot to the specific trauma of the poet's community: it assays the contrast between the numerous historical misfortunes that represent the condition of humanity and a more immediate disaster of monumental proportions for which uniquely, alas, there is truly no consolation (lines 14–16):

> For the accidents of fortune there is a consolation that makes them easy to bear,

yet there is no consolation for what has befallen Islam.
An event which cannot be endured has overtaken the peninsula;
one such that Uḥud has collapsed because of it and Thahlān has crumbled!
The evil eye has truck [the peninsula] in its Islam such that [the land]
decreased until whole regions and districts were despoiled of [the faith].

By rhetorically framing the catastrophe as what has befallen Islam, even before the peninsula is mentioned, the poem cleverly conditions its principal audience, which is not addressed directly until the final unit. Here the text anticipates and lays the groundwork for its appeal to Islamic solidarity beyond the borders of al-Andalus.

The poem's second unit (lines 15–24) shifts to catalog the fall of numerous prominent Andalusi cities and towns, transferring meaning from place to people, again deploying the conventional *ubi sunt* motif and asking, "Where have they gone?" (lines 17–19). The anaphoric sequence of rhetorical questions (*wa-ayna shāṭibatu am ayna jayyān . . . wa-ayna qurṭubatu . . . wa-ayna ḥimṣu*) has the poetic effect of creating anticipation, speeding up the conceptual rhythm of the lyric, and pushing its audience forward. Critical for our purposes is the depiction of society's disintegration: it accentuates the lapse of religious scholarship representing the domain of *dīn* (religion), on the one hand (regarding Córdoba, line 18), and the loss of pleasure, representing the sphere of *dunyā* (earthly matters), on the other (regarding Seville, line 19). Perhaps the latter is lent additional resonance by way of an oblique allusion to the Garden of Paradise depicted in the Quran (47:15, *fīhā anhar^{un} min maā'^{in} ghayri ʿās^{in}*/"There shall flow in it rivers of purest water"):

Therefore ask Valencia what is the state of Murcia; and where
is Játiva and where is Jaén?
Where is Córdoba, the home of the sciences, and many a
scholar whose rank was once lofty in it?

Clearly, the Muslims of al-Andalus, much as the Jews, endeavored to remember their ruin as singularly traumatic, as unique in kind—that is, as exceptional. Here the representation of ravaged and displaced religious structures and symbols heightens the emotional impact and the indignity of the Andalusi Muslims' loss of power (lines 21–24):

> The tap of the white ablution fount weeps in despair, like a
> passionate lover weeping at the departure of the beloved,
> Over dwellings emptied of Islam that were first vacated and
> are now inhabited by unbelief;
> In which mosques have become churches wherein only bells and
> crosses
> may be found.
> Even *miḥrāb*s weep though they are solid; even the pulpits
> mourn though they are wooden.

The picture of "dwellings emptied of Islam and now inhabited by unbelief" (line 22), along with the earlier image "regions and districts despoiled of the faith" (line 16), recall a powerful figure from another famous Andalusi Arabic poem, written more than a century earlier. Ibn Khafāja's ode memorializing the Muslims' recapture of Valencia from Alfonso VI in 1102, "Al-ān saḥḥa ghamāmu l-naṣri" (Victory's clouds have now flowed) triumphantly speaks of "stripping Valencia of unbelief."[38] But in al-Rundī's lyric, it is now Islam in full retreat and its faith that have been violently wrenched from the land. Accordingly, the poetic material employed in this passage of the elegy is designed to deepen and justify the mode of unrelieved sadness and despair that was established in the poem's reflective, universal introduction.

The images of the "passionate lover," "departed beloved," and "dwellings emptied," that is, uninhabited, have as their poetic source the classical and neoclassical Arabic *qaṣīda* repertoire of "bedouin encampment" motifs (*aṭlāl* and *nasīb*). But in the context of this lament, these traditional topoi have been appropriated to serve as emotive points of archaic literary reference that are replaced by more immediate and relevant associations of disintegrating holiness.[39] Depiction of the defilement of sacred places, artifacts, and items by what is derisively termed a "foreign religion" and, at the poem's conclusion, the pitiable representations of captivity and servitude utilizing gendered language and images ("Alas, many a mother and child have been parted as soul and bodies are separated," line 39) aim to stoke the audience's outrage at what has transpired. In the latter respect, the depiction resembles the rhetorical strategy deployed by the poet Ibn al-'Assāl reacting to the sack of Bobastro in 1064.[40] The emotional-rhetorical ploy also enlists the audience's resistance and, in theory, galvanizes it to resolve to restore the original and "natural" order of al-Andalus, in which Islam is sovereign over the peninsula.

Accordingly, al-Rundī's lyric does not conclude (lines 25–38) on a note of prayerful hope. Rather, it ends with an extended and impassioned plea for North African military assistance (as occurred under the Almoravids and Almohads, in succession, in the late eleventh and mid-twelfth centuries) in overturning the relentless Christian advance into the heart of the Andalusi domain of Islamdom. The poem's desperate appeal is couched in the form of a series of rhetorical questions designed to contest the listeners' complacency and stir them to action with ever more pathetic scenes of communal devastation and individual deprivation. Images of the Andalusis' humiliation and captivity are contrasted with figures of the power and extravagance that, the poet imagines, reside in the confines of the Islamic Maghrib (lines 28, 30):

> And you who walk forth cheerfully while your homeland diverts you,
> can a homeland beguile any many after [the loss of] Seville? . . .
> And you who are living in luxury beyond the sea enjoying life,
> you who have strength and power in your homelands.

There is a certain ironic reversal in the Andalusi Arabic poet's association of the Marīnid Berber rulers of the Maghrib with material extravagance. In the eleventh and twelfth centuries, the courtly Andalusis' supposedly lavish, indulgent, and intemperate ways, illicit excessive taxation of the populace, and purportedly lax observance of Islam were roundly condemned by the country's Mālikī religious scholars and jurists. These behaviors were said to cause friction between Andalusi party-kings and their nobility and the Almoravids and, more pointedly, the Almohads, who espoused a more austere revivalist Islam.[41] Indeed, Andalusi historiography and more than a few literary texts naturally blame the collapse of the Islamic polity and loss of territory to the Christian Iberian kingdoms on courtly, upper-class violations of Islam in favor of decadent and hedonistic behavior, party-kingdom payment of tribute to Castile, and instances of collaboration with it, as well as on Andalusi forfeiture of Islamic unity.[42] A famous quip attributed to the Almoravid leader Yūsuf b. Tāshufīn, doubtlessly under the sway of the Mālikī scholars of al-Andalus, denounces the emir al-Muʿtamid of Seville on account of his deplorable political, military, and religious failures. The ruler of the most important and powerful *ṭā'ifa* kingdom, who paid annual tribute to Alfonso VI of Castile rather confront the Christians in defense of al-Andalus and Islam, is said to revel in debauchery: "to an extent, his behavioral preoccupation was such that he never forsook the 'two orifices'" (Ar., *lā ya'dū l-ajwafayn*; i.e., digestive and sexual).[43] For the Almoravids (and then the Almohads), al-Andalus remained the "land of jihad" set forth in Islamic historiography and characteristic of frontier regions in Islamdom. But the pitiful Andalusis were deemed no longer capable of or committed to pursuing it in defense of the Muslims and Islam in their domain.[44]

In al-Rundī's case, the Andalusi poet issues the North Africans a call to action based on the ideals of valor and courage and the implicit Islamic obligation of jihad; they must strive in the path of God for the protection of fellow Muslims in distress and for the reestablishment of the political conditions necessary for the perfect practice of Islam in an Islamic polity (lines 33–34):

> What means this severing of the bonds of Islam on your behalf,
> when you, O worshipers of God, are brethren?
> Are there no heroic souls with lofty ambitions; are there no
> helpers and defenders of righteousness?

The poet finally challenges the Marīnid Muslims of the Maghrib to ignore his pleas for armed intervention in al-Andalus, if they dare (line 42):

> The heart melts with sorrow at such [sights]
> if there is any Islam or belief in that heart!

What are the cultural assumptions of *li-kulli shā'in idhā mā tamma nuqṣānu*? For the Muslims of al-Andalus, the progressive loss of territory and sovereignty signified not only displacement and exile but also dispossession and an unprecedented disempowerment that could not easily be understood, let alone accepted within the framework of classical Islamic history and culture. Here was a most unwelcome and unsettling form of Andalusi exceptionalism: nowhere but for al-Andalus was Islam ever in such retreat and Islamdom contracting, except for Islamic Sicily.[45] By contrast, territorial losses to the Byzantines in Syria (1076) and the crusader kingdoms in Palestine (beginning 1099) were temporary retreats from which Islamdom would eventually recover. The Mongol sack of Baghdad in 1258 also represented a short-term setback in these respects.

Andalusi religious intellectuals also were obliged to account for the Muslims' weakness and defeat at the hands of a Christian power going back to the eleventh century. They engaged in collective soul-searching and pietistic, diagnostic religious critique of Andalusi society, in general, and the party-kingdoms' and their rulers' failures to uphold the strictest standards of Islamic piety, justice, and Islamic unity, in particular. The religious intellectuals' verdict was predictably harsh regarding the lapse in religiously righteous political authority: they reasserted an unyielding Andalusi commitment to Islamic orthodoxy. Even some Andalusi poets who had been in the party-kings' service voiced a highly critical judgment of the *mulūk al-ṭawā'if.* For example, the aforementioned poet al-Sumaysīr responded to the fall of Toledo (1085) by accusing the party-kings of infidelity to Islam (*nādi l-mulūk wa-qul lahum*):

Call the kings and say to them
    "What have you brought about?
You have handed over Islam into enemy captivity
    and (yourselves) remain seated (and inactive)
We should rise up against you
    since you have given your support to the Christians
You take no account of the breaking of the bonds of community
    so that you have even broken the bonds of the community of
    the Prophet!"[46]

The following excerpt from a poem by Abū Ṭālib 'Abd al-Jabbār (d. 1106), replete with ironic paronomasia in the original,[47] condemns the illegitimate rulers for their impious, hedonistic, unrighteous, un-Islamic behavior, and odious political vassalage to the Castilians:

Then these *ṭā'ifa* [rulers] went to extremes
    and were replaced from their own people by womanly
    successors.
They professed the creed of injustice and deviance,
    Since the finest of their minds were plundered,
So they neglected the land and the people,
    and abandoned the frontier and jihad.

Their heads were consumed with wine,
with songs and listening to musical instruments.
And they compounded their ignorance and failure
by assisting the gang of the Cross.[48]

Because God is the author of history, Andalusi Muslim religious elites viewed their defeats in much the same way the Jews understood the significance of their ongoing exile—as divine judgment and punishment visited upon them for the slackness of their submission to the will of God. In particular, the eleventh-century savant and erstwhile Umayyad loyalist Abū Muḥammad ʿAlī ibn Ḥazm (d. 1064) was incensed by what he saw as a deterioration of devotion to Islam and thus loss of religious and political legitimacy among the ruling Andalusi party-kingdom elites. Here is how he looked back and framed the revolt of 1009, tracing Andalusi failure back to the disintegration of the unity state: "Except for those who sought protection of God, the revolt was an evil that will require detailed elaboration. For one thing, it ruined the religious beliefs in many respects. In brief, every ruler of a city or fortress throughout the width and breadth of al-Andalus was the enemy of God and His Messenger. These rulers pursued corruption on earth."[49]

Ibn Ḥazm devotes another famous treatise, "The Refutation (of Ibn al-Naghrīla, the Jew)," to decrying the socioeconomic and political positions assumed by Andalusi Jews and the prerogatives they attained under the party-kings. He issues a dire warning to the religiously errant Andalusi Muslim elites that they will share the wretched and accursed fate otherwise reserved for the Jews and the notoriously rebellious Israelites in the ultimate biblical prooftext, Deuteronomy 28.[50] By their association with the Jews, the treatise also upbraids the *ṭāʾifa* rulers for additional offenses against Islam and God, including their wanton materialism.[51]

Later in the century, the events that Spanish historiography deemed the beginning of the "Reconquista" imposed a new and even more problematic set of conditions upon the Muslims of al-Andalus, which called for a radical response. Reacting to the Castilian conquest of Toledo in 1085, the poet Abū Muḥammad ʿAbd Allāh al-Ghassāl (d. 1094) urges his fellow Andalusi Muslims to abandon their vanquished city:

O people of Andalusia, spur on your horses, for
staying here is a drastic mistake;

Garments begin to unravel at the seams, but now I see
that the peninsula is unraveling at the center.[52]

Was deserting regions formerly belonging to the polity of al-Andalus and the territory of Islamdom a properly Islamic answer? Mālikī authorities espoused an extremely stringent view on this question.[53] As documented in the fatwa compendium of the sixteenth-century Maghribi jurist Aḥmad al-Wansharīsī, Andalusi and Maghribi jurists repeatedly insisted that Muslims "staying on" (Ar., *mudajjan* or *ahl al-dajan*; Sp., *mudéjares*, as they came to be called) in lands formerly within the polity of al-Andalus were enjoined to abandon their homes and leave the country rather than accept subject status in the new Christian-dominated polity.[54] But before the demise of al-Andalus was fully complete in 1492, many Andalusis would endeavor to resist and revolt rather than depart for Islamdom's territory. According to the testimony of literary and historical sources, they repeatedly looked toward the Maghrib for the solution to their sociopolitical-religious plight.

The entreaty to the Maghribi Berbers for military intervention with which al-Rundī's poem concludes was not without important historical precedents going back to al-Muʿtamid ibn ʿAbbād of Seville's reluctant appeal to the Almoravids near the end of the eleventh century.[55] On the evidence of that plea and Ibn Mardanīsh's entreaty to Ḥafṣid Tunis for emergency aid to rescue besieged Valencia from James the Conqueror in 1238, it can be said that such requests conform to an explicit pattern in the history of al-Andalus.[56] Yet, given the unstable political situation in thirteenth-century Marīnid Morocco, a state of affairs of which al-Rundī was certainly aware, it is difficult to conceive of the lament's concluding supplication as eliciting or expecting much more than a limited response from the Maghribis.[57] Accordingly, the poem's appeal for intervention should be viewed primarily as a rhetorical device and gesture associated with a conventional literary topos. In this respect, al-Rundī's elegy closely resembles *Yā ḥimṣ a-qaṣduki l-maqduru* ("O Seville, was it your predetermined fate?"), another Arabic dirge on the fall of Seville, attributed to Abū Mūsā b. Hārūn and addressed to the Almohad ruler in Marrakesh.[58] Its rhetorical strategy also prefigures that of the anonymous elegiac ode written in 1501, *Salām^{un} karīm^{un} dā'im^{in} mutajaddad^{un}* ("A noble, enduring, ever-renewed peace do I attribute exclusively to his highness, the best of caliphs"), entreating the Ottoman sultan Bayazid II (r. 1481–1512) to intervene on behalf of the Muslims of Granada and its environs after the fall of the Naṣrid kingdom in 1492.[59] Such is the significance of the chroniclers of al-Andalus from Ibn ʿIdhārī down to al-Maqqarī who intone *aʿādhahā llāh* ("May God restore it to Islam") or similar expressions of "restorative nostalgia" when referring to al-Andalus writ large or toponyms of formerly Andalusi cities and towns.[60] The lament "Li-kulli shā'in" can thus be seen as signifying a gloomy poetic accommodation to the dispossession of Muslims and Islam from Andalusi territory. Such products of the literary imagination constructed a vanished world that exists only in memory but whose imagined restoration is sought with hope against hope.

For all the attention that the nostalgic sensibility has received, we should not isolate its persistent turn in the Arabic elegy from other expressions of Andalusi exceptionalism to which it is closely related. Nostalgia's rhetorical power rests not only on the ritualized reminiscence of experienced, remembered, and imagined loss but also—and, more particularly—on the community's recollection of exactly what was lost (as we read in al-Rundī's poem) and, especially, what survived. The elegists' wrenching yearning for formerly Andalusi cities and towns, their political and religious institutions, and outstanding poets and scholars, and for the vanished or diminished religious and communal and social life evoked in the laments and documented in the Arabic historiographical tradition was dependent upon the previous tenth-century construction of Andalusi exceptionalism. From the eleventh century onward, Andalusi Arabic literary tradition and its textual riffs on *faḍā'il al-Andalus* ("the virtues/merits of al-Andalus") and *mafākhir al-Andalus* ("the praiseworthy qualities of al-Andalus") continued to provide the substance informing the Andalusis' deep sense of loss and longing in the elegiac voice while justifying their claim to guardianship and ongoing practice of what made al-Andalus unique.

Let us now turn back to the seminal, quintessential yet idiosyncratic, and, in many quarters, notorious eleventh-century Andalusi literary and religious intellectual Ibn Ḥazm and his role, such as it is, in the history of the trope of Andalusi exceptionalism. Modern scholars frequently identify the polymath Ibn Ḥazm as the embodiment of what was unique about al-Andalus in classical Islamdom. While he never directly—or, at length—expressed the sentiment that al-Andalus and Andalusis were exceptional, several of his works gesture in this direction and were received as such by his readers.[61] Ibn Ḥazm, it should be recalled, once was fully immersed in Andalusi political life and, following his father's example, served as a court secretary-bureaucrat on several occasions. He is typically regarded as a staunch Umayyad loyalist. However, recent research identifies grounds for uncertainty regarding

Ibn Ḥazm's apparently negotiable political commitments and calls his orientation into question by connecting him as a young adult to a dedicated circle of ʿĀmirid activists.[62] In any case, Ibn Ḥazm fled the turmoil of Córdoba in life-altering circumstances. His exile took him first to Valencia, from whence he wandered. He is next found imprisoned in Granada, and then back in and out of Córdoba and Játiva, and in Dénia and Almería, among other towns and cities. Curiously, and for reasons that remain unclear, Ibn Ḥazm always remained well within Andalusi territory, and, unlike many Andalusi religious intellectuals, he never performed the obligatory pilgrimage to the holy sites in the Hijāz, let alone set out on an eastward trek in quest of sacred knowledge or spiritual refreshment.

Ibn Ḥazm's celebrated treatise on the manners of love, *Ṭawq al-ḥamāma fī l-ulfa wa-l-ullāf* (The Dove's Neck Ring), weaves personal reflections, autobiographical anecdotes, portraits of other political and literary figures, and poignant lyrics into a psychosocial and philosophical examination of friends and friendship and love and lovers within Ibn Ḥazm's privileged, courtly milieu. The work includes an important passage of direct interest to our subject. Appearing at the end of the chapter 24, devoted to the separation of lovers (*al-Bayn*), the passage represents a mournful prose-poetic depiction of and rumination on the devastation that befell Ibn Ḥazm's own home in Córdoba in 1013 during the *fitna*.

> One of those arriving from Córdoba informed me when I inquired of him what happened there that he had seen our home in Balāṭ Mughīth on the city's western side: its traces were eradicated, its features obliterated, its piazzas vanished, the rest disintegrated. It turned into desolate deserts from [a place of] liveliness, barren wastelands from [a place of] conviviality, shattered ruins from splendor, terrifying abysses from safe haven, places of shelter for wolves, instruments for ghouls, playgrounds for demons, and places for wild beasts instead of lion-like men and statuesque virgins whose hands shake off widespread kindness until their unity came apart and they were scattered to the four winds. Those ornate salons, those bedecked chambers that radiated like the sun, whose exquisite sight drove away anxieties, now resemble ruins, complete destruction, like the gaping mouths of predatory beasts announcing the end of the world and showing you the destiny of its inhabitants and informing you of what will become of all those

> you see abiding in it so that you will withdraw completely from the world, just as once you renounced leaving it behind.
>
> Then I recalled my days in it and my delights there, the months of my youth with voluptuous young women the likes of which [even] a reserved young man would desire. I pictured them to myself under the ground or in distant places and remote regions dispersed by the hand of exile, torn away by the claws of distance. I envisioned the destruction of that capital city that I had once known for its beauty and affluence and the established order in which I grew up, the emptiness of its courtyards, which had been congested with people. I imagined hearing the sound of the partridge and the owl over it instead of the bustle of the cohort among whom I was educated. Night would succeed day with movement of its residents and the meeting of its inhabitants; now day follows night in stillness and desolation. It brought tears to my eyes, inflicted pain in my heart, struck my innards with rocks, and compounded affliction in my core.[63]

This extended passage voices far more than the writer's reflective nostalgia for the past, with its comforts and glories. Ibn Ḥazm interweaves impressionistic recollections and melancholic feelings of a highly personal nature, what with his expression of angst on receiving the report about the physical remnants of his family's grand estate. The news he receives from the Córdoban traveler, perhaps a fellow exile, kindles the writer's memories of his home's surpassing beauty and luxuries, along with remembrance of its place of centrality in the conduct of the vibrant social, cultural, and intellectual scene frequented by members of Córdoba's aristocracy. Ibn Ḥazm recalls his home as open and closed, as a public as well as private urban space, as a space of desire and *adab* of the sort highly treasured in Umayyad Córdoba, where it signified political, social, and cultural authority in the tenth and early eleventh centuries. While Ibn Ḥazm and other intellectual elites would have to reckon with the demise of unified political authority, they honored the survival of social and cultural authority in the Arab and Islamic character of Andalusis and their traditions of religious scholarship and literary production. In so doing, they turned memory into an inspiration for literary art and the uninterrupted Andalusi pursuit of sacred and scientific knowledge.

Even if we set aside the murky matter of his family's own lineage (claiming clientage [*mawlā*] to the early Umayyads in the East) and when his ancestors supposedly arrived in al-Andalus as significant factors,[64] Ibn Ḥazm was intellectually invested in genealogical research. Recall that Arab genealogy was an important Andalusi pursuit and form of cultural memory, going back to Ibn Ḥabīb in the ninth century. As discussed in Chapter 1, aristocratic Islamic genealogy was a critical source of Umayyad political and religious legitimacy and thus one of the foundational signs of Andalusi exceptionalism.[65] Ibn Ḥazm's important work *Jamharat ansāb al-ʿarab* (Collection on the Genealogy of the Arabs) expands those Islam-based genealogical parameters. He identifies the Arab tribes that came to al-Andalus as conquerors at its outset and thereby establishes the Arab pedigree of significant figures in Andalusi history. Among the work's many subjects, the roster detailing the Arabs' kinship group practices and their elaborating their long history in al-Andalus is designed to confer nobility, ethnic continuity, and authenticity on Andalusi society and Andalusis, even after the downfall of the Umayyad state.[66] In effect, in their fixation on *ḥasab wa-nasab* ("noble lineage/descent") through the practice of *ʿilm al-nasab* ("genealogical inquiry"), Andalusi Muslim elites sought Islamic legitimacy for internal purposes, out of sensitivity to questions about their own worthiness and preoccupation with what the Easterners thought of them.[67] In the eleventh century, Arab genealogy was sufficiently valuable as a source of legitimacy that the Zīrid Berbers of Granada manufactured one for themselves (the fabrication was disputed by Ibn Ḥayyān), relying on earlier traditions of the Berbers' supposedly Shāmī (Levantine) or Ḥimyarī (Yemeni) Eastern origins.[68]

Andalusi literary intellectual Ibn Bassām al-Shantarīnī, who was forced to abandon his native town Santarém when it was overrun by Castilian forces in 1092, followed Ibn Ḥazm in privileging Arab-ness as a principal source of Andalusi virtuosity: "the noblest Arabs of the east conquered it [al-Andalus] and the chief armies of al-Shām and Iraq settled there. Thus, their descendants remained everywhere, with noble blood."[69] Al-Maqqarī also cites the twelfth-century Andalusi scholar Ibn Ghālib al-Gharnāṭī on the subject of the Andalusi character: "the people of al-Andalus are of Arab lineage, honor, pride, high-mindedness, eloquence of the tongue, cheerfulness, avoidance of inequity, impatience in enduring humiliation, generosity, freedom, and the elimination of infamy," explicitly linking their noble genealogy with their distinctive refinement in "clothing and food, cleanliness and purity, love of singing and partying, composing songs . . . devotion to seeking knowledge, as well as his [the Andalusi's] love of wisdom, philosophy, justice, and fair treatment."[70]

Ibn Ḥazm's untitled *risāla*, apparently produced midlife and revised,[71] sketched the merits of al-Andalus by highlighting the intellectual achievements of Andalusis. It was the earliest literary work supposedly devoted to this subject that other authors touched upon in miscellaneous comments and addressed in various passages of their works on other topics.[72] Transmitted by al-Maqqarī, the text is introduced as "an epistle of Abī Muḥammad ibn Ḥazm, the *Ḥāfiẓ* [an honorific for one who has memorized the entire Quran], recapping some of the excellences of the religious scholars of al-Andalus."[73] It is widely known as *Risāla fī faḍā'il ahl al-andalus* (Epistle on the Merits of the People of Andalus) or, as Ibn Khayr named it,[74] *Risāla fī faḍl al-andalus wa-dhikr rijālihā* (Epistle on the Merits of al-Andalus and Remembrance of Its Men [of Learning]). For historical and literary-historical reasons, it is no accident that the first literary efforts to capture the cultural feats of al-Andalus date from the eleventh century. As observed in Chapter 2, regarding the special case of Jerusalem, the genre represented an Andalusi manifestation of a broader cultural phenomenon in the lands of Islam: pride in local or regional character and place in Islamdom was textualized in the production of *faḍā'il* literature. Muslim literary intellectuals increasingly interested in attachment to their local and regional homelands commenced producing texts devoted to boasting of the noteworthy virtues and excellences of their own *waṭan* and its inhabitants. By the time Ibn Ḥazm sketched Andalusi scholarly and cultural achievements, the *faḍā'il* genre, to which his readers assigned the *Risāla*, had become a conventional literary vehicle for showcasing the singular religious, scholarly, or cultural merits of cities across an increasingly urbanized Islamdom. The genre's appearance and popularity during the tenth and eleventh centuries also draws upon a long-standing Arabic rhetorical penchant for juxtaposing competing claims and voices in several literary forms.[75]

According to the text's account, Ibn Ḥazm composed the epistle in response to reading a letter he came upon in a private library while attending a *majlis* at the home of an illustrious colleague, Muḥammad b. Aḥmad b. Isḥāq al-Muhallabī al-Isḥāqī.[76] The instigating letter was authored by Ibn Rabīb al-Tamīmī al-Qayrawānī and addressed to Abū l-Mughīra ibn Ḥazm, 'Alī's distinguished, intellectually gifted cousin and eventual rival. In the missive, Ibn Rabīb extols al-Andalus as "the depth of excellence, the wellspring of all that is good, the gist of all that is exquisite, and the trough of all treasures, the maxima of the desirous' hopes, and the utmost of the seekers' wishes."[77] But Ibn Rabīb al-Tamīmī indicts Andalusis for failing to dedicate themselves to extolling the virtues of their country and its residents in a literary work detailing the history of its prominent scholars' accomplishments and achievements and its rulers' exploits.[78]

Ibn Ḥazm ostensibly takes up the challenge in a short tract (eventually dispatched to his friend Muḥammad b. Aḥmad b. Isḥāq al-Muhallabī al-Isḥāqī, the host of the *majlis*) that partially follows the schema occasioned by Ibn Rabīb's condemnation of the Andalusis' negligence. But Ibn Ḥazm rejects Ibn Rabīb's premise that Andalusis alone were indifferent to the task of praising their own traditions. Instead, Ibn Ḥazm seizes the opportunity to respond in the service of his own, somewhat ambiguous, agenda. Following earlier *faḍā'il* texts on the religious merits of important cities in Islamdom such as Mecca and Jerusalem, he cites Islamic traditions. He includes a famous hadith in which Muḥammad foretold the conquest of an unnamed country that Ibn Ḥazm identifies as al-Andalus by "our ancestors, the *mujāhidīn*, whom the Prophet described as 'kings on [their] thrones'" (*al-mulūk 'alā l-usra*).[79] Because it establishes al-Andalus's classical Islamic bona fides, for Ibn Ḥazm this prophetic report "would be sufficient an honor to gladden now and delight in the future."[80] In the next passage, Ibn Ḥazm supplements Islamic tradition's high regard for al-Andalus, going back to the Prophet Muḥammad by citing the assessment of climatic theory (discussed in Chapter 1). The peninsula's favorable climatic location explains the Andalusis' intellectual aptitude and their forte for inquiry in all Islamic disciplines and the arts and sciences. The theme signals a discursive shift characteristic of the cultural turn of Andalusi exceptionalism from the eleventh century on. "Córdoba, the city of my birth, is located in the same clime as Samarra. Our intelligence and sharpness of mind are conditioned by the geographical situation of our climatic zone. . . . Al-Andalus is more privileged than most other countries. . . . The Andalusis have developed a mastery for the Islamic sciences such as reading and expounding the Quran, hadith studies and a great deal of Islamic jurisprudence; they have exhibited astuteness for Arabic grammar, poetry, lexicography, history, medicine, mathematics, and astronomy."[81]

Following an excursus on the use of patronymics in Islamic society, the missive turns to a rhetorically apologetic demonstration that Andalusis were not the only people in Islamdom that hitherto failed to devote a work to memorializing achievements associated with their cities and country. Next the epistle registers Ibn Ḥazm's assessment of his fellow Andalusis' envious reception or dismissal of his own cultural products, first citing the proverbial and universal nature of this experience. In this extended excursus, Ibn Ḥazm deems the Andalusis' temperament characteristically haughty by God's design. It predisposed them to judge others' cultural products harshly. Despite such psychological and social impediments, Andalusi thinkers and writers nevertheless have composed works of surpassing beauty.[82] Ibn Ḥazm, a habitually aggrieved, underappreciated, and alienated literary and religious intellectual, was, of course, speaking from considerable personal experience.[83] The irony of his complaint would not be lost on his readers, who have reckoned him, by turns, arrogant, petulant, self-aggrandizing, and irascible.

It is worth recalling Ibn Ḥazm's oft-cited *qaṣīda* vaunting his intellectual preeminence in which the poet airs his grievance regarding his underwhelming reception as a thinker and writer in his homeland.

> I am the sun which shines in the heavens of science,
> Although my only fault was to be born in the West;
> For if the light of my science appeared in the East,
> Surely all would then boast as if it were their own
> Of the prestige which none accords me here.
> My loving soul reaches out to Iraq,
> For it is no wonder that the passionate lover
> Desires with dejected longing to join his beloved!
> If in God's merciful commands it were written
> That I should be exiled forever to the land of Iraq,
> Then my countrymen would begin to mourn and weep for me.
> How many think I am contemptible, while they have me near,
> Yet if they were to lose me would gladly seek my doctrine in the books of Orient! . . .
> Truth to tell, a country which will not even let me live
> Is too small for me, far though its horizons
> Of gardens and wastelands may extend![84]

Lamenting the poet's reception and therefore the circumstance of his birth and place in the Islamic West, the complaint employs a conventional motif of neoclassical Arabic poetry—the passionate lover is spurned by his beloved. However, the theme's execution is ambiguous: the poet longs for Iraq only because he is rejected by his countrymen. Because of the rhetorical opposition of West to East, the poem ostensibly strikes the reader as an ironic admission of the primacy of the East over the West. Yet the text's ambiguity expresses ambivalence toward the estranged poet's homeland and especially its inhabitants for repudiation of their self-styled shining light.

To return to the *Risāla*: finally, well into the body of the text, Ibn Ḥazm reaches the crux of the work's supposed raison d'être, for which it became known and acquired its title: evidence of the merits of Andalusis and al-Andalus. He first surveys the key figures in Andalusi religious scholarship and their achievements in all the Islamic sciences, beginning with Mālikī jurisprudence, Quranic commentaries, hadith, and Arabic grammar and lexicography, before turning to sketches of the Andalusi contribution to poetry, historiography, biographical dictionaries and works of genealogy, and briefer notices on medicine, philosophy, mathematics, and theology. In nearly every case, the Andalusis' accomplishments are compared with the high standards of their Eastern rivals in each of the disciplines and are found, without exception, to measure up to their models, despite how far al-Andalus lies geographically removed from the "source from which knowledge flows and from the locale of the scholars," as the author reiterates near the end of the work.[85]

David Wasserstein discerns that the *Risāla* hardly reads as a genuine tribute to the merits of Andalusis and the excellence of al-Andalus—he suggests that it might represent a work in progress and characterizes it "basically, as we have it, just a list"—notwithstanding the titles or descriptions that its editors and transmitters assigned the work. Furthermore, Wasserstein insightfully observes: "Ibn Ḥazm was in a position to be conscious that al-Andalus had some sort of special identity within the medieval Islamic world. . . . We might have expected Ibn Ḥazm, because of his background, somehow to be part of the Andalusi equivalent or anticipation of that, to reflect in his writing something of that awareness of that special character. This *risāla* indeed forms part of our impression of al-Andalus as having that special character, but it must be said that does so merely because we have it, not because of any special virtues that it incarnates itself."[86] However, the titles that the *Risāla* acquired, predicated partly on the word *faḍl* appearing at the beginning of the letter, tell us that this is exactly how later authors received the work and how they proposed to read it.

Ibn Ḥazm's letter effectively germinated the genre of *faḍā'il al-andalus*, whose literary genealogy includes two important thirteenth-century authors. Writing during the Almohad age in response to very different socioreligious and political circumstances from what Ibn Ḥazm confronted, Ismā'īl ibn Muḥammad al-Shaqundī (d. 1231 or 1232) renewed the Andalusi formulation of this Arabic literary tradition. His *Risāla fī faḍl al-Andalus* (Treatise on the Merit of al-Andalus) is regarded as the more artistically accomplished *adab* work on the subject.[87] Al-Shaqundī was followed by Ibn Sa'īd al-Maghribī (1213–1286), a poet, geographer, and historian of the post-Almohad period, who also compiled *Rāyāt al-mubarrizīn wa-ghāyāt al-mumayyizīn*, the delightful collection of Andalusi and Maghribi Arabic lyrics cited above. Ibn Sa'īd's contribution to Andalusi *faḍā'il* literature takes the explicit form of an addendum to Ibn Ḥazm. Picking up where his predecessor left off and bringing the record of Andalusi achievement first in the Islamic sciences and then in literature, linguistics, geography, music, medicine, and philosophy down to his own time: "I will provide a supplement to [the epistle of] Abū Muḥammad ibn Ḥazm, the *wazīr* and *ḥāfiẓ*, on the praises of the people of al-Andalus."[88] By contrast with Andalusi figures of the eleventh century concerned over the status of a politically splintered al-Andalus and the stature of Andalusis in light of persistent Eastern stereotypical views of them and their country, al-Shaqundī and Ibn Sa'īd cast their comparative critical scrutiny on the Maghrib and what they deem the significant superiority of Arab over Berber culture.[89] Then, in the fourteenth century, the great Naṣrid court historian Ibn al-Khaṭīb devoted two rhymed prose works on the virtues of Andalusi cities relative to their Maghribi counterparts: *Mufākhara bayna mālaqa wa-salā* (Boasting Match Between Malaga and Salé); and the *maqāma Mi'yār al-ikhtiyār fī dhikr al-ma'āhid wa-l-diyār* (The Measure of Superiority in Mentioning Homes and Abodes), although not without ambivalence of the intimate connection between the two lands that he personally experienced.[90] In Ibn Khaṭīb's case, the genre's origins as a literary and rhetorical exercise are manifestly clear, especially in the title of the first work, unlike Ibn Ḥazm's *Risāla* or the contributions by al-Shaqundī and Ibn Sa'īd.

Each of these works represents agile literary responses to problematic images of Andalusis and al-Andalus in Islamic history and society. In an essay devoted to that subject, Manuela Marín observes that from the turn of the twelfth century on, the Andalusis came to be regarded widely as a militarily inferior and effete people subject to Christian or Maghribi rule. She notes the contrast between this reputation with "a set of general traits that Andalusis applied to themselves. In this respect it is interesting to note that the *mafākhir al-Andalus* texts written in al-Andalus emphasize the cultural production of the country. For the authors of these texts, the glories of al-Andalus are its poets and scholars, who compare favorably with poets and scholars from the Islamic East. Andalusis were naturally inclined to poetry and literature, a characteristic emphasized in many texts."[91] Was what I have categorized Andalusi exceptionalism's "cultural turn" really the consequence of the "Andalusi character," a ramification of geographical determinism, as the primary sources relate? Or was it an ideological contrivance and cultural construction designed to bolster self-esteem and recoup some relevance in Islamdom? We have seen that it became essential for Andalusi literary intellectuals to invest themselves in the trope of their refined literary and cultural predominance in counterpoint to their increasingly fragile and dire sociopolitical situation.[92] Muslim literary intellectuals sought to allay their experience of a decentered al-Andalus by reinforcing their sense of the uniqueness and superiority of Andalusi culture, that is, through advertising the uncommonly significant merits of Andalusis through building upon the remembrance of al-Andalus past, its people's potent genealogy, intellectual and literary brilliance, and the godsend blessings of the land. A case in point is al-Maqqarī's citation of a passage from *al-Mushib fī akhbār al-maghrib* (The Elaborate [Tract] of Accounts of the West) by the Andalusi geographer al-Hijārī (d. 1155), to this effect: "Al-Andalus is the Iraq of the West in might of genealogy and refinement of *adab*, in engaging the various sciences and mastering prose and poetry. . . . They are most gifted among humankind in poetry insofar as God, may He be exalted, blessed their country with abundance and placed before their eyes trees, rivers, fowls, and goblets."[93]

Historically, then, Ibn Ḥazm's *Risāla* set an agenda, however imperfectly, that was addressed in literary genres besides *faḍā'il al-Andalus*. For example, it was taken up by Ṣā'id al-Andalusi of Toledo, a near-contemporary of Ibn Ḥazm. Ṣā'id accentuates the Andalusi contribution to scientific study in the penultimate and extensive section of his biographical dictionary on the history of science *Ṭabaqāt al-umam* (Categories of the Nations).[94] The placement and length of the unit devoted to Andalusi mathematicians, astronomers, physicians, thinkers, and scholars of other related disciplines and the Islamic sciences identify the important place they occupy in the history of science as the tract's raison d'être. Naturally, the Umayyad caliphal epoch is emphasized, until political disorder undermined its support for scientific research. The author's party-kingdom period registers a significant number of accomplished scientists across the disciplines, despite Ṣā'id's own complaint regarding the *ṭā'ifa* rulers' diminished interest in scientific inquiry. For good measure, *Ṭabaqāt al-umam*'s final section highlights the Jewish contribution (*al-'ulūm fī banī isrā'īl*) to these branches of knowledge. Because it concentrates almost entirely on the Jews of al-Andalus—and on mostly recent or contemporary scholars, to boot—this concluding part also signals the book's chauvinistic agenda.[95] In similar fashion, al-Maqqarī devotes a chapter of *Nafḥ al-ṭīb* to Andalusi Jewish Arabic poets and another to Muslim women poets, intimating that the Andalusi endowment for literary excellence transcended the boundaries of its religious communities, and even gender.[96] For that matter, we can consider the long chain of religious intellectuals (from Ibn Ḥārith al-Khushanī [d. 971], Ibn al-Faraḍī [d. 1013], Ibn Bashkuwāl [d. 1183], Ibn 'Abbār [d. 1260], Ibn al-Zubayr [d. 1306], and Ibn 'Abd al-Malik al-Marrākushī [d. 1303]) who compiled biographical dictionaries of Andalusi *'ulamā'* and *fuqahā'*, frequently completing the work of predecessors, a significant demonstration of the vitality of Andalusi Islamic intellectual life. While reflecting a normative literary practice across Islamdom, the biographical dictionaries mark an interest in the provincial and indigenous, as opposed to the general or universal in writing the history of Islamic scholars and scholarship.[97]

At monumental length, Ibn Bassām al-Shantarīnī endeavored to provide for his readers the glorious substance of Andalusi *adab*. In the process, he demonstrates what it means be an Andalusi literary intellectual, representing himself as a guardian of the classical Andalusi cultural heritage who retains its authority to define Andalusi-ness, matters of no apparent interest to Ibn Ḥazm's *Risāla*.[98] Ibn Bassām relates in the introduction that he produced *al-Dhakhīra fī maḥāsin ahl al-jazīra*, a work that represents an outstanding textualization of the cultural turn of Andalusi exceptionalism, precisely to express the highest regard for the Andalusis' esteemed cultural accomplishments: "I have set forth this compilation which I have called *Treasury of the Merits of the People of the (Andalusi) Peninsula*, regarding the wonders of their learning and the marvels of their prose and poetry, that which is sweeter than the hushed talk of lovers."[99] Of course, Andalusi learning and its reputation as a land of scholarship were dependent on books and libraries going back to al-Ḥakam II's renowned collection, which also served as a visible material and symbolic sign of "Andalusi greatness." Accordingly, Ibn Bassām relates that the library of the Almerían Ibn 'Abbās was as impressive as the caliphal library.[100]

Al-Dhakhīra also turns defensive in combative response to the pervasive sense of the imitative, derivative nature of Andalusi culture and al-Andalus's systemic elision from a position of prominence in Islamdom. Notwithstanding the introduction, wherein he sets out the purpose of the work, Ibn Bassām admonishes his Andalusi readers for their reputation for slavish dependence on the East. In the following stinging rebuke he chastises the Andalusis for failing to respect their own traditions: "The people of these lands refuse but to follow in the footsteps of the Easterners. . . . If a crow should croak in those lands, or flies home somewhere in Syria or Iraq, they would kneel before the latter as before an idol and treat the crowing of the former as an authoritative text. . . . I was enraged by all this, and was full of disdain for such an attitude, so I took it upon myself to portray the merits of my own time, and to follow up the achievements of the people of my country. Whoever, I wished I knew, restricted learning to a particular time, and made [literary] excellence an Eastern preserve."[101] Indeed, Ibn Bassām dutifully transmitted traditions reflecting the Easterners' severe opinions toward their Western counterparts. He cites the philologist Abū 'Alī al-Baghdādī (Abū 'Alī Ismā'īl ibn al-Qāsim al-Qālī; 901–967), a resident of Baghdad who made his way to al-Andalus at the invitation of al-Ḥakam II: al-Qālī judged the people of Qayrawān and al-Andalus to be ignorant and lacking in understanding.[102]

Despite the Easterners' preconceived ideas about them, Andalusi literary intellectuals like Ibn Bassām refused to be defined by outsiders: they alone would control the signifiers of al-Andalus and Andalusi culture. Ibn Bassām's contemporary Abū Naṣr al-Fatḥ ibn Khāqān (d. ca. 1134) authored two rival anthologies, one of which partially survived. In *Maṭmaḥ al-anfus wa-masraḥ al-ta'annus fī mulaḥ ahl al-andalus* (The Aspiring Place for Souls and the Pasture for Familiarity), Ibn Khāqān levels his own complaint about, and intention to redress, the relative obscurity to which Andalusi poetry is confined, compared with that of the East.[103] For that matter we can read the suite of Andalusi Arabic literary anthologies, several incorporating Maghribi authors from the Almohad period, produced during the twelfth and thirteenth centuries by Ibn Bassām, Ibn Khāqān, Ibn Qaṭṭā' (d. 1121), Ibn Idrīs (d. 1202), Ibn Diḥya (d. 1235), al-Būnisī (d. 1253), and Ibn Sa'īd (compiler of *Rāyāt al-mubarrizīn* cited above), among others, as signs of the cultural turn in enhancing and promulgating Andalusi (and Maghribi including Sicilian) self-esteem based on the Islamic West's extensive literary artistic achievements.[104]

Andalusi Arabic literary historians also devoted themselves to continuous cultivation of the distinctively Andalusi strophic poetic forms, the *muwashshaḥ* and *zajal*. For example, the aforementioned historiographer Ibn al-Khaṭīb produced the second most important anthology of Andalusi *muwashshaḥāt*.[105] And Abū l-Khaṭṭab ibn Diḥya, the aforementioned thirteenth-century Andalusi literary historian who left for Baghdad, famously asserted that "the *muwashshaḥ* is the cream of poetry and its choicest pearl; it is the genre in which the people of the West excelled over those of the East."[106] These distinctively Andalusi strophic forms, their unique thematic repertoire, their introduction of new personae and voices into Arabic literature, and the *muwashshaḥ*'s postclassical form, "unorthodox" linguistic mix of the classical and vernacular, along with its frequent translingualism, represented a living Andalusi poetic and musical tradition that transcended temporal and geographic boundaries. The *muwashshaḥ* captured the attention and appreciation of the Egyptian scholar Ibn Sanā' l-Mulk (d. 1211), who became its first anthologist and most important theorist. The introduction to his treatise *Dār al-ṭirāz* (The House of Embroidery) refers to the *muwashshaḥ* as a treasure that the West has shared with the East, the "panache of the Age, enchantment of Babylon, amber of al-Shikhr, aloe wood of India, wine of al-Qufṣ, golden ore of the Maghrib."[107]

The motif of al-Andalus's agricultural bounty and the land's extraordinary beauty, discussed in Chapter 1, also found a conventional poetic outlet in the production of Andalusi Arabic "nature," "garden," and floral poetry (*nawriyyāt*).[108] For example, Abū l-Walīd al-Ḥimyarī (1020–1042) assembled a collection of such poems, *Al-Badī' fī waṣf al-rabī'* (Rhetorical Figures of Speech in the [Poetic] Description of Spring), and dedicated it to the founder of the 'Abbādid Seville, supposedly "to prove that the Andalusian litterateurs had attained a higher degree of perfection than the Eastern writers." This anthology thus explicitly links floral imagery and highly rhetorical ornate style with a *ṭā'ifa* political dynasty. In the work's introduction, al-Ḥimyarī complains about widespread sentiment that Eastern Arabic poetry always merits notice over Western verse.[109] Yet, like all Andalusi poets, he was an ardent consumer of the former himself.[110] Nature was not a new theme in Arabic verse. Andalusi poets avidly and expertly cultivated this subject as a segment in the polythematic *qaṣīda* and as a semi-independent genre. A few poems, such as the following lyric by Ibn Khafāja, explicitly consider the divinely bestowed richness of the Andalusi landscape, even as it suggests poetically a possibly ominous sociopolitical future:

O people of al-Andalus! God grant you abundance:
    water and shade and rivers and trees.
No garden of paradise but your homes;
    if I had a choice I would take you.

After this do not fear to enter hell;
after paradise you will not enter the fire.[111]

Whether we read it as pride of place, provincialism, chauvinism, apologetic, and defensive, or as authorizing a culturally powerful sense of Andalusiness in counterpoint to its political fragmentation and weakness, beginning in the eleventh century, comments and occasional passages about the merits of Andalusis and wonders of al-Andalus past and present were embedded in Andalusi Arabic texts of virtually every genre. Gestures to the greatness of al-Andalus and Andalusis are found in texts of such disparate literary character as the work of the sociologist-anthropologist Ibn Khaldūn, for whom "the Andalusis are found to have a sharpness of intellect, a nimbleness of body, and a receptivity for instruction such as no one else has"[112] and in imaginative texts such as al-Saraqusṭī ibn al-Ashtarkūnī's (d. 1143) *Al-Maqāmāt al-luzūmiyya*. The "*Maqāma* of the Berbers" in number 41 captures the trope vividly. The narrator al-Sā'ib ibn Tammām, who appears in this *maqāma* as an Arab from the East, reflects on Andalusis and al-Andalus as a place of desire from the vantage of Tangier across the Strait: "I had heard of the land of al-Andalus and of its culture, its festivities, and its refinement, and I had come to long for it with the longing of a passionate lover, and would have given old and valuable possessions in exchange for it. The qualities I observed in its inhabitants used to delight me, and the virtues I came to expect from its best and finest citizens used to please me, even though I had met only its newly weaned, rather than its experienced young camels, and merely viewed the foot of its summit."[113] It is worth observing that the *maqāma* narrator typically is identified with strong ties to a particular place, even as he travels widely in Islamdom, as opposed to his counterpart, the trickster-rogue figure with ties to no place, who makes an appearance in every place. Here, the figure of the narrator, al-Sā'ib ibn Tammām, is characterized as an Eastern Arab eagerly seeking passage to al-Andalus from North Africa. James Monroe offers a brilliant reading of this *maqāma*—of one of four *maqāmāt* that he detects as explicitly related to the author's resolute identification with al-Andalus and its culture—as a critique of Andalusi disdain for Berbers. He reads it as a call for unity of the Islamic *umma* of the Maghrib and al-Andalus in the face of Castile-León's encroachment on Islamic territory, such as we have noted in various Andalusi city elegies.[114]

The cultural turn of the trope of Andalusi exceptionalism left an indelible imprint on how al-Andalus and Andalusis would be remembered in

Islamdom. It survived down to al-Maqqarī in the seventeenth century, with the Naṣrid minister court historian and polymath Ibn al-Khaṭīb as the most important intermediary. The anonymous fourteenth-century Marīnid dynastic chronicle *Al-Dhakhīra al-saniyya fī ta'rīkh al-dawla al-marīniyya* (The Resplendent Treasure of the History of the Marīnid State) is a notable Maghribi text. The Marīnids' self-constructed legitimacy also imposed responsibility on them to engage in defensive jihad on behalf of Andalusi Muslims, an obligation that they dutifully performed during the Castilian Mudejar revolt of 1264–1266. Note how the court historian rehearses for his Maghribi patrons the second and third forms of the trope idealizing the wealth, refinement, religious knowledge, and intellectual and cultural achievements of Córdoba in the context of Marīnid support for their Andalusi allies, the Naṣrids of Granada:

> The capital city of Córdoba, since the island of Andalus was conquered, has been the highest of the high, the further of the far, the place of the standard, the mother of towns; the abode of the good and godly, the homeland of wisdom, its beginning and its end; the heart of the land, the fount of science, the dome of Islam, the seat of the imam; the home of right reasoning, the garden of the fruits of ideas, of the earth and the banners of the age, the cavaliers of poetry and prose. Out of it have come pure compositions and exquisite compilations. And the reason for this, and for the distinction of its people before and since, as compared to others, is that the horizon encompasses none but the seekers and searchers after all the various kinds of knowledge and refinement, Most of the people of the country are noble Arabs from the East who conquered it, lords of the troops of Syria and Iraq who settled there, so that their descendants remain in each district as a noble race. Hardly a town lacks a skilled writer, a compelling poet, who, has he praised it, the least would have been great.[115]

We have seen the how eleventh- and twelfth-century Andalusi intellectual elites represented themselves as unnerved by an acute sense of insecurity and powerlessness within Islamdom and by the Easterners' unaltered views of the marginality and relative inconsequentiality of al-Andalus. To compensate for this state of affairs, the Andalusis immersed themselves in narrating the history they remembered. They continued to depict Umayyad al-Andalus as a lush and fertile land capable of sustaining an affluent, religiously pious, and singularly idyllic Arabo-Islamic community that was endowed with a gift for rigorous intellectual inquiry and artistic production.

Whereas the unified Islamic polity vanished, the prosperity and cultural productivity of the *ṭā'ifa* kingdoms endured until the turn of the twelfth century and subsequently in different forms under Almoravid and Almohad rule. Even as Andalusi poets of the period were drawn to voicing conventional expressions of reflective and restorative nostalgia for what was lost, important scholars documented the outstanding cultural achievements of the past. More significantly, these literary intellectuals kept alive the practice and production of Andalusi *adab* traditions in all its forms. They promoted the idea that al-Andalus had been, and continued to be, the repository of great learning and magnificent cultural production despite its ruptured polity and geographic remove from the heartland of Islamdom. In so doing, they manufactured continuity between who Andalusis were in the past and, moreover, who they were in the present, and instituted an *adab*-based, empowering, virtual *'aṣabiyya* (group cohesion), to borrow Ibn Khaldūn's indispensable concept of social solidarity.[116]

The eleventh and twelfth centuries thus proved to be most critical in the history of Andalusi exceptionalism. The persistence of the cultural turn traced in this chapter produced the longest enduring inflection of the trope. Its echoes continued to resonate down to the early modern age, to modernity, and into the present and were expanded to incorporate additional elements of Andalusi intellectual life deemed unique in retrospect, a distinctively Andalusi philosophical-theological orientation, including a peculiar blend of philosophy and Sufism and unconventional scientific orientations such as anti-Ptolemaic astronomy.[117] In Robert Edwards's words, we might say that the trope endeavors "to rediscover and enact the values that are presumed to have governed the original order."[118] In reaching back to that lived, remembered, and then increasingly imagined past, the trope of Andalusi exceptionalism projects for Andalusis and those who identify with them a religiously, intellectually, and aesthetically powerful character rooted in an alluring vision of al-Andalus and its people throughout its history and long after its demise. The same can be said of Sefarad and Sefardi Jews, to whose discourses we return in Chapter 4.

Chapter 4

The Jerusalemite Exile That Is in Sefarad

Sefardi Exceptionalism (Eleventh and Twelfth Centuries)

> In the days of Ḥasdai (ibn Shaprūṭ) the Nasi, the poets began to chirp, and in the days of R. Samuel the Nagid, they burst into song.
>
> —Abraham ibn Daud

> They say: "The people of Sefarad have discovered
> the wonders of concealed knowledge."
>
> —Solomon ibn Gabirol

By the eleventh century, the fluid nature of the Andalusi Jews' affiliation with the Eastern rabbinical academies discussed in Chapter 2—pseudo-dependence turned virtual independence—was not a pressing issue of concern for either party. The Andalusis continued to engage the leaders of Iraqi academies with due reverence and financial support but increasingly more as respectful equals than as constituents seeking guidance, at least until after the death of Hayya Gaon in 1038. In exchange, the Eastern geonim showered Andalusi notables with grandiose titles that they alone were authorized to bestow at the time. Andalusi Muslims had to cope with an unprecedented sociopolitical situation with the demise of the Umayyad state and its replacement by competing party-kingdoms, followed by even greater trauma and loss in 1085. By comparison, the sociopolitical and religious condition of the Jews of eleventh-century al-Andalus and their cognitive-imaginative map of Sefarad remained relatively stable. In any case, Andalusi Jews were long accustomed to life as a religious minority in diasporic lands; and they inherited a long tradition of reflecting on and responding to their circumstance in various discourses.[1]

In Chapter 2, we read how tenth-century Andalusi Jewish elites led and sponsored by Ḥasdai ibn Shaprūṭ came to conceive of and represent Sefarad as an exceptional place inhabited by an incomparable community of Jews. What did the tenth-century invention of Sefardi exceptionalism portend in the eleventh and twelfth centuries for communal and intellectual elites, who also received the complex bundle of Jewish traditions regarding exile, Jerusalem, and redemption—traditions embedded in the canonical texts of rabbinic prayer recited daily as well as encoded in numerous religious practices? How did Andalusi Jewish communal and intellectual elites of the eleventh and twelfth centuries frame discursively their traditional devotional longing for restoration to the Land of Israel with their real-world connection to and affection for Sefarad? And how did they receive Ibn Shaprūṭ's efforts to represent the Jews of Sefarad as uniquely privileged among the Jewish communities of Mediterranean and other lands?

In posing these questions, I direct attention to a discrete manifestation of the conflicts that were a source of creative tension in Andalusi Jewish culture and that defined this Jewish subcultural communal, religious, and intellectual elite in an Islamic polity. I am referring to the territorial dimension of the Jews' complex loyalties and commitments and their competing geographical-cultural orientations. How did the Andalusi Jews' discourse, regarding their impassioned attachment to Sefarad, exist in creative rivalry with their textual expressions of pious devotional longing for the Land of Israel, a place most of them never saw except through the parallax imaginative lens of their sacred tradition and performance of their liturgical rituals? How does the geographical-literary imagination inflect these competing tropes in Andalusi Jewish culture, meditating the relation of their "exile in Sefarad" to space?[2]

Previous scholarship regarding Andalusi Jewish geographical-cultural orientation offers three fundamental approaches to these questions: acknowledging the Andalusi Jews' fulsome commitment to Sefarad; portraying them as living with the apparent contradiction; and highlighting the importance of those figures who turned away from dedication to life in Sefarad, whatever its benefits, in favor of renewed religious devotion to the spiritual value of living in the Land of Israel with or without certainty of the imminence of the messianic age. Speaking as a nineteenth-century German Jewish intellectual possessed by a deep attachment to his own country, its language, and culture, Heinrich Graetz quaintly defined the Jews' ties to medieval Iberia this way: "The Jewish inhabitants of this happy peninsula [Iberia] contributed by their hearty interest to the greatness of the country, which they loved as only a fatherland can be loved."[3] Gerson Cohen underscored the Andalusi Jews' attachment to Sefarad with greater nuance but no less boldly than Graetz. In his reading of Abraham ibn Daud's twelfth-century chronicle of Jewish tradition, *Sefer ha-qabbalah*, Cohen observed that the Andalusi Jewish elite "tried to live as though Andalus could become a second Palestine or its surrogate, and Granada and Seville latter-day Jerusalems."[4] At the same time, Cohen notes "the constant and passionate prayer for a return to the Holy Land that is echoed incessantly in the poetry of Andalus." According to Cohen, the two themes expressed in Andalusi Hebrew poetry (attachment to life in Sefarad while longing for the Land of Israel) and the cultural approaches informing them "were by no means mutually exclusive. The traditional messianic dream was a religious dogma that would be effected by God in His good time. In the meanwhile, a surrogate program could be translated into reality in Andalus as it had been in previous centuries in Babylonia."[5]

Samuel the Nagid (d. 1056) and Moses ibn Ezra (d. ca. after 1138), two of the four Andalusi Hebrew poets regarded by tradition and cultural history as the period's preeminent literary artists, are said to represent authoritative voices of a definitive tilt toward Sefarad among eleventh- and twelfth-century Jewish intellectuals. The Nagid is said to favor Sefarad because he was so immersed in the Andalusi political, sociocultural, and Jewish communal scene and Ibn Ezra because he yearned nostalgically for his former home in Granada and its intellectually minded Arabic-speaking cultural environment while he languished as a miserable exile in the Christian Iberian kingdoms. By contrast, in Cohen's interpretive scheme, Judah Halevi's (d. 1141) eventual turn in text and deed toward a stricter Jewish piety in the twelfth century signifies the most prominent challenge to his predecessors' and contemporaries' "Andalusi orientation" and to attempts to live with the tension of two competing points of geographical-emotional reference in Andalusi Jewish culture.

Halevi's later poetry frequently depicts West (al-Andalus) and East (the Land of Israel) in hierarchical opposition: even the semblance of balance between them seemed to this rendering of his lyric vision to prefer Sefarad and "all its prosperity" over Jerusalem and "the dust of its ruined shrine."[6] In the mature Halevi's scheme, his contemporaries' comfortable investment in Sefarad unduly signified betrayal of the special primordial connection that God ordained for the people of Israel and the Land of Israel. Indeed, modern scholars such as Nehemiah Allony and Ezra Fleischer,[7] following the historiographical approach that Yitzhak Baer launched,[8] have touted the compelling voice of tradition and piety that Halevi supposedly represents as the authentic expression of the Jewish ethos.[9] According to his poetry, his letters, and the *Kuzari Book*, Halevi struggled to abandon the pretense of Sefardi exceptionalism toward the end of his life, if not earlier, at least from the time of his disappointed messianic expectation, according to a poem dating to 1130 in which the disheartened poet grumbles.[10] Halevi supplanted the conceit of Sefardi exceptionalism with his conviction in Jewish chosenness, not merely in the traditional rabbinic sense but as an ontological category, that is, as an articulation of absolute "Jewish exceptionalism" in accordance with the divine order established at Creation.[11] Ironically, Halevi remained very much an Andalusi Jewish thinker and poet, even in his rejection of Sefarad, because he employed all the culture's linguistic, discursive, and intellectual tools against itself and his society.[12] I understand this paradox of Halevi's literary and intellectual identity as a sign of the Andalusi Jewish culture's inescapable power and authority.

Do Andalusi Jewish culture and Hebrew poetry before Halevi's revolt against social and religious convention really delineate so deep and unambiguous an attachment to Sefarad as Graetz imagined—or as Cohen asserted, in a more tempered manner? Was Halevi, the self-styled "prisoner of love" and "prisoner of desire,"[13] who invoked his estrangement from material existence ("Far from You I die while living / but if I cling to You I live through dying"),[14] the first Andalusi Hebrew poet to verbalize geographical desire for the East, or was Judah's twelfth-century literary, if not personal, reorientation prefigured by earlier authors? More to the point, how did the Andalusi Jewish literary intellectuals' affection for Sefarad coexist, compete, or become conflated with their ahistorical pious longing for their people's restoration to the Land of Israel? Was there room within the Andalusi Jewish cultural matrix for yet a fourth approach that appeared to favor neither Sefarad nor Jerusalem or the artful and edgy balancing of the two?

In Chapter 2, we learned that Andalusi Jews going back to Ḥasdai ibn Shaprūṭ and Dūnash ben Labrāṭ already grappled with the cultural dilemma underlying these questions, matters closely bound up with the history of the trope of Sefardi exceptionalism. The infectious Karaite agenda and activist approach toward settling the Holy Land, previously discussed, inspired and challenged Jewish religious intellectuals across Islamdom. It certainly played a significant role in testing the passivity of Rabbanite tradition regarding history, dispersion, exile, and redemption and thus in catalyzing a fundamental modification of Rabbanite thinking on these subjects. S. D. Goitein commented on this very shift: "between the death of Saadia Gaon in Baghdad in 942 and that of . . . Judah Halevi shortly after his arrival in Palestine in 1141, a considerable change seems to have occurred in the Rabbanite-Jewish attitude toward messianism. The matter assumed an aura of urgency, as if redemption were around the corner, as if one had to do something to hasten its realization."[15] He further observed: "The Karaite emphasis on the study of the Bible and Hebrew—their belief in the power of independent reasoning, and their call to live in the Holy Land, or at least to visit there, and lead an austere life, all invited examination and, at least partial emulation."[16]

Andalusi Jewish fascination with reports from Khazaria, Ḥasdai ibn Shaprūṭ's aforementioned correspondence with the Jewish regent of that independent and supposedly powerful Jewish realm,[17] and evidence of covert and overt messianic speculation among Andalusi Jews attest to a certain despiritualization in Andalusi Jewish culture of the classical rabbinic attitudes toward home, homelessness, homesickness, and homecoming—the traditional quietist attitudes that discouraged messianic speculation and activity. In Gerson Cohen's words, "at no time in the history of the Jews after the second century was there such a concentration of messianic speculation and of vigorous reaffirmation of the messianic hope as there was in Andalus in the eleventh and twelfth centuries."[18] At the turn of the twelfth century, Andalusi Jewish consciousness of their inconsequential role on the sidelines of the political struggle between Islamdom and Christendom for control of both the Holy Land and the Iberian Peninsula doubtlessly exacerbated the appeal of apocalyptic-messianism, with its promise of restoring Jewish sovereignty in the Land of Israel.

It is also worth recalling an eleventh-century Andalusi Arabic source—a skewed one, to be sure—that reports on a polemical exchange that the Muslim author supposedly held with a promising Andalusi Jewish scholar when they were both entering early adulthood. The episode is recounted by Ibn Ḥazm, whose profile as a historically eminent, but not especially influential, Andalusi Muslim religious and literary intellectual we encountered in Chapter 3. In his monumental work of heresiography, *al-Fiṣal fī l-milal* (Book of

Opinions on Religions, Sects, and Heresies), Ibn Ḥazm relates that he debated "Ismāʿīl b. Yūsuf the Levite, court secretary-scribe" (otherwise known as Samuel the Nagid), "the most knowledgeable and accomplished interlocutor among the Jews."[19] This is not the place to rehearse the details of the dispute, but one famous and significant note stands out for its specifically political valence: their divergent interpretations of a biblical verse narrated in a subchapter titled "The Torah Foretells the Conferring of Authority to Judah's Descendants." The prophetic verse in question is "The scepter shall not depart from Judah, nor the ruler's staff from between his feet till Shiloh [i.e., tribute] come [to him]" (Gen. 49:10). According to Ibn Ḥazm's account, the argument involved the contemporary significance of the ecumenical office of the exilarch (*ro'sh ha-golah*), head of the Jews, appointed and recognized by the Abbasid caliphs in Baghdad. Samuel ostensibly asserted that "to this day, the exilarchs are descendants of David and thus the offspring of Judah, and they possess authority, kingship, and rule." Ibn Ḥazm accepted the exilarchs' Davidic ancestry in accordance with Islamic reverence for the Prophet David but argued that these symbolic figures exercised no authority whatsoever in Islamdom.[20] Here we only read of Ibn Ḥazm's interpretation. But in light of the importance that rabbinic tradition attached to the continuity of the Davidic royal line, Andalusi Jewish interest in messianism going back to Ibn Shaprūṭ, the Nagid's title and correspondence with ecumenical heads of Jewish communities, and the audacious persona we encounter in his poetry, the biblical prophecy was arguably a significant literary touchstone for Samuel as a young man and for long thereafter.

The pronounced shift in the Jews' religious thinking regarding exile and redemption was inscribed in Andalusi Hebrew verse. Poetry in general and *piyyuṭ* (liturgical poetry) in particular served as important literary vehicles for inner Jewish resistance to the memory and condition of displacement, dispersion, and powerlessness. Ever since the age of the classical *piyyuṭ* in late antique Byzantine Palestine, liturgical poets composed lyrics on the theme of catholic Israel's exile, misery, and eventual, if long delayed, redemption. Their poems, while stylistically and linguistically opaque or inaccessible, were recited during the synagogue service as the final element of the *yoṣer* poetic cycle. During the Andalusi period, poetic embellishments to the rabbinic liturgy on the theme of communal redemption evolved into an independent strophic genre (*gᵉ'ullah*) that Andalusi Hebrew poets adopted, along with other genres devoted to the theme such as *sᵉliḥot* (penitential poems) and *tokhaḥot* (poems of admonition).[21]

Historical events also elicited literary responses, invariably in Hebrew poetry. When addressing the plight of the Jews of Palestine, Andalusi poets took note of their place of residence, which was unrivaled in religious importance. For example, the accomplished rabbinic scholar Joseph ibn Abītūr composed an elegy concerning the deprivations of the Jewish community during the Bedouin raids in Fāṭimid Palestine (1024), in which the poet speaks of Palestine as "their Homeland, the place of their desire" (*arṣam m^{e}qom ḥefṣam*).[22] It is noteworthy that a similar loaded phrase (*m^{e}ḥoz ḥefṣah*) appears in the famous elegy by Abraham ibn Ezra bemoaning the devastated Jewish communities of al-Andalus and the Maghrib at the outset of the Almohad period.[23] In the latter instance, its usage is ambiguous such that the reader is uncertain whether it refers to the Land of Israel, as one might expect, or to the Jews' homelands in the Islamic West.

Not every Andalusi Hebrew *g^{e}'ullah* adheres to a pure or standard agenda of a plea for eschatological homecoming such as we read in Halevi's "Ya'avor 'alai r^{e}ṣonkha."[24] Lyrics like the *muwashshaḥ* "Esb^{e}lah n^{e}dudi agilah v^{e}-galuti" (I bear my wandering / I rejoice in my exile), by Isaac ibn Ghiyāth,[25] the rabbinic authority from Lucena and head of its august academy, suggest a radical counter-approach that undermines the traditional rabbinic posture of waiting with prayerful hope. The poem's allusive biblical intertextual dynamics drawing on Lamentations, Deutero-Isaiah, and the Song of Songs are marshaled to welcome and revel in the suffering that God prescribes for Israel. Judah Halevi famously took up this uncompromising turn of the theme. His lyric "Me-'az m^{e}'on ha-ahavah" employs the language and images of social love poetry to render Israel's love for God in virtually sadomasochistic terms ("The taunts of foes for Your name's sake are sweet, / so let them torture one whom You tormented. . . . The day You hated me I loathed myself, / for I will honor none whom You disdain"), as if joyful acceptance of even greater suffering (at the hands of Muslims and Christians) might beget speedy redemption.[26]

Judah Halevi otherwise excelled in producing alternately haunting and buoyant lyrics on the traditional themes of exile and redemption, until he envisioned a course to experience personally (or inspire others and reestablish for many, according to another interpretation) the primeval metaphysical nexus between the God of Israel's manifest presence, the Land of Israel, and the people of Israel. Halevi's religious evolution—he refers to himself as "one whose homeland is Sefarad but whose destination is Jerusalem" (*S^{e}farad admato / vi-rushalayim m^{e}gamato*)[27]—appears to have unnerved his Andalusi

Jewish cohort, who regarded him as "the quintessence and embodiment of our country . . . our glory and leader, the illustrious scholar and unique and perfect devotee" (or, according to a different translation, "the heart and soul of our land").[28] As previously noted, Halevi remained an Andalusi Jewish intellectual, even in his rejection of Sefarad and its culture, in that he subversively turned the language and the artistic and intellectual tools of the culture against itself.

Samuel the Nagid (993–1056)

The competitive inflection and cultural turn of the trope of Andalusi exceptionalism engineered by Muslim elites discussed in Chapter 3 resonated among Andalusi Jews as well during the eleventh century. It took the form of a Sefardi exceptionalism even more grandiose and chauvinistic than we found in Ibn Shaprūṭ's ambitious blueprint for the Jews of tenth-century Sefarad. Much of the eleventh-century discourse related to the idea and significance of Sefarad, in fact, centers on the towering figure of Samuel (ben Joseph ha-Levi) the Nagid. By all accounts, Samuel was an accomplished rabbinic scholar, important Hebrew philologist-grammarian, virtuoso Hebrew poet, influential communal leader, and significant political player in Andalusi society as head vizier (prime minister) of Zīrid Granada. David Wasserstein's recent, characteristically judicious, biographical sketch of the Nagid sums up Samuel's singularly expansive field of operation:

> Samuel's active participation in the Islamic worlds of Granada and al-Andalus made possible also a far more powerful oscillation between worlds: it enabled him to play a great role in the Jewish world, itself part of the larger Islamic world, beyond the Iberian Peninsula. The wealth that he acquired enable him to send financial support to Jewish religious academies (yeshivot) as far away as Jerusalem and even Baghdad, to build a large library . . . to support students of holy writ at home and abroad, to fund copying and distribution of the Talmud and other religious texts in various cities all over the Islamic world, and—symbolically important—to send annual gifts of olive oil to the synagogues of Jerusalem.[29]

Aside from their role in the literary historical development of *g^e'ullot*, Andalusi Hebrew poets, including Samuel the Nagid, devoted lyrics of a personal and social nature to imaginative journeys to Palestine—symbolic, religious compensation, as it were, for their exilic/diasporic existence in Sefarad. Two generations after one of the voices in Dūnash ben Labrāṭ's poem "interrupted" his counterpart's invitation to a wine soirée in a lush Andalusi garden and conjured the disturbing image of the Jerusalem Temple grounds in Gentile hands, the Nagid produced several poems in which the poet's religious devotion to Zion figures prominently. It is instructive to recall that the Nagid supposedly championed the Rabbanite confrontation of Karaites in eleventh-century al-Andalus.[30] By contrast with Halevi, whose intellectual and religious trajectory had transformative consequences for his literary identity, Samuel the Nagid gives the impression of remaining steadfastly devoted to al-Andalus and Sefarad, even as he dutifully repeats the requisite pieties of yearning for the Land of Israel and the restoration of its biblical cultic and political institutions.

The Nagid does not seem to have composed many *piyyuṭim* per se but three of his forty-one Hebrew "war" poems (Ar., *al-ḥamāsa*) are introduced by elegies for Zion or odes to the Holy City. "B^{e}-libbi ḥom l^{e}-mifqad ha-n^{e}ʿurim" was written in 1047, on the occasion of Granada's defeat of the combined forces of Seville and Málaga. It begins with a first-person seventeen-line lament that serves as a lyrical introduction to a long poetic description of the battle (lines 18–58), before the poem concludes (lines 59–64) with a dedication to and praise of God. The introductory lament over Jewish life in exile contains a passage whose final lines appear to be a literary exercise or variation on the theme and rhetorical pattern established by Dūnash.[31] Seething on account of his and his people's condition "dwelling outside Zion, impure as a corpse," the poet wonders about and imagines restoration to the place and the socioreligious station of his Levite tribe—those assigned as singers in the Jerusalem Temple service:

> Will melodious song ever ring from my mouth or from my son's
> on the Levites' Temple platform?
> Will I ever see the children of the Living God
> whisked to Zion like clouds and doves?
> By the life of my living Redeemer! Until
> my dying day I hope for the ingathering of the dispersed!
> I do not claim: "I am mighty and majestic,

I belong among kings and eminent folk."
Neither do my urges tempt me to claim:
"You are a god, honored above men,
For what might you gain when Israel is redeemed?
What more could you attain when the dispersed are gathered in?"
Standing in the Sacred Precincts is best for my soul,
finer than ruling over everyone.
Quaffing rich drink on impure soil
is like swilling dregs to me!

The poet proceeds to imagine officiating as a Levite in the Temple cultic service,[32] only to be roused from the fantasy (awakening from a vision serves as a conventional transition formula in Arabic and Hebrew verse). Instead of serving as a Levite in the restored Jerusalem Temple, the poet's persona awakens to realize that instead, he is commissioned to compose Hebrew verse in praise of God as battle awaits him at Ronda. Samuel's rhetorical gifts, unique literary sensibility as a Hebrew poet, and his position of privilege in Granada (on which, see below) inform a fundamentally different approach to the vexing subject of Psalm 137 ("By the rivers of Babylon, there we sat, sat and wept, as we thought of Zion") and its Karaite interpretation.[33] So, too, the poetics of the *qaṣīda* form signify a symbolic transaction: composing Arabic-style Hebrew poetry replaces Levitic Temple service. The poet thus overcomes geographical and religious desire through the act of literary representation.

According to Andalusi Jewish tradition and the testimony of Muslim contemporaries, Samuel fulfilled his aspirations for Jewish communal leadership and public acclaim through his generosity and the influential positions that he occupied in the Zīrid courts of Ḥabbūs and his son Bādīs of Granada. Samuel was afforded the honorific title "Nagid" in 1027 as head of Granada's Jewish community, although the significance of this title in al-Andalus is uncertain.[34] In the twelfth century, Moses ibn Ezra reported on the unparalleled reach of the Nagid's intellectual-literary stature and communal standing: "All that pertains to his compositions and works and letters is known to the uttermost edges of east and west across the land and the sea, and up to the leaders of the Babylonian community and the sages of the Levant (i.e., Palestine) and the scholars of Egypt and the nagids of [North] Africa and the lords of the West and the Andalusi nobility."[35] The unique place that the Nagid occupied in the Andalusi Jewish social and cultural scene, as well as his political service to Berber Granada, did not escape the notice of Andalusi Muslims authors. Indeed, the attention he receives in the Arabic sources mark him as exceptional among the Jews of eleventh-century al-Andalus. Here is how Ṣāʿid al-Andalusi, born a generation after Samuel, noted his preeminence as a religious intellectual among the Jews of al-Andalus: "Among them [those learned in the law of the Jews] in al-Andalus was Abū Ibrāhīm Ismāʿīl ibn Yūsuf the Scribe, known as Ibn al-Naghrīla, who served Bādīs ibn Ḥabbūs al-Ṣinhājī, king of Granada and its territory, as administrator of the state. No one in al-Andalus before him had such learning in the law of the Jews and knowledge of how to use it and to defend it."[36]

Beyond his administrative service to the state and his exemplary control of Jewish law, the Nagid's command of the arts and sciences was noticed by Andalusi Muslims such as his contemporary, the great historian Ibn Ḥayyān (*apud* Ibn al-Khaṭīb): "He was an extraordinary man. He wrote in both languages: Arabic and Hebrew. He knew the literatures of both peoples. He went deeply into the principles of the Arabic language and was familiar with the works of the subtle grammarians. He spoke and wrote classical Arabic with the greatest ease. . . . He was excellent in the sciences of the ancients, in mathematics as well as astronomy. Also in the field of logic he possessed ample knowledge. In dialectics he even prevailed over his adversaries. . . . He assembled a beautiful library."[37]

Returning to Andalusi Jewish sources, *Sefer ha-qabbalah* casts Samuel the Nagid in a central role in the unfolding arc of Jewish history and in the emergence of Sefarad as its principal locus from the tenth century to the mid-twelfth century. He is represented as the veritable rabbinic "embodiment of three crowns: the crown of the Torah, the crown of kingship, and the crown of priesthood."[38]

> Besides being a great scholar and highly cultured person, R. Samuel was highly versed in Arabic literature and style. . . . Now R. Samuel was appointed as nagid in [4]787. He achieved great good for Israel in Spain, the Maghreb, Ifriqiya, Egypt, Sicily, indeed as far as the academy in Babylonia and the Holy City. He provided material benefits out of his own pocket for students of the Torah in all these countries. He also purchased many books—[copies] of the Holy Scriptures as well as of the

> Mishna and Talmud. . . . Throughout Spain and the countries just mentioned, whoever wished to devote full time to the study of the Torah found in him a patron. Moreover, he retained scribes who would make copies of the Mishna and Talmud, which he would present to students who were unable to purchase copies themselves. . . . He spread Torah abroad and died at a ripe old age after having earned four crowns: the crown of the Torah, the crown of power, the crown of a Levite, and towering over them all, by dint of good deeds in each of these domains, the crown of a good name.[39]

Note that *Sefer ha-qabbalah* attributes to Samuel the Nagid the mastery of religious knowledge and efforts to disseminate it widely, complete control of Arabic *adab* and its Hebrew adaptation, especially in the form of poetry, highborn genealogy, virtuous character, and the exercise of legitimate power—fundamental elements in the thematic matrix of the trope of Sefardi exceptionalism. Is it any wonder that among Ibn Daud's subsequent readers, Gerson Cohen was immensely influential for accrediting *Sefer ha-qabbalah* with effectively consolidating all the traditions marking Andalusi Jewish privilege? Cohen read it as presenting a programmatic vision of the providential trajectory of Jewish history in which Sefarad occupied the center of the Jewish world from the tenth century forward.[40]

Andalusi Hebrew poets in the Nagid's entourage and aspirants to his sponsorship naturally regaled him with encomiums projecting his authority far and wide. Poetic tributes to the Nagid have come down to us from poets he supported, such as Isaac ibn Khalfūn[41] and Solomon ibn Gabirol.[42] Panegyrics observe a conspicuous literary practice that Jonathan Decter recently studied as *Dominion Built of Praise* and that I ascribe to a psychosocial impulse to compensate for the Jews' relative powerlessness.[43] That is, Hebrew panegyrics for Jewish figures like the Nagid, following the stylized form and conventional content of Arabic poems of praise (*madīḥ*) addressed to Muslim dignitaries, were designed to impress, flatter, and secure reward for the poet. Panegyrics were also cultural products calculated to advertise the honoree's generosity and legitimacy and confer his communal standing and authority through literary representation.

Andalusi Hebrew poets represented the communal autonomy characteristic of Jewish life under classical Islam, going back to Ḥasdai ibn Shaprūṭ and continuing with influential Jewish notables such as Jacob ibn Jau in

ʿĀmirid Córdoba and Yequtiel ibn Ḥasan in Tujībid Saragossa,[44] as veritable rule. Those imaginative literary gestures were realized most fully in history in the person of Samuel the Nagid, who accrued and wielded unequaled political authority as *wazīr* in the kingdom of Granada for eighteen years. Consider Joseph ibn Ḥasdai's famous paean to Samuel dubbed "the orphan poem" or "the unique poem" (*shirah yᵉtomah*). The lyric tallies the full litany of conventional praises for the patron but formulates its tribute with the Nagid's own self-image in mind (see below), likening him to his biblical namesake, the priest and prophet Samuel, and hailing his Levitic descent, intellect, cultural sophistication, munificence, and eminence:

He soars like a tower over Israel,
raised high like a wall for his people;
renewed through him, for his tribe's devotion,
    is a place of honor over Orion.
Could it be that Shmu'el is Samuel—
    who was called to enter the Lord's Temple— . . .
If not—he's worthy in righteousness,
    pure in perfection of his soul,
His lips keep watch over all learning,
    and from his mouth the Law is taught
his glory glows just like the moon,
    his deeds are like a brook to thirst.
Virtue and merit are bound to his shoulder,
    authority's always sealed at his side.[45]

Poets also voiced praise of Samuel the Nagid by noting Sefarad's successful socioreligious and cultural competition for preeminence with the Jewish communities in the Islamic East and its leaders. The eleventh-century poet Solomon ibn Gabirol addressed an ode of apology by way of praise ("Qum ha-zman u-lvash ʿadanekha") to the Nagid, his erstwhile benefactor. It conjures with clarity the hierarchical opposition of Sefarad (with Samuel at its head) to Babylonia:

Through you the horn of Sefarad is raised
    from the day you were born till your old age.
Through you it [Sefarad] bellows at the folks of Shinhar (Iraq)
    who draw [water] from your well.[46]

A ninety-five-verse *qaṣīda* ("T^{e}hillat el b^{e}-ro'sh kol ha-t^{e}hillot"), by the rarely solicitous or unctuous Ibn Gabirol, offers an unnamed patron—almost certainly the irrepressible Samuel the Nagid, to whom a cluster of Ibn Gabirol's poems are addressed—the entire conventional catalog of generalized praise. However, in a remarkable passage midway through the lyric, the poet temporarily departs from rehearsing conventional *madīḥ* themes and exalts the addressee and Sefarad above the East and its "rival" rabbinic and cultural authorities. He envisions reception of the Nagid's wisdom by the Jewish communities of the Islamic East—ascribing to the Easterners bewildered consciousness of Samuel's rabbinic and intellectual acumen and accomplishment as belonging to Sefarad:

His *responsa* are read throughout Iraq
  and expounded by communal authorities.
In the councils of the heads of Nehardea and Sura
  the great towns of (rabbinic) jurisprudence
They elevate his *responsa* above the rest
  and inscribe them in scrolls with golden ink.
People say: "The Sefardim have discovered
  the wonders of concealed knowledge;
they behold the truth, their Master overpowers
  while we envision delusion.
Compared to them we dress in tatters
  while they're attired in finest apparel.
Their dignity resembles the lions';
  compared to them we are like ewe lambs.
They reap Wisdom's full-grown shoots
  while we clutch unripe ears of grain.
The eyes of their blind and the ears of their deaf are opened wide
  while our ears merely tingle.
The Master delights them and their joys abound;
  they revel in divulging his praises.
In his presence it's as though Rav Hayya never was,
  inadequately equipped to answer him with words."[47]

Such exaggeration arguably exceeds even the benefactor's expectation that the poem's rhetorical enthusiasm will promote his incomparable virtues. Indeed, the acclaim heaped upon the patron succeeds in elevating his entire community over its counterpart in the East, as it were, whose august leader's day has come and gone or, rather, "never was" (*w^e-rav hayya k^e-lo' haya l^efanaw*).[48]

The praises of the poets in his entourage aside,[49] conventional and otherwise, what can we learn from how the Nagid represented his own place in Sefarad and Jewish history and the grandiose vision that the poet constructed for himself? We cannot presume to know what Samuel actually thought, but we can certainly assess the political, propagandistic function of the public profile he promoted through his undertakings and the unique persona he exhibited and performed in his poetry. Samuel's determination to be a prominent or dominant player in Jewish affairs, scholarship, and literary life beyond the borders of al-Andalus led him to cultivate and maintain close ties with Jewish elites in North Africa, Palestine, and Iraq, as Ibn Shaprūṭ had done in the previous century. Through copying and circulating his works in Hebrew grammar, rabbinic scholarship, and his pathbreaking and masterful Arabic-style Hebrew verse, Samuel displayed a complete command of Jewish and Arabic learning and culture, the *adab* so highly valued in Andalusi society.

The Nagid's extensive network of correspondents across the Mediterranean included Hayya Gaon, whom he praised in three poems. He also authored a stirring eighty-verse lament on the occasion of Hayya's death in 1038.[50] Samuel had correspondence, such as epistolary lyrics or letters, with the exilarch Ḥezekiah in Baghdad,[51] Daniel ben 'Azaria Gaon, head of the Palestinian rabbinical academy,[52] Sahlān b. Abraham,[53] and 'Eli ben 'Amram, the respective heads of the Babylonian and Palestinian Rabbanite congregations in Fusṭāṭ (Old Cairo),[54] and Qayrawānī rabbinic luminaries Rabbeinu Nissim ben Jacob (to whose daughter Samuel's son Joseph was married),[55] and R. Ḥananel ben Ḥushiel and his son and successor R. Ḥushiel ben Ḥananel, among others.[56] With the exception of the unique role in Jewish history that Abraham ibn Daud assigns Samuel a century after his death, the reader might think that the various discourses and practices associated with Samuel the Nagid and the stature he achieved were shared, albeit to a lesser degree, by the other Jewish elites in the Mediterranean lands of classical Islam.

How did the Nagid's own poetry represent his place in Andalusi Jewish society and culture? Literary readings of the Nagid's poetry typically consider his consummate artistry and masterful control over the prosody, rhetoric, and thematic range of Arabic-style Hebrew verse. But there is another way to read the substantial corpus of compositions that the poet devoted to representing his communal and political life. That poetry served as the most important vehicle for portraying and marketing as unique the special place he occupied in Sefarad and in Jewish history. Viewed through the prism of his poetry, the Nagid's carefully calibrated public profile construes Samuel's political ascent and court service in Zīrid Granada as intimations of God's plan for history, as unmistakable signs of God's favor and his chosenness, and of his destined role in Jewish history as an incomparable communal, political, religious, intellectual, and cultural leader of the Jews of Granada, if not all of al-Andalus.

Armed with conventional rhetorical tools available in the stylized genre of the "boast" (Ar., *fakhr*), the poet repeatedly celebrates his aristocratic Levitic lineage. The Nagid's biblical ancestors "authorize" his composition of highly personal and idiosyncratic Hebrew songs of thanksgiving and praise to God:

> I am Kohath's descendant, Merari's progeny
> men of renown, musicians extraordinaire.[57]

The roster from the distant past is expanded in another poem and only seems shrouded in obscurity; the biblical names would be well known to educated Andalusi Jews:

> The heir of Merari, Sitri, and Assir,
> Elkanah, Mishael, Elzafan, and Assaf!
> How could a poem
> in my mouth be improper
> to the God who heals my wound?
> From Jedutun the singer of Psalms
> my father descends,
> and I from my father.
> For the Lord I sweeten my song in its discourse,
> as He embitters my enemy's heart.
> As He pledged to vanquish my foes,
> so I've pledged my song to please Him.[58]

Noble ancestry aside, the Nagid inventories the intellectual gifts that God bestowed upon him:

Do you remember that? And don't you remember when
He imparted
    you knowledge and intellect like elders?
When He enlightened you in His Scripture and Tradition,
    which are set apart at the apex of knowledge?
When He divulged to you the Greek sciences
    and imparted to you the knowledge of the Arabs. . . .
He made your name great and powerful
    beyond the sea and the lands of the West?[59]

Whether the reader regards it as warranted by his achievements or inflated and unjustified (he made rivals and enemies among the Jews of al-Andalus, to say nothing about some Muslim elites),[60] the Nagid's bravado and profile appear to reflect a carefully crafted image for public consumption. Some students view his self-presentation as apologetic, over-the-top rhetorical gestures informed by anxieties about his social and literary boundary-breaking. Other readers chalk it up to the poet's rhetorical derring-do. What discursive tool kit did the Nagid employ for this uncommonly bold scheme of self-aggrandizement, apart from the rhetoric and conventional themes that the audience expects in the "boast"? Andalusi Hebrew poets knew the Hebrew Bible by rote. At every turn, their poetry is replete with toponyms, figures, events, and themes drawn from the biblical Hebrew lexicon. Such references, associations, and allusions can be playful, decorative, or rhetorically significant to the artistry of the poem.[61] Compared with other poets, Samuel the Nagid was singularly adept at marshaling biblical references in crafting what Robert Hollander called typologies of "historical recurrence" that "guarantee or undermine authority."[62] Suffused with the cultural capital that Jewish tradition ascribed to prototypical figures, models, and institutions of ancient Israel, various typologies of historical recurrence inform the self-image that the Nagid publicized through his poetry. The literary evidence is so extensive that it is difficult to conclude that Samuel's Nagid's self-hype amounts only to a rhetorical gambit for apologetic purposes or a conventional, artistic show of force and talent.

The biblically inspired titles of three collections of poetry (*Ben Tᵉhillim*, *Ben Mishei*, *Ben Qohelet*) in the Nagid's *dīwān* edited by his son Joseph and the psalm-like designations of poems in *Ben Tᵉhillim* (particularly *tᵉhillah*, *nᵉginah*, *todah*), invite the audience to associate his verse with biblical texts attributed to the iconic Israelite kings David (Psalms) and Solomon (Proverbs and

Ecclesiastes). The Nagid devoted the aforementioned cluster of "war poems" to representing his political and military adventures as vizier of Zīrid Granada. In these unique Andalusi Hebrew lyrics the audience encounters a constellation of biblical allusions whose rhetorical effect surpasses biblical references of the conventional sort that abound in Andalusi Hebrew poetry. Here the Nagid's and the Berber Zīrids' Andalusi adversaries are cast as Israel and God's enemies and as latter-day descendants of ancient Israel's inveterate foes. Furthermore, biblical references to divine promises to the people of Israel are transformed into God's personal assurances to Samuel the Nagid. For example, toward the conclusion of one of his grandest battle poems, the warrior-poet requests that word of his (that is, Islamic Granada's) victory over (Islamic) Almería be dispatched speedily to the Jewish communities of North Africa, Egypt, Palestine, and Iraq. The poem establishes a typological correspondence (Samuel = Mordechai, the triumphant biblical Jewish courtier in the Book of Esther / Ibn 'Abbās of Almería = the notorious Amalekite enemy of the Jews, Haman the Agagite) authorizing the poet to call for commemorating "his" marvelous victory as a "second Purim," just as Mordechai instituted the late biblical festival following his defeat of Haman and rescue of the Persian Jews.[63]

Another famous lyric cited above represents what perhaps is the most brazen, extreme formulation of the Nagid's promotion of his peerless function and exclusive destiny in Sefarad. In response to an imagined interlocutor's interrogation, the poet likens himself or, rather, identifies himself with the biblical king David—psalmist, political leader, warrior—and, like Samuel, from the tribe of Levitic singers in the Jerusalem Temple:

> My friend, for me in my straits
>   The Rock rose up,
> Therefore I offer these praises,
>   My poem to the Lord. . . .
>   Someone objected:
>   Who are *you* to pay homage?
> I am, I answered, the David of my age![64]

The Nagid's noble Jerusalemite ancestry serves a dual purpose beyond the consent that it grants him as a Levite to compose Hebrew songs of praise to God. By likening himself to King David, the poet exploits his identification with the entire bundle of that emblematic figure's religious, literary, political, and genealogical attributes, aptitudes, and feats.

In the Nagid's case, poetic claims to divine election occur with such frequency as a form of self-promotion that they exceed the rhetorical parameters and conventional literary posture of the genre of "boast" in which the poet predictably sings his own praises.[65] Read together, nothing quite corresponds to these expressions of chosenness in the entire canon of medieval Hebrew poetry because no other poet inhabited simultaneously so many public roles so successfully or for so long a period of time. The poet implies that his genealogical roots with the Jerusalemite nobility confer this select status. So too, the "prophetic" dream-vision promising him divine favor and protection vouchsafed him at a young age (*Yom ṣar u-maṣoq*) is invoked in four "war poems." It likens him to his biblical namesake Samuel,[66] the priest and prophet; and additional messages that he "receives" from God, promising victory in battle, are fashioned so as to seem probative:

> The Lord is mine Who said: "Trust in Me.
>   and I will land you in delightful places.
> I will smash for you the teeth of lions.
>   I will lay low the sons of giants before you."[67]

Ibn Shaprūṭ's tenth-century program utilized his social status and economic largesse to enhance the prominence of a community without a polity, in order to turn his authority into ersatz dominion and put Sefarad on the map, so to speak. Samuel the Nagid's poetry, position, and exploits bestow on him cultural authenticity, political legitimacy, communal leadership, and genuine agency, if not outright rule and sovereignty. Through this persona, the Nagid became the embodiment of Sefardi exceptionalism by virtue of his unrivaled register of credentials in rabbinics, languages, poetry, and politics: his genealogy, intellect, religious knowledge, artistic skill, munificence, and communal and political authority are signs of election. In effect, Sefarad was exceptional because he was exceptional.

Solomon ibn Gabirol (1021/1022–ca. 1057/1058)

The reader encounters a textual journey of another sort than the Nagid's imaginative visit to Jerusalem, and with it an overlooked fourth position to the question of geographical orientation within the Andalusi Jewish cultural matrix, in the eleventh-century poet-philosopher Solomon ibn Gabirol.

Chronologically, Ibn Gabirol was the second of the four most artistically accomplished Andalusi Hebrew poets and a Nagid protégé, of sorts, for a time. One of his characteristically enigmatic poems is “Mah lakh y^{e}ḥidah tesh^{e}vi” (What's troubling you my soul, silent as a captured king?), a fifty-verse lyric that, as in so many of Ibn Gabirol's poems, blurs conventional generic and thematic lines between Andalusi Hebrew occasional-social and devotional poetry. This poem appears to relate the poet's contemplating a journey and quest, albeit with Gabirolian misdirection. The Arabic superscription is more specific, yet it only adds to the mystery: *wa-qāla ḥīna khurūjihi min al-andalus*, “verse he recited upon his departure from al-Andalus.”[68]

The poem consists of four or five thematic units whose divisions are skillfully marked by changes in tone and address, as well as sharp mood swings adroitly represented by transitional techniques. The lyric's pattern of metaphorical movements take us from mournful paralysis, motionless devotion, aimless futility, tentative journey, to the dynamic motion of swift flight; note the parallels with epithets for God: *yosh^{e}vi* (line 6, “from His throne,” in Cole's translation but more literally, “the Enthroned”) and *rokh^{e}vi* (line 38, “who rides the sky,” i.e., “the celestial Charioteer”). It may be outlined as follows:

1. counsel to the poet's soul
   a. lines 1–4 — poet's soul is deeply aggrieved and silent
   b. lines 5–10 — soul advised to renounce the world and await God
   c. lines 11–13 — the world is denounced
2. a solution for the soul and its specific problem
   a. lines 14–16 — soul urged to return to God and express itself
   b. lines 17–21 — soul's troubles with society
3. a second solution for the soul
   a. lines 22–30 — poet exhorts soul to leave al-Andalus for the East
4. lines 31–38 — more counsel to the poet's aggrieved soul
5. lines 39–43 — poet curses land of his foes
   a. Coda lines 44–50 — complaint with ascetic elements (in colloquial Andalusi Arabic)

In this lyric, the poet turns to his irate soul (frequently gendered in the Hebrew by use of the epithet *y^{e}ḥidah*, “my only one”) with questions, prodding, and counsel. Central to Neoplatonic thought is the notion that the soul, detached from the sublime source to which it will eventually return, wallows in the misery of corporeal existence. A thematic staple of Andalusi liturgical poetry thus involves admonishing the soul to abandon its worldly attachments.[69] In "Mah lakh yeḥidah," the soul has become so accustomed to its isolation, so inured in its desolation as to have severed its conjunction with God.[70] This condition also interferes with the soul's (and thus the poet's) capacity to express itself in songs of praise to God: the Neoplatonic poet's version of writer's block is captured beautifully in the image of a wounded (song)bird and through the rhetorical tropes (*muqābala* [parallelism] and *muṭābaqa* [antitheton] of line 2 [*kanfei renanim ta'sefi / u-khnaf yegonim tisḥavi*]).

What's troubling you, my soul,
    silent as a captured king—
that you've drawn in your wings of your hymns
    and drag them around in your suffering?
How long will your heart be in mourning?
    When will your weeping give way? . . .
Be still my soul, before the Lord—
    be still but don't despair. (lines 1–3, 5)

Hold on until he gazes
    down from his throne in heaven;
Close your doors behind you and hide
    until your anger has faded.
Whether you thirst or go hungry
    hardly merits attention:
The rewards to come will be greater—
    you'll count them all soon as a blessing.
Distance yourself from the world's concern,
    don't waste away in its prison. . . . (lines 6–10)

Return, my soul, return to the Lord,
    restore your heart to its place:
Pour out your tears like water,
    before him plead your cause. (lines 14–15)

Ibn Gabirol's persona, speaking here as a sage counselor to his soul, urges the soul to turn its silence (line 1), *Mah lakh yeḥidah teshevi / dumam ke-melekh* *ba-sh^{e}vi*, into stillness (line 5), *Dommi y^{e}ḥidati l^e-el / dommi w^e-al t^e'aṣ^{e}vi*) and to wait for God. Indeed, the poet's persona seems assured in the advice it offers; it seems to promise that such a seemingly passive course will actually restore a reciprocal relationship between God and soul (line 6). This anticipated mutuality is captured in the neatly wrought semantic balance, if not symmetry, of *'imdi w^e-ṣappi 'ad asher / yashqif w^e-yere' yosh^{e}vi* ("Hold on until he gazes down from his throne in heaven").

The text invites the reader to reflect on the final passage of this first section with the poem's opening passage in mind: denunciation of the world in line 11, *Mah lakh adamah vog^{e}dah?* echoes the rhetorical formula of the first line. However, the resemblance between the passages is more apparent than real because all the verbs and many of the nouns in the first two passages (*tesh^{e}vi*, *'imdi*, *dumam*, *ba-sh^{e}vi*, *davaqt b^e-yagon*, *qever*, *yosh^{e}vi*, *hinnaz-^{e}ri*, etc.) applied to the soul and God involve images of immobility. By contrast, the motion of the final passage of the first part of the poem—the motion of the material world—has the qualities of aimlessness, circularity, and duplicity (*tithall^{e}khi u-t^{e}sovavi*; *titni/tiqḥi*, *titnadd^{e}vi*). The opposing images set up the motion of the soul toward God in the poem's second part (line 14, *Shuvi y^{e}ḥidati l^e-el*). Its phrasing is perfectly parallel to the earlier instructions given the soul in line 5 (*dommi y^{e}ḥidati l^e-el*).

In the poem's key passage (end of second and the third unit), the intellectually exacting, socially alienated poet and his anguished soul seek understanding, appreciation, and recognition elsewhere. The soul's hoped-for release upward ("from the dungeon where you brood," line 16) harkens back to the image of it trapped in the grave of its own making (line 4).

> Perhaps he'll see to release you
>   from the dungeon where you brood
> with boors you've come to abhor,
>   who can't understand what you've written,
> or determine what's worth preserving
>   and what would be better erased—
> who can't hear what you're saying,
>   or know if it's true or mistaken.
> Rejoice in the day you leave them
>   and offer your thanks on an altar.
> Others elsewhere will know
>   the worth of the person you are. (lines 16–21)

Repeated references to the poet's embittered soul, its revulsion for the confines and corruption of earthly existence, its disgust for the taint of ignorance from having to live in society among boors, and its dreadful situation of existential exile, remind us that the poem only seems to belong with other familiar lyrical complaints. I have in mind Gabirolian lyrics such as "Niḥar b^{e}-qor'i g^{e}roni," on the poet leaving Saragossa,[71] and "N^{e}shamah me-asher tit'aw g^{e}du'ah," by Samuel the Nagid on the poet leaving Córdoba,[72] or nearly any poem from the cycle of lyrical complaints that Moses ibn Ezra composed in the Christian kingdoms of the north during his forty-year exile from Islamic Granada. As in the Arabic, these decidedly social and personal lyrics typically employ passages of *fakhr* (boast) in counterpoint to the poet's expressions of social and intellectual alienation (*taẓallum*) reminiscent of Ibn Ḥazm's posture discussed in the previous chapter. The boast thus redeems the poet symbolically from life among intellectual inferiors and from social rejection and isolation.

It should be noted that Samuel the Nagid's aforementioned poem "N^{e}shamah me-asher tit'aw g^{e}du'ah" also begins with mention of the soul, abstractly, in the third person and in opposition to the body (lines 1–4). However, in line 5, the Nagid's poem moves briskly into a conventional lyrical complaint about leaving Córdoba and escaping the misunderstanding of his friends (5–9). The poet's journey (10–19) is then outlined in self-aggrandizing terms, followed by panegyric (20–24). By contrast, Ibn Gabirol's ("Mah lakh y^{e}ḥidah") fusion of genres, themes, and voices involves deceptive reversals, internal contradictions, and ambiguities, as we shall presently see.

Rise, my troubled soul,
    rise up and take yourself there,
rise up and live where people
    will hold you in proper regard.
Leave your father and mother,
    and save your love for the Lord.
Rise up and race in pursuit of that place,
    be swift as an eagle or deer. (lines 22–25)

Although "that place" to which the poet's soul is bidden to swiftly flee is not yet identified, the injunction that it must depart immediately is decisive and the ensuing anticipated leave-taking absolute. The verbs *qumi*, *qumi*, *hityaṣ^{e}vi* (line 22) suggest that the poet's stance is rebellious and defiant: he exhorts his soul to gather itself and rise up against the social and spiritual constraints imposed upon it. The inner turmoil suppressed to this point in the poem is now released in the form of externalized action that will, like the patriarch Abram of the biblical allusion (line 24), replace meaningless social attachments with pious devotion to God. The next segment finally specifies the journey's itinerary, but not without ambiguous turns of its own.

When trouble and anguish confront you,
    don't let panic consume you.
Whether you'll need to take on
    mountain, gorge or wave,
put Andalusia behind you,
    and do it without delay—
until you've set foot near the Nile,
    the Euphrates or the Beautiful Land (of Israel),
where you'll walk in the power of pride,
    be lifted and held in awe. (lines 26–30)

The soul is counseled to abandon al-Andalus for Egypt, Iraq, and the Land of Israel. In the East, it will surely find the esteem it could not enjoy in al-Andalus. But this itinerary and its rationale raise more questions for the reader. Is the journey that the poem contemplates an actual journey, or an imagined and symbolic trek? Do the earlier references to captivity and the abundance of biblical allusions suggest a possible communal, rather than individual-minded, reading? And how are we to reconcile the personal, psychosocial motive for the journey's undertaking with its high-minded spiritual purpose? Certainly, the detail is so concrete as to suggest that the journey is real and not imagined (hills, valleys, seas, foreign lands). So are we to think of the soul's projected departure from al-Andalus for the East as akin to Samuel the Nagid's fantasy of Temple service, or more in the mold of Judah Halevi's lyrics anticipating and subsequently inscribing poetically the physical and spiritual route of his pilgrimage to Palestine? Or does the poem chart a singularly Gabirolian journey?

Once the poet exhorts his soul to exclusive love of God (line 24, *ṣurekh l^{e}vado ehevi*), it follows that the soul must seek love of the divine to the ends of the earth. Indeed, the proposed flight to the East is redefined in line 25 to swift pursuit of God (*qumi w^{e}-ruṣi aḥaraw*). Yet in the next passage, the poet must again urge on his soul, which remains reluctant to let go of its accustomed place in al-Andalus. The reader should note the shift from the concrete sense *beit m^e^gurekh*, "household" (line 32), to the metaphorical sense of *ger*, "stranger" (line 35). *Ger*, in the sense of "stranger," had another significance for Ibn Gabirol, as the loan translation of the Arabic term *gharīb*, in the sense of one who is spiritually estranged or alienated. The term was derived from a famous hadith ("Islam began as a stranger and shall return to being a stranger just as it began. Thus blessed be the strangers") cited widely by Sufi Muslims.[73] The motif of the soul's wandering upon the earth retroactively affirms the metaphorical nature of the proposed journey from al-Andalus to the East. Indeed, we are reminded in line 34 (*ki ṣel eloah ba'adekh/im tel^e^hki 'o tesh^e^vi*) that God is accessible anywhere and everywhere:

> Why, my troubled soul,
> why languish there in your longing?
> Is it leaving your people or household
> that holds you back in your grief?
> Keep them in mind as you go
> And your sorrow will find relief,
> For the Lord's shadow is with you,
> whether you leave or stay—
> And I'll be considered a stranger,
> until my bones are worn away.
> Remember the fathers in exile,
> keep them always in mind:
> Abram and tent-dwelling Jacob,
> and Moses who fled in haste:
> each in distance took refuge
> in the Lord who rides the sky. (lines 31–38)

Much could be said about the conclusion of the poem (lines 39–50). The reader will note dramatic changes in the poem's final two passages: (1) the poet initially ceases speaking to his soul and turns instead to "the land of my enemies" before again pressing his soul to depart ("My heart's desire is distance; how far will you manage to go"). This text's abrupt change in the speaker's stance and the addressee, as well as in its subject and tone, is reinforced and amplified by (2) a unique linguistic turn mid-verse from Hebrew to Andalusi Arabic (line 44b), deftly preserving both the meter and rhyme. The text's shift to colloquial language superficially resembles a *muwashshaḥ*'s *kharja*. However, "Mah lakh y^{e}ḥida" is not a strophic lyric but a polythematic monorhyming poem in quantitative meter.

Indeed, much more could be said about the whole poem, especially its pattern of metaphorical movements: mournful paralysis, motionless devotion, aimless futility, tentative journey, and the dynamic motion of swift flight (as noted above, compare reciprocal epithets for God at the beginning and toward the end of the poem, *yosh^{e}vi*, line 6, with *rokh^{e}vi*, line 34). We could also speak about its sharp mood swings, adroitly represented by transitional techniques.[74] But what is the significance of the unpredictable Gabirolian poetic twist and linguistic switch from Hebrew to Andalusi Arabic in line 44b of the poem's coda? The anaphoric sequence (*lahfa 'ala*; "I sigh for . . ." or "Woe for . . .") clearly sounds an impassioned cry that builds in intensity across lines 44b–48. Uttered with the immediacy of the colloquial language, the wail sharpens the lyrical complaint launched in line 39. Misunderstood, alone, rejected, frustrated, longing to depart, his poetry driven by acrimony, the figure of the poet appears to displace his soul as the subject. The poet laments that he is left to his own devices and nearly succumbs to the prospect of remaining in place. Was the devotional journey for the soul (plotted in the body of the poem) somehow premature? On the contrary, the poet's desperate plight and longing identifies him with the out-of-place position of the soul in the corporeal world. All that is left is pious resignation: *allāh ya'lam madhabī* (Cole: "God knows where I'm going!"; or "Only God knows my way!," line 50).

The ambiguity of motive and destination in Ibn Gabirol implies that the soul's proposed flight in the poem, however concretely rendered, is a spiritual quest. The ambiguity is also captured in line 48 of the Arabic coda: *lahfa 'alā saqa' l-ladhi / qad dāqa fihī maṭlabi*. Following Yarden's note, Peter Cole (87) translated the line "sigh for this world and its smallness / which can't contain my longing." Schirmann, however, understood *saqa'* in the sense of "home" or "land." It appears that Schirmann's understanding is correct, and the line should read: "sigh in a land that can't contain my longing."[75] The poet's problems with society yet attachment to it are symbolic of the soul's imprisonment in the corporeal realm—the myth-metaphor of the soul's exile in the material world and its longing to return and be gathered back to its sublime source. The text reminds us repeatedly (lines 24, 34, 38) of the soul's need to replace community and its collective aspirations with communion with God and to exchange the soul's social isolation and its temporary attachment to material existence for intimacy and oneness with God.

Baḥya ibn Paqūda, the eleventh-century "Jewish Sufi," as Diana Lobel identifies him,[76] acknowledges but appears to downplay the significance of the Andalusi Jews' condition of exile.[77] Rather, like Ibn Shaprūṭ in the previous century, Baḥya notes that the Andalusi Jews' prosperity and security are signs of God's perennial protective care for His people. However, like Ibn Gabirol in this poem, he suggests that the individual's interior spiritual life takes religious precedence over the relationship between God and Israel.[78]

When he is not speaking as a liturgical poet on behalf of the community, Ibn Gabirol tends to strip territory of religious significance. He has no use for al-Andalus and no particular or urgent need for the Land of Israel. Ibn Gabirol does not even seek what would now be called a diasporic intellectual community; rather, the poet's impulse to de-territorialize is matched by his sense of fulfillment as a solitary religious intellectual.[79] Ibn Gabirol's suppression of geographical desire, whether for al-Andalus or Palestine, to which other Andalusi Hebrew poets gave voice (and to which Ibn Gabirol gave ample voice as a liturgical poet),[80] as well as Samuel the Nagid's displacement of it through imaginative representation, reinforces our sense of the flexibility and untidy complexity of these competing tropes (Sefarad/Israel) and the varieties of their inflection in eleventh- and twelfth-century Andalusi Jewish culture as they relate to the notion of Sefardi exceptionalism.[81]

Moses ibn Ezra (ca. 1055–after 1138)

Chronologically the third of the four most accomplished Andalusi Hebrew poets, Moses ibn Ezra was born to privilege in Zīrid Granada around 1055, the year before Samuel the Nagid died. Sometime between 1090 and 1095, Ibn Ezra was driven from Islamic Granada to the northern Christian kingdoms, apparently a victim of the political turmoil surrounding the arrival of the Almoravid Berbers and toppling of the Zīrids in 1091. He died in exile from al-Andalus after 1138, the year Moses Maimonides was born, on the eve of the Almohad age. Hebrew literary history regards Moses ibn Ezra with great esteem on account of his penitential poems, introspective, philosophically minded lyrics, and for his professional mastery of all the formal structures, genres, rhetoric, and stylistic devices of Arabic-inspired Andalusi Hebrew verse. Ibn Ezra is also known for composing nostalgic expressions of profound sorrow over his fate, especially in a cycle of lyrical complaints—

laments, really—concerning his exile from Granada, a place to which the self-styled "prisoner of separation" (*asir peirud*) never returned.[82]

Recall how Samuel the Nagid appropriated biblical references and idioms to frame his individual exploits as historically and religiously significant for the Jewish community through typologies of historical recurrence. Ibn Ezra adeptly channels allusions and verbatim biblical citations referring to Israel's collective exile to underscore his dire personal misfortune—exile from al-Andalus—as well as his hope for restoration:

How long are my feet consigned to exile,
    yet to find a resting place? . . .
Let my right hand wither if I forget them, or if
    but among them I should care to rejoice.
If God will yet restore me to the splendor of
    Granada, my ways will prosper again.[83]

On account of such expressions of profound attachment to Granada and his ardent commitment to the Judeo-Arabic culture of al-Andalus, Moses ibn Ezra is frequently portrayed, like the Nagid and at variance with Judah Halevi, as "unduly" dedicated to Sefarad, as opposed to devoted to Jerusalem. Far more accurately, he is depicted as a partisan voice for the superiority of the Jews of Sefarad over Jewish communities of other lands, that is, for Sefardi exceptionalism. Indeed, one of his plaintive epistolary poems portrays Fate expelling him from "palaces of pleasure" (*heikhlei 'oneg*, i.e., al-Andalus) and casting him into Christendom (*bat 'edom*, i.e., the Christian kingdoms of northern Iberia) "amid boors who think themselves wise" in their foreign, uncivilized "forest" (*ba-'aṣei ya'ar*) environment.[84]

Ibn Ezra is also cast as the most Arabic of the Andalusi Hebrew poets. He cultivated the practices and nurtured the image of a neoclassical Arab poet, adhering strictly to the canons of Arabic rhetoric, poetics, and aesthetics, except that he wrote social and liturgical verse in Hebrew.[85] Furthermore, Ibn Ezra drew attention to the Andalusi Jews' complete acculturation to Arabic language, culture, and society (except for their steadfast adherence to Jewish tradition in matters of religious observance and practice). He cites two biblical prooftexts to validate this Jewish cultural turn, albeit with more than a touch of ambivalence and irony: "they mingled [*wa-yit'arvu* also means 'they Arabized'] with the nations and learned their ways" (Ps. 106:35); and "so that the holy seed has become intermingled [*w^e-hita'rvu*] with the peoples of the land" (Ezra 9:2).[86] The Judeo-Arabic prose work in which this citation appears contributed, above all, to the sense of Ibn Ezra's fidelity to Arabic *paideia* and Andalusi Jewish *adab.*[87]

Ibn Ezra authored *Kitāb al-muḥāḍara wa-l-mudhākara* (The Book of Conversation and Deliberation), the most important book about Arabic-style Hebrew poetry and poetics and Andalusi Jewish cultural history, during the later years of his protracted exile in the Christian north, far from the precincts of Islamic Granada. Consequently, expert readers of Ibn Ezra have drawn attention to the important question of Ibn Ezra's audience for a Judeo-Arabic cultural miscellany outlining and justifying Andalusi Hebrew poetry and celebrating its essential place in the Jewish literary tradition.[88] Who, exactly, were its readers supposed to be? Separated physically from his homeland and alienated from the surrounding society that he regarded with utter disdain, the pessimistic Ibn Ezra appears to have been an improbable Andalusi Jewish cultural emissary, unlike his younger contemporary the peripatetic Abraham ibn Ezra. Abraham's exile from al-Andalus in 1140 and his search for an audience to support and absorb his wide-ranging Andalusi Jewish learning and prolific literary output (Hebrew poetry and rhymed prose, biblical commentaries and grammatical works, theological-philosophical, mathematical, astronomical, and astrological studies and translations from Arabic into Hebrew) took him to England, France, and Italy.[89] Read in light of his own lyrical complaints, as well as occasional comments in the work itself, *Kitāb al-muḥāḍara* was composed by Moses ibn Ezra without a discernible receptive audience before him except for the imagined inquirer whose eight questions on poetry, literary history, and poetics supply the frame for the book's eight chapters.

Kitāb al-muḥāḍara's fifth chapter, "Regarding the Sheer Preeminence of the (Jewish) Exilic Community of al-Andalus over Others in Composing Poetry, Rhetorical Discourse, and Hebrew Epistles" (*Shufūf jāliyyat al-andalus fī qarḍi l-shi'r wa-taḥbīri l-khuṭab wa-l-rasā'il al-'ibrāniyya*), thematically mirrors the Arabic *faḍā'il al-andalus* and *mafākhir al-andalus* literature discussed in Chapter 3.[90] That is, like his eleventh- and twelfth-century Andalusi Muslim counterparts, Ibn Ezra emphasizes the centrality of Andalusi Jewish literary culture to Sefardi exceptionalism. Following chapters devoted to the Arabs' preeminence in composing poetry and the literary quality and prosodic form of the "poetic" books of the Hebrew Bible (Psalms, Job, and Proverbs), chapter 5 of *Kitāb al-muḥāḍara* relates the cultural history of the Jews of al-Andalus from its inception in tenth-century Córdoba to the early twelfth century. Alexander Elinson observes that Ibn Ezra begins by invoking the authority of biblical texts to justify the view of Andalusi Jewish distinction, just as Ibn Ḥazm employs a hadith to situate al-Andalus within Islamic tradition. Indeed, another passage in *Kitāb al-muḥāḍara* cites, decontextualizes, and recontextualizes a Talmudic tradition critiquing "the people of the Galilee who were not particular in their [Hebrew] speech" with the consequent loss of their knowledge of Torah, in marked contrast with the Judeans "who were particular in their [Hebrew] speech and whose [knowledge of] Torah endured,"[91] down to their descendants in Sefarad.[92] Elinson also notes that Ibn Ezra organizes the history of Andalusi Jewish culture according to generations of scholars and poets and by discipline.[93] The chapter begins as follows:

> Regarding the preeminence of the Jewish community of al-Andalus over others in composing poetry, rhetorical discourse, and Hebrew epistles—that is the response to the fifth query.
>
> There are several reasons. The first is that they are from the tribes of Judah and Benjamin as Scripture attests: "So the chiefs of the clans of Judah and Benjamin, and the priests and Levites, all whose spirit has been roused by God" (Ezra 1:5) and also: "These are the people of the province who came up from among the captive exiles whom King Nebuchadnezzar of Babylon had carried into exile to Babylon, who returned to Jerusalem and Judah, each to his own city" (Ezra 2:1). These aforementioned populations are people of the Noble Sanctuary, Jerusalem, the Holy City, may it be speedily rebuilt, and its environs, the exile released from Babylon, and the other exile to the lands of Rome and to al-Andalus, as Scripture testifies: "And that exiled force of Israelites [shall possess] what belongs to the Phoenicians as far as Zarephath, while the Jerusalemite exile community of Sepharad shall possess the towns of the Negeb" (Obad. 1:20). Our religious community received the tradition that Zarephath is the land of the Franks and Sepharad is al-Andalus in the language of the Arabs, associated with a person called Andalusān from the period of al-Izdihāq, the ancient king; and in the Romance language, Ishfāniyya, also derived from a ruler in the Roman country prior to the Goths, whose name was Ishfān, and whose capital was

> Ishbīliyya (Seville), on his account was it named, among the earliest (settlers) Isfamia.
>
> There is no doubt that the people of Jerusalem from whose exile community we hail were more learned in classical Hebrew literary language and in transmission of rabbinic knowledge than the communities of other places and towns [*kānat a'lama bi-faṣīḥi l-lugha wa-naql 'ilmi l-sharī'a min sā'iri l-bilād wa-l-qurā*], as said in Scripture: "If a case is too baffling for you to decide, be it a controversy over homicide, civil law or assault—matters of dispute in your courts—you shall promptly repair to the place that the Lord you God will have chosen" (Deut. 17:8). Its most lucid expression [in Scripture] concerns the anticipated promises [regarding the future]: "For instruction shall come forth from Zion, the word of the Lord from Jerusalem." (Isa. 2:3; Mic. 4:2)[94]

What are the "several reasons" for "the sheer preeminence of the (Jewish) exilic community of al-Andalus over others" in Hebrew literary creativity? Ibn Ezra accentuates the Andalusi Jews' aristocratic Jerusalemite lineage, their inheritance as the principal guardians of the classical Hebrew language, and, as Ibn Daud would "document" in the next generation, their station as authentic custodians of rabbinic tradition. In other words, *Kitāb al-muḥāḍara* valorizes the Andalusi Jews' lineage, learning, culture, and religious orthodoxy, the components constituting the trope of Sefardi exceptionalism.[95]

Ibn Ezra proceeds to expound upon the Andalusi Jews' unique gift for *adab* and their accomplishments in creating sophisticated cultural products, noting that Ḥasdai ibn Shaprūṭ's leadership and agency was instrumental in catalyzing the developments that initiated Andalusi Hebrew literary culture:

> When the Arabs conquered the peninsula of al-Andalus from the aforementioned Goths who themselves had been victorious over the Romans, its former masters, around three hundred before the Arabs conquered it during the period of al-Walīd bin 'Abd al-Malik bin Marwān of the Umayyad dynasty from Syria in the year 92 according to their calendar called al-Hijra, after a period of time our exile community made an effort to understand their tendencies and finally grasped their language, mastered their speech, fathomed their precise objectives, became accustomed to the true sense of their patterns, were mindful of their poems'

> sweetness, until God revealed to them the secrets of the Hebrew language and its grammar [*ḥattā kashafa (a)llah ilayhim min sirri l-lugha al-ʿibrāniyya wa-naḥwihā*], the weak letters, inversions, short vowels, the glottal stop, substitution, permutation, and assimilation of letters and other grammatical features, on which the proof of truth was adduced and by which the power of veracity was endorsed by Abū Zekhariah Yaḥyā b. David al-Fāsī, known as Ḥayyūj, and his followers, may God have mercy upon them. They quickly acquired rational methods of inquiry and understood that of which they were previously ignorant. The determination to investigate the speculative sciences and acquire reason-based knowledge stirred in a few of them. But their discursive eloquence was not strong and they were unprepared to compose poetry; they appreciated its sweetness and awakened to its marvels only after the seventh century of the fourth millennium since the Creation with the initial appearance of Abū Yūsuf Ḥasdai ibn Iṣḥāq b. Shaprūṭ, originally from Jaén, the communal leader, of Córdoba, may God have mercy upon him.[96]

Note the sequence of cultural and intellectual developments that the passage narrates. The Andalusi Jews' historic, intimate encounter with Arabs and Arabic culture, along with their mastery of the Arabic language and Arabic poetry, give rise to a dramatic revelation of sorts—the divinely inspired discovery of the hidden structures of classical Hebrew language and grammar. This marvelous account of intellectual and cultural history concludes by noting that the Andalusi Jews rapidly acquired rational methods of inquiry, interest in the speculative sciences, and, eventually, the imagination and knack for composing Hebrew poetry. The remainder of the chapter, like Ibn Ḥazm's roster of Andalusi Muslim savants and scholarship in the *Risāla*, reviews successive generations of numerous Andalusi Jewish literary and religious intellectuals, providing comments and evaluations on the literary skill and personal temperament of the Hebrew poets. It concludes with Ibn Ezra's reflections on the genuine poet's moral character and rhetorical expertise.

Ibn Ezra's account in chapter 5 of *Kitāb al-muḥāḍara* thus accentuates the significance of the Andalusi Jews' linguistic revolution and intellectual breakthrough as the first step in a series of interrelated cultural developments. Accordingly, *Kitāb al-muḥāḍara* broadens the disciplinary perspective adopted by Jonah ibn Janāḥ (b. ca. 985–990), the period's seminal scholar of Hebrew philology and grammar. At the beginning of the introduction to his Judeo-Arabic work on biblical Hebrew grammar, *Kitāb al-luma'*, Ibn Janāḥ asserts that expert knowledge of the Hebrew language is required for informed understanding and interpretation of Scripture.[97] For Ibn Ezra and all the Andalusi Hebrew poets, the Jews' turn to the rational and aesthetic study of the text and language of the Hebrew Bible was also an indispensable step in their creation of Arabic-style Hebrew poetry. Thanks to their highborn lineage and their embrace and practice of Arabic *adab*, the Jews of al-Andalus excelled across the entire classical Judeo-Arabic cultural curriculum—in rabbinics, scriptural exegesis, philosophy, science, and, above all, in their exceptional proficiency in Hebrew language and poetry.

Kitāb al-muhāḍara defines Ibn Ezra's literary identity as much as his poetry and textualizes his resolute ideological commitment to Arabic and Andalusi Hebrew *adab* that is centered in Sefarad and al-Andalus. In this respect, the work is analogous to *Sefer ha-qabbalah*, whose teleological history of the rabbinate culminates in Sefarad. Moses ibn Ezra imagines an ideal audience for his life's work attuned to Andalusi Jewish *adab*,[98] whether back home in al-Andalus or in posterity, as an act of cultural and historical preservation. As a document of Andalusi Jewish culture at a time of transition, *Kitāb al-muḥāḍara* served as a significant literary exercise of "restorative nostalgia" and as an iconic, definitive statement of Sefardi exceptionalism in the twelfth century.

Chapter 5

Out of Place with Exceptionalism on the Mind

Sefardi and Andalusi Travelers Abroad (Twelfth and Thirteenth Centuries)

There is no Islam except in lands of the West.

—*Riḥla*, Ibn Jubayr

When Easterners could not manage poetry, the Westerners' vision gushed prophetically.

—*Taḥkᵉmoni*, al-Ḥarizi

The literary motif of "the journey" is as old as the ancient Egyptian tale of Sinueh and the Babylonian epic of Gilgamesh. It is not surprising, then, that "the journey" appears as a compelling topos in various genres of Andalusi Arabic and Sefardi Judeo-Arabic and Hebrew literature. During the late classical Islamic period, all manner of travelers—pilgrims, pietists, migrants, adventurers, seekers, international merchants, craftsmen, literati, religious intellectuals, diplomats, agents, propagandists, political-religious refugees, and opportunists—set out from al-Andalus and Sefarad and the western frontier of Islamdom and Christendom and journeyed to North Africa or the northern Mediterranean, the Levant, and the Islamic East. Though frequently traversing the same terrain, the social meaning of their journeys varied considerably in accordance with their differing motives and the historically determined social and cultural matrices to which they belonged.

These intrepid souls composed accounts of their experiences and discoveries in letters, lyrics, travelogues, or imaginative narratives, necessarily framing their reflections in fidelity to the literary traditions within which they wrote. The travelers' differing purposes in leaving the West for the East found textual expression in accordance with representational practices associated with different literary genres, linguistic traditions, and religious cultures, even as the social meaning of their journeys varied according to their station and orientation. From the pilgrim-poet's exercise of his religious and literary imagination to the seeker's quest for knowledge, intellectual community, cultural refreshment, or patronage, to the refugee's search for safety and security, writing grounded in the venture of travel clearly lies at the intersection of social and cultural history. It also offers a different manifestation of the tropes of Andalusi and Sefardi exceptionalism.

Travel-based texts expose the instability and fluidity of sociocultural boundaries for Andalusi Muslims and Sefardi Jews. While operating within defined historical, religious, and cultural matrices, travel narratives, like other texts, have the potential to challenge and subvert their conventions by separating triumphalist and messianic socioreligious and political ideals from life as it is actually experienced, in all its complexity. As texts, they engage, resist, undermine, and dissolve the various borders and divisions imposed and policed by communal and historiographic orthodoxy, thereby mirroring the expanded social and cultural horizons of the traveler's experience.

I would like to focus on the twelfth and early thirteenth centuries, a period especially rich in diverse documentation of Muslim and Jewish travel originating in al-Andalus and Sefarad. These journeys and the textual reverberations they produced were undertaken during an extended moment of historical transition across the Mediterranean writ large. To remind us of only a few critical shifts informing the movement of people, goods, ideas, and texts across the region during this period: al-Andalus was incorporated into the Almohad Maghribi kingdom; the Andalusi Jewish community was thinned out in the process, with many refugees dispersed to North Africa and the Christian kingdoms of the north of the peninsula; the importance of French Mediterranean ports rose; and the activity of Italian merchants increased significantly in the wake of the Crusades.[1] During the twelfth and thirteenth centuries, apocalyptic eschatology, Mahdism, popular messianism, and millenarianism were very much in the air, reflecting social, political, and religious upheavals and turmoil over contested territory between Christendom and Islamdom in the Iberian Peninsula and the Levant. These socioreligious trends are attested by successive revivalist movements in North African Islam, in late rabbinic midrashim, documents of the Cairo Geniza, and the pilgrimage of groups of Jewish settlers from France and North Africa, among others "meeting in Jerusalem."[2]

Of course, cultural constructions of geography, territory, and place, central to the ways in which classical Islam and Judaism formally defined their place in history, conditioned what the traveler saw and how he represented it in textual form. Recall from Chapter 1 that in discussing the relationship between mental maps and ideology, Piotr Michalowski writes: "Geography is a human problem that involves both universals, which purportedly stem from the physical reality of mankind, as well as culturally independent variables. Certain conceptions of space . . . appear to differ little across societies. There do exist strong cultural variations, however, and one of the problems . . . is the question of mental or cognitive maps, that is, the ideas of space and its relative seriations that men and women carry in their heads, so to speak. These mental maps include notions of preference, as well as vague ideas and value judgments about places that speakers or authors have never seen."[3]

Turning back to the Andalusi Islamic and Sefardi Jewish traditions, with Michalowski's insights in mind, the architects of classical Islam clearly expected Islamdom to expand over time, even if it might occasionally contract under certain temporary circumstances. Their metaphorical conceptualization of Islam as an expanding "abode" essentialized the idea of unity for a religious community within a sprawling civilization that was as culturally varied, socially diverse, and geographically dispersed in practice as it was religiously connected in ideal and theory. The makers of classical Judaism institutionalized the concepts of "diaspora" and "exile" to address the historically and politically anomalous status of the "people of Israel"—the Jews in lands adjacent to and beyond Roman Palestine until such time as God would bring about the "ingathering of the exiles." The Jews' historical preoccupation with exile and return pervades their literature—a poetics and cultural practice that Sidra Ezrahi rather brilliantly called "booking passage."[4]

In the twelfth and early thirteenth centuries, "normative" religious and historical sensibilities pertaining to place—constituting, as Michalowski instructs us, the travelers' cultural baggage and ideology—informed but did not define our Andalusi and Sefardi travelers' cultural mentalities. Their travel constituted acts of imagination; and, as we shall read, travel narratives activated the capacity of the literary imagination and its representational practices to reshape and reconfigure experience. Because travel expands the horizons of the familiar, the unusual, the misunderstood, or the unknown, it engenders contact across social and cultural boundaries, thereby transforming established patterns of cultural meaning. As Eric Leed puts it: "The history of travel suggests that collective and individual identities arise from and are transformed by processes of mutual reflection, identification, and recognition in human relationships: that neither collective nor personal identities are implicit in the organism or collective but arise from relations to others."[5]

Let us turn to three paradigmatic late twelfth- and early thirteenth-century texts as case studies, based on the experience of travel from the Iberian Peninsula to the East, and inquire as to what extent and how Andalusi and Sefardi travelers abroad construed and deployed the trope of Andalusi and Sefardi exceptionalism.

Benjamin of Tudela

For the Jews of Sefarad, the social meaning of travel was circumscribed by their historical status as a small and widely dispersed minority in both Christendom and Islamdom. Sefardi Jews traveled around the Mediterranean for many reasons: for commerce, as evidenced in the Cairo Geniza; as an act of piety, as in Judah Halevi's voyage east in 1140–1141; on an intellectual quest, as in Isaac ibn Ezra's mission (1140–1142) to Egypt, then via Damascus to Baghdad, to study with the renowned philosopher Abū l-Barakāt al-Baghdādī; for religio-political sanctuary, as in Moses Maimonides' mid-twelfth-century journey from Córdoba to Fez and eventually Cairo, by way of Acre and Jerusalem; in search of patronage, as in Judah al-Ḥarizi's early thirteenth-century trek from Toledo in Castile, via Provence, to the Islamic East; for friendship; on diplomatic missions; on pilgrimage to holy sites in Palestine and Iraq; out of curiosity about reports of empowered or independent Jewish communities in remote places; and out of messianic hope or expectation. As we might expect, sources that have come down to us from each of these figures point to multiple and complex motives behind their journeys.

Benjamin of Tudela's *Sefer ha-massa'ot* (the Book of Travels, or the Itinerary) relates the author's round-trip journey visiting Jewish communities from Iberia to Iraq and Persia (and including hearsay reports regarding Central Asia, India, China, Arabia, Germany, and northern France) at some undetermined time after Moses Maimonides' arrival in the East.[6] In the words of the anonymous editor's preface to his "journal," Benjamin "made a record of all that he saw or was told by a trustworthy person—matters not previously heard of in the land of Sefarad. Also he mentions some of the sages and illustrious men residing in each place. . . . R. Benjamin is a wise and understanding man, learned in the Law and the halakha."[7]

Benjamin belonged to the long-established Jewish community of Tudela, which was incorporated into the modest-size kingdom of Navarre from Islamic al-Andalus, following the city's conquest in 1119.[8] Tudela's Jewish community was probably bolstered by the arrival of refugees from Almohad al-Andalus in the transitional period after 1147, "when all the nation had finished passing over [the border]" from the Muslim-controlled south to the Christian north, according to *Sefer ha-qabbalah*'s overstated formulation.[9] Though the Jews of Tudela apparently prospered under the rule of Sancho VI "the Wise," they fell victim to civil unrest in 1170 and needed special royal protection from Sancho VII "the Strong."[10] The cultural background of the *Book of Travels'* intended readers very likely reflected the vital mix of rabbinic and Judeo-Arabic Andalusi Islamicate learning still common in the Iberian Christian kingdoms through the thirteenth century.[11] As heirs to Andalusi Jewish culture, the *Book of Travels'* audience would have been very much aware of its own indebtedness to the former centers of Jewish learning in al-Andalus and the Islamic East. The text's occasional use of Arabic and mindfulness of the Jews' scientific, philosophical, exegetical, rabbinic, and literary indebtedness to Andalusi culture and the Islamic East indicate as much.

Like other examples of early geographical literature, the *Book of Travels* offers "descriptions of lesser-known parts of the world to inform a 'home population.'"[12] Setting out from Tudela, Benjamin probably followed the northern trans-Mediterranean itinerary favored by Christian merchants.[13] His route took him to Saragossa, Tarragona, Barcelona, and then to Provence; from Marseilles via the sea to Genoa and then on to Rome; to Greece, Constantinople, Cyprus, the Levantine coast, and overland to Jerusalem and the Islamic East, eventually returning to Navarre via Egypt and Sicily. Unlike his Muslim contemporaries, however, Benjamin had no travel-based or geographical literary tradition available to follow in setting forth his observations, comments, appraisals, and imaginings. Though he never explains why he set out on his journey or what inspired him to make a record of it, it seems likely that the intercommunal tensions and threats that the Jews of

Navarre experienced in 1170 constituted the background to Benjamin's journey and inform the *Book of Travels'* specific interest in lands where Jews "were not under the yoke of the gentile kings."[14]

The *Book of Travels'* entries range from tantalizingly brief notices devoted to places familiar to the Jews of Sefarad via correspondence, texts, and oral communications to somewhat more extensive and occasionally expansive reports about lands and communities farther afield. Storytelling occupies little place; indeed, the text is primarily descriptive, and it displays little narrative voice except for what is reported in the name of Benjamin's local informants. Rather, the *Book of Travels'* interest lies in the text's twelfth-century geographical sensibility and framing of the relationship between culture, commerce, religious community, territory, and power. In typically sober, occasionally enthusiastic tones, the book focuses on the size, institutions, prosperity, leaders, monuments, and learning of the Jewish communities that the traveler encountered. As Benjamin's near-contemporaries, the polymath Abraham ibn Ezra and the historian of rabbinic tradition and philosopher Abraham ibn Daud, remind their readers, the decline or disintegration of the Andalusi Jewish community meant that, to survive, its institutions, traditions, and learning had to be reconstituted in other places.[15]

While the principal concern defining the *Book of Travels'* geographic horizons is thus the state of the Jewish communities that Benjamin visited, the text is also keenly attuned to their surroundings, carefully situating observations regarding the Jews within more general remarks about their place of domicile. Montpellier, for example, is described as "a place well situated for commerce. It is about a parasang [about four miles] from the sea, and men come for business there from all quarters, from Edom (Christendom), Ishmael (Islamdom), the land Algarve,[16] Lombardy, the dominion of Rome the great, from all the land of Egypt, Palestine, Greece, France, Asia, and England."[17] Benjamin appears highly interested in the Christian and Islamic East. Constantinople and Baghdad receive the most comprehensive treatment. Cairo, Alexandria, Damascus, and Jerusalem are rendered in significant detail, with attention to socioreligious diversity and practices, sites, institutions, dignitaries, and sights that would be interesting and incredible to visitors from other lands. By contrast, North Africa and al-Andalus are ignored—apparently out-of-bounds to Benjamin's view of the world hospitable for Jews, no doubt signifying a late twelfth-century northern Iberian aversion to Almohad territory and rule. This attitude does not extend to Islamdom in general. On the contrary, in focusing on the Jewish communities of the Islamic East, the text draws attention to the generally favorable status that they enjoyed in the later twelfth century, at least from the perspective of a member of the recently embattled Jewish community of northern Iberia.

Benjamin's travels take him through a shared socioeconomic space, a region where individuals of diverse religious, ethnic, and cultural backgrounds interact extensively and relatively freely, especially in commercial enterprises. The *Book of Travels* signals that it is unremarkable for Jews to move freely among Christians and Muslims in and between Christendom and Islamdom, apparently confirming S. D. Goitein's construction of the high medieval Mediterranean as a "unified" world.[18] Although the text mentions persecution of Jews in Byzantium, it simultaneously affirms their role in Constantinople's open political economy: "[It] is a busy city, and merchants come to it from every country by sea or land, and there is none like it in the world except Baghdad, the great city of Islam. So the Greeks hate the Jews, good and bad alike, and subject them to great oppression, and beat them in the streets, and in every way treat them with rigour. Yet the Jews are rich and good, kindly and charitable, and bear their lot with cheerfulness."[19] The text is equally impressed with Alexandria as a hub of extraordinary international economic activity and opportunities for uncommon socioeconomic encounters: "Alexandria is a commercial market for all nations. Merchants come thither from all the Christian kingdoms."[20]

Among all the lands that Benjamin actually visited, he reserves his most rousing description for Baghdad. In addition to marveling at the expansive sights, commerce, services, and bustle of the Abbasid capital, *The Book of Travels* implicitly contrasts the Jews' idyllic situation there with its earlier depiction of their prosperity and persecution in the Byzantine Empire. The entire passage is exceptional for its sociopolitical perspective on the glories of Jewish life in the Islamic East, attributed in large measure to the just, wise, and learned caliph: "There the great king, the Abbasid caliph, holds his court and he is kind unto Israel, and many belonging to the people of Israel are his attendants; he knows all languages and is well versed in the law of Israel. He reads and writes the holy language [Hebrew]. . . . In Baghdad, there are about a thousand Jews and they dwell in security, prosperity and honor under the great Caliph, and among them are great sages, the heads of academies engaged in the study of the Law."[21] The segment is reminiscent, in its own way, of Ḥasdai ibn Shaprūṭ's portrayal of the Andalusi Umayyad caliph and the Jews of that realm in his tenth-century correspondence with the king of the Khazars, discussed in Chapter 2. Recall that Ibn Shaprūṭ, a court physician, scientist, diplomat, confidant of the caliph, and leader of the Jews of al-Andalus took note of the Jews' secure and prominent place under the protection of another enlightened Muslim ruler (ʿAbd al-Raḥmān III al-Nāṣir and al-Ḥakam II al-Mustanṣir) in Umayyad Córdoba ("We are dwelling peacefully in the land of our sojournings"). Yet the *Book of Travels* goes further, ascribing to the Abbasid caliph a cultural and religious intimacy with Judaism and Hebrew, as if he were a Judeophile or even pseudo-Jew himself. The documents of the Cairo Geniza show that, when necessary, Muslim authorities did occasionally take an interest in the inner affairs of the autonomous Jewish communities in their realm (in Cairo, Syria-Palestine, and Iraq). Nevertheless, the notion that a Muslim ruler—however enlightened, freethinking, and accommodating toward his Jewish subjects—would master their liturgical language and learn their sacred law is utterly fanciful.

This idealized portrait of the benefits that Abbasid rule conferred upon the Jews concludes with a thoroughly exaggerated scene of the lofty honor, nearly a co-sovereignty, that the Muslims extended (on the explicit authority of the Prophet Muḥammad, no less) to the exilarch, the hereditary—long since honorary and increasingly symbolic—office of the "Head of the Exile."[22]

> And at the head of them all is Daniel, son of Hisdai, who is styled, "Our Lord, Head of the Captivity of all Israel." He possesses a book of pedigrees going back as far as David, king of Israel. The Jews call him "Our Lord, head of the captivity," and the Muslims call him "Sayyidna bin Dawud," and he has been invested with authority over all the congregations of Israel at the hand of the emir al-Mu'minin the Lord of Islam. . . .
>
> There he appears before the caliph and kisses his hand, and the caliph rises and places him on a throne, which Muḥammad had ordered to be made for him, and all the Muslim princes who attend the court of the caliph rise up before him. And the head of the captivity is seated on his throne opposite the caliph, in compliance with the command of Muḥammad, to give effect to what is written in the Torah: "The scepter shall not depart from Judah" (Gen 49:10).[23]

This famous passage, a riff on the esteem with which Muslims regarded Jewish descendants of Islamic prophet (and biblical king) David (previously noted in Chapters 3 and 4), represents an ahistorical political-religious fantasy that projects power where little truly resides. By the tenth century, the caliph's authority, like the exilarch's (to which Muslim scholars such as the great sage al-Birūnī compared it) had waned.[24] The position was rendered largely ceremonial except for a revival under al-Nāṣir (1180–1225), successor to al-Mustaḍī' (1170–1180), the caliph in office during the time of Benjamin's visit.

The religious and historical regard that Muslims afforded descendants of the "House of David" is clearly attested. However, the *Book of Travels* transforms and amplifies Muslim acknowledgment of the exilarch's socioreligious genealogical nobility into a manifestly political symbol—as though any Islamic authority would ever assent to a sign or form of Jewish sovereignty or power-in-waiting in the lands of Islam. Indeed, the *Book of Travels'* biblical prooftext, "The scepter shall not depart from Judah" (Gen. 49:10), was long a point of profound contention in Jewish-Christian and then Jewish-Muslim polemics in eleventh-century al-Andalus, as we observed in Chapter 3, concerning Ibn Ḥazm's report of his debate with Samuel (ibn al-Naghrīla) the Nagid.[25] As the *Book of Travels'* report would have it, the titular head of the Islamic *umma* openly affirmed a critical condition for the fulfillment of Jewish messianism.

For the Jews of al-Andalus, the semblance of Jewish sovereignty that the *Book of Travels* imagines supposedly held great appeal as a harbinger of the messianic age. The Andalusi Jewish readiness to envision messianism began two centuries before Benjamin of Tudela, with Ḥasdai ibn Shaprūṭ's representation of the singularity of his position within the Umayyad polity, combined with his avid interest in the independent Khazar kingdom.[26] Frequently activist in form, this tradition endured when the centers of Sefardi Jewish life were transferred to the northern Christian kingdoms.[27] As discussed in Chapter 4, it is also evident in Samuel the Nagid's depiction of his unique political role in postbiblical Jewish history as the prime minister of the Islamic kingdom of Granada under the Zīrid Berbers.[28]

In the early thirteenth century, Judah al-Ḥarizi, who left Toledo for Provence and the Islamic East, depicts Jewish embrace of Islamic rule over the Holy Land. The "Jerusalem *Maqāma*" of *Taḥkemoni*, his collection of rhymed-prose rhetorical anecdotes discussed later in this chapter, portrays Ṣalāḥ al-Dīn's conquest of Jerusalem from the crusaders in 1187 as a sign of divine agency summoning Jews to return to the land and where they "now dwell under the shadow of sweet comfort."[29] Likewise, al-Ḥarizi's Arabic rhymed-prose work, *Al-rawḍa al-anīqa* (The Pleasant Garden), celebrates the benefit the Jews derived from the Ayyūbid victory over the crusaders in Egypt in 1221.[30] Where al-Ḥarizi's works contemplate the real-world effects of recent historical events, Benjamin's political sensibilities extended well beyond the geographical and historical bounds of the world with which he was familiar into the realm of the thoroughly imagined. For example, although Benjamin never reached Kurdistan, the *Book of Travels* relates the famous account of the legendary pseudo-Messiah David Alroy, who pledged in God's name to secure Jerusalem "and free you [the Jews of Kurdistan] from the yoke of the nations."[31] All such tales and reports enforce a borderless communal, rather than actual, geography and seem designed to galvanize the hopes and expectations of the Jews of late twelfth-century Navarre.

Beyond the *Book of Travels'* frequent observations about the holy sites, surroundings, topography, architecture, and commercial environment of the Jewish communities around the Mediterranean and in the Islamic East, its sense of place is more fundamentally defined by their well-being, safety, status, intellectual achievement, and political future. In this respect the *Book of Travels* calls to mind the cultural products of Andalusi Jews during the tenth and eleventh centuries. The text's view of geography is secondary and thus for all its detail almost incidental—it represents the geographical outlook of a small and scattered minority, the varied Jewish communities of the Mediterranean and the Levant. Indeed, as it moves easily and freely around the shores of the Mediterranean and beyond to adjacent lands, the *Book of Travels* collapses any sense of boundaries. As such, Sefardi exceptionalism in the form of Andalusi Judeo-Arabic cultural heritage and its potential for Jewish empowerment of a sort looms large behind the assumptions and agenda of the *Book of Travels* designed for a popular, rather than strictly elite, audience in the Jewish communities of Navarre and, more generally, all the Christian Iberian kingdoms.

Abū l-Ḥusayn Muḥammad ibn Jubayr (1145–1217)

Fortunately for the comparatist, it is possible to read Benjamin of Tudela's *Book of Travels* alongside that of an Andalusi Muslim near-contemporary.[32] Ibn Jubayr's *Riḥla* is the acclaimed report of his trans-Mediterranean and Levantine journey and pilgrimage from Granada to Mecca and back (1183–1185), on the first of three trips he undertook to the Islamic East. By the late twelfth century, journeys east in quest of knowledge and spiritual refreshment had long since become a defining practice of Andalusi Muslims eager to maintain first-hand contact with the Eastern centers of the Islamic world.[33] This religious and cultural routine, referred to and institutionalized as *riḥla*, was the Islamic equivalent of philosophical travel, often in the course of pilgrimage to sacred shrines.

Apart from its literary-historical significance as a paradigm for the *riḥla*-based literary tradition, Ibn Jubayr's travelogue, described as "a simple narrative of a voyage undertaken and experienced," is of interest to us in two respects.[34] First, it frames the Mediterranean and the Levant as shared terrains in which Muslims and Christians interact with a regularity that is both troubling and reassuring for the Andalusi traveler and his intended reader. Indeed, as Olivia Remie Constable observes, "the Iberian peninsula was one of two places in the western Mediterranean, together with the nexus of Ifrīqiya-Sicily, where Christian and Muslim shipping routes met."[35] Second, the text represents Islamic polities and societies in the Mediterranean and the Levant, except for the Almohad realm in al-Andalus and the Maghrib, as in desperate need of spiritual rejuvenation, righteous leadership, and social and political repair. Accordingly, Ibn Jubayr's *Riḥla* vigorously espouses Andalusi (and Maghribi) exceptionalism in a new religious and political sense. As such, the *riḥla* stands in stark opposition to *Ḥayy ibn Yaqẓān*,[36] the acclaimed philosophical allegory by Ibn Jubayr's older contemporary Ibn Ṭufayl (ca. 1110–1185). A trusted physician and counselor for the Almohad ruler Abū Ya'qūb Yūsuf, Ibn Ṭufayl nevertheless imagines a life of intellectual and spiritual discovery and fulfillment completely disconnected from family, community, and society.[37] Its cosmopolitan vision of the divine Presence is reminiscent of the conclusion of Solomon ibn Gabirol's Neoplatonic lyric studied in Chapter 4.

As an Andalusi Muslim from the region of Valencia (*Sharq al-andalus*) under the warlord Ibn Mardanīsh during the so-called second *ṭā'ifa* period of independent rulers between Almoravid and Almohad rule, Ibn Jubayr certainly would have been aware of the dangerous political divisions within Andalusi Islam until the Almohads secured hegemony over all of al-Andalus in 1172.[38] Ibn Jubayr also was intimately familiar with a society in which Muslims and Christians mixed and cooperated somewhat freely in various social sectors, commercial activities, and intellectual ventures. If such interactions (and the presence of non-Muslims as well as heterodox Muslims) diminished significantly under Almohad rule, they were nevertheless remembered. Andalusi traditions and patterns of social behavior were also reinforced as Andalusi Muslims continued to encounter Christians from the northern Iberian kingdoms as well as with Italian traders calling at Andalusi ports. By contrast, the persistent threat that Christendom posed to the territorial integrity of al-Andalus was an inescapable concern for Muslim scholars and Almohad political elites like Ibn Jubayr, who secured an administrative position in Granada sometime before his travels east in 1183.

Bearing the unlikely title *Tadhkīrāt bi-l-akhbār 'an ittifāqāt al-asfār* (Accounts of Events That Befell upon Certain Journeys), the text details, among other things, Ibn Jubayr's Mediterranean travels on Christian vessels. His pilgrimage from Almohad Granada to the Islamic East, shortly before Ṣalāḥ al-Dīn's capture of Jerusalem in 1187, begins on a Genoese ship that took him from Ceuta to Alexandria—the first leg of a journey that eventually took him to Cairo, Baghdad, Damascus, Mecca, and Medina.[39] Though the text does not indicate the purpose of his travels, al-Maqqarī famously, if apocryphally, reports that Ibn Jubayr set out on pilgrimage to Mecca and Medina to atone for his sin after the Almohad governor of Granada, for whom he worked as a secretary, forced him to drink seven cups of wine.[40] Other sources and readers have cited the "quest for knowledge" or ideologically minded information gathering for the Almohads regarding the Ayyūbids following Ṣalāḥ al-Dīn's vanquishing of the Fāṭimid caliphate in 1171.[41]

Notwithstanding the conflict raging over control of Iberian territory in the West and Syro-Palestine in the East, throughout Ibn Jubayr's work Muslims and Christians repeatedly cross paths, signaling how impossible it was for any trans-Mediterranean traveler performing the hajj to avoid encountering religious others, even when remaining strictly within the Muslim world. Such narratives, Mary Gergen asserts, typically position social, cultural, and religious others in relation to the self "discovered" in the course of the journey.[42] I am less certain of what we can say about any sense of "self" in these narratives; rather, I am primarily interested in the depiction of religious "others" and their behaviors as counter-models for what is socially and religiously normative. Instructive in this respect is the section describing Ibn Jubayr's passage through Lebanon, which categorizes the open social situation in the Mediterranean and the Levant under the rubric of *'ajā'ib*—the strange, unusual, unexpected, or astonishing circumstances that travelers witnessed on their journeys (similar to the "marvels and curiosities" [*Thoma*] that became a convention of "European" travel literature).[43] Here is how Ibn Jubayr puts it in his somewhat mystified response to them:

> It is strange [*wa-min al-ʿajab*] how the Christians round Mount Lebanon, when they see any Muslim hermits, bring them food and treat them kindly, saying that these men are dedicated to Great and Glorious God and that they should therefore share with them. . . .
>
> One of the astonishing things [*wa-min aʿjaba mā yuḥaddath bihi*] that is talked of is that though the fires of discord burn between the two parties, Muslim and Christian, two armies of them may meet and dispose themselves in battle array, and yet Muslim and Christian travelers will come and go between them without interference. . . .
>
> Between [the Hijaz road for overland passage of Muslims] and Jerusalem lies a day's journey or a little more. . . . This sultan invested it, and put it to sore straits, and long the siege lasted, but still the caravans passed successively from Egypt and Damascus, going through the lands of the Franks without impediment from them. In the same way, the Muslims continuously journeyed from Damascus to Acre (though Frankish territory), and likewise not one of the Christian merchants was stopped or hindered (in Muslim territories).[44]

Documentary material from the period provides uncensored information on commercial, social, and cultural arrangements and interactions between members of competing confessional communities. By contrast, the traveler's narrative voice is under no obligation to highlight or even comment on such relations in the manner of Ibn Jubayr's ambivalent wonderment at a Christian bridal procession in Tyre with Muslims and Christians in attendance together. Describing the bride's decorous beauty and elegance and the captivating appeal of the entire celebration, the passage concludes: "Leading them all were the musical instruments. The Muslims and other Christian onlookers formed two ranks along the route, and gazed on them without reproof. . . . We were thus given the chance of seeing this alluring sight, from the seducement of which God preserve us."[45]

Elsewhere, Ibn Jubayr's *Riḥla* manifests the unyielding hostility toward Christians that we would expect at a time of heightened political tension.[46]

The "note on the city of Acre," for example, invokes the pious formula "May God exterminate [the Christians in] it and restore it to the Muslims" (*dhikru madīnati 'akka dammarahā llāhu wa-'adāhā*), depicting a desolate religious landscape that draws upon the conventional language and imagery of Andalusi Arabic elegies for Iberian cities lost to the Christians: "Unbelief and unpiousness there burn fiercely, and pigs [Christians] and crosses abound. It stinks and is filthy, being full of refuse and excrement. The Franks ravished it from Muslim hands in the first decade of the sixth century, and the eyes of Islam were swollen with weeping for it; it was one of its griefs. Mosques became churches and minarets bell-towers."[47]

Yet the same note represents Acre as an uncommonly important commercial crossroads: "Acre is the capital of the Frankish cities in Syria, the unloading place of 'ships reared aloft in the seas like mountains' (Quran 15:24), a port of call for all ships. In its greatness, it resembles Constantinople. It is the focus of ships and caravans, and the meeting place of Muslim and Christian merchants from all regions."[48] Similarly, the "note on the fortress city of Tyre" alternates between the stock expression "May God Most High destroy it" and the qualitative observation and judgment: "Its people are by disposition less stubborn in their unbelief, and by nature and habit they are kinder to the Muslim stranger. . . . The state of the Muslims in this city is easier and more peaceful."[49]

From an Andalusi perspective, this paradigm of intercommunal relations, a century after the loss of Islamic Toledo (1085) to Alfonso VI of Castile, must have seemed especially familiar, vexing, and ironic in lands such as Palestine, Lebanon, and Sicily, where Christians likewise had snatched sovereignty away from Islamdom. Accordingly, the *Riḥla* adjures its readers as if they were the earliest Mudejares of Christian Iberia: "There can be no excuse in the eyes of God for a Muslim to stay in any infidel country, save when passing through it, while the way lies clear in Muslim lands. They will face pains and terrors such as the abasement and destitution of the capitation and more especially, amongst their base and lower orders, the hearing of what will distress the heart in the reviling of him [Muḥammad] whose memory God has sanctified, and whose rank He has exalted."[50]

Ibn Jubayr's account of his shipwreck and rescue at Messina en route home to al-Andalus reflects an equally paradoxical view of Christian-Muslim intercourse, as Karla Mallette has observed.[51] Although the text naturally attributes Ibn Jubayr's deliverance to Providence, the Norman king William II plays a prominent role in realizing God's design:

> The strangest thing that we were told was that this Rumi king, when he perceived some needy Muslims staring from the ship, having not the means to pay for their landing because the owners of the boats were asking so high a price for their rescue, enquired, this king, concerning them and, learning their story, ordered that they be given one hundred *ruba'i* of his coinage in order that they might alight. All the Muslims thus were saved and cried, "Praise be to God, Lord of the Universe." . . . Another sign of the loving-kindness and benevolence of Great and Glorious God toward us in this disaster was the presence of this Rumi king. But for that, all within the ship would have been robbed of everything, or all the Muslims might have been placed in servitude, for such was their custom.[52]

Ibn Jubayr's depiction of William's treatment of his Muslim subjects recalls Benjamin of Tudela's account of Abbasid Baghdad. In both cases, the ruler acquits himself justly toward his minority subjects, relies at court upon members of their community, and, incredibly, reads and writes their language. However, the *Riḥla* interprets William's largesse toward the Muslims in his realm not as a grateful, small minority accustomed to subject status might experience it (as the Jews of Baghdad in Benjamin's account) but rather as viewed by erstwhile rulers of a lost Islamic Sicily, wary of a very powerful rival who has displaced them and usurped their sovereignty over the island:

> Their king, William, is admirable for his just conduct, and the use he makes of the industry of the Muslims, and for choosing eunuch pages who all, or nearly all, concealing their faith, yet hold firm to the Muslim divine law. He has much confidence in Muslims, relying on them for his affairs, and the most important matters, even the supervisor of his kitchen being a Muslim. . . . William is engrossed in the pleasures of his land, the arrangement of its laws, the laying down of procedure, the allocation of functions of his chief officials, the enlargement of the splendor of the realm, and the display of his pomp in a manner that resembles the Muslim kings. . . . He pays much attention to his (Muslim) physicians and astrologers, and also takes great care of them. . . . May God protect the Muslims from his hostility and the extension

> of his power [*kafā llāhu l-muslimīna ʿadīyatahu wa-basṭatahu*]. One of the remarkable things told of him is that he reads and writes Arabic [*wa-min ʿajībi shāʾnihi l-muḥaddath bihi annahu yaqraʾu wa-yaktubu bi-l-ʿarabiyya*].[53]

In the pious imagination, King William's behavior, manners, and learning render him attractive and dangerously proximate to the Muslims. Like several Andalusi historiographical portrayals of the eleventh-century Granadan figure Samuel the Nagid, William is cast here as a powerful ersatz Muslim. His adoption of Muslim etiquette, his reliance on Muslim servants, bureaucrats, and scholars (who are consequently beholden to him), and his appropriation of Islamic knowledge—especially the Arabic language and use of formulas signifying Muslim piety—transgress socioreligious boundaries designed to protect Islam. Such behaviors and the blandishments of his power amount to clear and present social "seductions" for Muslims requiring God's protection.[54]

Clearly, Ibn Jubayr's *Riḥla* does not support a simplistic interpretation of the period as one defined by Crusade, Reconquest, and jihad. Rather, its ambivalence—alternately accepting and rejecting its religious others—reflects the complexity of a seemingly contradictory situation in which social, commercial, and cultural interactions existed alongside adversarial competition and conflict (including military clashes over contested territory), producing an abundance of polemical discourse.

Unlike Benjamin of Tudela, whose sparse reporting and reserved style does not signal much explicit consciousness of his Sefardi origin except for its intended audience and its suggestive message harking back to the Jewish experience in Umayyad al-Andalus, Ibn Jubayr frequently voices his sense of Andalusi-ness through expressions of profound satisfaction with the Almohad caliphate and the Maghrib. Ideology, rather than pride, drives the discourse as the *Riḥla* declaims the inimitable rightness of the Islam practiced in Western Islamdom. Indeed, the text denotes that Almohad authority merits universal recognition and extension over all Islamdom.

> Let it be absolutely certain and beyond doubt established that there is no Islam save in the Maghrib lands [*lā islāma ilā bi-bilādi l-maghrib*]. There they follow the clear path that has no separation and the like, such as there are in these eastern lands of sects and

> heretical groups and schisms, save those of them whom Great and Glorious God has preserved from this. There is no justice, right, or religion in His sight except with the Almohads [*lā ʿadla wa-lā ḥaqqa wa-lā dīna ʿalā wajhihi ilā ʿinda l-muwaḥḥidīna*]—may God render them powerful. They are the last imams of this time, all the other kings of the day follow another path, taking tithes from the Muslim merchants as if they were of the community of the *dhimma*, seizing their goods by every trick and pretext, and following a course of oppression the like of which, oh my God, has never been heard of. All of them, that is, except this just sultan, Saladin, whom we have mentioned for his conduct and virtues.[55]

Like other Muslim religious intellectuals of the period, Ibn Jubayr was bewildered and distressed by the divisions and discord in Islamdom and contemptuous of the avaricious Muslim rulers he witnessed on his journey. The *Riḥla*'s notice about the deplorable state of the sacred shrine in Mecca captures the consternation of a pious pilgrim. It prescribes genuine Islamic renewal through Almohad righteous hegemony: "And the House of God is in the hands of hordes who make an illegitimate living from it and make possession an excuse for pillaging wealth. . . . May God soon remedy this by a purification which will lift these ruinous innovations from the Muslims by the swords of the Almohads, the companions of the faith, the party of God, possessors of truth and honesty, guardians of the *haram* of—God Great and Mighty, eager [to maintain] His prohibitions, devoted to spreading His word and His mission and leading His faith to victory. He who brings to pass what He wishes."[56]

The *Riḥla* thus reads as an expression of activist allegiance to the Almohad caliphate and pious hope that its uncompromising advocacy of the doctrine of *tawḥīd* as correct belief, its religious reform and insistence on "commanding good and forbidding evil" would continue to expand eastward—it had already reached Ifrīqiya (Tunisia)—and that Ṣalāḥ al-Dīn's heroic uprightness would restore Islamic norms of social justice and religion in the East. The text's "religious geography" thus imagines universal restoration of a lost wholeness and just order in Islam newly found only in al-Andalus and the Maghrib. Its vision of Andalusi and Maghribi religious exceptionalism is in keeping with the mind-set of an ideologically committed penitent pilgrim but at variance with the intricate sociocultural accommodations of the age that Ibn Jubayr encountered and his *Riḥla* marveled at on his travels.[57]

Judah al-Ḥarizi (1165–1225)

Around 1208, the Arabic and Hebrew literary intellectual Judah al-Ḥarizi trekked from Arabophone Toledo in Castile via Provence and a sojourn there to the Levant and Islamic East in 1215. Al-Ḥarizi's travels, spanning the geography of Jewish communities of the Levant and Islamic East, are intertwined in complex ways with a corpus of Hebrew and Arabic texts that he authored in transit and in his final stop, a return visit to Aleppo.[58] Al-Ḥarizi's readers typically question the purpose of his trip and his motive for writing the literary works informed by it. He supposedly set out in search of Jewish patrons whose diminished largesse eluded him in Castile. There is evidence to the contrary, since while still in Toledo, al-Ḥarizi composed *Maḥbᵉrot iti'el*, his Hebrew "translation"-adaptation of al-Ḥarīrī's benchmark collection of Arabic *maqāmāt*.[59] He relates that Sefardi grandees commissioned him to undertake the translation: "The dignitaries of Sefard pleaded with me when I was still among them / to 'translate' this book for them / and I could not turn them away."[60] The introduction goes on to imply that al-Ḥarizi's compliance with the request to translate the Arabic masterpiece occasioned his abrupt departure from Toledo and Sefarad: "Now when I had fulfilled their desire and had translated the book, I forsook my home and wandered on roads, I sailed on ships. I crossed seas. I fled from the West and I shone in the East. And I realized that I had done foolishly, and my iniquity was greater than I could bear in having neglected to compose a book of our own poetry, and I had undertaken to translate a book of foreign poetry, as though the Living God were not among us."[61]

In any event, the quest for benefactors (rationale #1) occupies a prominent place in al-Ḥarizi's literary corpus: in *Taḥkᵉmoni*,[62] the collection of Hebrew *maqāmāt*—rhetorical and picaresque anecdotes—that he finished composing in the Islamic East;[63] in the so-called Maqāma of the Patrons,[64] an independent Hebrew composition detailing his itinerary and reported in al-Ḥarizi's own name; and in his interrelated Judeo-Arabic prose works authored during the same period.

Apart from al-Ḥarizi's search for sponsors, his works present the reader with a knotty, even jumbled, picture of what the author-traveler claims to seek and imagines that he will find in embarking for lands beyond his homeland. In Provence, for example, al-Ḥarizi presents himself as an emissary of Andalusi Jewish culture. Embracing the practice of *mujāwara* (disseminating knowledge), he presumes to educate and enlighten Provençal literary and religious intellectuals in Hebrew and Arabic culture (rationale #2). For a time, al-Ḥarizi even seems to have found that venture profitable in the form of his translations of various Jewish legal, philosophical, and *adab* texts from Arabic into Hebrew.[65] However, profound socioreligious and intellectual frictions in which al-Ḥarizi was embroiled already in Toledo loomed large in Provence—namely, the Maimonidean controversy and al-Ḥarizi's professional rivalry with Samuel ibn Tibbon working with competing methods and styles of translation.[66] Under these circumstances, al-Ḥarizi is thought to have followed intellectually minded Provençal rabbis among his supporters and intimates who left for the East in the hope of conferring with Abraham Maimuni (rationale #3) and with whom he would subsequently reconnect in Egypt and Jerusalem.[67] Naturally, al-Ḥarizi encountered socioreligious tensions within the Jewish communities there.

By contrast with the idea that al-Ḥarizi was hunting for benefactors or escaping a religious controversy in which he was enmeshed and consequently looking elsewhere for intellectual community,[68] al-Ḥarizi's introduction to *Kitāb al-durar* (The Book of Pearls), a collection of eleven "Divine Odes" and other Arabic poems and prose comments organized around his stations during the Eastern legs of his journey, characterizes his motivation in transparently conventional Arabo-Islamic terms. Judah traveled in pursuit of knowledge (*ṭalab al-ʿilm*) and in the prospect of absorbing tales of wonder (*ʿajāʾib*) found in far-off lands (rationale #4): "There I was, at the age of ambition, ere had waned the wish to wander, in order to sip the wine of wisdom and gather the blooms of knowledge, longing greatly to attend the meetings of the learned, and to hear of marvels of [distant] lands from the lips of strangers."[69]

The first and second of *Taḥkᵉmoni*'s Hebrew introductions sets forth yet another purpose for the journey East and the work: the author's fervent ideological-religious dedication to the Hebrew language and a Hebrew linguistic and literary program in opposition to the universal veneration of Arabic.[70] Al-Ḥarizi supposedly hoped to discover or stimulate a like-minded commitment that he could market among the Jewish communities of the East that would surely benefit from and appreciate his mastery of Andalusi Hebrew culture and support his literary endeavors (rationale #5). Here, three purposes merge: the ideological, the educational, and the commercial. However, *Taḥkᵉmoni*'s first Hebrew introduction also decries the Jews' preference for Arabic over Hebrew and "assigns" al-Ḥarizi the sacred task of redeeming the holy language and inspiring Jewish literary intellectuals to embrace this cultural agenda, especially from "Egypt to Baghdad," where it will enlighten and instruct Jews whose Hebrew is shoddy.[71]

The second Hebrew introduction (the first *maqāma*), in the form of an imagined meeting and consultation between the author's persona and one of his characters, concedes that Arabic is superior to other languages, except for Hebrew. Hebrew has been largely forgotten, on account of the Jews' protracted exile, but what remains of it is more than sufficient to produce enchantingly beautiful literature. Here, too, the Hebrew language finds its redeemer. This perspective on the cultural challenges of the day—competition with Arabic, protest about the sorry state of Hebrew knowledge among the Jews, and the holy language's enduring artistic capacity—reproduces conventional tropes of Jewish literature during the Andalusi and post-Andalusi periods.[72] Written in Arabic and in al-Ḥarizi's own voice, *Taḥkᵉmoni*'s third dedication is unsparing in its pessimistic perspective of the prospects for success in light of al-Ḥarizi's observations on the ground: "I have noticed that most of the Israelite community in these lands of the East are devoid of the Hebrew language and denuded of its beautiful garments. If one of them were asked about a Hebrew word, it would seem as if he were being addressed in a foreign language. . . . I consider this to be one of the most terrible misfortunes to come upon our nation during our exile. This disease continues to spread among them, to the extent that most of them are never capable of putting the [Hebrew] letters together."[73]

The text expresses nothing but utter contempt for the prominent people and poets of Eastern lands: they are vilified for their avarice and parsimoniousness, their obtuse anti-intellectualism, inept and amateurish poets, and their immorality. It represents the Islamic East, once long-standing home to the centers of Jewish life and scholarship, as an intellectual and cultural backwater, especially with respect to its communities' command of Hebrew and compared with the Jews of al-Andalus. At a supposedly subsequent stage, al-Ḥarizi appeared to come to terms with his new surroundings: *Kitāb al-durar* praises Easterners (with notable exceptions) for their largesse, scholarship, and moral stature, especially members of the rabbinic and social elites in Cairo, Alexandria, and Damascus.[74] But this might have represented a temporary accommodation, according to the testimony of his apparently final composition, "The Pleasant Garden," in which an embittered author grumbles about recent treatment by prominent members of the Baghdadi Jewish community.[75]

The meticulous, albeit positivist, editors of al-Ḥarizi's Hebrew and Arabic works say that "the purpose of al Ḥarizi's journey was to describe the communities from West to East" (rationale #6).[76] Indeed, the texts describe more than fifty Jewish communities, including Alexandria, Cairo, Acre, Safed, Damascus, Aleppo, Mosul, Baghdad, Wāṣit, and the shrines of the Prophet Ezekiel and Ezra the Scribe, near Basra. They also mention by name more than two hundred Jewish notables and poets in the East.

To complicate matters even further, *Taḥkᵉmoni*'s dedicatory poem alludes to Judah Halevi's pilgrimage lyrics and thus suggests a more pious motivation for al-Ḥarizi's trip East, a journey that he undertook around his fiftieth year. In all likelihood, al-Ḥarizi was aware from Halevi's verse that his illustrious precursor contemplated his pilgrimage at the same stage in his life (rationale #7):

> His land was the "Garden of God,"
> now exiled and banished from its fields,
> He left the land of his sojourn
> and raced trembling to the Land of the Lord.
> His name is known as Judah ben Solomon
> the name of his land and homeland, Sefarad.[77]

A fragment from a separate al-Ḥarizi text called "Iggeret lᵉshon ha-zahav" (Epistle of the Golden Language) depicts the trek in nearly identical terms:

> Sefarad is my land and the abode in which I lie down . . .
> And I have made Jerusalem my sought-after destination . . .
> And I left the district of Sefarad one morning,
> and went down to the
> swelling waves of the sea
> and hurried, trembling, to the Land of the Lord.[78]

Halevi's prose formulation—he referred to himself as "one whose homeland is Sefarad but whose destination is Jerusalem" (*Sᵉfarad admato / vi-rushalayim mᵉgamato*), in a letter to an Egyptian dignitary—certainly found an echo in al-Ḥarizi.[79] In *Taḥkᵉmoni*, the fictional narrator responds to a query about his place of origin by rephrasing Halevi: "Sefarad is my land, the Land of Israel my destination" (*S^efarad admati / we-ereṣ ha-ṣ^evi m^egamati*; *maqāma* 49:133).[80] The pious motivation is also related in the introduction to *Kitāb al-durar*: "Perchance, I would be granted to gaze upon the Holy Land and the divine landmarks, so that I could commune in pious prayer with God most high, who had bestowed upon me its benefit in that I would be able to inhale the perfumes of the land from the fragrance of its soil. Of the source of its wellsprings, perchance, I would be granted to catch a glance; yea, to capture wondrous marvels and astounding sights, at which souls faint with rapture, and hearts melt away at pining."[81] Such allusions sufficed for Schirmann-Fleischer to suggest that al-Ḥarizi purposefully framed his journey as a Halevi-inspired pilgrimage.[82]

As is well known, the individual chapters or installments of *Taḥk^emoni* are discontinuous, detached rhetorical anecdotes and thus do not represent a journey at all but, rather, irregular meanderings of the linguistic, imaginative, and textual kind. *Taḥk^emoni* claims to be further dissociated from the author's experiences and voice through the mediated reportage of its two conventional fictional personae, the characteristically staid and gullible narrator, Heman the Ezraḥite, and the uncommonly eloquent and provocative trickster-protagonist Ḥever the Qenite. In keeping with the conventions of the Hebrew version of the genre, al-Ḥarizi apprises the reader: "And I composed all the chapters in this book, put them in the tongue of Heman the Ezraḥite and Ḥever the Qenite. And even though none of them ever lived, and all that I quoted never existed, this is the rule of those who composed *maqāmāt*."[83] Yet, just as *Taḥk^emoni* seems to mark as indelible the line between the imagined and the real, it also endeavors to blur or even erase the line—a measure of its literary artistry.[84] The author's persona appears in the first *maqāma* and interacts with one of the fictional characters; and *Taḥk^emoni* includes ten direct and mostly ingenious references to the author's biblical namesake Judah or to his allotted territory in biblical Israel.[85] With a few exceptions, I read such passages of *Taḥk^emoni* and its allusions to the biblical figure Judah as little artistic treats left for the reader's literary pleasure, as tongue-in-cheek literary gestures, not as suggestions for the reader necessarily to identify the fictional characters with the author.

Taḥk^emoni is neither an account of al-Ḥarizi's travels nor a forthright, uncomplicated mouthpiece for expressing his thoughts, as some would have it.[86] From a literary-critical perspective, efforts to alternately identify either Heman or Ḥever with al-Ḥarizi, depending on the supposedly "autobiographical descriptions" of a particular *maqāma*, are frequently overdetermined except in a select few instances, such as *maqāma* 46 [39] ("Appraisal of the People"), which traces the itinerary while devoid of the sorts of narrative artifice that the reader encounters in other *maqāmāt*.[87] Readings fixated on capturing "autobiographical" details in an imaginative text easily can fall into the trap of circular reasoning insofar as they reflexively view *Taḥkᵉmoni*'s fictional landscapes and invented encounters in light of textual evidence that the Arabic and Hebrew prose travel accounts provide.[88]

Michael Rand's manuscript excavation of *Taḥkᵉmoni*'s compositional layers is an exception to the studies determined to pin down al-Ḥarizi's "identity." He keenly teases out *Taḥkᵉmoni*'s various conventional thematic polarities as evidence of its literary achievement. Rand also endeavors to identify more than a few passages wherein the fictional characters supposedly speak on behalf of the author because of a particular theme or a reference to the name of the biblical figure Judah.[89] Consequently, he concludes that *Taḥkᵉmoni* and al-Ḥarizi's journey are so completely entangled as to be virtually inseparable and that al-Ḥarizi produced a "narrative that included a strong element of his own autobiography as an itinerant poet and man of letters."[90] He sums up al-Ḥarizi's double venture: "Thus we see that the journey in the East, the composition and redaction of the *Taḥkᵉmoni*, and al-Ḥarizi's search for patronage are all intertwined, as biographical/geographical fact, ideological (and artistic) motive, and practical facilitation. In reality, all these aspects are united in the person of al-Ḥarizi. Seen from the point of view of the *Taḥkᵉmoni*, the rarefied journey literary product in which they are recorded, this means that the book and the journey are inseparable."[91]

Despite its professed fictionality, *Taḥkᵉmoni* certainly intersects indirectly with al-Ḥarizi's own travels. Indeed, the *maqāma* genre serves as a brilliant literary vehicle for the peripatetic author. Its stylized form is predicated on its restive characters' roving and directionless passages, their discontinuous comings and goings, arrivals and departures from *maqāma* to *maqāma*. The readers' sense of constant movement and the fluid rhythmic prose and the cadences of its rhymes within each *maqāma* are interrupted only by interlaced poetry. Moreover, the *maqāma* genre's conventional *adab* themes include discovery, foreignness, and wonderment, all of which serve an author on the move. Most significantly, *Taḥkᵉmoni* represents Judah on the make: his dogged pursuit of financial backing from the mercantile elites of Mediterranean Jewish society and his ideologically minded presentation of Hebrew literary history. It satirically reviews Eastern Jewish communities and their cheapskate patricians: "The Misers" (*maqāma* 12);[92] it calls out the inept versifiers he encountered in the Islamic East, compared with Sefarad: "Appraisal of the Poets of al-Andalus" (*maqāma* 3);[93] "The Era of the Hebrew Poets" (*maqāma* 18);[94] and bemoans the disappointing quest for patrons in the East staged as a literary debate between "Miserliness and Magnanimity" (*maqāma* 42): "Don't you see that in all the countries of the world, from Egypt to Persia / you will not find an uncrooked patron / except for one in a thousand."[95] In particular, "Appraisal of the People" (*maqāma* 46),[96] two versions of which have come down to us, resembles a travel narrative. Devoid of imaginative elements or narrative artifice, the *maqāma* draws directly on the author's itinerary, transforming, as it were, his movements into literary form as the rhetorically gifted grifter Ḥever the Qenite revisits all of al-Ḥarizi's way stations, from Toledo to Lunel and from Marseilles aboard ship to Alexandria and points east.

Thanks to the Arabic and Hebrew texts grounded in al-Ḥarizi's journey and to Joseph Sadan's discovery of an entry on al-Ḥarizi in a biographical dictionary of Arabic poets,[97] al-Ḥarizi's journey also can appear to resemble a form of "cultural refreshment" much like the "spiritual refreshment" (*al-murṭabāt al-rūḥiyya*) that Andalusi Muslim travelers bound for the Islamic East sought in response to changing, and often unsettling, social and political conditions in the West. Indeed, the introduction to *Kitāb al-durar* cited above as intimating the quest for knowledge or intellectual community also signals an expectation to find it in the Levant and Islamic East: "There I was, at the age of ambition, ere had waned the wish to wander, in order to sip the wine of wisdom and gather the blooms of knowledge, longing greatly to attend the meetings of the learned. . . . I had long dwelt in the lands of the West, yearning to sail the seas and wander afar, to visit the Levant and Iraq."[98] Thus al-Ḥarizi's readers ascribe the wanderlust that drew him eastward as an indication that he anticipated feeling more culturally at home in an Islamic society and a fully Arabic-speaking environment than was possible at the turn of the thirteenth century in Toledo (rationale #8).[99]

Rina Drory identified al-Ḥarizi's writings as products of new cultural circumstances in Christian Spain and Provence, in which the Andalusi tradition—Arabic employed for communicative and Hebrew for ceremonial purposes, characteristic of Jewish literature in the Arabic-speaking lands of Islam since Sa'adia Gaon—was replaced by Hebrew exclusivity (rationale #9).[100] While extremely insightful, this functional-instrumentalist scheme does not entirely account for the complexity of al-Ḥarizi's linguistic practice informed by his travels and experiences, expectations and disappointments, even if it illuminates his aesthetics and ideology. After all, al-Ḥarizi abandoned Toledo and Provence for the Islamic East and remained there until his death. Drory thus determines that *Taḥkᵉmoni*'s purpose was to indoctrinate Eastern literary intellectuals with Hebrew linguistic and literary tradition from Sefarad.[101] Rand's aforementioned study of *Taḥkᵉmoni*'s intricate textual history identifies "literary penance" (with Hebrew displacing Arabic) as "strongly implied" (rationale #10) for undertaking its composition.[102] And, of course, as imaginative literature with its humorous and satirical narratives and rhetorical flourishes, *Taḥkᵉmoni* means to entertain its audience, as the author signals in the book's introduction proper (rationale #11): "The word of Judah, son of Solomon the Sefardi, son of Ḥarizi: The Lord has given me a skilled tongue to rhyme nice words and special idioms . . . and [thus] to bring to every land joy and gladness to the Jews."[103]

Judah al-Ḥarizi—driven and drawn eastward, literary opportunist, cultural emissary, Arabic-speaking literary and religious intellectual out of place in Provence, pious pilgrim, Hebrew bard in search of Eastern patrons, Hebrew ambassador in the East, professional Arabic poet for Muslim and Jewish aristocrats, author of detailed travelogues, seeker of expiation for linguistic and literary sins: we can find textual evidence justifying each of these portraits of the author. How can we make sense out of this array or, rather, disarray of assessments of Judah al-Ḥarizi?

I prefer to pose the question of purpose and motive differently. How do al-Ḥarizi's writings illuminate his evolving literary identity, which is typically constructed in response to the professional dilemmas and social and cultural circumstances that he encountered on his travels? As we observed in the Introduction, literary identity, as opposed to "identity," a theoretically compromised term in some quarters,[104] makes no ontological claims and does not presume to recover or know with certainty what the author felt, thought, or intended. Rather, critical analytical interrogation of texts, in all their thickness, ambiguity, and internal and intertextual dissonance, produces a sense of the author's discursively constructed literary identity, informed by considerations of practice and artistic ethos drawing "on an exceptionally broad range of conventions and symbols, such as value-systems, religious beliefs, common practices, and scientific and artistic fashion."[105] In al-Ḥarizi's case, as with his preeminent Andalusi precursors and models Samuel the Nagid, Solomon ibn Gabirol, Moses ibn Ezra, and Judah Halevi, literary identity is inherently related to ideas about and representations of the al-Andalus/Sefarad and Jerusalem vector and thus to the trope of Sefardi exceptionalism.

The key to deciphering al-Ḥarizi's unstable, evolving, and multiply constructed literary identity and his espousal of Sefardi exceptionalism lies in reading his works as performances of that identity, as literary responses to his journey and social texts in dialectical relationship with his ideological commitment and mission on behalf of Andalusi Hebrew culture. For this reason, I am especially interested in the texts depicting interactions with and assessments of various audiences as well as al-Ḥarizi's professed ideological commitments and actual linguistic-literary practice: 1) *maqāma* 3, on the literary history of Andalusi Hebrew poetry, and *maqāma* 18, on the literary history of Hebrew poetry in al-Andalus and the Islamic East, each with a minimum of imaginative elements; 2) two recensions of *maqāma* 46 [39] ("Appraisal of the People"); 3) *Kitāb al-durar*; and 4) *Taḥkᵉmoni*'s three versions of an introduction, each providing its own framing of the book. These materials, by turns, praise and vilify the social, religious, literary, and intellectual elites of the Eastern communities that al-Ḥarizi visited. By contrast, they provide glowing perspectives on Andalusi Jewish communal figures, poets, and thinkers and portray al-Andalus, including Toledo in Christian Castile, as the unrivaled epicenter of Hebrew language and literature and Jewish culture.

Let me begin to unravel the confusing chaos of the author's ostensible purposes as traveler and poet by discussing the most important formal and conceptual elements of the "Jerusalem *maqāma*," whose literary oddities have been overshadowed by its solemn subject. Then I will briefly return to the significance of al-Ḥarizi's assessments of the Jewish sociocultural scene in the Islamic East compared with that of al-Andalus, the artistic ideological bearing of *Taḥkᵉmoni*'s introductions, and the interrelation of these elements in affording us a somewhat clearer understanding of his literary identity in the last decade of his life.

The Jerusalem *maqāma* depicts the fictional characters' encounter in the Holy City, whose Jewish community was reconstituted in 1187, when Ṣalāḥ al-Dīn retook Jerusalem from the crusaders a generation before al-Ḥarizi's visit in 1217.[106] It may be outlined as follows:

1. Heman, a Jew from Sefarad, addresses his soul and urges it to orient itself to Zion. (lines 1–13)

2. Heman recites a "Lament for Zion" (lines 14–63):[107]
   a. Heman addresses Zion and revels in praise of its glories. (lines 11–22)
   b. Elegy for Jerusalem's state and lament for the absence of its people in exile (lines 23–46)
   c. Hope for, and expectation of, redemption and return to Zion (lines 47–63)
3. Heman encounters a Jerusalemite who recounts the city's recent history and prays for an end to unspecified communal strife. (lines 64–124)
4. Recognition scene of Ḥever as the Jerusalemite and leave-taking after a month together (lines 125–128)

The Jerusalem *maqāma* finds Heman ha-Ezraḥi, who identifies himself as from Sefarad, in Egypt, impelled by an urgent need to "go up" to "Jerusalem's good." Touring holy ground, Heman recalls Jerusalem's once-grand stature (lines 1–10) and appears every bit the pilgrim ("Let me die now that I have beheld your appearance," line 9), vowing not to leave "this place." He then offers a lengthy mournful dirge to Jerusalem, indebted to Judah Halevi (as well as the Book of Lamentations), that underscores his identity as a Sefardi Jew whose spirit is drawn to religious experience in the Holy City (lines 11–60).[108] The incipit of the lyric's very peculiar formula—"A soul from Sefarad was exiled to Zion" (*nefesh le-ṣiyyon mi-sfarad galtah*) is all the more curious because of the lyric's devotional theme. In fact, its quizzical subversive note ("exile from Sefarad") echoes the ambivalent formula found in *Taḥkemoni*'s dedicatory poem ("His land was the garden of God / now exiled and banished from its field"). *Taḥkemoni* registers a similarly enigmatic allusion in "The Appraisal of the People," where the depiction of Toledo, al-Ḥarizi's home, casts it in biblical language reserved exclusively for Jerusalem ("For there have the tribes, Lord's Tribes, ascended," Ps. 122:4).[109] The reader will note the dramatic tonal shift nearly midway through the poem as the pilgrim's view of the Holy City is brought into sharper and more realistic focus. The city's otherworldly beauty that Heman remembers from texts and prayers, the image of the city that he imagines and extols, fades away because God's presence has departed ("Where is God's Glory and its ray of splendor?," lines 35–36). From this point on, the lyric confronts Jerusalem's present desolation and laments that the city is devoid of the community of Jews in exile for whom it is waiting to return.[110]

Wandering about in view of the ruins of the Temple Mount, a weeping, despondent Heman reaches an emotional nadir when he encounters a Jerusalemite who recognizes him as a visitor from abroad. Our narrator asks his local acquaintance for information about the Jews' return to Jerusalem, from which they were excluded during the crusader period. The resident offers a lesson in interpretive history that constitutes the text's longest "narrative" passage (lines 61–108): he recounts the Muslims' takeover of Jerusalem from the crusaders and subsequent opening of the city to Jewish resettlement as clear signs of God's providential intervention in history. Indeed, the Jews of Palestine "now dwell under comfort's sweet shadow," according to the Jerusalemite.[111]

But all is not so well within the Jewish community of Jerusalem: it is said to be rife with dangerous discord, contention, and dishonesty.[112] Recalling Heman's initial vision of Jerusalem in a bygone age, "wherein dwelt upright men of merit" (line 5, *mi-qedem shakhnu vah m^etei yosher u-zkhut*), Ḥever's prayer of supplication exhorts "upright men" (*m^etei yosher*, line 106) to overcome the unspecified communal strife. The tale concludes with the conventional *maqāma* formula, although without the protagonist's requisite leave-taking from the narrator. Heman inquires of his informant's name and, of course, the protagonist reveals himself to be Ḥever the Qenite, about whom Heman says, "I was glad to encounter him. . . . I delighted in his nearness the whole time I remained in his land" (lines 109–112).

If Jerusalem is a place unlike other places, does an imaginative text relating Heman's visit differ significantly from *Taḥk^emoni*'s other rhetorical exercises, anecdotes, narratives, encounters, and adventures set in other locales? While the Jerusalem *maqāma* is morphologically related to a few others in *Taḥk^emoni* with minimal or no narrative artifice to divert the reader from its somber theme, several unusual formal features and narrative elements are signs that the text stands apart as unique.[113] For one, the narrator Heman rarely assumes so prominent a role as the protagonist Ḥever; yet Heman's voice and perspective dominate the first half of the *maqāma*. So, too, for a trickster who lives by his wits, street smarts, and rhetorical genius, Ḥever's demeanor is uncharacteristically sober, consistent with the theme; and anagnorisis, the artistic ploy central to the *maqāma*'s narrative structure, falls flat, lacking any sense of its customary deception, double-dealing, trickery, and surprise. Indeed, the reader senses that these lapses in convention and inversions draw attention to a significant paradox: Ḥever the Qenite is an otherwise ubiquitous figure who alchemically turns up in every place but who belongs to no place. He is never rooted in a particular land and has no *waṭan* (homeland), not even the Land of Israel. At the end of the first *maqāma* and in *maqāma* 3, Ḥever identifies his encampment site as Elon b^{e}-Ṣa'ananim. An inconsequential figure with the same name, Ḥever the Qenite, is identified in the Hebrew Bible (Judg. 4:11) from just such a place. However, the biblical toponym also marks *Taḥk^{e}moni*'s fictional character as a drifter, since it is derived from the root *ṣ-ʿ-n* with the semantic sense of "travel/wander," cognate with the Arabic. Ḥever is, as his biblical surname also alludes, "a restless wanderer in the land," much like al-Ḥarizi himself.

Here and there, the reader finds minor textual gestures inviting some sort of identification of author with character. However, in several installments besides the first *maqāma*, Ḥever the Qenite appears as an Andalusi-style champion activist for Hebrew, supposedly as a surrogate for the author. In *maqāma* 39, for example, Ḥever sets out to visit Sefarad, arriving first in Toledo, al-Ḥarizi's presumed birthplace. The character is drawn by accounts that he has heard of its natural delights, a critical motif of the trope of Sefardi exceptionalism found in Ibn Shaprūṭ (as well as Isidore and al-Rāzī):

> In my youth I was told that Sefarad was
> a delight to the eyes,
> her light like the midday sun
> her soil's fragrance the scent of myrrh
> her fruits' taste like honey to the palate
> and her air like the life of souls
> her terrain the choicest terrain, the splendor of souls
> the delight of God and people
> and her gardens' flowers like the stars of heaven
> her land the rose of Sharon, the lily of the valley
> so a gust of impassioned
> desire raised me up
> to trod gulches
> and to cut through ponds and seas
> and I went through deserts
> split waves
> crossed passes
> and made Sefarad my destination
> from my land.[114]

Ḥever's craving to witness firsthand what he has heard about Sefarad is so urgent and his objective so beckoning that many readers focus on identifying the author jutting out from behind the mask of the character. But from the perspective of *Taḥkᵉmoni*'s sociocultural and artistic agenda, the message is more significant than the messenger.

The itinerant writer al-Ḥarizi also seems to invite the reader to associate the author with his other narrative figure, Heman the Ezraḥite, the Jew from Sefarad whose surname suggests rootedness in and attachment to a place, a singularly important place in *Taḥkᵉmoni*'s literary and geographical imagination. Indeed, the Jerusalem *maqāma* offers the reader two contrasting perspectives of the Holy City in the early thirteenth century, in keeping with the genre's rhetorical strategy of juxtaposing conflicting points of view: that of the visiting Sefardi pilgrim who views Jerusalem through the ahistoric exilic prism of Jewish religious tradition and liturgy; and that of the city's permanent resident, involved in all its messy social and political life.[115] Heman and Ḥever, and thus Sefarad and Jerusalem, do not stand in opposition but rather represent complementary figures, milieus, and geographic-emotional poles in *Taḥkᵉmoni*'s poetics of cultural identity and place.

Maqāma 12 also finds the two fictional figures in Jerusalem, attending a literary soirée of the sort that one would find in Sefarad. Ḥever the Qenite mounts a sustained, vicious critique of the Eastern Hebrew poets, from Alexandria to Baghdad. Ironically, not a single Hebrew litterateur is identified as residing in the Land of Israel, so the reader might wonder about the fictional salon's audience of cognoscenti. In a recent study, Uriah Kfir explains the significance of the Jerusalem setting: "So it is no coincidence that it is in Jerusalem, of all places, that al-Ḥarizi has Ḥever deliver his speech, and it comes as no surprise that the Jerusalemites are portrayed as drowning in a sea of 'puzzlement and doubt'; for there can be little doubt that al-Ḥarizi's purpose is to reposition Spain's Jews as the genuine inheritors of Jerusalem's glory and as the 'true' Jerusalemites."[116]

*Maqāma*s 3 and 18 are devoted to the literary history of Hebrew poetry and poets, Andalusi in the first instance and, at much greater length, Andalusi and Eastern in the second. Along with *Taḥkᵉmoni*'s introductions, these texts represent transparently ideological gestures of Sefardi cultural elitism.[117] In *maqāma* 3, Ḥever appears in the guise of a ravenous ill-mannered old-timer who rectifies Heman's cursory presentation on Andalusi Hebrew poets with a hectoring diatribe and lyrical review of the poets' respective merits, beginning with the following declamation:

For all the Sefardis' poems are powerful and sweet
hewn from a fiery flame
and drawn from a living source
and their poets are macho while all the poets of the world
are womanly.[118]

Maqāma 18 recounts Hebrew literary history more elaborately and relates how the Jews came to compose Arabic-style Hebrew verse.[119] It extols the Andalusi Hebrew literary tradition as the exclusive, transcendent paradigm for the production of elegant Jewish culture in Hebrew. The protagonist Ḥever the Qenite appears again in the guise of a sage holding court at a *majlis* set in Jerusalem. The erudite scholar attributes the development of Arabized Hebrew poetry to principles critical to the origins and trajectory of the trope of Sefardi exceptionalism articulated variously by Ibn Shaprūṭ's surrogates, Samuel the Nagid, Moses ibn Ezra, and Abraham ibn Daud: the Jews of Sefarad enjoy a noble Jerusalemite genealogy conferring Jewish leadership and stewardship of Hebrew language and culture on them alone;[120] and they reside in a climatically auspicious land befitting production of knowledge and sophisticated culture. "So after our religious community was exiled from its land, many came to reside with Arabs in their realm and became accustomed to speak their language and articulate as they do. By Arabizing with them [*u-vᵉ-hitʿarvam ʿimmahem*], they learned the craft of poetry from them, as Scripture attests: they mingled [*wa-yitʿarvu*] with the nations and learned their ways" (Ps. 106:35).[121] *Taḥkᵉmoni*'s play on words subverts and inverts the meaning of the biblical passage, also cited in Ibn Ezra's *Kitāb al-muḥāḍara* discussed in the previous chapter,[122] and draws ironic attention to the Jews' deep engagement with Arabic, its significant allure in Jewish literary and intellectual life, and for establishing the Arabic-style Hebrew poetry as a fundamental site of Andalusi Jewish culture.

The character Ḥever the Qenite's oration then evokes three familiar tenets of the trope of Sefardi exceptionalism: the Jews of Sefarad descend from the Jerusalemite nobility (evidenced by Obadiah, v. 20); as Judean elites, they are stewards of the Hebrew language and its cultural products; and (in an assertion recalling the Andalusi geographer al-Hijārī's perspective, above Chapter 3) Sefarad, like Baghdad, resides in the fourth clime, which is most suitable to civilization and sophisticated cultural production.

Now, since some of the tribe of Judah escaped to Sefarad / as it is said: . . . "And the exile of Jerusalem that is in Sefarad," and the

> boundary of Sefarad is directly opposite the middle of the heavens / under the equatorial meridian and since the Babylonians are at this line in the East and the Sefardis are at the other extremity of this line in the West, therefore scientific inquiry spread to these two extremities in kind . . . for the scholars of the world were formerly in Babylon / and also in Sefarad, scholars in the rhetorical art of poetry, both metrical verse and rhymed prose. Therefore their [Hebrew] speech was preserved in its purity.[123]

Hebrew literary history is summarized in verse:

> When scholars were screened from chanting song
>   sages of Sefarad assembled to sing;
> And when Easterners could not manage poetry
>   the Westerners' vision gushed prophetically.[124]

Ḥever proceeds to paint an adulating portrait of Ḥasdai ibn Shaprūṭ, inaugurating Sefarad as the epicenter of Jewish intellectual life. His enterprise is rendered pseudo-prophetic:

> He issued a proclamation: Let he who is for the Lord, let him come to me. Let all his wants lie upon me.
>
> Then every great scholar and every sage gather unto him from Christendom and Islamdom, from East and West. . . .
>
> From that time on, the sciences in Sefarad made a breakthrough. . . .
>
> In his day culture spread throughout Israel for he was a patron and liberator of learning.[125]

The ambiguities, ambivalences, and inconsistencies that we find in al-Ḥarizi's interrelated texts afford us clues to his negotiable and multiply constructed literary identity. Rather than attempting to reconcile the ostensible contradictions of motive and purpose that the Ḥarizian texts set forth, I read them as a representation of the rich creative paradoxes that characterized Andalusi Jewish culture (to which al-Ḥarizi was resolutely committed) and its reception in other domains that al-Ḥarizi visited and in which he settled. Jonathan Decter states that "possessing *adab* was [for al-Ḥarizi] the highest cultural ideal, one that signified continuity with the Andalusian past."[126] Indeed, the opening (extant) passage of *Kitāb al-durar* characterizes the Jews of Fusṭāṭ as "endowed with the characteristics of *adab*" (*dhāt al-shiyam al-adabiyya*) and of Cairo as "possessing *adab*-minded people" (*dhāt al-nufūs al-adabiyya*).[127] The thematic inconsistencies we have observed in al-Ḥarizi's works thus signal the author's complicated and evolving attitude toward Hebrew and Arabic. Al-Ḥarizi's stance toward these languages could be quite pragmatic. Yet the aesthetic and ideological complexities of his linguistic-literary identity were authentically rooted in Andalusi Jewish *adab*—in its cultural ideals, values, and practices—that the author claims as his very own and from which he derives his cultural authority.

Born in a Christian polity two hundred years after the era of Ibn Shaprūṭ and thus removed temporally and geographically from his models, al-Ḥarizi's literary identity offsets dedication to Sefarad with devotion to Jerusalem and balances Arabic expertise and an ideological commitment to Hebrew with full knowledge of Andalusi Hebrew literature's deep structural relationship to Arabic. Al-Ḥarizi's self-fashioned literary identity as a curator of Andalusi Jewish tradition represents him as a zealous, empowered heir to Sefardi cultural capital. It defines a foreigner in Eastern lands as a self-styled Andalusi abroad, thoroughly invested in campaigning for the idea of Sefardi exceptionalism.[128]

Conclusion

Andalusi, Sefardi, and Spanish Exceptionalism

Reclaimed, Repudiated, Reimagined

The past is never dead. It's not even past.

—William Faulkner

A thing of beauty is a joy forever: its loveliness increases.

—John Keats

No doubt al-Andalus and Sefarad are more than subjects of historical study. Nearly eleven centuries since their genesis in Umayyad Córdoba (fourteen centuries, if we consider Isidore and Hispania), the tropes of Andalusi and Sefardi exceptionalism continue to beguile, enchant, inspire, irritate, and infuriate. How have practitioners of modern historiography and literary, religious, intellectual, and art history viewed and handled the tropes of Andalusi and Sefardi exceptionalism and the closely related trope of Spanish exceptionalism? And why do al-Andalus, Sefarad, and "medieval Spain" live on in the imaginative lives of various modern literary artists, cinematic auteurs, and musicians who find such cachet in the memory of their exceptionalism? Nostalgia, Orientalism, nationalism, and postmodern cosmopolitanism continue to draw scholars, thinkers, and writers to al-Andalus and Sefarad as sites of memory (*lieux de mémoire*) and meaning "because they are no longer milieux de mémoire, real environments of memory."[1]

History Interpreted and Its Uses

Modern scholars such as Américo Castro popularized the notion of *convivencia* ("living together") as characteristic of the society and culture of "medieval Spain," with its singular European heritage of *las tres culturas* ("the three cultures").[2] María Rosa Menocal was doubtlessly the foremost devotee of Castro's approach to medieval Iberian history and culture. Writing as a public intellectual in the aftermath of September 11, 2001, Menocal deemed medieval Iberia under Islam "a first-rate place" and endeavored to explain "How Muslims, Christians and Jews Created a Culture of Tolerance in Medieval Spain" (the subtitle of her *Ornament of the World*).[3] Castro and Menocal, to name only two of the most prominent proponents of this perspective, however, were not the first to cast the medieval Iberian Peninsula in an uncommonly positive light. Reinhart Dozy (1820–1883), the Dutch Orientalist and historian of "Spanish Islam," established the Romantic framework for representing the trope's classical inheritance whose origins, inflections, and trajectory we have studied in this book. Referring to the near-universal literacy purportedly achieved under the rule of the intellectually minded Umayyad caliph al-Ḥakam II al-Mustanṣir (961–976), Dozy revels in esteem for al-Andalus: "All branches of learning flourished under so enlightened a prince. The primary schools were good and numerous. In Andalusia nearly everyone could read and write, while in Christian Europe persons in most exalted positions—unless they belonged to the clergy—remained illiterate."[4]

Dozy's contemporary, the great Arabist-Orientalist Pascual de Gayangos (1809–1897), is a representative figure among anticlerical, liberal, nationalist Spanish scholars of the nineteenth century. Gayangos forged a new, inclusive vision that integrated, rather than simply incorporated, the story of Muslims and Islam into the grand narrative of Spanish history. His work sought to transform modern Spain's conception of its past and thus of itself in his own day.[5] Gayangos also contributed mightily to the liberal European Romantic awakening to the glorious memory and model of al-Andalus, especially through his partial translation of the first part of al-Maqqarī's epic early modern composition.[6] Gayangos's translator's preface to al-Maqqarī engages in a series of offsetting assertions, although his historical sympathies are sufficiently clear:

> The followers of Mohammed, whether considered as enthusiastic warriors, whose victorious arms spread terror and consternation over our continent, or as the cultivated race who led the way for us in the career of letters and civilisation, are certainly entitled to a prominent place in the annals of Europe. . . . It was from Spain that issued those dreaded expeditions which threatened more than once the liberties of Europe; in Spain shone the first rays of that civilisation which subsequently illumined the whole of the Christian world; in the Arab schools of Cordova were gathered, and carefully preserved for us, the dying embers of Greek learning; and it is to Arab sagacity and industry that we owe the discovery and dissemination of many of the most useful and important modern inventions.[7]

Dozy and Gayangos echoed the most often observed of Andalusi exceptionalism's predominant forms of expression: the Andalusi Muslims' nostalgic longing for the grandeur and richness of al-Andalus as it was in tenth-century Umayyad Córdoba or, more accurately, as it was remembered, especially in North Africa. From the twelfth century onward, Andalusi identity and the legacy of al-Andalus became even more inextricably intertwined with the Maghrib.[8] Andalusi exiles and Maghribi scholars invested or interested in al-Andalus preserved and transmitted Andalusi traditions and offered their own reflections upon them, mediated by the social, political, and religious concerns of their own time and place and their temporal and geographical distance from the remembered and imagined wholeness of the Umayyad past. During these later centuries, writing Andalusi literary and social history inclined toward recalling a vision of the past so as to preserve and transmit the idea of al-Andalus intact into the present and for the future.[9] Accordingly, Gayangos deliberately introduced his readership to al-Maqqarī, the seventeenth-century North African scholar writing in Egypt more than a century after Naṣrid Granada fell to the Catholic monarchs. According to Aziz al-Azmeh, al-Maqqarī's monumental work on the cultural history of al-Andalus (*Nafḥ al-ṭīb min ghuṣn al-andalus al-raṭīb*) "is a vast celebration of the excellences of bygone al-Andalus . . . an Andalus of the imagination, one that is constructed not from vision but from nostalgia."[10]

Various European elites of the early modern period also were caught up in the enthusiasm for "Moorish Spain." For example, Heinrich Heine (1797–1856), who concocted for himself a Sefardi "Marrano" identity from his mother's side, devoted one of his *romanceros* among his "Hebrew Melodies" to an epic meditation and poetic tribute to the incomparable poet Judah Halevi. He also celebrated the open and civilized society of Islamic Spain in the tragic verse play *Almansor.*[11] Visiting Spain in 1830 on a trans-Mediterranean odyssey of self-discovery, a youthful Benjamin Disraeli, whose family fabricated an aristocratic Sefardi identity before its conversion to Christianity, imagined that he had found in Granada a place of majesty, culture, belonging, and even ownership in the glorious Alhambra. As he was taking in the splendor of the structure and its grounds and a local attendant took him for a "Moor," Disraeli is said to have exclaimed: "This is my palace."[12]

In the nineteenth century, a party of late Ottoman Turkish writers, intellectuals, and politicians encountered works of European scholars interested in Moorish Spain and enthusiastically recovered, reclaimed, and popularized the notion of a glorious Andalusi Golden Age.[13] They found it deeply appealing for reasons having to do with their own modernizing aspirations and the transformations that they sought in Turkish society and culture.[14] By the 1930s, Philip Hitti, writing as a committed Arab nationalist, would paint a mesmerizing picture of tenth-century Islamic Córdoba in *A History of the Arabs* (1937). Reading Hitti, one cannot help but notice the pride that a Lebanese Maronite intellectual takes in the lustrous cultural scene of the capital of Arabo-Islamic "Spain," compared with two great cities of western Christendom:

> Córdoba took its place as the most cultured city in Europe and, with Constantinople and Baghdad, as one of the three cultural centers of the world. With its one hundred and thirteen thousand homes, twenty-one suburbs, seventy libraries and numerous bookshops, mosques, and palaces, it acquired international fame and inspired awe and admiration in the hearts of travelers. It enjoyed miles of paved streets illuminated by lights from the bordering houses, whereas seven hundred years after this time there was not so much as one public lamp in London, and in Paris, centuries subsequently, whoever stepped over his threshold on a rainy day stepped up to his ankles in mud.[15]

What with this startling cultural repossession and the ease of modern travel to relevant sites in Spain, the veneration of al-Andalus as an Islamic land of uncommon greatness spread to postcolonial Islamic societies as far removed temporally and geographically from it as Pakistan, which hosted its own commemorations of 1492 and all the wonders that came before. More than any other country, al-Andalus and its proximate historical connection to the Maghrib serves as an especially powerful marker of modern Moroccan culture and identity, even as it also was used to authorize Spanish colonial ambitions in North Africa.[16]

Representations of al-Andalus as a uniquely enlightened, inspired, and still-inspiring land and society also abound in modern scholarship on the history of ideas. For our purposes, four illustrations will suffice. Oliver Leaman's study of Moses Maimonides frames the twelfth-century rabbinic philosopher's Andalusi cultural background as extraordinary for its time: "Spain, *al-Andalus*, was a repository of considerable intellectual effort, with skillfully constructed libraries, observatories, and circles of scholars quite consciously setting themselves up in opposition to the traditional fount of both Islam and early Islamic theoretical thought in the east of the empire. This opposition was not in terms of opposition to the principles of Islam, but rather an assertion of the specific climatic, intellectual, and political virtues of the West (*al-faḍā'il* [sic] *al-Andalus*)."[17] In an essay devoted to the "shared passion for certain intellectual subsystems" within which "intercourse between Spanish Muslims and Jews flourished," Steven Wasserstrom writes: "And it was specifically Spanish emigrants who shipped a propensity for *convivencia* with them in their luggage, as it were, and who maintained such characteristically Spanish conversations abroad."[18] Mohammad 'Abid al-Jabiri, a contemporary Moroccan thinker, offers his own historically minded assessment of the unique intellectual venture of Andalusi Islam in *Arab-Islamic Philosophy: A Contemporary Critique*. Chapter 5 of the work, "The Andalusian Resurgence," asserts that "intellectual activity [in the Maghrib and al-Andalus] met with a different fate than in the East" because of "the absence of a pre-Islamic heritage" and because Andalusis "had remained independent from, and ideologically in conflict with, the Abbasid caliphate and likewise with the Fatimids subsequently creating a constant cultural competition."[19] For his part, William Gallois identifies the social basis of the cultural distinctiveness of al-Andalus. Responding to Todorov's *The Conquest of America: The Question of the Other*, Gallois asserts that "from his vantage point in Early Modern Spain Todorov need not have looked far for an ideal encounter between selves and others, for he would have found such a meeting in cosmopolitan Umayyad al-Andalus."[20] To put it another way: Leaman and others have come to posit an Andalusi intellectual and/or social exceptionalism within premodern Islam, despite their awareness of the constant movement of scholars, traders, and pilgrims across the different Muslim polities, East and West—or rather, precisely on account of the continuous exchange of ideas and competition within the cultural unity of Islamdom that these various movements signify.

Various literary, art, and architecture historians, social and intellectual historians, and historians of material culture, archaeologists, musicologists, and ethnographers also embrace the trope of Andalusi cultural exceptionalism. A few examples should serve to illustrate its appeal, albeit in the service of widely divergent ideals. Henri Pérès, one of the earliest European literary historians of al-Andalus, follows the major trend in early modern Spanish historiography by regarding the Arabo-Islamic element of medieval Iberian culture as a temporary foreign transplant onto the soil of the peninsula. Pérès identifies and admires the Andalusis' uncommonly delicate poetic sensibility and achievement, such as that embodied in Ibn Ḥazm's famous treatise on the manners of love, *Ṭawq al-ḥamāma* (The Dove's Neck Ring), from which we read in Chapter 3. However, Pérès racializing perspective attributes both the sensibility and accomplishment to the Andalusi poets' Ibero-Romance lineage and views their literary production as a progression of that cultural bearing and heritage rather than as a development of Arabo-Islamic civilization on the western frontier of Islamdom.[21] A. R. Nykl presented his translations of and commentary on "Hispano-Arabic love poetry" to an English-reading audience as evidence of its connection to early Provençal lyric verse.[22] Troubadour historian Roger Boase asserts: "Many people in North Africa today still regard al-Andalus as the lost Garden of Eden. . . . This is hardly surprising because in Muslim Spain Arab civilization reached a level of artistic and intellectual refinement unattained elsewhere."[23] Among archaeologists of medieval Iberia, James Boone refers to al-Andalus as "a lost civilization," partly on account of "its uniqueness. Spain and Portugal are the only nations in Europe with a substantial Muslim and specifically Arab past (only Sicily has a similar trajectory, and parts of southeastern Europe under Turkish rule). As such, Iberia in the Middle Ages doesn't 'fit in.' Too 'Eastern' for traditional European medievalists and too 'Western' for traditional Middle Easternists."[24]

Historians of science,[25] historians of religious thought, and historians of Islamic and Jewish law and legal theory also define the ways in which thinking in the Islamic West took peculiar turns.[26] From its first figure, the ascetic and mystically inclined Mu'tazilite thinker Ibn Masarra (d. 931) in the tenth century, to Ibn Bājja (the Latin Avempace; d. 1139), who is credited with the "Andalusi revival" of neo-Aristotelianism, in the late eleventh and early twelfth centuries, and Ibn Rushd (the Latin Averroës; b. 1126) in the twelfth, Islamic thought in al-Andalus is said to diverge from the course of Islamic theology and philosophy in the East in several respects, including in its preference (with the exception of Ibn Ṭufayl, d. 1185–1186) for al-Fārābī and Aristotle over Ibn Sīnā and emanationist Neoplatonism.[27]

As for ethnographers, John Fox, Nada Mourtada-Sabbah, and Sulayman Khalaf identify al-Andalus as a dynamic, open, and socially tolerant society and, consequently, a place where traditional Arab gender roles broke down and "became less conservative and exclusionary,"[28] while ethnomusicologist Jonathan Glasser identifies Andalusi musical practice in modern and contemporary North Africa as the paradoxically endangered and prestigious "Lost Paradise" of "Islamic Spain."[29] Critical theorists are also drawn to contemplate the significance of al-Andalus. Gil Anidjar, for example, reconsiders "what is meant today by al-Andalus as a literary and cultural object of Arab Jewish letters."[30] For Anidjar, al-Andalus is a context that has vanished from view; nevertheless, it is inscribed today in various discourses and thus constitutes a rhetorical event that is not reducible to its literary, cultural, and historical contexts. That is, "al-Andalus" is a literary trope that takes place or resides solely in texts. In another essay, Anidjar offers a biting critique of the contemporary deployment of the memory of medieval Spain with which "we persist in thinking of Europe as an exemplary and exceptional site of peaceful coexistence."[31] Gonzalo Fernández Parrilla speaks of Spain as uniquely colonizing, orientalizing, and orientalized and observes "the singularity of Spanish history" that "ended up establishing al-Andalus as a 'domestic Orient.'"[32] Similarly, literary critic Anouar Majid appeals to the trope by identifying modern absolutisms, fundamentalisms, and extremisms as characteristic of the "post-Andalusian age."[33]

Cultural critic John Docker explores the intellectual, literary, and political consequences for Jews, Arabs, Indians, and modernity of the pre-1492 "lost world."[34] And the essays in a recent number of the *Journal of Postcolonial Writing* devoted to "the enduring legacy of al-Andalus" reflect critically on many of the aforementioned authors, for whom "the sense of al-Andalus and its lingering resonances five hundred years later as an integral part of a quest for answers by expatriate Muslims to contemporary issues of migration, identity, belonging, mutation and change."[35] Elena Arigata, a scholar of contemporary Islam, examines "Spain—the al-Andalus legacy" post–September 11, 2001. Her interrogation of the interference of the Islamic legacy of al-Andalus on the modern nation-state observes: "al-Andalus represents a unique legacy within the context of Europe. From a historical standpoint, eight centuries of continuity, and the remarkable cultural and scientific achievements make al-Andalus unique."[36] And *Critical Muslim* recently devoted an entire issue of the journal (titled *Reclaiming al-Andalus*) to a collection a dozen essays, each of which speaks to the trope's contemporary social agency or offers historical or critical reflections on it.[37]

As for Sefarad, Sefardi refugees from the traumas of the late fourteenth to late fifteenth centuries carried with them an abiding connection to their former homeland inscribed in their languages (Judeo-Arabic and Ladino) and culture. For example, the Gavison (or Gavishon) family of rabbinical scholars from Seville and subsequently Granada fled in 1492 to Tlemcen, where they enshrined Andalusi Jewish tradition at the center of the Sefardi culture that they practiced in North Africa.[38] Solomon ibn Verga, author of *Shevet Yehudah* (ca. 1520), who escaped to Ottoman Turkey, and early modern Italian Jewish intellectuals of Sefardi ancestry who espoused Sefardi exceptionalism such as Elijah Capsali (ca. 1483–1555) and Joseph ha-Kohen (1496–ca. 1578), served as cultural intermediaries between early modern Sefardi intellectuals and early modern writers of the European Jewish Haskalah (enlightenment). By the same token, Ottoman Jewish intellectuals of Sefardi lineage living in Middle Eastern lands, such as Raphael Solomon ben Samuel Laniado (d. 1793), the chief rabbinic judge of the Jewish community of Aleppo, were instrumental in what has been called the "emergence of Sefardi studies."[39]

Drawing upon images of the Jews and culture of classical Sefarad conveyed in the writings of early modern Sefardi exiles in Ottoman lands,[40] modern Jewish historians famously deemed the mid-tenth through mid-twelfth centuries as the Golden Age of Hebrew literature, Jewish culture, and the Jews in Spain. This arresting appellation-cum-characterization of the period has endured ever since.[41] Jewish enlightenment cognoscenti and Jewish scholars of that era, such as Abraham Geiger (1810–1874), uniformly exalted Jewish life and culture in the lands of classical Islam, where Judaism "developed its own fullest potential in closest union with Arabic civilization."[42] They singled out Sefarad as the outstanding example of Jewish cultural achievement and sociopolitical security in premodern Islamdom. Performing a sign of their increasing resistance to the norms of traditional Jewish practice and belief, these scholars preferred the ethos of worldliness, sociocultural openness, and literary, scientific, and philosophical accomplishments that they associated with Sefarad over the assumed insularity and excessive piety of Ashkenaz (Franco-Germany).[43] Heinrich Graetz, a pillar of *Wissenschaft des Judentums* (Science of Judaism), a scholarly movement in nineteenth-century Germany, doubtless was thinking of his own attachment to Germany and its high culture when he defined the Jews' ties to medieval Iberia and commemorated their cultural accomplishments (1894):

> While the history of the Jews in Byzantium, Italy, and France possesses interest for special students, that of their brethren in the Pyrenean peninsula rises to the height of universal importance. The Jewish inhabitants of this happy peninsula [Iberia] contributed by their hearty interest to the greatness of the country, which they loved as only a fatherland can be loved, and in so doing achieved worldwide reputation. . . . When Judaism had come to a standstill in the East, and had grown weak with age, it acquired new vigor in Spain, and extended its fruitful influence over a wide sphere. Spain seemed to be destined by Providence to become a new center for the members of the dispersed race, where their spirit could revive, and to which they could point with pride.

Graetz concluded: "Jewish Spain became the home of civilization and of spiritual activity—a fragrant garden of joyous, gay poetry as well as the seat of earnest research and clear thought."[44] Such judgments would be echoed more prosaically in the pioneering work of the great German Jewish scholar-bibliographer Moritz Steinschneider (d. 1907).[45]

Arguably the most remarkable example of scholarly interest in al-Andalus and Sefarad from that period came from Abraham Shalom Yahuda (1877–1951). A self-identified Arab Jew from a Jerusalemite family, Yahuda served at the University of Madrid as professor of Jewish history and literature *and* of Arab culture. Yahuda appealed to the Jews' and Arabs' social and cultural convergence in al-Andalus during the Golden Age that they shared as a model to guide the two peoples in living together in British Mandate Palestine. For example, in an address delivered in classical Arabic to Jerusalemite Arabs in 1920, Yahuda called upon his audience "to revive the legacy of al-Andalus": "Only when the spirit of tolerance and freedom that prevailed in the golden age of Arab thought in al-Andalus . . . will return to prevail today, in a way that will enable all peoples, without religious or ethnic prejudice, to work together for the revival of enlightenment in the Eastern nations, each people according to its unique character and traditions, can an all-encompassing Eastern enlightenment be reborn that will include all Eastern nationals and peoples."[46] In similar fashion although with a different political horizon and purpose in mind, Abraham S. Halkin concluded a synthetic essay, "The Judeo-Islamic Age," by paying tribute to the lasting impact of the Golden Age of Hebrew literature and hoping that Jewish life in Israel would reclaim "for modern times the glory that was Spanish Jewry."[47]

The culture of Sefarad also has served as the touchstone for contemporary Sefardi and Middle Eastern Jewish scholars such as Haïm Zafrani, José Faur, Ammiel Alcalay, and Nissim Rejwan. For Zafrani, the Andalusi Golden Age, with its cultural concord between Muslims and Jews, always bridged the strait and found a permanent home in Morocco after the events of 1492.[48] Faur's postmodernist rabbinic intellectual regimen is rooted in what he refers to as the Judeo-Arabic literature of "Old Sepharad."[49] Alcalay's critical essays (as well as his creative writing) are informed by a profound investment in what he deems "Levantine culture," the Jewish culture produced from ninth-century Baghdad to thirteenth-century al-Andalus.[50] Likewise, the self-identified Arab Jew Nissim Rejwan found inspiration in the culture that Jews shared with Arabs for centuries in the lands of Islam. For Rejwan, the Jewish culture culminating in al-Andalus was a model for what he deemed the unrealized potential of "Israel's place in the Middle East."[51]

Regarding modern and contemporary uses of the idea of Sefarad, Yael Halevi-Wise devises the term "Sephardism" to identify a new type of discourse, a contemporary trope as "a politicized literary metaphor."[52] Analyzing the origins of modern historical romances, Halevi-Wise observes: "With growing intensity from the end of the eighteenth century onwards, writers with completely different viewpoints from Germany, England, Latin America, North Africa, and even India found in Spain's roller-coaster history a useful metaphor, remarkably well suited to reimagining the image and political status of minorities in competing nationalist agendas."[53] Tabea Alexa Linhard explores the place of the Jews and "Jewish Spain" in twentieth-century Spain through examining the discourses about them informing the ongoing public debates about Spanish identity.[54] And ethnomusicologist Ruth Davis introduces a collection of essays on the afterlife of al-Andalus in the Jewish musical tradition with observations about the paths of exile that music took as a principal repository of Jewish memory.[55]

History Contested

The interrelated cultural tropes of Andalusi, Sefardi, and Spanish exceptionalism, in their varied inflections, are highly contested in modern scholarship and letters, precisely on account of the contemporary work that they can perform.[56] Bracing critiques of the idea of the uniqueness of al-Andalus, Sefarad, or Spain and resistance to its enthusiasts' formulation of it take different forms. In most instances, repudiating the claim of Andalusi or Sefardi exceptionalism outright or at least diminishing credence of its historicity turn on reassessing the sociopolitical situation of a premodern multiethnic, multireligious, multicultural land. Various scholars challenge the nature, scope, and significance of the socioreligious tolerance that is said to have prevailed in al-Andalus. What, they ask, was the actual extent of what Castro termed *convivencia*?[57] Alex Novikoff draws welcome attention to the shifting subject, the implications of divergent notions of *convivencia*, and the history of the polemic surrounding it: Does it refer to social tolerance, to cultural openness and fusion, or to both?[58] One can wonder further whether *convivencia* is supposed to apply exclusively to al-Andalus or to medieval Iberia in its entirety.[59]

Spanish historiography and social thought have long grappled with a wide range of contending perspectives on the trope of Spanish exceptionalism.[60] Following Isidore, a constellation of prominent modern nationalist Spanish historians, including Marcelino Menéndez y Pelayo, Julián Ribera, Miguel Asín Palacios, and Ramón Menéndez Pidal, championed the assured and unaltered essential continuity of Spain, Spanish, and Spanishness from the time of the Visigoths.[61] They envisioned a temporarily "occupied" Spain (what Pierre Guichard remarked that they treated as a "historical parenthesis")[62] untainted by centuries of Islamic rule and uncontaminated by the extended Muslim and Jewish presence in the peninsula and their extensive social, economic, and cultural interactions with Christians.[63] The Spanish philosopher Julián Marías Aguilera, for example, devotes chapter 1 of his *Understanding Spain* to critical dissection of the elements of what he deems "Spain's supposed abnormality," including its "cultural mosaic" and assumptions about the superiority of "civilized Moors" over "primitive Christians."[64]

The long-standing debate among Spanish scholars and its spillover effect among the reading public in Spain show no signs of letting up anytime soon, as evidenced by a recent provocative book by Alejandro García Sanjuán and the lively scholarly and public intellectual exchanges it prompted.[65] Bruno Soravia, for instance, takes North American postmodernists (María Rosa Menocal is singled out as the principal and influential purveyor of the idea) to task for what he regards as their ahistorical construction of the "myth" of al-Andalus as an "interfaith utopia": the "fascinating cultural achievements of Islamic Spain cannot obscure the fact that it was never an example of peaceful *convivencia*."[66] Recently, Darío Fernández-Morera argued (in the service of an extensive broadside against other historians' political correctness, as he sees it) that "Spain" (Hispania/Spannia/Spania), not "Iberia," served medieval Christians as the geographical term for the entire peninsula, regardless of historical period or religious polity. He also claims that, on occasion, prominent Muslim authors from the ninth through seventeenth centuries, such as al-Ṭabarī, al-Maʿsūdī, al-Idrīsī, Ibn Khaldūn, and al-Maqqarī referred to the land as Isbāniya, that is, "Spain."[67] Accordingly, Fernández-Morera labels the Muslims' eventual settling on "al-Andalus" as the Arabic name of the territory as a "well-known colonialist maneuver," as if they were historically obliged to adhere to the geographic term in another language associated with a different religion and favored by those who previously ruled the land.[68] Even American historians have joined the fray. Brian Catlos's synthetic narrative history of Islamic Spain, geared to a public audience, subtly but unmistakably endeavors to serve as what the author views as a corrective to Menocal's presentation, especially as it pertains to what *convivencia* signifies.[69]

For modern Spain and its students, it seems, high historical stakes—the very identity of Spain—concern the extent and significance of the sociocultural role played by Muslims and Jews in premodern Iberia. Specifically, what is the significance of their service as transmitters of exquisite literary forms and themes, Greek science, and rational thought to Christendom through their translations into and out of Arabic?[70] What sort of place of belonging in Spanish history of the premodern age do Iberian Muslims and Jews merit? Alternatively, should Muslims and Jews be marginalized in the history of Spain or even excluded from the category of what is Spanish?[71] Notwithstanding such debates among the Spanish, Yosef Hayyim Yerushalmi noted with considerable satisfaction that since the nineteenth century, the modern Spanish academy devoted resources and attention to the study of Jews: "Despite certain limitations and slants, Spain remains the only European country in which the record of medieval Jewry is claimed somehow as an organic part of the national patrimony."[72] The same could be said regarding the important place that Andalusi Arabic and Islamic studies occupy in Spanish universities, institutes, and publishing. Ironically, though predictably, market forces in modern Spain's tourist industry have rushed to turn the nationalist historiographers' paradigm inside out, promoting all things *convivencia*, "Moorish," and Jewish in a profitable new commercial campaign infused with an unmistakably Romantic-Orientalist sensibility.[73]

In Islamic studies and Jewish studies, the virtues of Andalusi Muslim and Jewish cultural production and society relative to other places and times also have been questioned and their lasting significance challenged. In Islamic studies, for example—apart from outstanding work being done by members of the contemporary Spanish academy as well as a select few American historians of Arabic literature and social, religious, and legal historians of Islam—al-Andalus is still frequently neglected; or al-Andalus is consigned to a marginal position on account of its place on the far western frontier of Islamdom and Christendom and its supposedly peculiar social, political, and religious history.[74] One of the early and solitary cautionary voices advocating a sober assessment of the place of al-Andalus and its cultural production in Arabo-Islamic letters belongs to the pioneering Hungarian Islamicist Ignáz Goldziher. Although Goldziher specifically set out to dispel the view that al-Andalus ever attained cultural superiority over the Islamic East, he framed the contested subject in 1876 remarkably, as though he were party to the current debate on the significance of al-Andalus in the history of civilization:

> There is a widespread opinion, both in historical works and with the educated people, that the medieval Spanish Arabs were above the general cultural level of the Muslims; that their civilization was superior to that of all the other Muslim peoples; that scholarship was more cultivated by them than by other Muslim groups; that their philosophical erudition mitigated Muslim intolerance and fanaticism; that they were more sensitive and susceptible to the beautiful in both life and art than their Eastern kinsmen—in a word, that from the viewpoint of humanism Andalusian Islam is the most pleasing phenomenon of Muslim cultural history, one in which civilized man delights more than in Eastern Islam. It is remarkable that this prejudice has not only misled the conceptions

of European scholars but has falsified the views of many medieval Arab scholars as well. . . .

[I]t is undoubtedly true and undeniable that the Spanish Arabs had great and lasting merits in improving civilization in the Europe of the ninth century. It is true that these merits are, even in recent times, ridiculously exaggerated above their correct level by careless and superficial enthusiasts.[75]

The eminent Anglo-Arab historian Albert Hourani strikes the reader as considerably more judicious than his predecessors in observing that "in the far west, there developed an Andalusian civilization which was different in some ways from what existed in the east." Hourani suggests that al-Andalus was distinctive on account of its "fruitful mixture of different elements: Muslims, Jews and Christians; Arabs, Berbers, indigenous Spaniards, and soldiers of fortune from western and eastern Europe."[76] Social historian Ira Lapidus is prudent in a different way from Hourani in his monumental study *A History of Islamic Societies*. Employing glowing language and rendering arresting images reminiscent of Hitti but without his comparative judgment, Lapidus pays tribute to the unique accomplishments and ambiance of al-Andalus:

> Muslim Spain bears the aura of glory. The great mosque of Cordova, the gardens, fountains and courtyards of the Alhambra, the *muwashshahat* and *zajal* poetry with their Arabic verses and occasional romance language refrains, the irrigated gardens of Seville and Valencia, the wisdom of philosophy and science—these are the monuments of Spanish Islam. Spain was the focal point for the transmission of Greek philosophy from the Arab world to Europe. No less important was the drama of defeat of this brilliant Muslim civilization by its European enemies, the expulsion of the Arabs, and the reabsorption of Spain into Christian Europe.

However, Lapidus minimizes the geopolitical place and historical significance of al-Andalus within the wider orbit of classical Islamdom: "For all its brilliance, Muslim Spain was a province of the Arab Caliphate."[77]

David Wasserstein has since sketched the most astute view of what was unquestionably unique about al-Andalus relative to other lands of Islamdom:

it was the only Islamic polity without "a land frontier in common with any other Islamic territory." So, too, al-Andalus's geographical remoteness from the central lands of Islam meant that it remained protected from external military invasion at the hands of other Muslims from the foundation of the Umayyad emirate in the mid-eighth century until nearly the turn of the twelfth.[78] To this assessment we can note several additional sociohistorical differences between al-Andalus and the Islamic East. Unlike other lands of Islamdom, pre-Islamic Hispania was neither a part of the Byzantine nor the Sassanian empire, and its population, excluding the tiny Jewish minority, was Hispano-Roman and German and spoke and wrote languages that bore no relationship to Arabic, unlike the peoples of the pre-Islamic Near East.

Most notably, María Rosa Menocal's early scholarly work *The Arabic Role in Medieval Literary History: A Forgotten Heritage* (1987) indicted the field of Romance studies by arguing that there had been a deliberate, ideologically informed, forgetting of the Muslims' and Jews' salient impact on the universally admired achievements of medieval "Spanish" culture and, through its mediation, European culture.[79] Menocal then demonstrated exactly what those contributions were and how they came about.[80] Recall that Bernard Lewis traced the modern origins of the Muslims' enthusiastic recovery of al-Andalus to the nineteenth-century Turkish discovery of the translated works of European scholars interested in "Moorish Spain."[81] Lewis took modern Muslim historiographers to task for obscuring what he regarded as the European discovery of the subject and then for employing it on behalf of what he deemed their own excessive, apologetic nostalgic-romantic agenda. Oddly enough, Lewis seems to have forgotten that North African Muslims of Andalusi origin required no such discovery: they kept their cultural traditions very much alive and thus their identity intact and distinct for centuries. By contrast, Menocal was among the first medievalists to consider how the critical insights that Edward Said articulated in *Orientalism* (1978) might benefit the study of premodern Iberia as a unique crossroads of Christendom and Islamdom. She sought to undermine the presumed binary of Islam and Europe, to erase the ontological distinction between "Orient" and "Occident," and to dissolve the epistemological division between their respective cultural productions. Al-Andalus, properly studied, was the missing link. To her credit, Menocal was very much aware of the risk of substituting one narrative for another, although she was resolute about its edifying, rather than destructive, purposes in history and in the nuanced manner in which she articulated her views.[82] Menocal's final project, *The Arts of Intimacy*,[83] unpacks a complex aspect of the hybrid cultural "identity" of a premodern Castile that was constructed in part "out of Arabic." In the same year, Barbara Fuchs demonstrated the centrality of constructions of Moorishness in the cultural history of early modern Spain.[84]

Even Oleg Grabar, doyen of Islamic art historians, frames an otherwise nuanced essay on "the first four centuries of the brilliant Arab Islamic presence in Spain," authored for the catalog of a Metropolitan Museum of Art exhibition that observes the "uniqueness" of al-Andalus mediated by the particular perspective of the viewer:

> The Muslim Spain of the eighth to the eleventh century was unique within pre-Romanesque Europe and the newly created Islamic word culture. From the point of view of the rough and cold Christian north, it was a haven of warmth, sophistication, and refinement in every aspect of life—from the clothes that were worn to the buildings that were built to the ideas that were created and the knowledge that was pursued. From the point of view of the Iraqi centers of Islamic culture, it was an upstart province that had succeeded in creating a literature and systems of thought that competed with the finest Arabic poetry and philosophical discourse of the past or present. . . . For the Iberian Peninsula itself, it was an astounding achievement: a land in which a totally new language and religion first overwhelmed and the interacted with a native tradition to produce a complex and original mixed culture that was to enrich the nature of Spanish civilization throughout its subsequent history.[85]

For social and literary historians of al-Andalus, the Andalusis' sense of dependence upon, and cultural competition with, the Islamic East and the difficulties that Andalusi rulers encountered in pacifying, controlling, and absorbing Berber elements in Andalusi society—before and after al-Andalus was incorporated into the Almoravid (end of the eleventh century) and Almohad kingdoms (mid-twelfth century)—typically inform Andalusi cultural and historical self-definition and claims to Islamic legitimacy.[86] Anna Akasoy reframes the question of a distinctive Andalusi identity by drawing attention to the frequently overlooked or underestimated role of regional diversity, especially regional intellectual culture in classical Islamdom and the complexity and multiplicity of intellectual tendencies and affiliations.[87]

What of Sefarad? Writing in the shadow of the late interwar twentieth century, long before the current stage in the historiographical battle was joined and these salvos were issued, Yitzhak Baer, author of the authoritative history of the Jews in the Christian Iberian kingdoms, devoted a section of the work's introduction to "Moslem Spain" and a segment of chapter 1 to "intellectual currents during the Reconquest," featuring comments on the Andalusi literary-religious intellectuals Moses ibn Ezra and Judah Halevi.[88] In the former, and implicitly through the body of the work, Baer expresses a striking preference for the "authentically" and "intrinsically" Jewish orientation and tradition of the Jews of the Christian kingdoms over what he regarded as the rationalist, elitist, and hedonistic courtly culture of the Jews of al-Andalus. In his own gesture toward Sefardi exceptionalism, Yom Tov Assis refutes Baer's view:

> Sefarad was not an assimilationist trend that intended to destroy Jewish tradition. Sefarad is not Spain. . . . Sefarad is a name for a brand of Judaism that emerged as a result of the fusion of Jewish tradition with elements of Greco-Arabic civilization and elements from Romance culture brought by the *Reconquista*. . . . Sefarad was an experiment in Jewish history that was unique in its attempt to create a Jewish trend that was in many respects contradictory to the exilic conditions that dominated Jewish life for centuries. It was an attempt to liberate Judaism from its exilic restrictions. The experiment may not have been able to survive forever, but it was probably the formula that was best suited to a people living in its cultural and religious milieu.[89]

Bernard Lewis, who deemed the persecution of Andalusi and Maghribi Jews under the Almohads during the twelfth century to be exceptional "in Muslim history west of Iran," nevertheless leveled a stinging critique of "the myth of Spanish Islamic tolerance" and what he deemed its modern, politically informed uses.[90] A recent related, and decidedly tendentious, condemnation of the myth, framed for the reading public rather than a scholarly audience, requires viewing the Jewish experience in classical al-Andalus through the political lens of modern Zionism and its own contested history in the modern Middle East. Hillel Halkin, in particular, critiques Menocal and other authors whose work interprets the Andalusi Jewish experience in any sort of a positive historical, socioreligious, or sociopolitical light.[91]

Yosef Hayyim Yerushalmi suggests that "the profusion of personal and historical accounts emanating from the Spanish expulsion must somehow be related to the traditionally high, even inflated, degree of self-awareness on the part of Spanish Jews of their special identity and destiny as 'the exile of Jerusalem that is in Spain.'" Yerushalmi's prooftext for this Sefardi attitude is the famous passage by Isaac Abravanel cited above in the Introduction (page 2). Popularizing authors like Howard Sachar paint a similar picture of the Golden Age of Spanish Jewry in "Moslem Spain" "sustained by self-satisfaction. Iberia's affluent Jews envisaged themselves as the aristocrats of the Diaspora. In its condescension, the assessment evinced at once economic success, superior education, and often a highly cultivated, characteristically Iberian elegance of personal demeanor."[92]

Eminent historians of the Jews, such as Ivan Marcus and Ismar Schorsch, take a radically different critical approach. Responding in part to the idea of Sefarad as a frequent foil for Ashkenaz in modern Jewish historiography,[93] they assail a scholarly fixation on what they call the "Sefardi mystique,"[94] an approach to Jewish historiography supposedly valorizing the cultural achievement of the Jews of medieval Iberia over those of northern European lands that is said to inflate the actual role and importance of Sefardi Jews in Jewish history.[95] In response to a state of the field essay in which Marcus reiterates his critique of Sefardi-centered modern scholarship, the historian of thought Hava Tirosh-Rothschild breaks down the "Sefardi mystique" into distinct yet related phenomena. For our purposes, its two most important manifestations insofar as they pertain to the Andalusi period are: the Jewish scholarly preoccupation with Sefardi Jewry; and a fascination with the rationalist and "secularist" sensibilities of the Sephardi "courtier class," resulting from its high degree of "assimilation" in Islamic society. For Tirosh-Rothschild, these impulses "reflect a pro-Sephardic bias among Jewish historians, inadvertently revealing overt assimilationist and reformist tendencies" that "created a myth of a golden age that never was."[96] She nevertheless acknowledges that scholarly focus on this branch of the Jewish people is justified in part by the realization that the overwhelming majority of the world's Jews lived in the lands of classical Islam; interest in them was further catalyzed by the discovery of the Cairo Geniza.

Historian of religion Aaron Hughes traces the intellectual history of the very idea of the Golden Age. Dissecting its uses in Geiger, Graetz, Baer, and Goitein, Hughes argues that the Golden Age was and remains a historical imaginary and invented tradition that has much to say about the field of modern Jewish studies.[97] Menahem Ben-Sasson, one of the most accomplished and respected Israeli historians of the Jews, hews closely to Zionist historiography in contesting the idea of the Golden Age of the Jews of Spain. He endeavors to undermine the image that Andalusi Jews themselves constructed of their (diasporic) experience and venture: "This paper will briefly survey the history of the 'Golden Age' image and then submit the claims underlying that image to a critical examination. It signals the fact that Spain was never the first in any field of creativity, even in those that reached high levels of development. It also emphasizes that in a few important areas, there was no 'golden' state as imagined and described in scholarly works. . . . [I]t present[s] the possibility that in many respects Spanish-al-Andalus-Jewry was, until the twelfth century, quite similar to other Jewish communities under Islam."[98] Reviewing many of the scholarly sources noted above, Ben-Sasson argues that the "Golden Age" appellation should apply only to the Andalusi Jewish experience, in the very limited sense of its literary creativity, if at all.

No less a social historian than S. D. Goitein, the incomparable student of the documentary Cairo Geniza and one of the dominant scholarly figures of the twentieth century, referred to the literary production of the Jews of Iberia as "the Spanish miracle."[99] One of Goitein's students, Norman Stillman, attributes the basis of an assumed Andalusi uniqueness not to its peculiar religious or ethnic diversity but rather to its geographic position. He identifies "an exclusivist tendency manifest in the Iberian Peninsula—not only among the Sefardic Jews and not only during the Islamic period, but throughout the course of Spanish history. . . . Spanish exclusivism derived from its isolated position at the western extremity of the Dar al-Islam on the very doorstep of Christian Europe. We must bear this salient geographical fact in mind in order to properly understand the individuality of Andalusian culture."[100] However, as we saw in the previous chapters, while distant from the center of the Islamic world, al-Andalus was never as remote and isolated as some have argued or imagined.

Prominent twentieth-century Islamicists such as Bernard Lewis and Jacob Lassner, who turned their attention later in their scholarly careers to the history and place of the Jews in Islamic society, also regard al-Andalus and the status of its Jews as exceptional primarily because of its distance from the Eastern heartland of classical Islam. Lewis notes that "with the striking exception of Spain and Arabia, Islamic regimes were more tolerant at the center than at the periphery, indeed becoming more repressive the further they were from the heartlands of Islamic civilization." Accordingly, the specific persecution of Andalusi and Maghribi Jews under the Almohads during the twelfth century is likewise said to be exceptional "in Muslim history west of Iran."[101] Lassner views the Andalusi Jewish experiences as unusual on account of its outlying locus: "Indeed the Jewish experience in the Iberian peninsula was often cited as typical of Jewish experiences everywhere in the medieval Muslim world, although serious scholars who focus more narrowly on Islamic history have always appreciated how al-Andalus, the western periphery of the Islamic realm, was very different in so many ways from the other regions. There is, nevertheless, a general consensus regarding the achievements of Andalusian Jewry."[102] Those cultural accomplishments and the high social standing of Jewish elites are very much admired and even glorified throughout Eliyahu Ashtor's canonical study of the Jews of al-Andalus, which narrates their history to the mid-eleventh century.[103]

Social historians of the Jews of Iberia variously observe, endorse, and celebrate, or repudiate and debunk the Jews' self-fashioned identity-relating traditions, often with a minimum of critical reflection or sense of the trope's complex, evolving expression and trajectory.[104] By contrast, Esperanza Alfonso judiciously analyzes the ways in which Andalusi Jewish identity was established in self-conscious awareness of Islam and the Andalusi Muslim majority, a perspective that enriches our understanding of the nexus of Andalusi and Sefardi exceptionalism.[105] For others, such as Jonathan Ray, the identification of Sefarad with *convivencia* is overdetermined, and the treatment of Sefarad as stable and unchanging is soundly critiqued. However, Ray allows that as an "imagined community," "Sepharad was an influential idea around which Iberian Jewry was able to organize itself."[106]

In the Creative Imagination

Aside from the unique place that al-Andalus and Sefarad have come to occupy in modern historiography, the history of thought, and cultural history, the idea of a tolerant, multicultural, and intellectually and artistically vibrant Iberia has inspired the modern literary imagination and critical thought. Authors writing in various European languages as well as in Hebrew and Arabic, as William Granara and Reuven Snir have shown, and in other languages in which Islamic culture is conducted, as Yaseen Noorani has demonstrated, have come to depict al-Andalus or Sefarad variously as a place of great sociocultural accomplishment and sociopolitical tolerance, a "multicultural garden" (said of Córdoba, in particular), and a "paradise lost" (typically in reference to Granada).[107] For contemporary Arab and Muslim literary intellectuals, such as the Egyptian writer Radwa Ashour, and Palestinians like Maḥmūd Darwīsh and his *Eleven Stars over Andalusia* (2002), in particular,[108] nostalgic visions of al-Andalus appear to capture an idealized cultural and political identity for the present age and its many discontents.[109] For the great Syrian poet Adūnīs (Adonis), Andalusi philosophers serve as transgressive figures who resist the hegemonic authority of religion over the individual. In *Destiny* (*Al-Maṣīr*, 1997), the Egyptian cinematic auteur Youssef Chahine reimagines the philosopher Ibn Rushd and his al-Andalus as the site of a struggle between humanistic intellectuals and artists, on the one hand, and religious zealots and political opportunists, on the other. The Tariq Ali–produced documentary *The Final Solution: Islam in Spain* (1991) features renowned Spanish writers Juan Goytisolo and Antonio Muñez Molina. As its title insinuates, the film represents a biting polemic connecting the fifteenth-century expulsion of Muslims from Spain with historiographical denial of the "Arab roots of European culture." Above all, various colonial and postcolonial Moroccan intellectuals, writers, musicians, and festival promoters lay Morocco's claim to the heritage of al-Andalus.[110]

Zofloya or, The Moor (1806), by Charlotte Dacré; *The Manuscript Found in Saragossa* (ca. 1815), by Jan Potocki; Sir Walter Scott's *Ivanhoe* (1820); Heinrich Heine's verse play *Almansor* (1821); Robert Browning's (1864) reflective-didactic lyric "Rabbi Ben Ezra";[111] Washington Irving's *Tales of the Alhambra* (1832); Muḥammad Iqbal's Urdu-language philosophical lyric (1933) to *convivencia* recalled in "The Mosque of Córdoba," the inspiration of al-Andalus in the Egyptian Aḥmad Shawqī's poetry (1868–1936); Federico García Lorca's lyrical evocations of the Andalusian landscape in what he called *casedas* and *gacelas*;[112] *These Are the Travels of Rabbi Judah Halevi* [Hebrew] (1959), by Yehudah Burla, the Israeli novelist of Turkish ancestry; Anthony Mann's cinematic epic *El Cid* (1961); Yehuda Amichai's brief Hebrew poetic meditations on Ibn Gabirol and Judah Halevi (1948–1958),[113] as well as references to Sefardi figures in his surrealistic "The Travels of the Last Benjamin of Tudela" (1968) and his stylistic affinity for the model of Samuel the Nagid's verse;[114] the first book of *Leo Africanus* (1988), retold by the Lebanese exile Amin Maalouf;[115] José Saramago's *The History of the Siege of Lisbon* (1989; trans., 1996);[116] *The Death and Life of Miguel de Cervantes* (1991), by Stephen Marlowe; Tariq Ali's *Shadows of the Pomegranate Tree* (1992); Salman Rushdie's *The Moor's Last*

Sigh (1995) and his *Two Years Eight Months and Twenty-Eight Nights* (2015), which assigns Ibn Rushd (Averroës) Scheherazade's role in a retelling of the *1001 Nights*; A. B. Yehoshua's *Journey to the End of the Millennium* (1997), which represents, among other things, a Hebrew-language idealization for a contemporary Israeli audience of the Andalusi Jewish experience and culture, in opposition to that of Franco-Germanic Ashkenaz; *The Last Kabbalist of Lisbon* (1998), by Robert Zimler; the historical sketches published as *Sepharad* by Antonio Muñoz Molina (2001); Almog Behar's reflective essay-memoir "Dreams in Spain" [Hebrew];[117] Laila Lalami's *The Moor's Account* (2014); G. Willow Wilson's *The Bird King* (2019), the story of the preferred concubine of the last Naṣrid emir of Granada; and Borges's iconic story "Averroës's Search" (1947): these are only a few of the more inspired works of fiction, verse, or film set in or drawing upon images, figures, and themes from medieval Iberia.[118]

With their reputation for relative social harmony, marvelous cultural production, and premodern multicultural situation, al-Andalus and Sefarad (as well as medieval Iberia) occupy a special place in the theoretical regimen, historical study, and literary and cinematic imagination of scholars, thinkers, writers, filmmakers, and musicians who are inclined to find it interesting, appealing, compelling, or disturbing for reasons having to do with their own time, place, sociopolitical circumstance, and cultural condition. The ideas of "al-Andalus" and "Sefarad" remain potent and arguably more powerful and prevalent than they were in the past. In sum, eleven hundred years of history—the trope's longevity, multiple incarnations, and various audiences—suggests that al-Andalus and Sefarad were and remain truly exceptional as enduring tropes of Islamic and Jewish culture originally advanced in tenth-century Córdoba.

Notes

INTRODUCTION

Iberian Moorings does not intervene directly in the acrimonious, persisting debates about al-Andalus and Sefarad as uncommonly magnificent and remarkable in terms of their social and cultural profiles. While it is clear enough from this study that al-Andalus and Sefarad were indeed different, distinctive, unique, and exceptional, I deliberately leave it to readers to make any qualitative judgments about their history, society, and culture.

Notes to epigraphs: Ibn Khaldūn, *Al-Muqaddima*, 1:141; Ibn Khaldūn, *The Muqaddimah*, 1:179. Ibn Khaldūn's family roots were in Seville; although born in Tunis, he served for a time in Granada at the Naṣrid court. Note that the Arabic original reads *li-ahli l-andalus*, meaning "the people of al-Andalus"—i.e., "Andalusis" not "Spaniards," as found in Franz Rosenthal's translation. Judah al-Ḥarizi, *Taḥk^{e}moni* (2010), 64 (introductory poem). Yosef Hayyim Yerushalmi, "Medieval Jewry," 16.

1. "Moorish Spain" and the less commonly used term "Arab Spain" are fraught with historical problems. On the former, see Brann, "The Moors."

2. See below, the Conclusion for a critical review of these debates in Spanish, Jewish, and Islamic historiography and culture.

3. Throughout this study, I employ "trope" when referring to "exceptionalism," on account of its transhistorical trajectory and social agency. I reserve "topos" to refer to its occasional manifestations as a literary theme.

4. See Harvey, "A Morisco Collection of Apocryphal *Ḥadīths*."

5. Yerushalmi, "Exile and Expulsion in Jewish History," 19. Isaac ben Judah Abravanel, *Commentary on the Former Prophets* [Hebrew] (Jerusalem: Torah w^{e}-da'at, 1954–55), 422–423 (the autobiographical section of the introduction to his *Commentary on the (biblical) Book of Kings*), connects the original Jerusalemite exile to Babylonia and the exile of the Jews from Sefarad. An anonymous Hebrew account of the expulsion from ca. 1495 was published by Marx, "The Expulsion of the Jews from Spain." Marx, 248–249, reviews the sixteenth century reports authored by Abraham Zacuto, Elijah Capsali, the anonymous chronicler and the various dates they assigned to the expulsion. My thanks to Martin Jacobs for pointing me to these sources.

6. For a translation of the edict, see "Charter of Expulsion," trans. E. Peters.

7. Isaac ben Judah Abravanel, *Commentary on the Later Prophets*, 311 (*Commentary on Jeremiah* 2:24), appears to be the source for the tradition-legend that the expulsion originally scheduled for July 31, 1492 = 7th of Av was delayed for the multitudes including Abravanel

himself until August 2 = 9th of Av. Heinrich Graetz, *Geschichte der Juden*, 8:349 [missing from the English translation] popularized the 9th of Av dating. Marx and Yitzhak Baer, *History of the Jews in Christian Spain*, 2: 439 and 512 [note 14], dismissed its historicity.

8. Kammen, *Imagining Spain*, 1–37, reviews the various efforts to create the myth of a premodern national history and dates the nation of Spain from a "community of nations" to the early nineteenth century.

9. Dangler, "Edging Toward Iberia," treats the instability of the markers "España" and "al-Andalus," and, now in expanded form, her critique of the epistemological and methodological problems in the study of premodern Iberia, *Edging Toward Iberia*.

10. Wolf translates "corn," which I have changed to "grain," so as not to mislead about a "New World" crop not found in seventh-century Iberia. In a private correspondence, Wolf tells me that he used "corn" in the broader, non-American sense of "grain."

11. Isidore of Seville, "History of the Kings of the Goths," trans. Wolf, *Conquerors and Chroniclers of Early Medieval Spain*, 81. For a different translation, see *History of the Goths, Vandals and Suevi*, trans. Donini and Ford, Jr., 1–2.

12. *The Chronicle of 754*, in Wolf, *Conquerors and Chroniclers*, 133 (#56–57), 132 (#54).

13. The history of these toponyms is reviewed below.

14. Corriente, "Coptic Loanwords of Egyptian Arabic," 116.

15. Blau, "'At Our Place in al-Andalus,' 'At Our Place in the Maghreb,'" 293–294, "Maimonides, al-Andalus, and the Influence of the Spanish-Arabic Dialect on His Language," and "Maimonides' 'At Our Place in al-Andalus' Revisited." Kraemer, "Maimonides and the Spanish Aristotelian School," 40–42, draws attention to Maimonides' "Andalusian affinities" across the advanced curriculum.

16. Maimonides, *The Guide of the Perplexed*, 1:177 (Chapter 1 Section 71).

17. Ibid., 2:268.

18. Goitein, *A Mediterranean Society*, 2:274.

19. Akasoy, "Identity and Diversity in Islamic Intellectual History," 340–341.

20. Abū l-Walīd Muḥammad ibn Rushd, *Talkhīṣ al-āthār al-ʿulwiyya*, 103–104, cited by Stroumsa, "Thinkers of 'This Peninsula,'" 47.

21. Akasoy, "Al-Andalus in Exile," 329–343. Below, Chap. 5, examines the literary responses of three prominent travelers.

22. Lefebvre, *The Production of Space*, 53 (emphasis added).

23. For the significance and evolution of the term *adab*, see Hämeen-Antilla, "Adab, Arabic." Regarding divergent views of the term and its range, see Pellat, "Variations sur le thème de l'adab"; Bonebakker, "*Adab* and the Concept of Belles-Lettres"; and Holmberg, "*Adab* and Arabic Literature."

24. I borrow the term "Arabo-Islamic humanism" and the underlying concept from Kraemer, *Humanism in the Renaissance of Islam*.

25. Bourdieu, "The Forms of Capital." I am indebted for this reference to Zeitler, "Legacy of Muslim Spain," 64–65.

26. To avoid giving the impression of asserting any ontological claims regarding what Andalusi Muslims and Jews felt or thought, I employ phrases such as "self-representation" or "self-fashioning," "Andalusi-ness," and "Sefardi-ness" when referring to how Andalusi Muslims and Jews portray themselves in relation to other peoples and places. In the main I try to avoid ascribing to them "attitudes," "self-perceptions," or the loaded modern term "identity."

27. Gregory, *Geographical Imaginations*, 104.

28. I am indebted here to the critical discussion concerning nostalgia in Trilling, *The Aesthetics of Nostalgia*, 3–27.

29. Stillman, "Aspects of Jewish Life in Islamic Spain," 61, points to "an exclusivist tendency manifest in the Iberian Peninsula" and to "self-conscious pride . . . concerned with purity of lineage, language and religious tradition, . . . a hallmark of Hispano-Arabic society" (65). Wasserstein, "The Muslims and the Golden Age of the Jews in in al-Andalus," 194, among a few others, have also noticed the connection.

30. Glick, *Islamic and Christian Spain in the Early Middle Ages*, xxi. Glick also reviews the various theories regarding the origins of the name.

31. Miles, *The Coinage of the Umayyads of Spain*, 1:20–21.

32. Vycichl, "Al-Andalus (sobre la historia de un nombre)," 449–450.

33. Wexler, *The Non-Jewish Origins of the Sephardic Jews*, 76.

34. Lévi-Provençal, *Histoire de l'Espagne musulmane*, 1:71–73. Torres Balbas, "Al-Andalus," 1:486; Helm, "Al-Andalus und Gotica Sors," 252–263, and "L'Origine du nom *al-Andalus*," 49–55.

35. Bossong, "Der Name *al-Andalus*: Neue Überlegungen zu einem alten Problem."

36. Vallvé Bermejo, "El Nombre de al-Andalus," 353, and "Mater Spania (siglos VIII–XIII)."

37. Corriente, *Diccionario de arabismos y voces afines en iberromance*, 215.

38. Corriente, "Coptic Loanwords of Egyptian Arabic in Comparison with the Parallel Case of Romance Loanwords in Andalusi Arabic," 117. The symbol "*" is used in phonology to indicate the word does not obey the phonotactics.

39. Ramírez del Río, "Acerca del origen del topónimo al-Andalus." García Sanjuán, "Al-Andalus, Etymology and Name," reviews the various scholarly hypotheses and their weaknesses.

40. Transmitted, among others, by the geographer Ibn 'Abd al-Mun'im al-Ḥimyarī, *al-Rawḍ al-mi'ṭār fī khabar al-aqṭār*, 2.

41. Miquel, "Al-Iṣṭakhrī," 4:222–223; Tibbetts, "The Balkhi School," 114, 119, observes that al-Iṣṭakhrī appears to treat al-Andalus and the Maghrib as one area. Accordingly, the Maghrib, in the sense of the Islamic West, includes al-Andalus and not only Morocco, a notion encoded in Moses Maimonides' usage, on which see above, page 5. A facsimile of an 1173 manuscript copy of al-Iṣṭakhrī's map can be found in Harley and Woodward, *The History of Cartography*, pl. 6.

42. Aḥmad ibn Muḥammad al-Maqqarī, *Nafḥ al-ṭīb min ghusn al-andalus al-raṭīb*, 1:125, 147. All references to this work refer to the 'Abbās 1968 edition unless otherwise noted.

43. See Lipinski, "Obadiah 20"; and Rabinowitz, "Sefarad."

44. See Krauss, "The Names Ashkenaz and Sepharad"; Laredo and Gonzalo Maeso, "El nombre de 'Sefarad'"; and Harkavy, "Toldot r. shmu'el ha-nagid." M. R. Cohen, "The Origins of Sephardic Jewry in the Medieval Arab World," 24, suggests that the Aramaic translator "rendered 'Sepharad' by the word 'Aspamia,' presumably thinking of Apamea, a city in Mesopotamia." "Sefarad" is used in the Babylonian Talmud to signify a faraway place. See Oppenheimer, "From Qurtava to Aspamya," 57. See also Roth, "A Note on the Meaning of Sefarad," who reviews many of these interpretations and sources and cites additional contributions to the discussion.

45. Abū l-Walīd Marwān ibn Janāḥ, *Kitāb al-uṣūl*, 496.

46. Brutzkus, "Sfarad un Ṣorfat," 1:11, cited by Wexler, *The Non-Jewish Origins of the Sephardic Jews*, 76–77.

47. Wexler, *The Non-Jewish Origins of the Sephardic Jews*, 77–78. Wexler also discusses the vexing matter of usage, whether and when Sefarad applied to the peninsula in its entirety or to its specifically Islamic or Christian domains. Roth, "Note on the Meaning of Sefarad," 245–246, cites the nineteenth-century philologist Antonio García Blanco as the first to derive *i sephanim* from the Semitic.

48. Solà-Solé, "Semitic Elements in Ancient Hispania," 490–491 (184–185).

49. Pons, "The Origin of the Name Sepharad," 311; Pons also reviews the entire history of scholarly attempts to identify the place name Sefarad.

50. Aslanov, "*S^{e}fārad* as an Alternative Name for *Hispania*," 239.

51. Ramírez del Río, "Acerca del origen del topónimo al-Andalus (II)," 710–714.

52. Gelston, *The Peshiṭta of the Twelve Prophets*, 86.

53. The text was edited by Ben-Shammai and Chiesa, "Q^{e}ṭa'im mi-peirush rasa"g li-mgilat eikhah," 70. My thanks to Moshe Yagur for bringing this source to my attention.

54. *Seder 'olam zuṭa*, in *Mediaeval Jewish Chronicles*, 1:71. See Hacohen, "The Jerusalem Talmud in the Teachings of the Early Spanish Sages," 113–117, for additional geonic-era sources.

55. Three versions of the text of *Midrash 'eser galuyot* were published in *Oṣar midrashim*, 2:433–439. The reference to Sefarad is found in the third version (originally published by Carmoli as "Sefer 'Uqṭān d^{e}-mar ya'aqov"), 439. The dating of *Midrash 'eser galuyot* is uncertain, but R. Ṣemaḥ Gaon, head of the Palestinian academy for thirty-one years, refers to it in the ninth century in correspondence, supposedly with the Jews of Qayrawān, regarding tales of the mysterious apocalyptic figure Eldad ha-Dani. See *Sefer Eldad ha-Dani*, 1:40, cited by G. Cohen, *The Book of Tradition*, 251.

56. Kraemer, *Maimonides*, 493n39. Beaver, "Nebuchadnezzar's Jewish Legions," studies the early modern Christian Spanish uses of this Sefardi legend and their sources, going back to Islamic polemics against Jewish Scripture.

57. Text: Poznański, "The Arabic Commentary of Abu Zakariya Yaḥya (Judah ben Samuel) ibn Bal^{c}am on the Twelve Minor Prophets," 34–35.

58. Cairo Geniza, DK 184a, ed. Gil, *In the Kingdom of Ishmael*, 2:63 (doc. 19, line 10); and Gil, *Jews in Islamic Countries in the Middle Ages*, 195–196. Among the earliest Andalusi Hebrew poets, "Ispamya" is occasionally employed for metrical purposes as the equivalent of Sefarad. See Isaac ibn Mar Shaul, "Ṣ^{e}vi ḥashuq b^{e}-ispamya," in Schirmann, *New Hebrew Poems from the Genizah*, 158 (#66); and Samuel the Nagid, "M^{e}odam b^{e}-mar'ehu w^{e}-'arev l^{e}-shotehu u-mazug b^{e}-ispamyā," in Schirmann, *Hebrew Poetry in Spain and Provence*, 1:163.

59. This important letter to Joseph, king of the Khazars, is discussed below, Chap. 2.

60. Moses ibn Ezra, *Kitāb al-muḥāḍara wa-l-mudhākara*, 54 (29a).

61. Abraham ibn Daud, *Dorot 'olam*, 124–127.

62. Assis, "Sefarad," 31.

63. Ray, *After Expulsion*, 13.

64. Decter, *Iberian Jewish Literature*, 5–6.

CHAPTER 1

In this chapter, I am indebted to the pathbreaking series of studies by Maribel Fierro, as well as to the work of Manuela Marín, Gabriel Martínez-Gros, Nicola Clarke, Janina Safran, David J. Wasserstein, James T. Monroe, and others for definitive studies on how the tenth-century Umayyad caliphs employed various textual, material, and performative tools to ground their authority in the language of Islamic legitimacy. Rather than undertaking an exhaustive study of these legitimacy-conferring discourses and performances, I endeavor to synthesize what is known and draw selective attention to paradigmatic illustrations from written sources and material culture because I assign them an agency over and above their import for articulating Umayyad political and religious legitimacy and power. For the most part, I concentrate on illustrations drawn from the earliest available sources, with the notable exception of al-Maqqarī, who preserves fragmentary versions of what is otherwise lost. Accordingly, I set aside the always important and notoriously difficult question of source criticism, transmission, and redaction: who borrowed from whom and when and where and for what purpose.

Note to epigraph: Al-Rāzī *apud* al-Maqqarī, *Nafḥ al-ṭīb*, 1:129.

1. Sumner, "The Chronology of the Early Governors of al-Andalus to the Accession of 'Abd al-Raḥmān I."

2. For the history of the conquest, the governors' period and the early Umayyad emirate, see Collins, *The Arab Conquest of Spain, 710–797*; 'Abd al-Wāḥid Dhannūn Ṭāhā, *The Muslim Conquest and Settlement of North Africa and Spain*, 84–109, 183–253; and Kennedy, *Muslim Spain and Portugal*, 1–16. Of late, Spanish historiography has become embroiled in a polemical contest over the history of the early eighth century, on which, see the Conclusion below.

3. Fierro, "Mawālī and Muwalladūn in al-Andalus, 228–229, explains that before the mid-tenth century, the term *muwallad*, typically understood as "converts to Islam," actually "designates someone who was 'Arabized' but not necessarily 'Islamized.'" Fierro further demonstrates (195–245) just how complex the social and ethnic situation was in al-Andalus prior to the tenth century and how the various terms for the convert population shifted over the first two Islamic centuries.

4. An account of the circumstances surrounding the declaration and text of the decree is preserved in *Crónica Anónima de 'Abd al-Raḥmān III al-Nāṣir*, 75–80, trans. Cobb, in Constable, *Medieval Iberia*, 87–90.

5. Lévi-Provençal, *Histoire de l'Espagne Musulmane*, 2:1–164, recounts the political history of 'Abd al-Raḥmān III al-Nāṣir's reign.

6. See ibid., 2:78–110.

7. Bulliet, *Conversion to Islam in the Medieval Period*, 114–127. For discussions of Bulliet and the specific methodological and statistical problems of the study of conversion in al-Andalus, see Penelas, "Some Remarks on Conversion to Islam in al-Andalus"; Wasserstein, "Where Have All the Converts Gone?"; and Harrison, "Behind the Curve," which offers a reconsideration of Bulliet in light of the dearth of sources and the survival of a significant Andalusi Christian community. See Bulliet, "The Conversion Curve Revisited," 71, where Bulliet responds to what he regards as misinterpretation of his "technique and conclusions" "with regard to Spain"; and Fierro, "The Islamisation of al-Andalus."

8. Said, *Orientalism*, 332, famously articulated the universality of this process in producing cultural self-definition. On social boundaries in al-Andalus, see J. Safran, *Defining Boundaries in al-Andalus*.

9. Wasserstein, *The Caliphate in the West*, 17. Cf., however, Wasserstein's earlier perspective in *Rise and Fall of the Party-Kings*, 28–29.

10. J. Safran, *The Second Umayyad Caliphate*, 10–11.

11. See Fierro, "Sobre la adopcíon del título califal por 'Abd al-Raḥmān III"; Martínez-Gros, *L'idéologie omeyyade*; Martínez-Gros, *Identité andalouse*; and Monroe, "Hispano-Arabic Poetry During the Caliphate of Córdoba."

12. See Taḥṭaḥ, *Al-ghurba wa-l-ḥanīn fī l-shi'r al-andalusī.*

13. Gellens, "The Search for Knowledge in Medieval Muslim Societies," 51.

14. Selheim, "Faḍīla." My understanding of the discourses of place in classical Islamdom has benefited from Antrim, *Routes and Realms.*

15. Fierro, *'Abd al-Raḥmān III*, 7. I do not address Pierre Guichard's *Al-Andalus: Estructura antropológica de una sociedad islámica en Occidente* question of the social reality, i.e., whether cleavage between Berbers and Arabs continued unabated into the eleventh century or whether the distinct Andalusi "identity" that the Umayyads sponsored widely took hold in the tenth. See Wasserstein, *Rise and Fall of the Party-Kings*, 164–165.

16. Here I employ the idea of "myth" in its original significance as *mythos*, "the thing told," and without any of the pejorative connotations it accrued.

17. The geographical imagination of the Jews of al-Andalus, by contrast, did not construe their community as quite so isolated. It engaged questions of center and periphery but in a fundamentally different way from Andalusi Muslims. Chapters 2, 4, and 5 below treat this matter regarding the Jews of al-Andalus and the communities of the Islamic East.

18. Marín, "Historical Images of al-Andalus and Andalusis."

19. See du Mensil, *Géographes d'al-Andalus*, 95–119.

20. Michalowski, "Mental Maps and Ideology," 131.

21. García-Arenal, *Messianism and Puritanical Reform*, 80, citing Fierro, "Le mahdī Ibn Tūmart et al-Andalus," who observes (48): "among Muslims, traditions had already circulated in the 2nd–8th century predicting that their settlement in the Iberian Peninsula would be transitory and was destined to end tragically."

22. See D. Cook, *Studies in Muslim Apocalyptic*, 77, citing Nu'aym ibn Ḥammād al-Marwazī, *Kitāb al-fitan*, 267, 279, 288.

23. On the political upheavals of the early ninth century and the uprisings directed against the autocratic regime of the Umayyad emir al-Ḥakam I (r. 796–822), see Kennedy, *Muslim Spain and Portugal*, 42–44. Refugees from the revolts resettled in Fez, where they established the renowned Andalusi quarter (*Madīnat al-andalusiyyin*) anchored by the Andalusi mosque.

24. 'Abd al-Malik ibn Ḥabīb, *Kitāb al-Ta'rīkh*, 136–156 (chap. devoted to al-Andalus), carefully studied by Safran, *The Second Umayyad Caliphate*, 143–150. Dangler, "Edging Toward Iberia," reviews Safran on Ibn Ḥabīb in brief. On Ibn Ḥabīb, see Campoy and Serrano Niza, "Ibn Ḥabīb al-Ilbīrī." Andalusi historiography proper dates to the tenth century and the Umayyad royal chroniclers Aḥmad ibn Muḥammad al-Rāzī (d. 955) and his son 'Īsā (d. 989), whose work was partially preserved by Ibn Ḥayyān. See Pellat, "The Origin and Development of Historiography in Muslim Spain."

25. The "Córdoba Martyrs' Crisis" broke out shortly before Ibn Ḥabīb's death. On that famous episode, see Wolf, *Christian Martyrs in Muslim Spain.*

26. Stearns, "Representing and Remembering al-Andalus."

27. The eleventh-century Andalusi geographer Abū 'Ubayd 'Abd Allāh ibn 'Abd al-'Azīz al-Bakrī, *Jughāfiyat al-andalus wa-ūrūbbā min kitāb al-masālik wa-l-mamālik*, 130. Later Andalusi geographers such as al-Ḥimyarī, *al-Rawḍ al-Mi'ṭār*, 3, and historians of Andalusi traditions such as al-Maqqarī, *Nafḥ al-ṭīb*, 1:144–145, upheld and preserved this theme as idyllic Islamic markers of Andalusi historical identity long after it had ceased to have any meaning

in the Naṣrid and post-1492 ages, respectively. For example, the Naṣrid writer and jurist, Ibn Hudhayl (d. 1409), *Tuḥfat al-anfus*, 68, celebrates al-Andalus for its "purest soil" and its inhabitants' "accumulated merit of martyrdom." García-Arenal, *Messianism and Puritanical Reform*, 80–85, makes the connection between early Umayyad confrontations in Syria with Christian Byzantium and Andalusi Umayyad battles against the Christian kingdoms of the northern peninsula. Accordingly, Islamic traditions cast Syria, like al-Andalus, as a land of jihad and site of future apocalyptic battles.

28. Saleh, "Paradise in an Islamic *'Ajā'ib* Work," 2:933–936, discusses the history of the distinct thematic strands and instances of their blending into one.

29. See Todorov, *The Fantastic*, 46.

30. Juberías, *La península imaginaria*, 306.

31. Ibid., 25–76, for a complete study of the "City of Copper."

32. For a complete study of the legend of "Solomon's Table," see ibid., 208–248, as well as Clarke, *The Muslim Conquest of Iberia*, 84–101; and López Lázaro, "Rise and Global Significance," 271.

33. On Alexander/Dhū l-qarnayn and his association with Mérida, Saragossa, and Toledo in Arabic sources, see Marín, "Legends on Alexander the Great in Moslem Spain," 71–89. On the "Pillars of Hercules," see Lévi-Provençal, "La description de l'Espagne d'Aḥmad al-Razi," 93–94. Juberías, *La península imaginaria*, 108–119, also reviews the various sources.

34. Of course, al-Andalus shares many of these traditions with distant frontier regions in the Islamic East that were also cast as sites of wonders.

35. On the political turmoil of the first half of the thirteenth century, see Kennedy, *Muslim Spain and Portugal*, 249–280.

36. Abū 'Abd Allāh Muḥammad ibn Aḥmad al-Qurṭubī, *Al-Tadhkīra fī aḥwāl al-mawtā wa-umūr al-ākhira* (Remembrance of the Affairs of the Dead and Matters of the Hereafter), 165–166.

37. Fierro and Faghia, "Un nuevo texto de tradiciones escatológicas sobre al-Andalus." See Fierro, "Ways of Connecting with the Past," 71–72, which traces al-Fakhkhār's sources back to the eleventh century.

38. The Eastern geographer's work connected physical geography and human geography as an early form of ethnography. On the abundant traditions regarding al-Andalus as a strange place of wonders, see Juberías, *La península imaginaria*, 249–343. Like Walid Saleh's literary categorization of *'ajā'ib* motifs, Nicola Clarke's discussion of Islamic courtly geographical tradition, *'ajā'ib* themes, and otherness from the perspective of the Islamic East, *Muslim Conquest of Iberia*, 69–83, differentiates classes of wonders—wonders of creation and the like from dangerous, threatening wonders associated with lands on the periphery of and beyond Islamdom. Clarke notes (81) that these traditions could serve to enhance al-Andalus's prestige.

39. Abū l-Ḥasan 'Alī ibn Bassām al-Shantarīnī, *Al-Dhakhīra fī maḥāsin ahl al-jazīra*, 1:14, cited and translated by Kassis, "Roots of Conflict," 153.

40. Al-Bakrī, *Jughāfiyat al-andalus*, 65–66; and al-Ḥimyarī, *Rawḍ al-mi'ṭār*, 1.

41. On the "encircling ocean" (*baḥr al-muḥīṭ*) in Islamic geographical and historical discourse, see Pinto, *Medieval Islamic Maps*, 147–185.

42. See Romm, "Continents, Climates, and Cultures," 221–223; Silverstein, "The Medieval Islamic Worldview," 274; and Hopkins, "Geographical and Navigational Literature," 303–304. Du Mensil, *Géographes d'al-Andalus*, 119–133, reviews this topos in the geographers' works.

43. Al-Maqqarī, *Nafḥ al-ṭīb*, 1:129–130, trans. Decter, "a Myrtle in the Forest," 137. Al-Andalus's merit based on its position in the perfect "clime" figures in al-Bakrī, *Jughāfiyat al-andalus*, 70.

44. Muḥammad ibn Aḥmad al-Muqaddasī, *Kitāb aḥsan al-taqāsīm fī maʿrifat al-āqālīm*, 215–248, trans. Collins, *The Best Divisions for Knowledge of the Regions*, 183.

45. Abū l-Qāsim ibn Ḥawqal, *Kitāb ṣūrat al-arḍ*, 108–109, trans. Marín, "Historical Images of al-Andalus and Andalusians," 409.

46. Abū l-Qāsim Muḥammad ibn Ḥawqal, *Kitāb ṣūrat al-arḍ* (1938), 111, cited by Constable, *Trade and Traders in Muslim Spain, 900–1500*, 22.

47. See Glick, "Tribal Landscapes of Islamic Spain," 123–126.

48. Glick, *Islamic and Christian Spain in the Early Middle Ages*, 69–70.

49. See Anderson, *The Early Islamic Villa in Early Medieval Spain*, 157, citing al-Fārābī (d. 950), *Fuṣūl al-madanī*, 50. The concept is more clearly articulated as the "Circle of Power" assigning "cultivators" a significant role alongside rulers and religious leaders in social well-being appears to be pre-Islamic Iranian in origin.

50. Abū Muḥammad ibn Qutayba, *Kitāb al-sulṭān* (The Book of Government) in *ʿUyūn al-Akhbār*, 1:63. See Black, *The History of Islamic Political Thought*, 55, citing Horovitz, "Ibn Qutaiba's ʿUyūn al-Akhbār," 193. My thanks to Joseph Lowry for alerting me to the notion of "Circle of Power" in Islamic thought and its Iranian background, and for pointing me to Anthony Black.

51. ʿArīb ibn Saʿd al-Kātib al-Qurṭubī, *Le Calendrier de Cordoue*. See Anderson, *The Islamic Villa*, 158–159. Christys, *Christians in al-Andalus, 711–1000*, 116–127, points to some oddities about the Arabic text of the Calendar and raises the possibility that an Andalusi Christian authored it.

52. Al-Maqqarī, *Nafḥ al-ṭīb*, 1:125–126.

53. Ibn Khaldūn, *The Muqaddimah*, 2:279.

54. Prado-Vilar, "Circular Visions of Fertility and Punishment," 21.

55. On which, see below, Chap. 3.

56. Martínez-Gros, *L'idéologie omeyyade*, 29. Except for Ibn Ḥabīb, all the Andalusi or Maghribi historiographical or annalistic sources treating genealogy date to the tenth century or later, and our interest here lies with the earliest. For a complete survey of the twenty-one Islamic sources on genealogy devoted to or including al-Andalus, see Viguera Molíns, "The Muslim Settlement of Spania/al-Andalus," 1:13–38.

57. See F. Rosenthal, *A History of Muslim Historiography*, 100; and Kennedy, "From Oral Tradition to Written Record in Arabic Genealogy."

58. Martínez-Gros, *L'idéologie omeyyade*, 29.

59. Ibn ʿAbd Rabbihi, *Al-ʿIqd al-farīd* (2006), 4:469–494, trans. Monroe, *Hispano-Arabic Poetry*, 74–129.

60. At issue was the Islamic debate going back to the period following the death of Muḥammad over whether legitimacy of the community's leadership is derived from immediate family kinship with the Prophet, the position of the Shīʿa, or from following the model of pious behavior that he set, the position of the Sunnis. See Afsaruddin, *Excellence and Precedence*, 146–196.

61. Monroe, "The Historical Arjūza of ibn ʿAbd Rabbihi," 67–95 (citation from 74).

62. Khoury, "The Meaning of the Great Mosque of Córdoba in the Tenth Century," 97 n62, suggests this line of thought and notes a few of the important later sources that follow

this pattern, such as Ibn ʿIdhārī's (al-Marrākushī) early fourteenth-century *al-Bayān al-mughrib* and Ibn al-Khaṭīb's (d. 1375) *Kitāb aʿmāl al-aʿlām*.

63. See Manzano-Moreno, "Oriental 'Topoi' in Andalusian Historical Sources," 43–44; and Safran, *The Second Umayyad Caliphate*, 130, in which Safran examines in detail the representational linkage in historiography between ʿAbd al-Raḥmān I and III. *Akhbār majmūʿa fī fatḥ al-andalus wa-dhikri umarāʾihā* briefly relates the conquest and its aftermath, followed by the era of the Umayyad emirate until ʿAbd al-Raḥmān III (119–140).

64. *Akhbār majmūʿa*, 107–108, discussed by Safran, *The Second Umayyad Caliphate*, 130–131.

65. Ibn al-Qūṭiyya, *Taʾrīkh iftitāḥ al-andalus*.

66. Ibn Ḥabīb, *Kitāb al-Taʾrīkh*, 140, cited by Clarke, *The Muslim Conquest of Iberia*, 34–35.

67. Ibn ʿIdhārī, *Al-Bayān al-mughrib fī akhbār mulūk al-andalus wa-l-maghrib*, 41.

68. *Akhbār majmūʿa*, 56; the story is also told with a few different details in *Fatḥ al-andalus*, 70 (64).

69. Ibn Ḥabīb, *Kitāb al-Taʾrīkh*, 136–137.

70. The story is preserved by al-Maqqarī, *Nafḥ al-ṭīb*, 1:254–255. See Delpech, "Du héros marqué au signe du Prophète," cited by García-Arenal, *Messianism and Puritanical Reform*, 81. Delpech observes the transcultural dimensions of this motif and cites Jabert, "The Birth-mark in Folk-Belief, Language, Literature and Fashion."

71. Clarke, *The Muslim Conquest of Iberia*, 34–35.

72. Ibn al-Qūṭiyya al-Qurṭubī, *Taʾrīkh iftitāḥ al-andalus* (1994), 76=*Early Islamic Spain: The History of Ibn al-Qūṭiyya*, 51.

73. Ibn al-Qūṭiyya, *Taʾrīkh* (1994), 76–77 = *The History of Ibn al-Qūṭiyya*, 52. It is subsequently reported in al-Maqqarī, *Nafḥ al-ṭīb*, 1:231, citing Ibn Bashkuwāl as his source.

74. Maḥmūd ʿAlī Makkī, "Egypt and the Origins of Spanish Arabic Historiography."

75. Ibn Ḥabīb, *Kitāb al-Taʾrīkh*, 136, on which, see Marín, "Ṣahāba et Tābiʿūn dans al-Andalus," 5–49; and Turki, "La vénération pour Malik et la physionomie du malikisme andalou."

76. Ibn al-Faraḍī, *Taʾrīkh ʿulamāʾ l-andalus*, 125, 212, 310.

77. Al-Maqqarī, *Nafḥ al-ṭīb*, 1:278, 288. Al-Maqqarī cites a now-lost work, *Ṭabaqāt al-fuqahāʾ wa-l-tābiʿīn*, by Ibn Ḥabīb, and another work, supposedly authored by Ibn Bashkuwāl, as among his sources.

78. Maribel Fierro interrogated these traditions regarding Muʿāwiya b. Ṣāliḥ and argues convincingly they are ninth-century projections. See Fierro, "Muʿāwiya b. Ṣāliḥ al-Haḍramī al-Ḥimṣī," and "The Introduction of Ḥadīth in al-Andalus," 70–73.

79. See Fierro, "Ways of Connecting with the Past," and "Anṣārīs in al-Andalus." For more on Andalusi origin myths, see Terés, "Linajes árabes de al-Andalus según la 'Yamhara' de Ibn Ḥazm."

80. Scholars of classical Islam frequently avoid using the terms "orthodox" and "orthodoxy," which, strictly speaking, apply to doctrine rather than law and practice central to Sunni Islam. On this question, see Henderson, *The Construction of Orthodoxy and Heresy*, 49–60.

81. See the classic study by F. Rosenthal, *Knowledge Triumphant*, and, for al-Andalus in particular, Heath, "Knowledge."

82. The notion *ṭalab al-ʿilm* can refer narrowly to travel in search of hadith traditions or, more broadly, to travel in search of religious knowledge in all the Islamic sciences. It can refer even to seeking knowledge in the general sense, as implied in the famous hadith in which the Prophet encourages Muslims to journey and "seek knowledge even to China."

83. Touati, *Islam and Travel in the Middle Ages*, 1.

84. Based on her study of the earliest biographical dictionary of Andalusi religious scholars compiled by Muḥammad ibn al-Ḥārith b. Asad al-Khushanī, *Akhbār al-fuqahā' wa-l-muḥaddithīn*, Ávila, "The Search for Knowledge," 126, notes that 225 of the work's 527 biographies explicitly mention that the subject traveled to the East in quest of knowledge (*raḥala ilā l-mashriq*). Lombard, *The Golden Age of Islam*, 80–83, among others, refers to the Andalusi processing of Arabo-Islamic culture during the ninth century as "orientalization," the conscious (and self-conscious) importation of Eastern models in government organization, religious studies, building style, and literature.

85. Such as the famous scholars Ziyād b. 'Abd al-Raḥmān al-Lakhmī, called Shabṭūn (d. second decade of ninth century). Ibn al-Faraḍī, *Ta'rīkh al-'ulamā'* (part 1), 154–155 (#458), who is said to have been among the Andalusis who studied with Mālik b. Anas in Medina and was responsible for transmitting his doctrines in al-Andalus and Abū Zakariyyā Yaḥyā b. Mālik (d. 985); Ibn al-Faraḍī, *Ta'rīkh al-'ulamā'* (part 2), 193 (#1599), who is credited with having "collected more hadiths than any of those who travelled East for the sake of study."

86. Forcada, "Books from Abroad."

87. See Ellenblum, *The Collapse of the Eastern Mediterranean.*

88. On new technologies in Andalusi agriculture, see Glick, *Islamic and Christian Spain in the Early Middle Ages*, 42–112, 253–268. On irrigation specifically, Glick, *From Muslim Fortress to Christian Castle*, 64–91.

89. Ibn al-Faraḍī, *Ta'rīkh al-'ulamā'* (part 2), 112–113 [#1400]. Ibn al-Faraḍī's habit of listing and treating *ghurabā'* separately was followed in subsequent Andalusi biographical dictionaries of religious scholars.

90. Fierro, "Heresy and Political Legitimacy in al-Andalus," 51–76, demonstrates that the religious situation in classical al-Andalus was more complex and nuanced than the traditional sources and modern scholarship assert. E.g., 'Abd al-Raḥmān III seems to have promoted the idea, if not the complete practice, of Sunni "pluralism" in counterpoint to Fāṭimid exclusive truth-claims. See Fierro's earlier discussion on Mālikism and legal pluralism in al-Andalus, "Why and How Do Religious Scholars Write About Themselves?"; and Aguadé, "Some Remarks About Sectarian Movements in al-Andalus."

91. Scholars disagree on exactly why al-Andalus embraced Mālikism. Fierro, "Proto-Malikis, Malikis, and Reformed Malikis in al-Andalus," examines the contending theories and proposes new ideas.

92. Fierro, "Heresy and Political Legitimacy in al-Andalus," 65, and "Why and How Do Religious Scholars Write About Themselves?," 415–416.

93. Muḥammad ibn Muḥammad al-Rā'ī, *Intiṣār al-faqīr al-sālik li-tarjīḥ madhhab al-imām al-kabīr mālik*, 165–166, trans. Dutton, *Original Islam*, 48. See also the *Intiṣār*'s passage (136–138, trans. Dutton, 32–34) on "The *Ḥadīth* of the Prophet About 'the People of the West.'"

94. The complex history of Andalusi Mālikism, with its modifications, reforms, and accommodation to Almohad rule and thought is perhaps a sign of Andalusi difference. It is a vast subject in and of itself. See Fierro, "Proto-Malikis, Malikis and Reformed Malikis"; and Urvoy, "*The 'Ulamā'* of al-Andalus."

95. Al-Muqaddasī, *Aḥsan al-taqāsīm*, 236–237. Fierro, *La heterodoxia en al-Andalus durante el periodo omeya*, 176, has shown that al-Muqaddasī's views were shaped by reports of Andalusi society under the reign of the chamberlain-cum-absolute ruler Muḥammad ibn Abī 'Āmir (al-Manṣūr, r. 977–1002).

96. Kennedy, *Muslim Spain and Portugal*, 41. Kennedy adds, contrary to the modern reputation of al-Andalus, "if Córdoba was spared the conflicts that convulsed Baghdad, it also saw none of the intellectual excitement that accompanied them."

97. Al-Ḥumaydī, *Jadhwat al-Muqtabis fī dhikr wulāt al-andalus*, 112–113. A translation by Dozy appeared in his book review of Renan, *Averroès et l'averroïsme*, 93. For a study of the account and its sources with a new translation, see M. Cook, "Ibn Saʿdī on Truth-Blindness," 169–178.

98. Ibn Jubayr, *Riḥla*, 87. Ibn Jubayr is discussed below, in Chap. 5.

99. Their literary intellectual counterparts joined them in fashioning the image and disseminating the reputation of al-Andalus as an exemplary site for the cultivation of various forms of sophisticated inquiry and scientific and humanistic knowledge and literary creativity, as we shall see below, in Chap. 3.

100. Fierro, "Heresy and Political Legitimacy," 61–63, and "Opposition to Sufism in al-Andalus." Idem, *ʿAbd al-Raḥmān III*, 23, explains the sociopolitical benefit to the Umayyads of the adoption of Mālikī law as it pertains to converts who became clients of the religious community in its entirety, not of specific Arab tribes. On the Umayyads and Mālikism in al-Andalus, see Idris, "Reflections on Mālikism Under the Umayyads of Spain."

101. Kennedy, *Muslim Spain and Portugal*, 90–91, cites al-Rāzī (*apud* Ibn Ḥayyān), *al-Muqtabis* 5:160–161: "benefitting the people and completing the attributes of his sovereignty."

102. Khoury, "The Meaning of the Great Mosque of Córdoba," 86. Zadeh, "From Drops of Blood," speaks of the codex as "a broader metaphor of exchange and rivalry along the western frontier of Islam" (323). The ʿUthmānic *muṣḥaf* also turns up in other Islamic lands. See Meri, *The Cult of Saints Among Muslims and Jews in Medieval Syria*, 114–116.

103. Al-Maqqarī, *Nafḥ al-ṭīb*, 4:460.

104. Al-Sharīf al-Idrīsī, *Waṣf al-masjid al-jāmiʿ bi-qurṭuba* (Description de la Grande Mosquée de Cordoue), 8–11, cited by Dodds, *Architecture and Ideology in Early Medieval Spain*, 100–101; 167. See Khoury, "The Meaning of the Great Mosque of Córdoba," 80–81; and Dodds, "The Great Mosque of Córdoba."

105. Fierro, "The Movable *Minbar* in Córdoba."

106. Fierro, "Red and Yellow," 79–83.

107. Ibid., 81. Another, different dimension of the Umayyad quest for legitimacy involved the diplomatic recognition and symbolic prestige afforded them by the Byzantine emperors from the time of al-Ḥakam I in the mid-ninth century. See Wasserstein, "Byzantium and al-Andalus."

108. M. Weber, *Economy and Society*, 215.

109. S. Stetkevych, "The Poetics of Ceremony and the Competition for Legitimacy."

110. Prado-Vilar, "Circular Visions of Fertility and Punishment"; and Holod, "Luxury Arts of the Caliphal Period."

111. Barceló, "The Manifest Caliph."

112. Anderson, *The Islamic Villa in Early Medieval Iberia*, examines the various symbolic and political functions of the Andalusi *munya* (137–167). See also Ruggles, *Gardens, Landscape, and Vision in the Palaces of Islamic Spain*, which examines many of the same matters.

113. Ibn al-Faraḍī, *Taʾrīkh al-ʿulamāʾ*, part 1, 69 (#223). It should be noted that in al-Fārābī's epistemology, the linguistic sciences (*ʿulūm al-lugha*) were considered foundational to all other scientific pursuits. See Netton, *Al-Fārābī and His School*, 44–45, discussing the place of language study in *The Catalogue of the Sciences* (*Iḥṣāʾ l-ʿulūm*).

114. Vallejo Triano, "Madīnat al-Zahrā'," and "Madinat al-Zahra'"; Fierro, "Madīnat al-Zahrā', Paradise and the Fatimids," offers another theory of the significance of the complex, its decorative elements, and its name, specifically related to the Umayyads' rivalry with the Fāṭimids and recent turns of events in the Fāṭimids' favor.

115. Wasserstein, "The Library of al-Ḥakam II al-Mustanṣir and the Culture of Islamic Spain"; and al-Khushanī, *Kitāb al-qudāt bi-qurṭuba*, 5–6.

116. Fierro, "Heresy and Political Legitimacy in al-Andalus," 68.

117. I use these terms in a somewhat more capacious sense than Bourdieu, *The Field of Cultural Production*, 270, who conceived of them for theorizing and critiquing the material political economy of artistic production and for those "trading in the sacred" (76) but who do not create it.

118. Manifestations of the trope after the tenth century are typically ascribed to nostalgia for the grandeur of the Umayyad caliphal age. Chapter 3 below explores additional ways of understanding the trope's social agency in the post-Umayyad period.

119. Vesser, *The New Historicism*, xi, observes: "every act of unmasking, critique, and opposition uses the tools it condemns."

CHAPTER 2

Notes to epigraphs: Moses ibn Ezra, *Kitāb al-muḥāḍara*, 54 [29a]; and Schirmann, *Hebrew Poetry in Spain and Provence*, 1:38 (vv. 52–54).

1. Benbassa, *Suffering as Identity*, 51. For important reflections on theme of exile with reference to medieval Iberia, see Yerushalmi, "Exile and Expulsion in Jewish History." On the broader, transcultural significance of diaspora, see Barkan and Shelton, *Borders, Exiles, Diasporas*, 5. For studies of the specifically Jewish issue in the modern period, see Eisen, *Modern Jewish Reflections on Homelessness and Homecoming*; and Ezrahi, *Booking Passage*.

2. Noted by Wasserstein, "The Muslims and the Golden Age of the Jews in al-Andalus," 194.

3. On the various estimates by scholars such as Ashtor and Torres Balbás that amount to guesses, see Wasserstein, "Jewish Elites in al-Andalus," 106–109. In "The Muslims and the Golden Age of the Jews," 181, Wasserstein cautions us regarding unsubstantiated overstatements about westward migration of Jews to al-Andalus.

4. Goldberg, *Trade and Institutions in the Medieval Mediterranean*, 313–319, studies economic documents from the Geniza and points to the changing status of al-Andalus in East–West trade, with a proportional decline of Geniza traders doing business there in the later eleventh century.

5. See García Iglesias, *Los judíos en la España antigua*, 44–81 (Roman Hispania), 161–181 (Visigothic Iberia).

6. On the Jews of the Iberian Peninsula before al-Andalus, see Katz, *The Jews in the Visigothic and Frankish Kingdoms of Spain and Gaul*; and Bachrach, "A Reassessment of Visigothic Jewish Policy," 589–711.

7. For a source-based summary of the history of rabbinical scholarship in Sefarad to the eleventh century, see Margaliot, *Sefer hilkhot ha-nagid*, 1–10. For more details on these ties to the Pumbedita and Sura academies, based on *responsa* and correspondence, including appeals for financial support going back to the turn of the ninth century, see D. Rosenthal, "Rav

Paltoi Gaon and His Place in the Halakhic Tradition," 603–609. My thanks to Marc Herman for bringing this article to my attention.

8. The fabulous legend of Naṭrūnai's paranormal journey (*qᵉfiṣat ha-derekh*) to al-Andalus is related in an early twelfth-century source: Judah ben Barzillai al-Bargeloni, *Peirush sefer yᵉṣirah*, 103–104, 321. Rosenthal, "Rav Paltoi Gaon," 607, cites another fantastic legend: the geonic tradition that the sages of Palestine advised Alexander the Great, who sought to ascend to the heavens. They reportedly counseled him to go to Spain to consult with the wise scholars who had resided there since the First Exile. A brief (non-fantastical) mention of Naṭrūnai leaving Baghdad for the Maghrib is found in *Iggeret Shᵉrira Ga'on*, in *Mediaeval Jewish Chronicles*, 1:36 = *Iggeret shᵉrira ga'on* (1921), 104. See also Ginzberg, *Geonica*, 1:17–20. For details on the exilarchs ("Ro'sh ha-golah"; "Reish gālūtā"; "Head of the Diaspora") and their office, see Gil, *Jews in Islamic Countries in the Middle Ages*, 83–116. On the exilarch as the "secular" of two ecumenical authorities, see Goitein, *A Mediterranean Society*, 2:17–23.

9. Judah ben Barzillai al-Bargeloni, *Sefer ha-'Ittim*, 267, who ascribes his source for the tradition to Samuel the Nagid.

10. Ashtor, *The Jews of Moslem Spain*, 1:139. For particulars on the geonim, their authority, and communal and literary activities, see Brody, *The Geonim of Babylonia and the Shaping of Medieval Jewish Culture*; Gil, *Jews in Islamic Countries*, 117–206; and Goitein, *A Mediterranean Society*, 2:5–17. The political and economic tensions between the Babylonian and Palestinian Jewish centers of authority were naturally grounded in differences in halakhic opinion and practice. See Margulies, "The Differences Between Babylonian and Palestinian Jews."

11. See G. Cohen, *The Book of Tradition*, xvi–xxvi, for examination of Ibn Daud's intellectual background.

12. Abraham ibn Daud, *Sefer ha-qabbalah*, 79.

13. Ibid., 78.

14. Ashtor, "Un Mouvement migratoire au haut Moyen Age"; and Baron, "Saadia's Communal Activities," 99–100.

15. Ben-Sasson, "Varieties of Intercommunal Relations in the Geonic Period," 17–18.

16. See Fishman, *Becoming the People of the Talmud*, 65–76.

17. Ben-Sasson, "Religious Leadership in Islamic Lands," 1:183–187.

18. Grief, "Reputation and Coalitions in Medieval Trade," 861.

19. Scheindlin, "Merchants and Intellectuals, Rabbis and Poets," is devoted to the broad sweep of Jewish culture under classical Islam, including North Africa, and so represents an important departure from convention. My own earlier work, *The Compunctious Poet*, acknowledges and details the significance of philological scholarship in North Africa for developments in al-Andalus but still adheres too closely to the prevailing narrative.

20. The comment is found in the introduction to Abraham ibn Ezra, *Sefer Mo'znayim* (also known as *Mo'znei lᵉshon ha-qodesh* [Scales of the Holy Language]), Jiménez Paton), 4 (Hebrew section), in which Ibn Ezra reviews the history of the sages of Hebrew grammar from Sa'adia to Sefarad. Following Sa'adia, fourteen of fifteen are Maghribi or Andalusi scholars.

21. For recent studies of Sa'adia incorporating findings from the Cairo Geniza unavailable to earlier scholars, see Brody, *Rabbi Sa'adia Gaon*; Stroumsa, *Saadia Gaon*; Steiner, *A Biblical Translation in the Making*; Ben-Shammai, "The Exegetical and Philosophical Writing of Sa'adya Gaon"; and Tobi, "Sa'adia Gaon, Poet-*Paytan*."

22. Dāwūd ibn Marwān al-Muqammaṣ, *'Ishrūn maqāla* (Twenty Chapters).

23. On al-Qūmisī, see Nemoy, *Karaite Anthology*, 30–41; and Polliak, *The Karaite Tradition of Arabic Bible Translation*, 23–36.

24. For a brief review, see Khan, "The Early Karaite Grammatical Tradition," 72–80; for a representative text and study, idem, *The Early Karaite Tradition of Hebrew Grammatical Thought*.

25. Aharon Maman and others identify Abū l-Faraj Hārūn ibn al-Faraj with Abraham ibn Ezra's unnamed "Jerusalemite scholar" in the introduction to *Sefer Mo'znayim*, 4 [Hebrew]. See Maman, *Comparative Semitic Philology*, 375–380. For a roster of Karaites whom Ibn Ezra mentions, always unfavorably, in his commentaries on biblical books, see Melammed, *Bible Commentators*, 676–678. In the introduction to his *Commentary on the Torah*, 1:2–6 ["the second approach"], the staunchly Rabbanite Ibn Ezra censures the Karaites' interpretation of the Hebrew Bible for their rejection of the (Rabbanite) transmission of oral tradition.

26. Drory, *Models and Contacts*, 146–157.

27. Notable exceptions are the intellectual historians Kraemer, "Maimonides and the Spanish Aristotelian School," 40, for whom, following Maimonides' experience and thought, "Andalusia and the Maghrib formed a single *Kulturkreis*"; and Stroumsa, *Maimonides in His World*, 23.

28. Abraham ibn Daud, *Sefer ha-qabbalah*, 44.

29. Parts of the Judeo-Arabic original were published by Friedlander, "The Arabic Original of the Report of R. Nathan Hababli," 747–761. A medieval Hebrew translation appears in Neubauer, *Mediaeval Jewish Chronicles*, 2:78–88. See Ben-Sasson, "The Structure, Goals, and Content of the Story of Nathan ha-Babli."

30. The standard work on Israeli is Altmann and Stern, *Isaac Israeli*.

31. *Le Commentaire sur le Livre de la Création de Dunash Ben Tamim de Kairouan (Xe siècle)*. See also Hayman, *Sefer yeṣira*, 29–30. Ibn Tamīm's other philological and scientific works are no longer extant.

32. Sa'adia's theological work is *Kitāb al-amānāt wa-l-i'tiqādāt*, trans. as *The Book of Beliefs and Opinions*.

33. Schlanger, *La Philosophie de Salomon Ibn Gabirol*, 97–101; and Joseph ibn Ṣaddīq, *The Microcosm of Joseph ibn Ṣaddīq*. By the eleventh century, al-Andalus had supplanted North Africa as well as the Islamic East as the principal locus for Jewish theological speculation and philosophical activity.

34. Judah ibn Quraysh, *Risāla*. Zwiep, *Mother of Reason and Revelation*, studies the history of Jewish philological research and demonstrates its centrality to intellectual thought in general. Alfonso, *Islamic Culture Through Jewish Eyes*, 10–14, examines the Jews' discourse on language and the process of Jewish identity construction in al-Andalus.

35. David ben Abraham al-Fāsī, *Kitāb Jāmi' l-alfāẓ*.

36. These details are studied by Maman, *Comparative Semitic Philology in the Middle Ages*; and Sáenz-Badillos, "Menahem and Dunash in Search of the Foundations of the Hebrew Language." In this respect, too, Sa'adia and his followers were adapting to Hebrew the Arabo-Islamic doctrine *i'jāz al-qur'ān*, the "inimitable wondrousness of the form and content of the Qur'ān," espoused in exegetical literature by the end of the ninth century, on which, see Grunebaum, "I'djāz," and Aleem, "'Ijazu' l-Qur'an."

37. Relying on the testimony of the acrostic "signature" in one of his liturgical poems as well as a comment by Moses ibn Ezra in the twelfth century, a few scholars conclude that Dūnash ben Labrāṭ was born in Baghdad into a Maghribi family that had migrated east. See Schirmann, *The History of Hebrew Poetry in Muslim Spain*, 119–120.

38. First articulated in his Hebrew introduction to *Sefer ha-Egron* (*Kitāb uṣūl al-shi'r al-'ibrānī*); and Dotan, *The Dawn of Hebrew Linguistics*.

39. The ambiguous comment that his teacher supposedly made is reported by Dūnash, *Sefer t^eshuvot dūnash ha-lewi ben labrāṭ 'al rabbi sa'adiyah ga'on*, 31. See Schirmann-Fleischer, *The History of Hebrew Poetry in Muslim Spain*, 121. Some scholars dispute the identification of this text with Dūnash. See Sáenz-Badillos, "Sobre el autor de las *Tešubot 'al Se'adyah*."

40. Menaḥem Ben Sarūq, *Maḥberet*.

41. *Tešubot de Dūnash ben Labrāṭ* is a critique of Menaḥem's *Maḥberet*. Their respective students' ensuing literary row: *Tešubot de los discípulos de Menaḥem contra Dunaš Ben Labraṭ*; and *Teshubot de Yehudi Ben Sheshet*. Drory, *Models and Contacts*, 191–207, explains the intricate linguistic and phonetic details of Dūnash's prosodic system and the different explanations that scholars have given for the metrical choices involved. See also Schirmann-Fleischer, *History of Hebrew Poetry in Muslim Spain*, 119–143.

42. Solomon ibn Gabirol, Brody-Schirmann, *Secular Poems of Ibn Gabirol*, 5; and Moses ibn al-Taqāna, Schirmann, *Hebrew Poetry in Spain and Provence*, 1:287.

43. Moses ibn Ezra, *Kitāb al-muḥāḍara*, 58; and Judah al-Ḥarizi, *Taḥk^emoni*, 109.

44. Ibn Daud, *Sefer ha-qabbalah*, 73 (trans. G. Cohen, *Book of Tradition*, 102).

45. Robles, *Tešubot de los discípulos de Menaḥem contra Dunaš Ben Labraṭ*, 15–16; and Sáenz-Badillos, "Los discípulos de Menahem sobre métrica hebrea." The debate had other implications as well, insofar as it involved two divergent theories of the origins and nature of language, natural or conventional. See Sáenz-Badillos, "Menahem and Dunaš in Search of the Foundations of Hebrew Language."

46. Text: Sáenz-Badillos, *Teshubot de Dunash*, 5; Dūnash, *Poems*, 73, lines 15–16; and Valle Rodríguez, *El Diván Poético de Dunash Ben Labraṭ*, 508. Allony (Dūnash, *Poems*, 139), followed by Ray, "The Jews of al-Andalus," 258, note the putdown of the "sages of Sefarad."

47. Important exceptions to this general rule came in the form of highly accomplished Eastern poets such as Moses ben Abraham Dar'ī (twelfth-century Egypt) who embraced Andalusi style and the scholar Tanḥūm ben Joseph Yerushalmi (thirteenth-century Egypt) who was a staunch devotee of Andalusi Jewish culture in all its respects. At the same time, Judah al-Ḥarizi, who left Christian Toledo for the Islamic East in the early thirteenth century, complains about the supposedly very sorry state of Hebrew knowledge, linguistic studies, and poetic composition among the Easterners he encountered, studied below, Chap. 5.

48. Dotan, "The Vicissitudes of Arabic Impact on Hebrew Language Study in the East and in Spain," 135–136.

49. Ray, "The Jews of al-Andalus." G. Cohen, "The Story of the Four Captives," 179, 205–206n214, was the first to speak of Sefardi "nativism" in interpreting this controversy as well as the conflict between the Ibn Shaprūṭ–Ibn Falīja faction against the Ibn Jau party and the struggle between their respective candidates—Ḥanokh b. Moses (who apparently formalized his ties to the Ibn Falīja family through marriage) and Isaac (ben Jospeh) ibn Abītūr—to assume leadership of the rabbinical academy. Cohen cites Salo Baron's earlier observation of Iraqi Jewish nativism in response to the rise of the Egyptian (i.e., "foreign") Sa'adia Gaon assuming leadership of the Sura academy. See Baron, "Saadia's Communal Activities," 422n93.

50. Ray, "The Jews of al-Andalus," 255.

51. E.g., Dūnash ben Labrāṭ, *Poems* (1947), 70, lines 35–38. So, too, Ḥasdai ibn Shaprūṭ backed his son Ḥanokh ben Moses over the "local" candidate, Joseph ibn Abītūr in the struggle over succession in rabbinical leadership following Moses ben Ḥanokh's death.

52. The maneuver to import or welcome distinguished rabbinic talent to enhance the local scene was not unique to tenth-century al-Andalus but commonplace among the Jewish communities of Islamdom.

53. Although there are problems with its dating, among other difficulties, scholars such as Allony, "Judah ben David and Judah Ḥayyūj," identify Ḥayyūj (full name: Abū Zakariyya Yaḥyā ben David al-Fāsī) with the Judah ben David who was among the partisans of Menaḥem ibn Sarūq.

54. Abraham ibn Ezra, *Sefer Mo'znayim*, 5.

55. Judah Ḥayyūj (Abū Zakariyya ibn Dāwūd of Fez), *The Weak and Geminative Verbs in Hebrew*; *Three Treatises on Hebrew Grammar by R. Judah Hayyuj*; *Kitāb al-nutaf*; and *El Libro de Hayyūy*.

56. Cano, *Yishaq ibn Jalfun*; and Schirmann-Fleischer, *The History of Hebrew Poetry in Muslim Spain*, 172–182.

57. See Brener, *Isaac ibn Khalfun*.

58. Samuel the Nagid, *Ben Tehillim*, 256–260 (#107), composed a poetic letter of condolence in Aramaic to Ḥananel ben Ḥushiel on the occasion of his father's death; trans. Kobler, *Letters of Jews Through the Ages*, 1:135–138.

59. Beeri, "'Eli he-Ḥaver ben 'Amram," 279–280, observes that al-Andalus and Palestine competed as centers of Hebrew poetry in the tenth century. Their divergent preferences in matters of form and content reflect the mutual ambivalence with which Eastern and Western Hebrew poets were regarded. By the eleventh century, the commanding influence of the forms and some of the content of Andalusi Hebrew poetry had penetrated the East.

60. Thanks to the Cairo Geniza, it is now apparent that other eleventh-century liturgical poets of the East, such as David ben (Ḥezekiah) ha-Nasi, were well aware of and guardedly experimenting with aspects of Andalusi Hebrew-style poetics. See Beeri, "Between Spain and the East," and "*Tochakha*: Un poème de remontrance de David Hanassi."

61. *T'shuvot ha-g'onim*, 27 (#60).

62. *Iggeret rav sh'rira ga'on*, 15. Writing a century after the disappearance of the Iraqi geonim, Abraham ibn Daud constructs a view of the history of rabbinic scholarship that implicitly asserts that authority was transferred from Babylonia to al-Andalus in the tenth and eleventh centuries. According to Ibn Daud's account, the Jews of North Africa also achieved de facto separation from the Iraqi centers about the same time, with Ḥushiel ben Elḥanan's establishment of a rabbinic academy in Qayrawān. Whether Ibn Daud's account is historically accurate is less important than what it tells us about the rise of regional rabbinic centers in North Africa and al-Andalus in the tenth century: their first teachers came to them from Baghdad, indicating that rabbinic learning literally was in the process of passing from East to West.

63. Nissim also composed a Judeo-Arabic folkloristic-didactic work modeled after the Arabic genre *al-faraj ba'da shidda* ("relief after adversity"), in *Rav Nissim Gaon: Five Books—Remnants from His Compositions*.

64. *Perush ha-Mishnah*, 47. Twersky, *Introduction to the Code of Maimonides* (*Mishneh Torah*), 160.

65. Ta-Shma, *Talmudic Commentary in Europe and North Africa*, 145–153.

66. While the history of Hebrew poetry in al-Andalus and the Islamic East has benefited immensely from the discovery of texts in the Geniza, it has been underutilized for what it reveals about the cultural contacts between the Jews of the Islamic West and East, as opposed to the well-documented and studied socioeconomic interconnections.

67. Goitein and Friedman, *India Traders of the Middle Ages*, 9.

68. On Jewish physicians in general, see Goitein, *A Mediterranean Society*, 2:240–261. On Abraham ibn 'Aṭā, the illustrious "N[e]gid ha-golah" (early eleventh century), see Goitein, "Three Letters from Qayrawān Addressed to Joseph ben Jacob ben 'Awkal"; and Hirschberg, *A History of the Jews in North Africa*, 1:112–113, 198–199, 211–213. Comparable figures are Abū l-Faḍl Mevorakh b. Sa'adia in Fāṭimid Egypt and Moses Maimonides in Ayyūbid Egypt, among others.

69. Documents: Mann, *Texts and Studies in Jewish History and Literature*, 1:3–30. For the comparative dimension, see Decter, "Before Caliphs and Kings." An expansive and frequently imagined romanticized portrait of Ḥasdai ibn Shaprūṭ may be found in Ashtor, *Jews of Moslem Spain*, 1:155–227. Aside from Abraham ibn Daud's remarks about Ḥasdai, see the comments of Moses ibn Ezra, *Kitāb al-muḥāḍara wa-l-mudhākara*, 57; and Judah al-Ḥarizi, *Taḥk[e]moni*, [12] 212, lines 80ff., discussed below, in Chaps. 4 and 5.

70. Wasserstein, *Rise and Fall of the Party-Kings*, 196, casts doubt on the historicity of Muslim accounts of Ḥasdai's diplomatic mission to the Byzantines. Wasserstein, "The Muslims and the Golden Age of the Jews in al-Andalus," 186, is also skeptical about reports of Ḥasdai's high rank. For a contrasting view, see Stroumsa, "Thinkers of 'This Peninsula,'" 49–51.

71. Ibn Abī Uṣaybi'a, *'Uyūn al-anbā' fī ṭabaqāt al-aṭibbā'*, part 2, 50. This detail of the portrait of Ḥasdai appears tailored to fit the familiar mold of the Jewish physician-scholar of religious law. See also the passage regarding Ḥasdai in Ṣā'id ibn Aḥmad al-Andalusī, *Kitāb ṭabaqāt al umam*, 81.

72. According to a poem by Dūnash, Schirmann, *Hebrew Poetry in Spain and Provence*, 1:37 (v. 38), Iraqi geonic authorities may have conferred upon Ḥasdai the title "Ro'sh kallah," normally reserved for a high-ranking rabbinic scholar. No doubt they endeavored to preserve their formerly close ties to the Andalusi Jewish community and its leaders. See Bareket, "*Head of the Jews* in Spain in Comparison with *Head of the Jews* in Egypt." By the eleventh century, the title "nagid," a territorial head of the Jews without a genealogical connection to the line of David, appeared exclusively in the Islamic West—specifically, al-Andalus and Egypt. On the values and symbolic language of literary representations of Jewish political legitimacy in the Mediterranean lands of classical Islam, see Decter, *Dominion Built of Praise*, 90–127.

73. Abraham ibn Daud, *Sefer ha-qabbalah*, 42, 49, 68, 73. Ibn Daud (51) reports that following Ḥasdai's death, the Umayyad vice-regent nominally ruling on behalf of the minor caliph Hishām II, al-Manṣūr (ibn abī 'Āmir), appointed the silk merchant Jacob ibn Jau *nasi* of the Jews "from Sijilmassa to the river Duero." See Wasserstein, *Rise and Fall of the Party-Kings*, 196–197.

74. On this office, see Franklin, *This Noble House*.

75. Notable examples from the tenth century are the Fāṭimid Jewish courtiers Menashshe ibn al-Qazzāz and Abū Sa'd al-Tustarī. On Ibn al-Qazzāz, see Rustow, *Heresy and the Politics of the Community*, 125–132. On al-Tustarī, see Gil, *The Tustaris*.

76. See Scheiber and Malachi, "Letter from Sicily to Ḥasdai ibn Shaprut"; and J. Mann, "Ḥisdai ibn Shaprūṭ and His Diplomatic Intervention on Behalf of the Jews in Christian Europe," in J. Mann, *Texts and Studies in Jewish History and Literature*, 1:3–30.

77. Recall that Ḥasdai ibn Shaprūṭ and Andalusi Jewish social and intellectual elites regarded "Sefarad" as equivalent to al-Andalus. Obviously, "Sefarad" came to connote the mental and geographic space occupied by Iberian Jews in the Christian kingdoms following the Almohad invasion of the mid-twelfth century. See Decter, *Iberian Jewish Literature*, 5–6.

As late as the fourth decade of the twelfth century, Moses ibn Ezra, an exile from Almoravid Granada living in the Christian north, asserts (highlighted in an epigraph to the Chapter): "Sefarad is al-Andalus in the language of the Arabs."

78. Ed. Ḳoḳovtsov, *Evreisko-khazarskaia*, 10–19. On the manuscript history of the correspondence and discoveries in the Cairo Geniza, see Golb and Pritsak, *Khazarian Hebrew Documents of the Tenth Century*, trans. Kobler, *Letters of Jews Through the Ages*, 1:98–106.

79. The eleventh-century pietist Baḥya ibn Paqūda of Saragossa, *Al-Hidāya ilā farā'iḍ al-qulūb*, 119 (The Book of Direction to the Duties of the Heart, 171), strikes a note similar to Ḥasdai's, albeit without reference to the community's noble origins.

80. Schirmann, *Hebrew Poetry in Spain and Provence*, 1:35–40. The twelfth- to thirteenth-century author Judah al-Ḥarizi (*Taḥkᵉmoni*, chap. 18, in Schirmann, *Hebrew Poetry*, 3:135) paid tribute to Ibn Shaprūṭ and his instrumental role in the establishment of Andalusi Jewish society and culture as follows: "He convened around him every gaon and rabbinic scholar, from Christendom and Islamdom, from East and West and set a table of his generous bounty before them." For a complete discussion of al-Ḥarizi's look back westward, see below, Chap. 5.

81. On the Khazars, see Zohori, *The Khazars, Their Conversion to Judaism and History in Hebrew Historiography*; D. M. Dunlop, *The History of the Jewish Khazars*; and Golden et al., *The World of the Khazars*.

82. Ḳoḳovtsov, *Evreisko-khazarskaia*, 10–19, trans. Kobler, *Letters of Jews Through the Ages*, 1:98–106.

83. "Afudat nezer lᵉ-sheveṭ moshlim," in Schirmann, *Hebrew Poetry in Spain and Provence*, 1:6–8. See Alfonso, "Constructions of Exile in Medieval Hebrew Literature," and "The Uses of Exile in Poetic Discourse."

84. Alfonso, *Islamic Culture Through Jewish Eyes*, 89–93, following Cohen and Goitein who argued that *Sefer ha-qabbalah* relayed an esoteric messianic message, reads these texts as reflecting an eschatological urgency among Andalusi Jewish elites. She further suggests that Ḥasdai's messianism parallels in the Umayyad quest for Islamic legitimacy.

85. I am aware, of course, that this reading is dependent upon the conventional dating of the document, something that the late manuscript does not necessarily support.

86. Text: Poznański, "Ibn Balᶜam on the Minor Prophets," 34–35.

87. It is worth recalling that in his famous *responsum* to Obadiah, the proselyte (*Tᵉshuvot ha-rambam*, 2:548–550 [#293]) Maimonides associated himself with this hallowed tradition: "Thus says Moses b. R. Maimon of the descendants of the exile from Jerusalem in Sefarad" (548).

88. Wasserstein, "The Khazars and the World of Islam," 381–382.

89. Gil, "The Babylonian Yeshivot," 82.

90. *Iggeret rav shᵉrira ga'on* (1991), 143–144 = *Epistle of Sherira Gaon* (1921), 104.

91. Judah ben Barzillai al-Bargeloni, *Sefer ha-'ittim*, 267. Al-Bargeloni amplified the tradition by elevating Naṭrūnai's appearance in al-Andalus to a "miraculous journey." See Lewin, "Geniza Fragments."

92. Text: Ginzberg, *Ginzei Schechter*, 2:139–147, 504–573; and Spiegel, "On the Polemic of Pirqoy ben Baboy." For a study of the sources, see Brody, *Pirqoy ben Baboy and the History of Internal Polemics in Judaism*.

93. Brody, *The Geonim of Babylonia*, 26–30, summarizes the general usefulness and problems of this source. Ben-Sasson, "The Structure, Goals, and Contents of the Story of Nathan ha-Babli," published Judeo-Arabic fragments of the original.

94. Nathan the Babylonian, *Seder 'olam zuṭa*, in Neubauer, *Mediaeval Jewish Chronicles*, 2:78. The specific issues in the dispute apparently involved 'Uqba's attempt to alter the traditional formula for dividing diaspora contributions to the two rabbinic academies.

95. The highly doubtful historicity of this figure is secondary to the legend, for which there is evidence from before the mid-twelfth century with the so-called *Book of Eldad*, ed. Epstein, *Eldad ha-Dani*, 22–29. For the jumbled history of the fanciful tradition, see Jacobs, *Reorienting the East*, 43–44, 186–187, 196, and Jacobs's extensive bibliographical notes. Ben-Dor Benite, *The Ten Lost Tribes*, 86–100, reads three Eldad traditions (*The Book of Eldad*; the Qayrawānīs' correspondence with Ṣemaḥ Gaon, Epstein, *Eldad*, 3–8; and a later text ascribed to the Jews of Qayrawān, Epstein, *Eldad*, 83–136, with Epstein's notes in which Eldad describes for them certain Jewish rituals slightly inconsistent with rabbinic practice) as an ethnographer and identifies Eldad as a historical figure who was actually a trickster.

96. Epstein, *Eldad*, 25 (#11).

97. The correspondence with a (certain) R. Ṣemaḥ Gaon survived only in late manuscripts, casting serious doubts on its historicity. See Jacobs, *Reorienting*, 240n111. For English translations, see Neubauer, "Where Are the Ten Tribes?"; and Adler, *Jewish Travellers in the Middle Ages*, 15–21.

98. Judah ben Barzillai al-Bargeloni (b. 1070), text ed. Ḳoḳovtsov, *Evreisko-khazarskaia*, 127–128, was the first author to cite the Ibn Shaprūṭ–King Joseph correspondence. On al-Bargeloni's comments about the authenticity of the tradition and the historicity of the episode, see Assaf, *Texts and Studies in Jewish History*, 91–99. Abraham ibn Daud, *Sefer ha-qabbalah*, 64, cited it shortly thereafter. The most famous and extensive, albeit literary, reference to the Khazar king is Judah Halevi, *The Book of Refutation and Proof on the Despised Faith* (*The Khazarī Book*).

99. Ḳoḳovtsov, *Evreisko-khazarskaia*, 18, trans. Kobler, *Letters of Jews Through the Ages*, 105. Some readers see it as a confirmation that Eldad visited al-Andalus. All we can say with certainty is that a tradition developed about his visit to the peninsula.

100. *Seder Rav 'Amram*, ed. Goldschmidt.

101. The forms in which it has come down to us do not represent the original text but various adaptations: Ginzberg, *Geonica*, 1:119–154, 2:301–345; and Kobler, *Letters of Jews Through the Ages*, 75–76. Brody, "The Enigma of *Seder Rav 'Amram*," 21–34, examines the many problems with the textual history of the material that has come down to us.

102. Edited by Gil, *In the Kingdom of Ishmael*, 2:63, doc. 19.

103. Goitein, *Mediterranean Society*, 1:30, 400n2.

104. Gil, "The Babylonian Yeshivot and the Maghrib in the Early Middle Ages," documents the primary relationship with the Sura academy until the first half of the tenth century, when contacts with Pumbedita were initiated.

105. Writing two centuries later and in a radically different historical context, the chronicler Abraham ibn Daud (*Sefer ha-qabbalah*, 63–66) credited Providence for the creation of a new center in al-Andalus for rabbinic scholarship of the highest order. For Ibn Daud and historiographers who follow him, Moses ben Ḥanokh's arrival in the tenth century to serve as head of the rabbinical academy at Lucena marked the (arguably exaggerated) launch of Sefarad's divinely orchestrated autonomy from Iraqi geonic authority.

106. *Ṭabaqāt al-umam*, 88–89, trans. Wasserstein, "The Muslims and the Golden Age," 189–190.

107. Mann, *Texts and Studies*, 1:121. In the eleventh century, there is evidence of Andalusi Jewish sensitivity to its movement toward virtual independence from the authority of the Iraqi academies. See below, Chap. 3.

108. See Ben-Sasson, *Emergence of the Local Jewish Community in the Muslim World*, 173, 237; Fishman, *Becoming the People of the Talmud*, 65–90; and Herman, "Situating Maimonides' Approach to the Oral Torah in Its Andalusian Context," identify additional ways in which Maghribi-Andalusi rabbinic tradition charted an independent course in departing from the geonim and adopted a Mālikī-like epistemology and reliance on rabbinic oral tradition, with its unimpeded chain of transmission. Herman (38–39) examines a noteworthy illustration involving interpretation of the Talmudic dictum "A sage is superior to a prophet" by the eleventh-century Andalusi rabbinic master of Lucena, Isaac ibn Ghiyāth, subsequently cited by Baḥya ibn Paqūda, Joseph ibn Migash, and Moses ibn Ezra.

109. Many scholars have made this observation previously. Wasserstein, "The Muslims and the Golden Age," 194, senses more than a hint of this Andalusi-centered worldview in Ṣā'id's idiosyncratic portrait of Ibn Shaprūṭ.

110. On the institution of courtly and private intellectual gatherings, see papers in Lazarus-Yafeh, *The Majlis*; and on the literary salon, Ali, *Arabic Literary Salons in the Islamic Middle Ages*.

111. The historicity of Abraham ibn Daud's account of this foundational event in his *Sefer ha-qabbalah* is secondary to its importance in tradition.

112. Text: Schirmann, *Hebrew Poetry in Spain and Provence*, 1:34–35, trans. Scheindlin, *Wine, Women, and Death*, 41–42. See also the discussion of the poem by Granat, "Polémica, Equívico, o Ambivalencia?"

113. Nevertheless, it also appears to have existed or been transmitted as an independent lyric. See Elizur, "Ḥiddushim b^{e} -ḥeqer ha-shirah w^{e}-ha-piyyuṭ."

114. Brann, *The Compunctious Poet*, 32–33.

115. Drory, *Models and Contacts*, 147–157, delineates "three major Karaite contributions to tenth-century Jewish culture": introduction of an option for a change in Jewish literature (Arabic models); introduction of writing as an official mode of text production (institutionalized writing of literary works); and preparation of language-setting for the new writing models (division of function between Hebrew and Arabic). It should also be noted that in the political struggle for Ibn Shaprūṭ's favor, Dūnash appears to have accused his rival Menaḥem of Karaism, or at least of holding Karaite sympathies, predicated on a cluster of Ibn Sarūq's biblical interpretations. See Dūnash ben Labrāṭ, *Teshubot*, 5, lines 19–21. The indictment was picked up by Rabbeinu Tam in his commentary on Dūnash's *Sefer t^{e}shuvot dūnash ben labrāṭ 'im hakhra'ot rabbeinu ya'aqov tam*, 8. On the history of the allegation, see Allony, "Karaite Views in 'Maḥberet' M^{e}naḥem."

116. Dūnash, *Poems* (1947), 60, lines 4–6. See also idem, 57, lines 6–8; 58, lines 3–4, 7.

117. Ben-Shammai, "The Karaites," 201.

118. Simon, *Four Approaches to the Book of Psalms*, 64–65.

119. Mann, "A Tract by an Early Karaite Settler in Jerusalem," 257–298; cited excerpts trans. Nemoy, *Karaite Anthology*, 34–39. For the complete text, see Nemoy, "The Pseudo-Qumisian Sermon to the Karaites."

120. F. Peters, *Jerusalem*, 220–224.

121. Yahalom, "The Temple and the City in Liturgical Hebrew Poetry," 283, cites Goitein, "Al-Ḳuds." On the status of Jerusalem during this period, see Sivan, "Le caractère sacré de Jérusalem dans l'Islam aux 12e–13e siècles."

122. Ibn 'Abd Rabbihi, *Al-'Iqd al-farīd* (1983), 7:29–93.

123. Peters, *Jerusalem*, 235.

124. Abū Bakr Muḥammad b. Aḥmad al-Wāsiṭī, *Faḍā'il al-bayt al-muqaddas*. See Sivan, "The Beginnings of the Faḍā'il al-Quds Literature," 263; and Isaac Hasson, "Muslim Literature in Praise of Jerusalem."

125. Goitein, *A Mediterranean Society*, 5:362.

126. Yahalom, "The Temple and the City," 283; and Zulay, "The Poem of Adonim Halevi of Fez," 24–25. In this context, it is worth recalling that Baḥya ibn Paqūda, in *Al-Hidāya ilā farā'iḍ al-qulūb* (The Book of Direction to the Duties of the Heart), derides the individual "intoxicated by the wine of this worldliness succumbing to his animal lusts" (38). It warns the Andalusi reader (400) to "beware of excessive drinking of wine, of quaffing, of drinking in company, for these are most serious ills for religion and the world"; cited by B. Safran, "Baḥya ibn Paquda's Attitude Toward the Courtier Class," 171.

CHAPTER 3

Notes to epigraphs: Ibn 'Idhārī, *Al-Bayān al-mughrib*, 3:110, quoting an anonymous poet; and al-Maqqarī, *Nafḥ al-ṭīb*, 1:153, here attributed to an unidentified religious scholar. Iḥsān 'Abbās, the text's editor, notes that the couplet is repeated in *Nafḥ*, chap. 4, where it is attributed to Abū Muḥammad b. 'Atiyya l-Muḥāribī.

1. The Umayyad caliphate did not end formally until 1031, with the death of Hishām III. The chaotic period from 1009 until 1031 witnessed the popular revolt and then the Berber sack of Córdoba in 1013, and the appearance of assorted claimants to rule, including futile efforts to install various Umayyad pretenders and restore the caliphate. Regarding a particularly tumultuous time labeled "The Year of the Four Caliphs," see Wasserstein, *The Caliphate in the West*, 192–195.

2. J. Safran, *Second Umayyad Caliphate*, 185–186.

3. For a full roster of its Quranic usages, see Kassis, *A Concordance of the Qur'an*, 449.

4. The Arabic term *ṭā'ifa* means "faction" or "division" and thus stands in opposition to the ideal of the united Islamic *umma*. On the ethnic dimensions of sociopolitical conflict during this period, see Wasserstein, *Rise and Fall of the Party-Kings*, 55–81; and Kennedy, *Muslim Spain*, 105–129.

5. See Wasserstein, *Rise and Fall of the Party-Kings*, 82–160. He identifies thirty-eight such states, including temporary, short-lived polities (83–98). Seville, Granada, Almería, Toledo, Valencia, and Saragossa stand out as among the most important. On the intellectual and cultural richness of the period, see Marín, "La actividad intelectual"; and Garulo, *La literatura árabe de al-Andalus durante siglo XI*.

6. On the two dynasties and their history, see Bennison, *The Almoravid and Almohad Empires*.

7. For a study of the battle as symptomatic rather than causative of transformative historical developments, see Gómez-Rivas, "Las Navas de Tolosa, the Urban Transformation of the Maghrib, and the Territorial Decline of al-Andalus"; on problematic nationalist uses of this battle, see Fromherz, "Making 'Great Battles' Great," 38.

8. Kennedy, *Muslim Spain and Portugal*, 266–272.

9. O'Callaghan, *A History of Medieval Spain*, 248–249; and Harvey, *Islamic Spain, 1250–1500*, 9–16.

10. See Garulo, *La literatura árabe de al-Andalus durante siglo XI*.

11. Ibn ʿIdhārī (al-Marrākushī), *al-Muʿjib fī talkhīṣ akhbār ahl al-maghrib*, 117.

12. Boym, *The Future of Nostalgia*, 41–55.

13. See Decter, "A Myrtle in the Forest"; Garulo, "La Nostalgia de al-Andalus"; Enderwitz, "Homesickness and Love in Arabic Poetry"; Arazi, "Al-ḥanīn ilā l-awṭān entre la Gāhiliyya et l-Islam"; Elinson, *Looking Back at al-Andalus*, which also contrasts the Andalusi and Eastern Arabic poetic traditions of *rithā' l-mudun*; Tarbieh, *Nostalgia and Elegy for Cities in the Andalusian Arabic and Hebrew Poetry*; and Masarwah and Tarabieh, "Longing for Granada in Medieval Arabic and Hebrew Poetry."

14. Ferris, *The Genre of Communal Lament in the Bible and the Ancient Near East.*

15. For a comparative study of Ibn ʿAmmār and Moses ibn Ezra, see Schippers, "Two Andalusian Poets on Exile."

16. Arazi, "Shiʿr."

17. Ibn Shuhayd, *Dīwān*, 64–67 ("Mā fī l-ṭulūli min al-aḥibbati mukhbir").

18. Cited by Elinson, *Looking Back*, 27.

19. Ibn Zaydūn, *Poesías* 30–37 ("A-qurṭubatu l-gharrā'u hal fīki matmaʿ"), 39–43 ("Saqā janabāti l-qaṣri ṣawbu l-ghamā'im") = Ibn Zaydūn, *Dīwān*, 198, 269–270.

20. Robinson, "*Ubi Sunt.*"

21. Elinson, *Looking Back*, 25, 38–49.

22. Al-Sumaysīr was the name by which Abū l-Qāsim Khalaf b. Faraj al-Ilbīrī was known. The poem was originally preserved in al-Maqqarī, *Nafḥ al-ṭīb*, 1:527–528. It was recently published in *Shiʿr al-Sumaysīr*, 76. For other translations and comments, see Elinson, *Looking Back*, 6–7; and Ruggles, "Arabic Poetry and Architectural Memory in al-Andalus."

23. For a study of the entire tradition, see ʿAbd Allāh Muḥammad al-Zayyāt, *Rithā' l-mudun fī l-shiʿr al-andalusī.*

24. Monroe, *Hispano-Arabic Poetry*, 214–217.

25. Ibid., 228–241.

26. "Inna li-l-jannati bi-l-andalusi," *Dīwān ibn khafāja*, 136 (#88).

27. Al-Maqqarī, *Nafḥ al-ṭīb*, 4:484. Discussed briefly by S. Stetkevych, *The Mute Immortals Speak*, 106–107; and Elinson, *Looking Back*, 28. For additional illustrations, see Lévi-Provençal, "La 'Description de l'Espagne,' d'Aḥmad al-Rāzī," 61–62; and Terés, "Textos poéticos árabes sobre Valencia," 292–295.

28. Monroe, *Hispano-Arabic Poetry*, 322–331.

29. Text in al-Zayyāt, *Rithā' l-mudun*, 698, discussed briefly by Elinson, *Looking Back*, 29.

30. Monroe, *Hispano-Arabic Poetry*, 366–371.

31. Ibid., 376–389.

32. Al-Maqqarī, *Nafḥ al-ṭīb*, 1:7–12.

33. Ibn Rashīq al-Qayrawānī, *Dīwān ibn rashīq al-qayrawānī*, 143–148 ("Kam kāna fīhā min kirām^{in} sādat^{in}," #221).

34. Ibn Ḥamdīs, *Dīwān ibn Ḥamdīs*, 274–276, trans. Mallette, *The Kingdom of Sicily, 1100–1250*, 134–137.

35. Text in al-Maqqarī, *Nafḥ al-ṭīb*, 4:487–488, trans. Monroe, *Hispano-Arabic Poetry*, 332–337. For additional translations, see Ebied and Young, "Abū 'l-Baqā' al-Rundī and His Elegy on Muslim Spain," who also study the textual history of the poem and its subsequent imitations; and Nicholson, *Translations of Eastern Poetry and Prose*, 168–169.

36. On this conceptual model, see Scheindlin, *Form and Structure in the Poetry of al-Muʿtamid ibn ʿAbbād.*

37. See J. Stetkevych, "Spaces of Delight," 14–15. The aforementioned elegy by the Naṣrid emir Yūsuf III bemoaning the fall of Anteqera in 1410 adopts the same rhetorical strategy.

38. Ibn Khafāja, *Dīwān*, 208–209, esp. line 11.

39. On this type of transformation, see Stetkevych, "Spaces of Delight," 15–16.

40. Al-Ḥimyarī, *al-Rawḍ al-mi'ṭār*, 40–41, trans. Melville and Ubaydli, *Christians and Moors in Spain*, 3:73.

41. Hopkins, *Medieval Muslim Government in Barbary Until the Sixth Century of the Hijra*, 137.

42. In this discussion and for some of the sources, I am indebted to Wasserstein, *Rise and Fall of the Party-Kings*, 274–291; and Marín, "Historical Images of al-Andalus and Andalusis."

43. Al-Maqqarī, *Nafḥ al-ṭīb* (1949), 6:109.

44. The widespread reputation of Andalusis as disinterested in jihad—in this case, an offensive mission—is observed by the Zīrid ruler of Granada, 'Abd Allāh b. Bullugīn, in his self-serving memoir, *Kitāb al-tibyān*. Speaking of their reluctance to follow al-Manṣūr into expeditionary battle, he writes: "The citizens of al-Andalus were unequal to such a task and complained to him of their inability to fight and of the fact that expeditions would prevent them from cultivating their lands. Moreover, they were not a warlike people." *Mudhakirāt al-amīr 'abd allāh al-musammāt bi-kitāb al-tibyān*, 17; and *The Tibyān: Memoirs of ᶜAbd Allāh b. Bullugīn, Last Zīrid Amīr of Granada*, 44, cited with slightly revised translation by Marín, "Historical Images of al-Andalus and Andalusians," 411. On the elastic nature of jihad in al-Andalus, see Urvoy, "Sur l'evolution de la notion de gihād dans l'Espagne musulman," 335–371.

45. On Islamic Sicily, see Ahmad, *A History of Islamic Sicily*.

46. *Shi'r al-Sumaysīr*, 118, preserved by Ibn Bassām, *al-Dhakhīra fi maḥāsin ahl al-jazīra*, 1 (part 2), 430, trans. Wasserstein, *Rise and Fall of the Party-Kings*, 280. Wasserstein (281) also cites an anonymous poet's lament for the same event, holding Andalusis in general to account.

47. E.g., *takhlafuhum min ālihim khawālifu* = "and were *replaced* from their own people by *womanly successors*."

48. Ibn Bassām, *al-Dhakhīra*, 1 (part 2), 943.

49. "Risālat al-talkhīṣ li-wujūh al-takhlīṣ," in *Rasā'il ibn ḥazm*, 3:173–174, trans. Chejne, *Ibn Ḥazm*, 32–33.

50. Ibn Ḥazm, "Al-Radd 'alā ibn al-naghrīla al-yahūdī," in *Rasā'il ibn ḥazm*, 3:41, 68–69.

51. Ibid., 3:45. I studied some of the ambiguities and contradictions in, and the significance of, this work in Brann, *Power in the Portrayal*, 75–90.

52. "Yā ahla andalus^{in}," appears in Ibn Sa'īd al-Maghribī's collection, *Rāyāt al-mubarrizīn wa-ghāyāt al-mumayyizīn*, 81 (#59), trans. Bellamy and Steiner, *The Banners of the Champions*, 138. The poet's name is sometimes transcribed as al-'Assāl. Another poem on the same theme with the identical incipit is preserved in al-Maqqarī, *Nafḥ al-ṭīb*, 4:352, alongside al-Ghassāl's (al-'Assāl's) poem.

53. Abou El Fadl, "Islamic Law and Muslim Minorities," 146, 150–151, 153–157.

54. The text of al-Wansharīsī's fatwa, along with a compilation of opinions on this subject by earlier legal authorities, is found in "Usnā 'l-mutājir," edited by Ḥusayn Mu'nis, 148ff. See also Harvey, *Islamic Spain*, 56ff.

55. Al-Maqqarī, *Nafḥ al-ṭīb*, 1:287, 2:568.

56. See Harvey, *Islamic Spain*, 9–10. For details of the Ḥafṣid response and its rationale, see Abun-Nasr, *A History of the Maghrib*, 139.

57. On the Marīnid military campaign against Christian forces in the peninsula and North Africa, see Abun-Nasr, *History of the Maghrib*, 122.

58. The text of the poem appears in Ibn ʿIdhārī, *Kitāb al-bayān al-mughrib [qism al-muwaḥḥidīn]*, 381–383.

59. Text in Monroe, *Hispano-Arabic Poetry*, 376–389.

60. Wasserstein, *Rise and Fall of the Party-Kings*, 281–282, cites this prominent rhetorical gesture in Ibn Bashkuwāl, Ibn Saʿīd, Ibn al-Khaṭīb, and al-Maqqarī.

61. Ormsby, "Ibn Ḥazm."

62. See Soravia, "A Portrait of the ʿĀlim as a Young Man."

63. *Ṭawq al-ḥamāma fi l-ulfa wa-l-ullāf*, 182–183.

64. See Puerta Vilchez, "Abū Muḥammad ʿAlī Ibn Ḥazm," 3. Wasserstein, "Ibn Ḥazm and al-Andalus," 69–72, is far more cautious in his approach and skeptical about the claim of prestigious *mawlā* ancestry from a family of early Persian converts.

65. Terés, "Linajes Arabes en al-Andalus," 55–57.

66. *Jamharat ansāb al-ʿarab*. For Wasserstein, *Rise and Fall of the Party-Kings*, 60, this work represents "an assertion of the new Andalusian, or Andalusian-Arab, ethnic solidarity and identity." Arab genealogy continued to serve as a source of political legitimacy down to the Naṣrids of Granada. See Fierro, "Ways of Connecting with the Past." Viewed historically, genealogy, genealogical claims, and ethnic identification are immensely complicated subjects, partly on account of Andalusi Arab marriages to women of every available background. What matters here is the constructedness of their Arab identifications and the agency imbued therein.

67. Fierro, *La heterodoxia en al-Andalus*, 78, 8n26.

68. See Shatzmiller, *The Berbers and the Islamic State*, 17–27. Ibn Gharsiyya's epistle represents resistance to this feature of Andalusi society. See Monroe, *The Shuʿūbiyya in al-Andalus*. Wasserstein, *Rise and Fall of the Party Kings*, 55–74, provides the clearest articulation of the issues involved in interpreting the ethnic divisions in Andalusi society in the eleventh century.

69. Al-Maqqarī, *Nafḥ al-ṭīb*, 3:154, trans. Elinson, *Looking Back*, 118.

70. Al-Maqqarī, *Nafḥ al-ṭīb*, 3:150–156, trans. Elinson, *Looking Back*, 118.

71. Pellat, "Ibn Ḥazm bibliographe et apologiste de l'Espagne musulmane," 55, cited and discussed by Wasserstein, "Ibn Ḥazm and al-Andalus," 79.

72. Al-Maqqarī, *Nafḥ al-ṭīb*, 3:158–179, and *Rasāʾil ibn Ḥazm*, 3:171–188. It has been studied most recently by Martínez-Gros, "L'Ecriture et la 'Umma';" Elinson, *Looking Back*, 123–130; and Wasserstein, "Ibn Ḥazm and al-Andalus," 78–84. Previously, Pellat, "Ibn Ḥazm bibliographe et apologiste de l'Espagne musulmane," introduced the text and translated it into French.

73. Al-Maqqarī, *Nafḥ al-ṭīb*, 3:156.

74. Cited by the text's editor, Iḥsān ʿAbbās, *Nafḥ al-ṭīb*, 3:156n1.

75. On the genre's widespread appearance and longevity in Egypt, see Haarman, "Regional Sentiment in Medieval Egypt," esp. 57. On Arabic literary debate going back to al-Jāḥiẓ in the ninth century, see Van Gelder, "Arabic Debates of Earnest and Jest"; and Heinrichs, "Rose Versus Narcissus."

76. Al-Maqqarī, *Nafḥ al-ṭīb*, 3:159.

77. Ibid., 3:156.

78. Ibid.

79. See Pellat, "Ibn Ḥazm," 64n1, for the hadith's source.

80. Al-Maqqarī, *Nafḥ al-ṭīb*, 3:161.

81. Ibid., 3:163.

82. Ibid., 3:166–167.

83. Observed by Marín, "Historical Images," 414.

84. The poem appears in Ibn Bassām, *al-Dhakhīra*, 1:173, trans. Puerta Vilchez, "Ibn Ḥazm," 1–14, drawing on Asín Palacios, *Abenhazam de Córdoba y su historia crítica de las ideas religiosas*, 1:237–238.

85. Al-Maqqarī, *Nafḥ al-ṭīb*, 3:177.

86. Wasserstein, "Ibn Ḥazm and al-Andalus," 83.

87. Transmitted by al-Maqqarī, *Nafḥ al-ṭīb*, 3:186–237. It is studied by Elinson, *Looking Back*, 134–142. Four *faḍā'il al-Andalus* texts (including Ibn Ḥazm's letter) drawn from al-Maqqarī were published together and introduced by Ṣalāḥ al-Dīn al-Munajjad as *Faḍā'il al-andalus wa-ahlihā.*

88. Al-Maqqari, *Nafḥ al-ṭīb*, 3:179.

89. For Andalusi texts on this score designed to set Andalusis apart from Berbers, see García Gómez, *Andalucía contra Berbería*. The attitude informing their work denigrating Berbers naturally was met with Berber resistance. Shatzmiller, *Berbers and the Islamic State*, 31, traces to the eleventh century the earliest textual expressions of *mafākhir al-barbar* (praiseworthy qualities of the Berbers) and *maḥāsin ahl al-maghrib* (the merits of the people of the Islamic West)—echoes of Berber resistance to Arabic acculturation. Roughi, "The Andalusi Origin of the Berbers," problematizes many of the prevalent assumptions about the Berbers, especially as they pertain to the Muslims' advance into North Africa in the seventh century and to the Iberian Peninsula in the eighth.

90. Lisān al-Dīn ibn al-Khaṭīb, *Mufākhara bayna mālaqa wa-salā*, 57–65, trans. García Gómez, "El 'Parangón entre Málaga y Saé' de Ibn al-Jatib," 183–196. Ibn al-Khaṭīb's contribution is studied by Elinson, *Looking Back*, 142–150.

91. Marín, "Historical Images of al-Andalus and Andalusians," 413, 421.

92. Ibid., 421.

93. Al-Maqqarī, *Nafḥ al-ṭīb*, 3:155. Here, the richness of the land also provides the poets with visual material informing Arabic poetic genres and themes.

94. Ṣā'id al-Andalusī, *Ṭabaqāt al-umam*, 62–87; and *Ṭabaqāt al-umam* (1998), 84–108.

95. Ṣā'id al-Andalusī, *Ṭabaqāt al-umam* (1912), 87–90 = *Ṭabaqāt al-umam* (1998), 109–112. On the work's specifically Andalusi agenda and emphasis on Saragossa, see Wasserstein, "The Muslims and the Golden Age of the Jews in al-Andalus."

96. Al-Maqqarī, *Nafḥ al-ṭīb*, 3:522–530 (Andalusi Jewish poets), 4:166–179 (Andalusi women poets).

97. Gilliot, "Prosopography in Islam," 43–44.

98. Wasserstein, "Ibn Ḥazm and al-Andalus," 82–83.

99. Ibn Bassām, *al-Dhakhīra*, 1:14.

100. Ibid., 1 (part 2): 664–665, cited by Wasserstein, "Ibn Ḥazm and al-Andalus," 82.

101. Transmitted by Ibn Bassām, *al-Dhakhīra*, 1:12, trans. Abu-Haidar, "The Muwaššaḥāt in Light of the Literary Life That Produced Them," 116.

102. Ibn Bassām, *al-Dhakhīra*, 1:14–15.

103. Abū Naṣr al-Fatḥ ibn Khāqān, *Maṭmaḥ al-anfus wa-masraḥ al-ta'annus fī mulaḥ ahl al-andalus*, 53.

104. Ibn Qaṭṭā, *al-Durra al-khaṭīra min shu'arā' l-jazīra*; Ibn Idrīs, *Zād al-musāfir wa-ghurrat muḥayyā l-adab al-sāfir*; Ibn Diḥya, *al-Muṭrib min ash'ār ahl al-maghrib*; al-Būnisī, *Kanz al-kuttāb wa-muntakhab al-adāb.*

105. Lisān al-Dīn ibn al-Khaṭīb, *Jaysh al-tawshīḥ.*

106. Stern, *Hispano-Arabic Strophic Poetry*, 107, citing Ibn Diḥya, *al-Muṭrib min ash'ār ahl al-maghrib*, fol. 150v. The passage may be found in the edited text of *al-Muṭrib min ash'ār ahl al-maghrib,* 176.

107. Ibn Sanā' l-Mulk, *Dār al-ṭirāz fī 'amal al-muwashshaḥāt*, 29.

108. On the Andalusi urban garden, see Dickie, "The Islamic Garden in Spain."

109. Abū l-Walīd Ismā'īl b. Muḥammad al-Ḥimyarī, *al-Badī' fī waṣf al-rabī'*, 1–2.

110. Stoetzer, "Floral Poetry in Muslim Spain," 179. Stoetzer references the debate among Arabic literary historians Pérès, García Gómez, Hoenerbach, and Schuler, regarding the extent of the Andalusis' dependence on Eastern poetic models of this theme and genre.

111. Ibn Khafāja, *Dīwān*, 364 (*Yā ahla andalus^{in}*). See also "Inna li-l-jannati fī-l-andalus" (*Dīwān Ibn Khafāja*, 136 [#88]). For additional illustrations, see Lévi-Provençal, *Histoire de l'Espagne musulmane*, 61–62; and Terés, "Textos poéticos," 292–295.

112. Ibn Khaldūn, *al-Muqaddima* 1:400; *The Muqaddimah* 1:179.

113. Al-Saraqusṭī ibn al-Ashtarkūnī, *al-Maqāmāt al-luzūmiyya*, 418.

114. Monroe, *al-Maqāmāt al-luzūmiyya*, 46–54.

115. *Al-Dhakhīra al-saniyya*, trans. (without citation of the Arabic source) Hillenbrand, "The Ornament of the World," 112. Originally published in 1921 by Mohammed Ben Cheneb as an anonymous chronicle of Marīnid rule, and subsequently in 1972 by 'Abd al-Wahhāb Binmanṣūr, the text is now frequently ascribed to the fourteenth-century Marīnid court historian ^{c}Alī ibn ^{c}Abd Allāh ibn abī Zar' al-Fāsī, author of the dynastic chronicle *al-Anīs al-muṭrib bi-rawḍ al-qirṭās fī akhbār mulūk al-maghrib wa-ta'rīkh madīnat fās*, which contains passages repeated verbatim from *al-Dhakhīra*. For a recent study of the entire work, see Ramírez del Río, "Al-Ḏajīra al-saniyya." I have read through both published editions of the text without identifying the passage that Hillenbrand cites.

116. Levanoni, "'Aṣabiyya."

117. These modern interpretations of Andalusi intellectual history as unique are discussed below, in the Conclusion.

118. Edwards, "Exile, Self, and Society," 25.

CHAPTER 4

Notes to epigraphs: Abraham ibn Daud, *Sefer ha-qabbalah*, 73; and Brody-Schirmann, *Ibn Gabirol: Secular Poems*, 47 (#85), v. 46.

1. Levin, *Tannim w^{e}-khinnor*, 96–108, 174–183, 275–299.

2. Kaminsky, *After Exile*, xvi.

3. Graetz, *History of the Jews*, 3:41.

4. G. Cohen, *The Book of Tradition*, 287. Yerushalmi, "Exile and Expulsion in Jewish History," expresses the opposition in Jewish history by using the terms "exile" and "domicile."

5. Cohen, *Book of Tradition*, 287.

6. Ibid., 295–299. The poetic images are drawn from Halevi's celebrated lyric "My heart is in the East and I in the farthest West" ("Libbi v^{e}-mizraḥ wa-anokhi b^{e}-sof ma'arav"),

Schirmann, *Hebrew Poetry in Spain and Provence* [hereafter, *HPSP*], 2:489 = *Yehuda Ha-Levi: Poemas*, 422 (#114), trans. Cole, *Dream of the Poem*, 164. The poem "Y^{e}feh nof m^{e}sos tevel," Schirmann, *HPSP*, 2:489 = *Yehuda Ha-Levi: Poemas*, 430 (#116) represents a closely related variation on this theme.

7. E.g., Allony, "The Reaction of Moses ibn Ezra to 'Abrabiyya," and "Ha-kuzari: Sefer ha-milḥamah b^{e}-'arabiyya"; and Fleischer, "Yehuda Halevi" and "The Culture of the Jews of Spain and Their Poetry According to the Findings of the Geniza."

8. Baer, *A History of the Jews in Christian Spain*, 1:67–76.

9. For a fuller discussion of his evolving literary identity and the debate among Andalusi Jews as well as Halevi's modern readers, see Brann, *The Compunctious Poet*, 84–118.

10. "Namta w^{e}-nirdamta w^{e}-ḥared qamta," in Schirmann, *HPSP*, 2:480 (#202) = *Yehuda Ha-Levi: Poemas*, 318 (#86), trans. Cole, *Dream of the Poem*, 158.

11. For the most recent and compelling studies of this aspect of Halevi's thinking and experience, see Krinis, *God's Chosen People*; and Scheindlin, *The Song of the Distant Dove.*

12. Brann, "Judah Halevi."

13. The penitent poet characterizes himself as *asir ta'awah*, in "Ṣiyyon ha-lo' tisha'li," line 5. Schirmann, *HPSP*, 2:485–489 (#208) = *Yehuda Ha-Levi: Poemas*, 424–428 (#115), trans. Cole, *Dream of the Poem*, 162–164; and as *asir tiqwah*, in "Qir'u 'alei vanot u-mishpaḥot" (line 2), Schirmann, *HPSP* 2:503–504 (#214 *gimel*) = *Yehuda Ha-Levi: Poemas*, 502 (#133), trans. Scheindlin, *Song of the Distant Dove*, 223–225.

14. Schirmann, *HPSP*, 2:521–523 (#228) ("Adonai negd^{e}kha kol ta'awati," lines 6–7) = Judah ha-Levi, *Liturgical Poetry of Rabbi Judah Halevi*, 1:78–81 (#32, line 4), trans. Cole, *Dream of the Poem*, 159–160.

15. Goitein, *A Mediterranean Society*, 5:391.

16. Ibid., 5:365.

17. See above, Chap. 2, pp. 60–66. In Judah Halevi's *al-Kitāb al-khazarī*, 227–228, the Khazar king, perhaps like the elite Andalusi Jewish audience that was Halevi's principal audience, appears satisfied with life in exile and shows no interest in joining the sage in his journey to the Land of Israel.

18. Cohen, *Book of Tradition*, 288.

19. Ibn Ḥazm, *al-Fiṣal fī l-milal*, 1:245.

20. Ibn Ḥazm's principal interest in the verse is that it supplies additional evidence of the Jews' corruption-falsification (*taḥrīf*) of God's revelation. On the office of the exilarch and its role in the historical imagination of the Jews of Sefarad, see below, Chap. 5.

21. Scheindlin, *The Gazelle*, 36; and Elbogen, *Jewish Liturgy*, 169.

22. Schirmann, *HPSP*, 1:64–65 (#12), trans. Cole, *Dream of the Poem*, 31–32.

23. "Ahah yarad 'al s^{e}farad," in *Abraham ibn Ezra Reader*, 102, line 37, trans. Cole, *Dream of the Poem*, 181–182. The episode occasioned an oft-imitated dirge by Abraham ibn Ezra. In this classical exercise of "reflective nostalgia," after the fashion of Arabic city elegies, the poet bundles a literary response to the tribulations of Seville, Córdoba, Jaén, and Almería, together with the concurrent ordeals suffered by the Maghribi communities Dar'a, Sijilmassa, Tlemcen, Ceuta, Meknes, and Fez. Elsewhere, Brann, "Constructions of Exile in Hispano-Hebrew and Hispano-Arabic Elegies," 53–54, I have offered a reading of Ibn Ezra's lyric alongside al-Rundī's Arabic elegy studied in Chap. 3 and shown how the former spiritualizes the Andalusi and Maghribi Jews' sense of home and homelessness and crosses the boundaries formally separating Arabic-style Hebrew social poetry and Hebrew liturgical verse. In style, it stands apart from more traditional and numerous Andalusi

Hebrew liturgical gestures lamenting the interminable exile of catholic Israel as well as liturgical poems bemoaning specifically Andalusi disasters such as Isaac ibn Ghiyāth's dirge on the death of Joseph ibn al-Naghrīla and the events of 1066 in Granada; Isaac ibn Ghiyāth, *Poems*, 219–220 (#120).

24. Schirmann, *HPSP*, 2:464 (#187) = *Yehuda Ha-Levi: Poemas*, 340 (#92).

25. Ibn Ghiyāth, *Poems*, 182–183 (#87) = Schirmann, *HPSP*, 2:324–325 (#127), trans. Cole, *Dream of the Poem*, 112–113.

26. Schirmann, *HPSP*, 2:467 (#192) = *Yehuda Ha-Levi: Poemas*, 356 (#98), trans. Scheindlin, *Song of the Distant Dove*, 67. See also "Yiṭav b^e-'einekha n^{e}'im shiri," Schirmann, *HPSP*, 2:523–524 (#230).

27. Judah Halevi's letter to Samuel ben Ḥanania the Egyptian Nagid, in Yahalom, "The Immigration of Rabbi Judah ha-Levi to Eretz Israel in Vision and Riddle," 44–45.

28. Ar., *jumlat bilādinā wa-ma'nāhā*, from the testimony of a personal letter from 1130 preserved in the Cairo Geniza published by Goitein, "Judeo-Arabic Letters from Spain (Early Twelfth Century)," 341. Scheindlin, *Song of the Distant Dove*, 15, 255, renders the Arabic phrase "the heart and soul of our land," but the implications for Halevi's standing in Andalusi Jewish society are the same, regardless of which translation is favored.

29. Wasserstein, "A Family Story." Wasserstein's study and some of the historical sections of chap. 3 in Schirmann-Fleischer, *History of Hebrew Poetry in Muslim Spain*, 181–256, replace earlier papers by Schirmann, "The Wars of Samuel ha-Nagid," and "Samuel Hanagid: The Man, the Soldier, the Politician"; and the somewhat fanciful extended narrative presentation by Ashtor, *Jews of Moslem Spain*, 2:158–194.

30. Abraham ibn Daud, *Sefer ha-qabbalah*, 69–72; and Cohen, *Book of Tradition*, 94–101.

31. Samuel the Nagid, *Poemas*, 1:106–110 (#25).

32. The theme is also taken up by Judah Halevi. See "Elohai mishk^{e}notekha y^{e}didot," Schirmann, *HPSP*, 2:517 (#223).

33. On which, see above, Chap. 2. See also the Nagid's "L^{e}vavi b^e-qirbi ḥam," Schirmann, *HPSP*, 1:112–115 (#32) = Samuel ha-Nagid, *Poemas*, 1:41–44 (#8), whose fifteen-line introduction is a lament over Zion's ruin preceding the transition (lines 15–16) to the poetic description of Granada's battle against rebel forces (lines 16–37); and the *t^{e}hillah* "Ha-e'eṣor naḥalei 'einai w^e-anuḥah," Samuel ha-Nagid, *Poemas*, 1:136–141 (lines 1–7) (#31).

34. Some important scholars attach great significance to the title. See Schirmann-Fleischer, *History of Hebrew Poetry in Muslim Spain*, 200–204. According to Gil, *In the Kingdom of Ishmael*, 1:197, it was conferred upon Samuel by Hayya Gaon. During the same period in the East, it was an actual office with territorial authority over the Egyptian Jewish community. See Goitein, *Mediterranean Society*, 2:23–40; and, in greater detail, M. R. Cohen, *Jewish Self-Government in Medieval Egypt*.

35. Moses ibn Ezra, *Kitāb al-muḥāḍara wa-l-mudhākara*, 62 (33a).

36. *Ṭabaqāt al-umam*, 90, trans. Wasserstein, "Muslims and Golden Age of the Jews," 191–192. Aspects of the text and its historical context are also discussed in Brann, *Power in the Portrayal*, 28–36.

37. Lisān al-Dīn ibn al-Khaṭīb, *al-Iḥāṭa fī akhbar gharnāṭa*, 1:438–439, slightly emended from the translation by Schippers, "Literacy, Munificence and Legitimation of Power During the Reign of the Party Kings in Muslim Spain," 80. This text is also analyzed in Brann, *Power in the Portrayal*, 36–42.

38. BT Avot 4:17.

39. Abraham ibn Daud, *Sefer ha-qabbalah*, 53–56; and Cohen, *Book of Tradition*, 71–75.

40. *Sefer ha-qabbalah*, 71–72 [Hebrew, 53–55]; and Cohen's comments, *Book of Tradition*, 269–273.

41. Isaac ibn Khalfūn, *Poems*, 119 (#46), 130–133 (#49), and 133–134 (#50), among others. Ibn Khalfūn's poems to the Nagid are not uniformly poems of praise. According to the poetry, their relationship was complicated. For five of the Nagid's poems to Isaac, see Ibn Khalfūn, *Poems*, 158–171.

42. Schirmann, *HPSP*, 1:204 (#71), 205–206 (#72).

43. Decter, *Dominion Built of Praise.*

44. Unlike the Nagid, Ibn Jau and Yequtiel fell victim to court intrigue typical of the period. See Wasserstein, "Ibn Jaw, Jacob." For Yequtiel ibn Ḥasan, see Schirmann-Fleischer, *History of Hebrew Poetry in Muslim Spain*, 273–278. I deliberately avoid mentioning high-ranking Jewish officials who may or may not have converted to Islam, such as Abū l-Faḍl Ḥasdai ibn Yūsuf, on which, see Stroumsa, "Between Acculturation and Conversion in Islamic Spain."

45. Schirmann, *HPSP*, 1:172–175 (#54), trans. Cole, *Dream of the Poem*, 71–73.

46. Brody-Schimrann, *Ibn Gabirol: Secular Poems*, 73 [126], ll. 52–53.

47. "Tᵉhillat el bᵉ-rosh kol tᵉhillot," Brody-Schirmann, *Ibn Gabirol: Secular Poems*, 46 (#85), ll. 43–51.

48. Alfonso, *Islamic Culture Through Jewish Eyes*, 40, identifies Ibn Gabirol's praise of the Nagid as a parallel to Ibn Ḥazm's famous lyric juxtaposing his western "rise" opposite the eastern sunrise (discussed above, Chap. 3).

49. For discussion of these lyrics and additional illustrations of poems praising Samuel the Nagid and other figures while designating Sefarad as the cultural center and other lands the periphery, see Kfir, *A Matter of Geography*, 11–36. Kfir engages literary-historical study spanning three centuries of the dynamic relationship of post-Andalusi Hebrew literature, especially in thirteenth-century Provence, to its "classical" tenth- through mid-twelfth-century Andalusi model. He dissects the critical notions of "center," "periphery," and "de-territorialization," especially significant since the Jewish authors live in different lands but think of themselves as connected by language, religion, and history. The theoretical importance that Kfir attaches to the hegemonic function of the notion of the Andalusi "center" obliged him to consider other "peripheries," such as Egypt, Iraq, and Italy, that had to wrestle with the canonical status projected by the Andalusi poets.

50. Samuel ha-Nagid, *Dīwān* [*Ben Tᵉhillim*], 91 (#27, line 44), 209 (#63, line 16), 229 (#83, line 3), 231–236 (#85).

51. Ibid., 134–138 (#39).

52. Ibid., 139–142 (#40).

53. To Sahlān: Samuel ha-Nagid, *Dīwān* [*Ben Tᵉhillim*], 200–202 (#62).

54. Regarding ʿEli ben ʿAmram and the Nagid, see Bareket, *Eli Ben Amram and His Companions*, 60–61, citing Gil, *Palestine During the First Muslim Period (634–1099)*, 1:488–489. For ʿEli ben ᶜAmram's correspondence with Samuel and his extending additional honorifics to the Nagid, see Beeri, "ʿEli he-ḥaver b. ʿAmram, Hebrew Poet in Egypt," 282–283.

55. Samuel ha-Nagid, *Dīwān* [*Ben Tᵉhillim*], 196–199 (#60–61) = Samuel ha-Nagid, *Poemas* 2:43–46 (#60–61).

56. Schirmann, *HPSP*, 1:256–260 (#107), a letter and poem in Aramaic to R. Ḥananel; to R. Ḥushiel, Schirmann, ibid., 1:153–154 (#46).

57. "Ha-tedaʿ et peʿalai la-ḥakhamim," Schirmann, *HPSP*, 1:158–160 (#52b) (lines 37–40) = Samuel ha-Nagid, *Poemas* 2:163–166 (#136).

58. "Sh^e'eh minni 'amiti wa-ḥaverai," Schirmann, *HPSP*, 1:109–111 (#31) = Samuel ha-Nagid, *Poemas* 1:37–40 (#7), trans. Cole, *Dream of the Poem*, 52–53.

59. "Sh^emu'el qadmah yoshev k^eruvim," Schirmann, *HPSP*, 1:120–124 (#37) = Samuel ha-Nagid, *Poemas* 1:76–80 (#18), lines 22–26.

60. Additional texts authored by Andalusi Muslims are studied in Brann, *Power in the Portrayal*, 24–118. On possible expressions of doubt, see the poems mentioned in Brann, *Compunctious Poet*, 55–56, although these, too, might be conventional in nature.

61. Brann, *Compunctious Poet*, 39–46.

62. Ibid., 47–58; and Hollander, "Typology and Secular Literature," 3–19.

63. "Eloah 'oz w^e-el qano' w^e-nora'," Schirmann, *HPSP*, 1:85–92 (#25) = Samuel ha-Nagid, *Poemas* 1:3–14 (#2), trans. Scheindlin, "The Battle of Alfuente," 61–69, reads the poem (55–61) as an expression of doubt and as a defensive rhetorical apology addressed to Andalusi Jews who feared for the repercussions that Samuel's activities might bring on the Jewish community.

64. "Sh^e'eh minni 'amiti wa-ḥaveri," Schirmann, *HPSP*, 1:109–11 (#31), line 38 = Samuel ha-Nagid, *Poemas* 1:37–40 (#7), trans. Cole, *Dream of the Poem*, 52.

65. On this genre in Andalusi Hebrew poetry, see Levin, *The Embroidered Coat*, 1:150–208.

66. Schirmann, *HPSP*, 1:78–79 (#21) = Samuel ha-Nagid, *Poemas* 1:2 (#1).

67. "Ha-li ta'as b^e-khol shanah fi'alim," Schirmann, *HPSP*, 1:94–102 (#27) = Samuel ha-Nagid, *Poemas*, 18–28 (#4), lines 64–65.

68. Brody-Schirmann, *Solomon ibn Gabirol, Secular Poems*, 12–13, trans. (with exceptions noted) Cole, *Selected Poems of Solomon ibn Gabirol*, 85–87.

69. Scheindlin, *Gazelle*, 42–43. See, e.g., Tanenbaum, *The Contemplative Soul*, 84–105, which studies Ibn Gabirol's strophic *piyyuṭ* to the soul "Shabb^eḥi nafshi l^e-ṣureikh," Solomon ibn Gabirol, *Liturgical Poems*, 2:537–538.

70. Abstinence and seclusion, expressions of the Arabic topos *dhamm al-dunyā*, are also paired motifs in Ibn Gabirol's *zuhdiyya* "Mah tifḥadi nafshi" (Brody-Schirmann, *Solomon ibn Gabirol, Secular Poems*, 128, trans. Cole, *Selected Poems of Ibn Gabirol*, 105). This lyric is nearly a miniature study exercise for the first three thematic units of our poem:

> Why are you troubled and frightened, my soul?
> Be still and dwell where you are.
> Since the world to you is small as a hand,
> you won't, my storm, get far.
>
> Better than pitching from court to court
> is sitting before the throne of your Lord;
> if you distance yourself from others you'll flourish
> and surely see your reward.
>
> If your desire is like a fortified city,
> a siege will bring it down in time:
> You have no portion here in this world—
> so wake for the world to come.

71. Schirmann, *HPSP*, 1:207–210 (#74).

72. Ibid., 1:83–84 (#23) = Samuel ha-Nagid, *Poemas* 2:58–59 (#67).

73. For the sources, its popularity, and additional usages in al-Andalus, see Fierro, "Spiritual Alienation and Political Activism." Here is how Ibn Bājja (d. ca. 1139), *Tadbīr al-mutawaḥḥid*, 11, defined it: "These are those whom the Sufis mean in speaking of 'strangers' [*ghurabā'*] because although they are in their native lands and among their companions and neighbors, they are strangers in their views and they journey in their thoughts into other levels which are their true native lands," cited by Ormsby, "Ibn Ḥazm," 249.

74. The text's relationship to the Arabic genre *zuhdiyya*, to *Rasā'il ikhwān al-ṣafā'*, and to Neoplatonic thought in general is especially prominent. On the Neoplatonic thought and Ibn Gabirol, see Goodman, *Neoplatonism and Jewish Thought*; and Leibes, "The Book of Creation in R. Shelomoh Ibn Gabirol and a Commentary of His Poem 'I Love You.'" On Ibn Gabirol and *zuhdiyya*, see Scheindlin, "Ibn Gabirol's Religious Poetry and Arabic *Zuhd* Poetry." Scholarly opinion is divided on the precise dating of the *Rasā'il ikhwān al-ṣafā'*, but the encyclopedia arrived in al-Andalus in the tenth century. On the *Epistles of the Pure Brethren* and Ibn Gabirol, see Schlanger, *La philosophie de Salomon ibn Gabirol*, 94–97; and Levin, *Mystical Trends in the Poetry of Ibn Gabirol*, 137–167.

75. Muḥammad ibn Mukarram ibn Manẓūr, *Lisān al-'arab*, 4:2040–2044, identifies one of its meanings as well as its dialectical variant *saqa*ᶜ as "home"/"land"/"dwelling." In a personal communication, Peter Cole told me that he would amend his translation accordingly.

76. Lobel, *A Sufi-Jewish Dialogue*.

77. Baḥya ibn Paqūda, *al-Hidāya ilā farā'iḍ al-qulūb* (1998), 121, trans. Mansoor, *Book of Direction to the Duties of the Heart*, 171–172.

78. Lobel, *Sufi-Jewish Dialogue*, 21–50, examines the philosophical-mystical parallels between Ibn Gabirol and Ibn Paqūda.

79. In the meditative work *Tadbīr al-mutawaḥḥid*, Ibn Bājja, like Ibn Gabirol, is principally concerned with the individual's intellectual-spiritual contact with the divine. So, too, the protagonist of Abraham ibn Ezra's *Ḥay ben Meqiṣ* (text in Levin, *Abraham ibn Ezra Reader*, 121). This Hebrew adaptation of Ibn Sina's philosophical allegory, *Ḥayy ibn Yaqẓān*, narrates a vertical journey that begins on the same note as Ibn Gabirol's:

I have abandoned my house
Walked away from my possessions.
I left my home
My birthplace, my people.
The sons of my mother put me in charge
But they did not let me attend to my vineyard.
I arose to travel
In search of tranquility.
My spirit called out for relaxation
My soul demanded peace
I was in need of seclusion.

80. E.g., the poet laments Israel's exile and pleads for or imagines its eventual redemption-restoration in a poetic introduction to the second benediction of the daily prayer ("Shallah ruḥakha lᵉ-haḥayot giweinu"), Ibn Gabirol, *Liturgical Poems*, 2:337–338 (#107). See also Ibn Gabirol's admonition to the soul ("Nafshi de'i mah tif'ali"), *Liturgical Poems*, 1:291–293 (#88), and counsel to the soul ("Sᵉ'i 'ayin yᵉḥidati lᵉ-ṣureikh"), *Liturgical Poems*, 2:333–334 (#102).

81. It also reminds us of just how many prominent Andalusi Hebrew poets left al-Andalus for the Islamic East (Joseph ibn Abītūr, Isaac ibn Khalfūn, Judah Halevi, Isaac ibn Ezra, and Judah al-Ḥarizi).

82. Ibn Ezra represents an outstanding early example of what Wachs, *Double Diaspora in Sephardic Literature*, deems the "double diaspora" of Sefardi authors.

83. Moses ibn Ezra, *Secular Poems*, 1:66–67. The poet employs the "prisoner of separation" (*asir peirud*) to represent himself in the lyrics of the last verse (34). Brann, *The Compunctious Poet*, 44–46, discusses the allusive artistry in this poem. Elinson, *Looking Back*, 81–115, studies several of Ibn Ezra's odes for their nostalgic tenor and the ways in which they preserve al-Andalus and Sefarad in memory, analogous to the Andalusi Arabic elegies.

84. Moses ibn Ezra, *Secular Poems*, 1:113–114 (#112), vv. 14, 30–31. Decter, *Iberian Jewish Literature*, 37, discusses the importance of the opposing spatial metaphors for urbane al-Andalus and the uncivilized Christian kingdoms.

85. For the most comprehensive study of Ibn Ezra's poetry and poetics, see Pagis, *Secular Poetry and Poetic Theory*.

86. Moses ibn Ezra, *Kitāb al-muḥāḍara*, 48 (25b–26a). The negative valence of the second prooftext is unambiguous. In the century following Ibn Ezra, Judah al-Ḥarizi, *Taḥk^{e}moni* (18:36–40), in Schirmann, *HPSP*, 3:133 (#312), would deploy the first of these prooftexts to similar effect; see below, Chap. 5.

87. The most comprehensive study of this work is Dana, *Poetics of Medieval Hebrew Literature According to Moshe Ibn Ezra*.

88. Decter, *Iberian Jewish Literature*, 52–53; Drory, *Models and Contacts*, 210–215; Sadan, "Identity and Inimitability"; and Scheindlin, "Rabbi Moshe Ibn Ezra on the Legitimacy of Poetry."

89. Levin, *Abraham ibn Ezra*, 23, speaks of Abraham's "pedagogical urge" to impart the Judeo-Arabic heritage and worldview of Sefarad to the Jewish communities of Christian Europe.

90. Moses ibn Ezra, *Kitāb al-muḥāḍara*, 54–87 (28b–47b). Recall al-Hijārī's (*apud* al-Maqqarī) nearly identical framing of Andalusi Muslim exceptionalism above in Chapter 3, 99. Elinson, *Looking Back*, 130–134, examines the text according to the specifications of the Arabic genre.

91. BT 'Eruvin 53a: *B^{e}nei y^{e}hudah she-hiqpidu 'al l^{e}shonam nitqayy^{e}mah toratam b^{e}-yadam; b^{e}nei galil she-lo' hiqpidu 'al l^{e}shonam lo' nitqayy^{e}mah toratam b^{e}-yadam*. I have inserted "Hebrew" in brackets to indicate that this is how Ibn Ezra is reading the Talmudic tradition.

92. Moses ibn Ezra, *Kitāb al-muḥāḍara*, 52 (28a). The preeminent Andalusi grammarian of Hebrew, Abū l-Walīd Marwān Jonah ibn Janāḥ, *Kitāb al-luma'*, 8, also cites this Talmudic tradition.

93. Elinson, *Looking Back*, 132.

94. Ibn Ezra, *Kitāb al-muḥāḍara*, 54–56 (28b–30b). The chapter's title recalls the first chapter of al-Tha'ālibī's *Yatīmat al-dahr*, 1:6, "On the Superiority of the Poets of Syria over the Poets of Other Lands" (fī faḍl shu'arā' l-shām 'alā shu'arā' sā'ir al-buldān).

95. Hebrew texts from later twelfth-century authors originating or writing in the Christian kingdoms but still enamored of the Andalusi Jews' Judeo-Arabic heritage, e.g., Abraham ibn Ezra, Abraham ibn Daud, and Judah al-Ḥarizi, followed this cultural turn. Their cultural self-definition was portable, as long as they nurtured its aesthetic, literary, intellectual, and scientific values in Arabic and in Arabic-to-Hebrew translation.

96. Moses ibn Ezra, *Kitāb al-muḥāḍara*, 54–56 (29b–30a). The twelfth–thirteenth-century author Judah al-Ḥarizi rehearses Ibn Ezra's view on the origins of Hebrew poetry in al-Andalus. His perspective on Sefardi exceptionalism is discussed below, in Chap. 5.

97. Jonah ibn Janāḥ, *Kitāb al-luma'*, 2, and in Judah ibn Tibbon's (b. ca. 1120) medieval Hebrew translation, Jonah ibn Janāḥ, *Sefer ha-riqmah*, 10. Ibn Tibbon's introduction to his translation of *Sefer ha-riqmah*, 2–3, follows Ibn Ezra in remarking that God aroused the scholars of the Jerusalemite exile in Sefarad to the study of the Hebrew language and grammar.

98. Ibn Ezra, *Kitāb al-muḥāḍara*, 80 (43b), refers the reader to another of his related tracts, a nonextant work titled *Maqāla fī faḍā'il ahl al-ādāb wa-l-aḥsāb* (On the Merits of Men of *Adab* and of Noble Character).

CHAPTER 5

1. Balard, "A Christian Mediterranean," 187–88.

2. Goitein, *A Mediterranean Society*, 5:391–406.

3. Michalowski, "Mental Maps and Ideology," 131.

4. Ezrahi, *Booking Passage*, 3–23.

5. Leed, *The Mind of the Traveler*, 20.

6. Jacoby, "Benjamin of Tudela and His 'Book of Travels,'" 135–164, reviews the "gaps and inconsistencies" and other problems in the text still awaiting a critical edition. Jacoby asserts that two medieval editors abridged and revised Benjamin's original text. He further reconstructs a "plausible itinerary" and an "approximate time frame for several stages of Benjamin's journey." For a different treatment of the *Book of Travels*, which contests the numerous positivist readings of the work, see Jacobs, "A Day's Journey," expanding upon Jacobs's excellent treatment of the work in *Reorienting the East.*

7. Benjamin of Tudela, *Sefer ha-massa'ot*, 1–2, trans. *The Itinerary of Benjamin of Tudela*, 55.

8. For the history of this community and its place in Navarre, see Leroy, *The Jews of Navarre in the Late Middle Ages*, 1–33.

9. Abraham ibn Daud, *Sefer ha-qabbalah*, 72, trans. G. Cohen, *Book of Tradition*, 99. On the specifically cultural transition, see Gampel, "A Letter to a Wayward Teacher," 389–447.

10. Assis and Magdalena, *The Jews of Navarre in the Late Middle Ages*, 30.

11. Assis, "The Judeo-Arabic Tradition in Christian Spain," 111–124.

12. Matthews and Herbert, *Geography*, 2.

13. Constable, "Muslim Merchants in Andalusi International Trade," 759–773.

14. Signer, *Itinerary of Benjamin of Tudela*, 223, and Signer introduction, 29, 32.

15. Ibn Daud, *Sefer ha-qabbalah*, 63–103.

16. A textual corruption (*al-'rwh*) is frequently rendered "Algarve" (i.e., southwest Portugal), as in Adler's translation; sometimes, it is translated simply as "Portugal." Wasserstein, "Does Benjamin Mention Portugal?," 193–200, demonstrates that it should be rendered "Morocco."

17. Benjamin of Tudela, *Massa'ot*, 2–3; *Itinerary*, 60.

18. Goitein, "The Unity of the Mediterranean World in the 'Middle' Middle Ages," 296–307.

19. Benjamin of Tudela, *Massa'ot*, 24; *Itinerary*, 72.

20. Benjamin of Tudela, *Massa'ot*, 105–106; *Itinerary*, 134.

21. Benjamin of Tudela, *Massa'ot*, 54–55, 60; *Itinerary*, 96, 99.

22. Goitein, *Mediterranean Society*, 2:19. On the decline of the exilarchate even as its social nobility endured for the Jews, see Brody, *The Geonim of Babylonia and the Shaping of Medieval Jewish Culture*, 80–82; and Gil, *Jews in Islamic Countries in the Middle Ages*, 105–116.

23. Benjamin of Tudela, *Massa'ot*, 40; *Itinerary*, 100.

24. Crone, *God's Rule*, 221; Fischel, "'The Resh-Galuta' in Arabic Literature," 181–187; and Gil, *Jews in Islamic Countries*, 88–91.

25. Brann, *Power in the Portrayal*, 72–74.

26. Alfonso, *Islamic Culture Through Jewish Eyes*, 89–90.

27. G. Cohen, "Messianic Postures of Ashkenazi and Sephardim," 271–297.

28. Brann, *Power in the Portrayal*, 130–139.

29. Judah al-Ḥarizi, *Taḥkᵉmoni*, 264; and Brann, *Power in the Portrayal*, 155–156.

30. Yahalom and Blau, *The Wanderings of Judah al-Ḥarizi*, xvii. The benefits of Jewish life under Ayyūbid sovereignty are also expressed in Judah al-Ḥarizi, *Kitāb al-durar*, 110 [trans. 79*].

31. Benjamin of Tudela, *Massa'ot*, 77–81; *Itinerary*, 54–56. On Alroy, see Golb, "Al-Rūjīi, Solomon and Menahem," 4:190–194.

32. See E. Weber, "Construction of Identity in Twelfth-Century Andalusi," 1–8. Weber writes (4): "Benjamin and Ibn Jubayr's writings defined what it meant to be from Andalusia (or not) to large numbers of people."

33. Gellens, "The Search for Knowledge in Medieval Muslim Societies," 59.

34. Netton, *Seek Knowledge*, 40, 95; and Pellat, "Ibn Djubayr," 3:755.

35. Constable, *Trade and Traders in Muslim Spain*, 16.

36. Ibn Ṭufayl, *Ḥayy ibn Yaqẓān*. The bibliography on this work is especially rich. A noteworthy recent contribution is Ben-Zaken, *Reading Ḥayy Ibn-Yaqẓān*.

37. Attar, "Beyond Family, History, Religion, and Language," reads the tale in the pluralistic social context of Almohad al-Andalus during the intellectually minded rule of Ibn Ṭufayl's patron Abū Ya'qūb Yūsuf (r. 1163–1184). That was to change under his stern successor, Abū Yūsuf Ya'qūb al-Manṣūr (r. 1184–1199), coinciding with the first of Ibn Jubayr's voyages. My thanks to Esperanza Alfonso for alerting me to Attar's article.

38. On Almohad legitimacy and al-Andalus, see Fierro, "The *Mahdī* Ibn Tumart and al-Andalus."

39. Ibn Jubayr, *Riḥla* (1992), 23; *The Travels of Ibn Jubayr*, 26.

40. Al-Maqqarī, *Nafḥ al-ṭīb*, 2:385.

41. Dejugnat, "La Méditerranée comme frontière dans le récit de voyage (*riḥla*) d'Ibn Gubayr," 33.

42. Gergen, "Narrative Structures in Social Explanation," 96, cited in Euben, *Journeys to Other Shores*, 9.

43. Recall that we read in Chap. 1 of *'ajā'ib* in the sense of "the fantastic." Its semantic range covers the various words employed in the chapter, including "strange," "unusual," "remarkable," or "astonishing," depending on the context. Hartog, *The Mirror of Herodotus*, 230, cited in Leed, *Mind of the Traveler*, 106. Arabic storytellers thoroughly embraced the theme of *'ajā'ib* as a genre unto itself. See also Bynum, "Wonder."

44. Ibn Jubayr, *Riḥla*, 362–364; *Travels*, 300–301.

45. Ibn Jubayr, *Riḥla*, 388–389; *Travels*, 320–321.

46. Netton, *Seek Knowledge*, 133–136.

47. Ibn Jubayr, *Riḥla*, 385; *Travels*, 318.

48. Ibid.

49. Ibn Jubayr, *Riḥla*, 386–387; *Travels*, 319.

50. Ibn Jubayr, *Riḥla*, 390–391; *Travels*, 321–322.

51. Mallette, *The Kingdom of Sicily*, 1–4.

52. Ibn Jubayr, *Riḥla*, 410–411; *Travels*, 337–338.

53. Ibn Jubayr, *Riḥla*, 413–414; *Travels*, 340–341.

54. Brann, *Power in the Portrayal*, 91–118.

55. Ibn Jubayr, *Riḥla*, 87; *Travels*, 73.

56. *Riḥlat Ibn Jubayr* (1907), 77–78, cited by Beninson, "Liminal States," 18, where Beninson refers to Ibn Jubayr expressing "both militancy and a sense of superiority towards the parlous state of the Eastern Islamic world."

57. Netton, *Seek Knowledge*, 134.

58. Yahalom-Blau, *Wanderings of Judah al-Ḥarizi*, reckons with five distinct accounts of this journey.

59. Judah al-Ḥarizi, *Maḥberot iti'el*. On the Arabic *maqāma* in al-Andalus and its Hebrew adaptation, there and in the Christian kingdoms, see Drory, "The Maqama."

60. Judah al-Ḥarizi, *Taḥkemoni*, 78 (author's introduction, lines 359–360).

61. Al-Ḥarizi (Yahalom-Katsumata), *Taḥkemoni*, 78.

62. An earlier edition of *Taḥkemoni* was published by Y. Toporowsky, trans. (1965–1973) Victor Emanuel Reichert. There is a freer rhymed prose translation by Segal, *The Book of Taḥkemoni*. I cite page numbers from the Yahalom-Katsumata edition but follow Toporowsky's numbering of *maqāmāt*, noted in parentheses ( ) and Yahalom-Katsumata's ordering in brackets [ ].

63. See Rand, *The Evolution of al-Ḥarizi's Taḥkemoni*, for an excellent new study on the text's manuscript transmission and recension history and its literary motifs in relation to al-Ḥarizi's travels and al-Ḥarīrī's Arabic prototype.

64. Yahalom-Blau, *Wanderings of Judah al-Ḥarizi*, 77–89: "Be not lazy in seeking your / means of support and make a caravanserai your nest" (line 19).

65. E.g., *Ādāb al-falāsifa*, by Ḥunayn ibn Isḥāq, trans. as *Musrei ha-filosofim*; *Maqālat al-ḥadīqa fī ma'nā l-majaz wa-l-ḥaqīqa*, by Moses ibn Ezra, trans. as *'Arugat ha-bosem*; and *Dalālat al-ḥā'irīn*, by Moses Maimonides, trans. as *Moreh nevukhim*.

66. See Baneth, "R. Judah al-Ḥarizi and the Chain of Translations of Maimonides' Treatise on Resurrection." On the very complex translation issue, see Pearce, *Andalusi Literary Intellectual Tradition*, 171–191. The century-long struggle that came to be known as the "Maimonidean controversy" turned important sectors of the Sefardi elite in the Christian kingdoms of northern Iberia to embrace some values of their Franco-German neighbors' intellectual and spiritual orientations in a new synthesis of cultural stimuli. In so doing, they challenged the supremacy of the Andalusi Jewish rationalist and aesthetic traditions. On the controversy in general, including references to al-Ḥarizi, see Septimus, *Hispano-Jewish Culture in Transition*; and Silver, *Maimonidean Criticism and the Maimonidean Controversy, 1180–1240*.

67. Judah al-Ḥarizi, *Kitāb al-durar*, 92–108 [trans. 72–77*], offers an extended prose and poetic encomium to Maimonides, along with references to the controversy and complaints about his opponents. Al-Ḥarizi's Arabic panegyric for Abraham Maimuni appears in Yahalom-Blau, *Wanderings of Judah al-Ḥarizi*, 247. *Kitāb al-durar* appears more interested in Jewish religious intellectual figures than al-Ḥarizi's other works.

68. Jacobs, *Reorienting the East*, 47, mentions "emulating Judah Halevi" and participating in "a wider movement of primarily French Jewish intellectuals . . . who flocked to Palestine during the late Crusader period" as factors in al-Ḥarizi's excursion.

69. Al-Ḥarizi, *Kitāb al-durar*, 44 [trans. 55*].

70. There are four in all, two in Arabic. On the recensions and dedications, see Rand, *Evolution*, 24–41.

71. Al-Ḥarizi, *Taḥkemoni* [2010], 77 [al-Ḥarizi's introduction].

72. Brann, *Compunctious Poet*, 26, 37–39, 82.

73. Al-Ḥarizi, *Taḥkemoni* [2010], 55, trans. Drory, *Models and Contacts*, 221.

74. Al-Ḥarizi, *Kitāb al-durar*, 109–120, 124–144 [trans. 78–91*].

75. Yahalom-Blau, *Wanderings of Judah al-Ḥarizi*, 160–162.

76. Al-Ḥarizi, *Kitāb al-durar*, 37*. By contrast, Yahalom-Blau, *Wanderings of Judah al-Ḥarizi*, xvii, conclude: "In the end we were unable to definitively establish what motivated Alḥarizi's journey."

77. Al-Ḥarizi, *Taḥkemoni* [2010], 3.

78. Ibid., 598.

79. In *maqāma* 3, Halevi is the artistic standard by which all other Andalusi Hebrew poets are judged.

80. Judah Halevi's letter to Samuel ben Ḥanania the Egyptian Nagid, in Yahalom, "The Immigration of Rabbi Judah ha-Levi to Eretz Israel in Vision and Riddle," 45.

81. Al-Ḥarizi, *Kitāb al-durar*, 44 [trans. 55*].

82. Schirmann-Fleischer, *Hebrew Poetry in Christian Spain*, 155–156. So, too, Yahalom-Katsumata, *Taḥkemoni* [2010], ix, note that al-Ḥarizi "saw himself not merely as an adventurer but as a holy pilgrim."

83. Al-Ḥarizi, *Taḥkemoni* [2010], 78–79.

84. On this specifically Ḥarizian rhetorical gambit, see Huss, "It Never Happened, Nor Did It Ever Exist," 75–77.

85. Al-Ḥarizi, *Taḥkemoni* [2010], xv, where Yahalom-Katsumata provide a list of the book's references to the biblical figure Judah.

86. E.g., Dishon, "Medieval Panorama in the Book of Taḥkemoni," 11–27, and the more nuanced Oettinger, "The Characteristics of Satire on Jewish Communities in Yehudah al-Ḥarizi's 'Book of Taḥkemoni,'" 59–87.

87. Decter, *Iberian Jewish Literature*, 194–196, observes that in contrast to Benjamin of Tudela, al-Ḥarizi is uninterested in topographical details and concentrates exclusively on individuals, communities, and the state of Jewish learning and culture that he found on his visits.

88. E.g., disagreements among experts regarding dating *Taḥkemoni*'s recensions and redactions frequently are driven by al-Ḥarizi's other works that do not belong to the category of imaginative literature. For my purposes, I am setting aside questions of *Taḥkemoni*'s compositional stages.

89. Rand, *Evolution*, 10–23.

90. Ibid., 66.

91. Ibid., 9.

92. Al-Ḥarizi, *Taḥkemoni* [2010], 193–208 [11].

93. Ibid., 103–116 [3]. Arabic title: "Maqāmat shuʿarāʾ ʾl-andalus." Thirty Andalusi poets are discussed.

94. Al-Ḥarizi, *Taḥkemoni* [2010], 209–233 [12]. Arabic title: "Maqāmat ʿaṣr al-shuʿarāʾ l-ʿibrāniyyin." Six Andalusi poets are considered.

95. Al-Ḥarizi, *Taḥkemoni* [2010], 415 [36], ll. 124–125.

96. Ibid., 433–457 [39].

97. Sadan, "R. Judah al-Ḥarizi as a Cultural Junction."

98. Al-Ḥarizi, *Kitāb al-durar*, 44 (introduction, lines 15–20) [trans. 55*].

99. Scheindlin, "The Jews in Muslim Spain," 198; and Decter, *Iberian Jewish Literature*, 124, 212–213.

100. Drory, *Models and Contacts*, 25.

101. Ibid., 225.

102. Rand, *Evolution*, 59.

103. Al-Ḥarizi, *Taḥkᵉmoni* [2010], 69.

104. Brubaker and Cooper, "Beyond 'Identity.'"

105. Reedon, *Ideology*, 60.

106. Al-Ḥarizi, *Taḥkᵉmoni* [2010], 261–266 (#28) [16]. Cf. *Taḥkᵉmoni* [2010], 436 (#46) [39], "Appraisal of the People," which incorporates Ḥever's three-line mention of his visit to Jerusalem. Al-Ḥarizi's travels took him to Jerusalem in 1218 while heading from Cairo overland to Syria and Iraq. We read additional brief accounts of this visit in the "Maqāma of the Patrons," an independent text reported in al-Ḥarizi's own name and that is not part of *Taḥkᵉmoni* (Yahalom-Blau, *Wanderings of Judah al-Ḥarizi*, 77–83) and in *Taḥkᵉmoni*'s "Aleppo Dedication," al-Ḥarizi, *Taḥkᵉmoni* [2010], 595. *Maqāma* 19 of *Maḥbᵉrot iti'el*, al-Ḥarizi's translation-adaptation of al-Ḥarīrī's *maqāmāt*, transposes to Jerusalem the original text's imaginative visit to Mecca.

107. Al-Ḥarizi, *Taḥkᵉmoni* [2010], 529 (#50), contains two additional poems to Jerusalem in the poetic miscellany: "Shalom lᵉ-'ir shalem" and "Ṣiyyon sha'afah nafshi." Recall that that pilgrimage is also mentioned in *Taḥkᵉmoni*'s first introduction and in "Iggeret lᵉshon zahav."

108. Al-Ḥarizi, *Taḥkᵉmoni* [2010], 261 [notes], and Segal, *Taḥkᵉmoni*, 553–554, cite parallels to Halevi's legendary pilgrimage lyrics.

109. Al-Ḥarizi, *Taḥkᵉmoni* [2010], 450 [#46] (#46).

110. Cf. al-Ḥarizi's 110-line Arabic *qaṣīda* in praise of Jerusalem; Yahalom-Blau, *Wanderings of Judah al-Ḥarizi*, 252–256.

111. As noted above, *Taḥkᵉmoni* shares this view of the benefits of Jewish life under Ayyūbid sovereignty with *Kitāb al-durar*, 110 [trans. 79*] and *al-Rawḍa al-anīqa*, in Yahalom-Blau, *Wanderings of Judah al-Ḥarizi*, xvii.

112. Kedar, "The Jews of Jerusalem, 1187–1267, and the Role of Naḥmanides in the Reestablishment of Their Community," 123–24, surmises that the internecine troubles obliquely mentioned involved tensions among the composite of groups from France, North Africa, and "Ashkelon," i.e., Levantine Jews, among others.

113. In Brann, *Power in the Portrayal*, 150, I categorize *Taḥkᵉmoni*'s various types of discourse as: (1) anecdotes in which the narrative element exists merely or primarily as a setup for rhetorical exercises; (2) accounts of an adventure or a rescue; (3) tales involving a ruse or some other form of deception; and (4) *maqāmāt* that are vehicles for descriptive or didactic discourse.

114. Al-Ḥarizi, *Taḥkᵉmoni* [2010], 450. Decter, *Iberian Jewish Literature*, 181, discusses *Taḥkᵉmoni*'s idyllic depictions of lush gardens as "a place remembered that evokes Andalusian culture."

115. I am skeptical of readings of the "Jerusalem *maqāma*" such as Segal, *Taḥkᵉmoni*, 552–557, which assign it messianic overtones. Al-Ḥarizi identifies himself as a staunch enthusiast of Maimonides, who opposed popular messianic speculation and activity. Rather, the *maqāma*'s critique summons the community to righteous behavior that can only improve its diminishing lot more in accordance with Maimonides, *Maqāla fī tᵉḥiyyat ha-meitim*, 34* [#48]; *Moses*

Maimonides' Treatise on Resurrection, 174: "their conditions did not follow the course of the conditions of the rest of the nations, but they are set apart through this great miracle: namely, that the improvement of their conditions or their ruin is always associated with their actions."

116. Kfir, *Matter of Geography*, 79.

117. Judah Halevi is deemed the standard according to which all Hebrew poets are measured.

118. Al-Ḥarizi, *Taḥkemoni* [2010], 109 (lines 160–162) [(#3)].

119. Unlike *maqāma* 3, *maqāma* 18 deems Solomon ibn Gabirol, who groused about his countrymen's pitiful ignorance of the holy language, their inferior poetic talent, and inadequate intellect, the quintessential model of an Andalusi Hebrew poet.

120. Kfir, *Matter of Geography*, 78–79, draws attention to the high irony of the lecture's tribute to the Sefardi Jews' Jerusalemite origins before an imagined audience of clueless present-day denizens of the Holy City.

121. Al-Ḥarizi, *Taḥkemoni* [2010], 210–211 (#18) [12].

122. Moses ibn Ezra, *Kitāb al-muḥāḍara*, 25b.

123. Al-Ḥarizi, *Taḥkemoni* [2010], 211 [12].

124. Ibid., 212.

125. Ibid., 211–212 [12].

126. Decter, *Dominion Built of Praise*, 144.

127. Al-Ḥarizi, *Kitāb al-durar*, 44.

128. Cole, *Dream of the Poem*, 208, calls al-Ḥarizi an "Andalusian writer through and through," despite a literary style that incorporates post-Andalusi elements. Kfir, *Matter of Geography*, 71, observes that "none of Alḥarizi's predecessors matched his own profuse efforts, in either poetry or prose, to aggrandize Spanish Jewry at the expense of other Jewish communities."

CONCLUSION

1. I follow the distinction delineated by Nora, "Between Memory and History," 7.

2. Castro, *The Structure of Spanish History*, represents an elaboration of his work originally published in 1948 as *España en su historia*. Glick, *Islamic and Christian Spain in the Early Middle Ages*, 290–299, discusses and glosses the significance of Castro's ideas. For sketches of the notion *convivencia*, see Glick, "Convivencia." See also Akasoy, "Convivencia and Its Discontents"; Szpiech, "The Convivencia Wars"; Ray, "Between Tolerance and Persecution"; Wolf, "Convivencia in Medieval Spain"; Novikoff, "Between Tolerance and Intolerance in Medieval Spain"; and Soifer, "Beyond Convivencia," all of which provide critical reviews of the subject.

3. See Menocal, "Visions of al-Andalus," and her volume for the reading public, *Ornament of the World*, whose opening chapter is titled "A First-Rate Place." Menocal's book takes its title from a comment by Hrotsvit of Gandersheim, the tenth-century author writing about a Christian martyr in Córdoba. See the sources cited by Cole, *Dream of the Poem*, 343n12. Kikim Media recently released the documentary *Ornament of the World* (2019), produced and directed by the late Michael Schwarz. The film, years in the making, is based to some extent on Menocal's book.

4. Dozy, *Spanish Islam*, 455.

5. On the sociopolitical context of Gayangos's vision for liberal Spain, see Ginger, "The Estranged Self of Spain"; and Álvarez Ramos, "Gayangos and Politics in Spain." On Dozy's

correspondence with Gayangos, see Marín, "Scholarship and Criticism." The conclusion of Kimmel, *Parables of Coercion*, 175–178, titled "Excavating Islamic Spain," comments on the role of early modern Spanish scholars like Gayangos in defining a new Spanish nationalism predicated on "celebrating a multi-cultural history of the three faiths." Monroe, *Islam and the Arabs in Spanish Scholarship*, studies the entire arc of early to contemporary Spanish scholarship on Arabic and Islam.

6. Gayangos, *History of the Mohammedan Dynasties of Spain*.

7. Ibid., 1:vii.

8. The Andalusi quarter in Fez was established early in the ninth century by exiles from an unsuccessful revolt against the Umayyad emir al-Ḥakam I in Córdoba. See Kennedy, *Muslim Spain and Portugal*, 44. These Andalusi refugees were also responsible for construction of the Andalusi mosque that is a twin of the more iconic Qarawiyyin mosque.

9. Hermes, "Nostalgia for al-Andalus in Early Modern Moroccan *Voyages en Espagne*."

10. Al-Azmeh, "Mortal Enemies, Invisible Neighbours," 260.

11. "Jehuda ben Halevi," Draper, trans., *The Complete Poems of Heinrich Heine*, 659–677, in which Moses ibn Ezra is also lionized and Solomon ibn Gabirol plays an important role; *Almansor*, 179–237. Heine also composed a lyric ballad, "Moor's Serenade," trans. Draper, 164, that appears in his *Book of Songs*. On this facet of Heine, see Goldstein, "A Politics and Poetics of Diaspora"; and Schonfield, "Heine and Convivencia."

12. See Kuhn, *The Politics of Pleasure*, 120–121. On Disraeli's romanticism and his fluid identity, see Rozen, "Pedigree Remembered, Reconstructed, Invented."

13. B. Lewis, *History Remembered, Recovered, Invented*, 72–78.

14. B. Lewis, "The Cult of Spain and the Turkish Romantics," 129–133.

15. Hitti, *A History of the Arabs from the Earliest Times to the Present*, 526.

16. See Calderwood, *Colonial al-Andalus*.

17. Leaman, *Moses Maimonides*, 5.

18. Wasserstrom, "Jewish-Muslim Relations in the Context of Andalusian Emigration," 69.

19. Al-Jabiri, *Arab-Islamic Philosophy*.

20. Gallois, "Andalusi Cosmopolitanism in World History," 75.

21. Pérès, *La poésie andalouse en arabe classique au onzième siècle*, 473–75. García-Arenal translated Pérès's book (originally published in 1937) into Spanish under the noteworthy title *El Esplendor de al-Andalus: La poesía andaluza en árabe clásico en el siglo XI*.

22. Nykl, *Hispano-Arabic Poetry and Its Relations with the Old Provençal Troubadours*, xiii.

23. Foreword to Ibn Sa'īd al-Maghribī, *The Banners of the Champions*, v.

24. Boone, *Lost Civilization*, 10, citing (without page citation) J. Safran, *The Second Umayyad Caliphate*.

25. See Langermann, "Another Andalusian Revolt?"; and Sabra, "The Andalusian Revolt Against Ptolemaic Astronomy."

26. For studies on law and legal theory, see Hacohen, "The Jerusalem Talmud in the Teachings of the Early Spanish Sages," 113–176; and Herman, "Situating Maimonides' Approach to the Oral Torah in Its Andalusian Context." For the practical application of Mālikī law in al-Andalus, see Hendrickson, the suggestively titled "Is al-Andalus Different? Continuity as Contested, Constructed, and Performed Across Three Mālikī *Fatwās*."

27. Nasr and Leaman, *The History of Islamic Philosophy*, 1:275–364, group thinkers accordingly. See also Cruz Hernández, "Islamic Thought in the Iberian Peninsula"; Stroumsa and Sviri, "The Beginnings of Mystical Philosophy in al-Andalus"; Conrad, "The World of Ibn Tufayl," 12–13; and Akhtar, *Philosophers, Sufis, and Caliphs*. For Jewish thought, see

Stroumsa's work identifying Moses Maimonides as a "Mediterranean thinker" and an "Almohad thinker," *Maimonides in His World*, 6–13, 53–83. By the eleventh century, al-Andalus had supplanted North Africa and the Islamic East as the principal locus for Jewish theological speculation and philosophical activity. This relocation would have significant consequences for the history of Jewish thought.

28. Fox, Mourtada-Sabbah, and Khalaf, "Ethnography and the Culture of Tolerance in al-Andalus," 146.

29. Glasser, *The Lost Paradise.*

30. Anidjar, *Our Place in al-Andalus*, 3. In another work, "Medieval Spain and the Integration of Memory," Anidjar offers a biting critique of the contemporary deployment of the memory of medieval Spain with which "we persist in thinking of Europe as an exemplary and exceptional site of peaceful coexistence" (221).

31. Anidjar, "Medieval Spain and the Integration of Memory," 221.

32. Fernández Parrilla, "Disoriented Postcolonialities."

33. Majid, *Freedom and Orthodoxy.*

34. Docker, *1492.*

35. Shamsie, *Journal of Postcolonial Writing.*

36. Arigata, "Spain," 224.

37. Sardar and Yassin-Kassab, *Critical Muslim.*

38. Alfonso, "From al-Andalus to North Africa," identifies the Gavisons' exegetical activity, as inspired by Castilian rabbis, alongside their fealty to Judeo-Arabic and Hebrew culture.

39. J. Cohen and Stein, *Sephardi Lives*, 387–390.

40. See B. Lewis, "The Pro-Islamic Jews," 148.

41. The term "Golden Age" (of the Hebrew literature of the Jews of Spain) appears to have been coined by the Lutheran theologian Franz Delitzsch, *Zur Geschichte der jüdischen Poësie vom Abschluss der heiligen Schriften Alten Bundes bis auf die neueste Zeit*, 44–45 ("das goldene Zeitalter"), cited by Ben-Sasson, "The So-Called 'Golden Age,'" 125.

42. Cited by Efron, *German Jewry and the Allure of the Sephardic*, 198.

43. The modern German Jewish fascination with Iberia and its Jews and the usefulness of the trope of Sefardi exceptionalism for their own cultural project is now the subject of two books: Efron's aforementioned *German Jewry*; and Schapkow, *Role Model and Countermodel.* See also Gerber, "Reconsiderations of Sephardic History;" Stillman, "The Judeo-Islamic Historical Encounter," 3–6; M. R. Cohen, *Under Crescent and Cross*, 3–6; and Frenkel, "The Historiography of the Jews in Muslim Countries in the Middle Ages."

44. Graetz, *A History of the Jews*, 3:41–42.

45. Steinschneider, *Jewish Literature from the Eighth to the Eighteenth Century with an Introduction on Talmud and Midrash*, 61–62.

46. Evri, "Translating the Arab-Jewish Tradition," 5ff. Evri analyzes the political implications of Yahuda's speech against the background of deep divisions in Palestinian politics as well as his outlier status among his contemporary Jewish scholars.

47. A. Halkin, "The Judeo-Islamic Age," 263.

48. Zafrani, *Juifs d'Andalousie et du Maghreb.* Schroeter, "The Shifting Boundaries of Moroccan Jewish Identities," studies the relation of Zafrani's project to the construction of Moroccan Jewish identity and "Moroccan-style *convivencia.*"

49. Faur, *Homo Mysticus*, ix.

50. Alcalay, *After Jews and Arabs*, 119–194.

51. Rejwan, *Israel's Place in the Middle East*, 48–80.

52. Halevi-Wise, "Introduction: Through the Prism of Sepharad," 1.

53. Ibid., 6.

54. Linhard, *Jewish Spain*.

55. Davis, *Musical Exodus*, xxx.

56. Islamic Sicily, the only other Islamic polity to disappear into memory, has received similar attention as the site of an exceptionally tolerant society defined by its cultural symbiosis. See Abulafia, "The End of Muslim Sicily," 103; and Simonsohn, "Sicily."

57. Szpiech, "The Convivencia Wars," reframes the scholarly debate over *convivencia* as rooted in epistemology and, accordingly, in modern disciplinary struggles and their relationship to nationalism.

58. Novikoff, "Between Tolerance and Intolerance," 8, further identifies the origins and traces the history of the trope in Spanish historiography.

59. The idea of a "multicultural Spain" has come to compete with *convivencia* as a descriptive term for the idea of the "uniqueness" of Spain. See Martín and Martínez-Carazo, *Spain's Multicultural Legacies*, for a collection of essays on this theme.

60. Barkai, *Spanish Mythology*. Note that modern Hebrew has no other word for "Spain" than "Sefarad," so to the Hebrew reader, Barkai's book is ambiguously titled "Sefardi Mythology."

61. The contradictory trends in Spanish historiography are reviewed by González Alcantud, "The Beginning and End of the *Good* Myth of al-Andalus."

62. Guichard, *Al-Andalus*, 24.

63. See Monroe, "The Hispano-Arabic World," 70. Novikoff, "Between Tolerance and Intolerance in Medieval Spain," reviews the debate in Spanish historiography.

64. Marías Aguilera, *Understanding Spain*, 1–11.

65. García Sanjuán, *La conquista islámica de la península ibérica y la tergiversación del pasado*, debunks the views of notorious "denialists" such as Ignacio Olagüe Videla and Emilio González Ferrín, who aver that Muslims never even conquered the Iberian Peninsula. For a valuable self-described "outsider's" reading of García Sanjuán and his interlocutors, see Wolf, "Negating Negationism." On the ways in which the history of modern Spain is intertwined with nationalism and identity, see García Sanjuán, "Rejecting al-Andalus, Exalting the Reconquista." For a different review of the historiography and an analysis of the related sociopolitical issues in contemporary Spain, see Hirschkind, "The Contemporary Afterlife of Moorish Spain."

66. Fernández-Morera, "The Myth of Andalusian Paradise," and his book-length assault on the Castro-Menocal school on the same theme, *The Myth of the Andalusian Paradise*. See also Fanjul, "El mito de las tres culturas," which is aimed at Castro's contribution. That issue of the journal is titled *Al-Andalus Frente a España: Un Paraíso Imaginario*.

67. Fernández-Morera, *The Myth of the Andalusian Paradise*, 15, 246 (notes). Such usages by Muslim authors are stripped of their context.

68. Ibid., 16.

69. Catlos, *Kingdoms of Faith*.

70. See Viguera Molíns, "Al-Andalus como interferencia"; and Aidi, "The Interference of al-Andalus." The Spanish historian Ignacio Olagüe Videla offered his readers a novel and extreme expression of the idea of "eternal Spain," as indicated by the title of his work, *Les Arabes n'ont jamais envahi l'Espagne*.

71. Note that the Modern Language Association's annual bibliography of literary studies includes, in the category of "Spanish literature," all works written in premodern Iberia,

regardless of language (i.e., including Hebrew and Arabic). Glick, *Islamic and Christian Spain*, 291, who finds value in much of Castro's contribution, nevertheless critiques his numerous ahistorical assertions "of the singularity of the Spanish situation," as evidenced in Castro's expressions such as "the essential uniqueness of the phenomenon" and "uniquely Spanish circumstances."

72. Yerushalmi, "Medieval Jewry," 15–16.

73. See Calderwood, "The Invention of al-Andalus." On related uses of *convivencia* in contemporary Morocco, see Boum, "The Performance of Convivencia." On the significance of al-Andalus in contemporary southern Spain, see Rogozen-Soltar, "Al-Andalus in Andalusia."

74. See comments of Menocal, "Visions of al-Andalus," 13. Yet equally significant, if not greater, religious diversity was prevalent in the Islamic East, with its dynamic mix of Zoroastrians, multiplicity of Christian churches, and Rabbanite Jews, aligned, by turns, with the Palestinian or Iraqi academies and Karaite Jews and varieties of Shiite Muslims throughout the region.

75. Goldziher, "The Spanish Arabs and Islam," 1:370–71. Marín compares critically the positions of Goldziher and Nykl, "Dos calas en la visión sobre al-Andalus del orientalismo europeo."

76. Hourani, *A History of the Arab Peoples*, 189. It is interesting that scholars such as Hourani do not point to the more complex linguistic situation in al-Andalus in which Romance was spoken alongside the Andalusi Arabic dialect as a potential factor in Andalusi "difference" when compared with the Islamic East.

77. Lapidus, *A History of Islamic Societies*, 378–379.

78. Wasserstein, *Rise and Fall of the Party-Kings*, 15.

79. In effect, Menocal was returning, albeit with much greater sophistication, to the literary-historical project launched by Nykl in *Hispano-Arabic Poetry and Its Relations with the Old Provençal Troubadours* (1946).

80. Menocal, *The Arabic Role in Medieval Literary History*.

81. Lewis, *History Remembered, Recovered, Invented*, 72–78.

82. Menocal, *The Arabic Role in Medieval Literary History*, 16.

83. Menocal, Dodds, and Balbale, *The Arts of Intimacy*.

84. Fuchs, *Exotic Nation*.

85. Grabar, "Islamic Spain, the First Four Centuries," 8–9.

86. See Safran, *The Second Umayyad Caliphate*.

87. Akasoy, "Al-Andalus in Exile," 329–343.

88. Baer, *Die Juden im christien Spanien*; *History of the Jews in Christian Spain* [Hebrew]; *A History of the Jews of Christian Spain*, 1:22–38, 59–77. On Baer and his historiography, see Yuval, "Yitzhak Baer and the Search for Authentic Judaism."

89. Assis, "Sefarad," 35.

90. For his views on "the myth of Spanish Islamic tolerance," see Lewis, *History Remembered, Recovered, Invented*, 71–78.

91. H. Halkin, "Out of Andalusia," 39–45, and his book *Judah Halevi*, the last chapter of which assails Menocal's *Ornament of the World*. Halkin was preceded by R. Lewis, "Muslim Glamour and the Spanish Jews," and "Maimonides and the Muslims," among others, who endeavored to dismantle any semblance of the Jews' sense of rootedness and being at home anywhere or at any time in premodern Islamic society, contrary to S. D. Goitein.

92. Sachar, *Farewell España*, 19.

93. E.g., Zimmels, *Ashkenazim and Sephardim*, 1, famously went so far as to assert that "there was almost no department in which [Ashkenaz and Sefarad] did not differ." On the cultural creativity of medieval Ashkenaz, see the authoritative study by Kanarfogel, *The Intellectual History and Rabbinic Culture of Medieval Ashkenaz.*

94. Marcus, "Beyond the Sephardic Mystique."

95. Schorsch, "The Myth of Sephardic Supremacy."

96. Marcus, "Medieval Jewish Studies," 114–115; Tirosh-Rothschild, "Response," it should be noted, does not always find undue emphasis on Sefardi history and culture, as Marcus would have it. It is also worth drawing attention to Ruderman, "The Impact of Early Modern Jewish Thought on the Eighteenth Century," which examines evidence of complex early modern Italian Jewish attitudes toward the cultural authorities of classical Sefarad.

97. Hughes, "The 'Golden Age' of Muslim Spain."

98. Ben-Sasson, "Al-Andalus."

99. Goitein, *A Mediterranean Society*, 5:425.

100. Stillman, "Aspects of Jewish Life in Islamic Spain," 61–62, and "Al-Andalus," 1:106.

101. B. Lewis, *The Jews of Islam*, 41, 52.

102. Lassner, *Jews, Christians, and the Abode of Islam*, 201–202.

103. Ashtor, *History of the Jews in Muslim Spain* [Hebrew] = *The Jews of Moslem Spain.*

104. Additional illustrations are Gerber, *The Jews of Spain*; and M. A. Cohen, "The Sephardic Phenomenon," 79.

105. Alfonso, *Islamic Culture Through Jewish Eyes.*

106. Ray, "Images of the Jewish Community in Medieval Iberia," 196.

107. Granara, "*Extensio Animae*"; Snir, "Al-Andalus Rising from Damascus"; Noorani, "The Lost Garden of al-Andalus"; and Shannon, "There and Back Again."

108. Ashour, *Granada.* On Darwīsh and al-Andalus, see Xavier, *Mahmoud Darwich et la nouvelle Andalousie.*

109. Aidi, "Let Us Be Moors."

110. Calderwood's recently published *Colonial al-Andalus Spain and the Making of Modern Moroccan Culture* argues that charting the memory of Christian, Muslim, and Jewish coexistence in al-Andalus served as a vehicle for authorizing Spanish colonialism in North Africa. Civantos, *The Afterlife of al-Andalus*, studies the various ways in which al-Andalus is used as the site of memory by modern and contemporary Arabs and Spaniards. On al-Andalus as the inspiration for contemporary musical performance, see Shannon, *Performing al-Andalus.*

111. Browning, *The Complete Poetic Works*, 383–385.

112. In *Divan El Tamarit.* See Morris, *Son of Andalusia.*

113. Amichai, *Poems, 1948–1962*, 25–26.

114. See Rosen, "As in a Poem by Shmuel Ha-Nagid," 83–106. Pearce, "His (Jewish) Nation . . . and His Muslim King," analyzes Amichai's academic study of the poet Samuel the Nagid.

115. Filios, "Expulsion from Paradise," discusses works of Chahine and Maalouf, among others.

116. Although not set in premodern Iberia, Saramago's *The Stone Raft* (1986) narrates a fabulous tale of Iberian "otherness."

117. Almog Behar, "Halomot b^{e}-espaniya," https://almogbehar.wordpress.com/חלומות-באספניה. Ben-Porat, "'Golden Age' Poetry in Contemporary Israeli and Palestinian

Poetry," 127–143, interrogates the canonic but "inactive" and marginal status of Andalusi Hebrew poetry in Israeli culture, in contrast to the "active Andalusian model" for a Palestinian poet writing in Hebrew.

118. The first part of Calderwood, "Invention of al-Andalus," 27–31, identifies Romantic writers besides Washington Irving who "invented the romantic and modern al-Andalus."

Bibliography

PRIMARY SOURCES

'Abd Allāh b. Bullugīn. *Mudhakkirāt al-amīr 'abd allāh al-musammāt bi-kitāb al-tibyān*. Edited by Évariste Lévi-Provençal. Cairo: Dār al-ma'ārif, 1955.

———. *The Tibyān: Memoirs of 'Abd Allāh b. Bullugīn, Last Zīrid Amīr of Granada*. Translated by Amīn T. Tibi. Leiden: E. J. Brill, 1986.

Abraham ibn Daud. *Dorot 'olam* (Generations of the Ages). Edited by Katja Vehlow. Leiden: Brill, 2013.

———. *Sefer ha-qabbalah* (The Book of Tradition). Edited and translated by Gerson D. Cohen. Philadelphia: Jewish Publication Society, 1967.

Abraham ibn 'Ezra. *Sefer Mo'znayim* (also known as *Mo'znei l^eshon ha-qodesh* [Scales of the Holy Language]). Edited by Lorenzo Jiménez Paton and Angel Sáenz-Badillos. Córdoba: Ediciones el Almendro, 2002.

Abraham ibn Ezra Reader [Hebrew]. Edited by Israel Levin. New York: Israel Matz Hebrew Classics and I. Edward Kiev Library Foundation, 1985.

———. *Commentary on the Torah* [Hebrew]. 3 volumes. Edited by Asher Weiser. Jerusalem: Mosad Harav Kook, 1977.

Abū Bakr Muḥammad b. Aḥmad al-Wāsiṭī. *Faḍā'il al-bayt al-muqaddas*. Edited by Isaac Hasson. Jerusalem: Magnes, 1979.

Abū l-Walīd Muḥammad ibn Rushd. *Talkhīṣ al-āthār al-'ulwiyya*. Edited by Jamāl al-Dīn al-'Alawī. Beirut: Dār al-gharb al-islāmī, 1994.

Abū Naṣr al-Fatḥ ibn Muḥammad ibn 'Ubayd Allāh ibn Khāqān. *Maṭmaḥ al-anfus wa-masraḥ al-ta'annus fī mulaḥ ahl al-andalus*. Edited by Madīḥa al-Sharqāwī. Cairo: Maktabat al-thaqāfa al-dīniyya, 2001.

Abū l-Walīd Ismā'īl b. Muḥammad al-Ḥimyarī. *Al-Badī' fī waṣf al-rabī'*. Port Sa'īd: Maktabat al-thaqāfa al-dīniyya, n.d.

Akhbār majmū'a fī fatḥ al-andalus wa-dhikri umarā'ihā. Edited by Ibrāhīm Abyārī. Cairo: Dār al-kitāb al-maṣrī, and Beirut: Dār al-kitāb al-lubnānī, 1989.

'Amram Gaon. *Seder Rav 'Amram*. Edited by Daniel Goldschmidt. Jerusalem: Rav Kook Institute, 1971.

'Arīb ibn Sa'd al-Kātib al-Qurṭubī. *Le Calendrier de Cordoue*. Edited and translated by Charles Pellat. Leiden: Brill, 1961.

Baḥya ibn Paqūda. *The Book of Direction to the Duties of the Heart*. Translated by Menahem Mansoor. Portland, OR: Littman Library of Jewish Civilization, 2004.

———. *Al-Hidāya ilā farā'iḍ al-qulūb*. Edited by Joseph Qāfiḥ. Jerusalem: ha-Va'ad ha-k^elali li-yhudei teiman, 1998.

———. *Al-Hidāya ilā farā'iḍ al-qulūb*. Edited by A. S. Yahuda. Leiden: E. J. Brill, 1912.

al-Bakrī, Abū ʿUbayd ʿAbd Allāh ibn ʿAbd al-ʿAzīz. *Jughāfiyat al-andalus wa-ūrūbbā min kitāb al-masālik wa-l-mamālik*. Edited by ʿAbdurraḥmān ʿAlī El-Ḥājjī. Beirut: Dār al-irshād li-l-ṭibāʿa wa-l-nashr wa-l-tawzīʿ, 1968.

Benjamin of Tudela. *The Itinerary of Benjamin of Tudela: Travels in the Middle Ages*. Introductions by Michael A. Signer, Marcus Nathan Adler, and A. Asher. Malibu, CA: Joseph Simon Pangloss, 1987.

———. *Sefer ha-massaʿot* [The Itinerary of Benjamin of Tudela]. Edited and translated by Marcus Nathan Adler. London: 1907; repr., Jerusalem: Feldheim, n.d.

al-Būnisī, Abū Isḥāq Ibrāhīm. *Kanz al-kuttāb wa-muntakhab al-ādāb*. Abu Dhabi: al-Majmaʿ al-Thaqāfī, 2004.

Crónica Anónima de ʿAbd al-Raḥmān III al-Nāṣir. Edited by E. Lévi-Provençal and Emilio García Gómez. Madrid: Consejo Superior de Investigaciones Científicas, 1950.

David ben Abraham al-Fāsī. *Kitāb Jāmiʿ l-alfāẓ*. 2 volumes. Edited by Solomon L. Skoss. New Haven, CT: Yale University Press, 1936–1945; repr., New York: AMS, 1981.

Al-Dhakhīra al-saniyya fī ta'rīkh al-dawla al-marīniyya. Edited by ʿAbd al-Wahhāb Binmanṣūr. Rabat: Dār al-Manṣūr li-l-ṭibāʿa wa-l-wirāqa, 1972.

———. Edited by Mohammed Ben Cheneb. Algiers: Jules Carbonel, 1921.

Dūnash ben Labrāṭ. *Sefer teshuvot dūnash ha-lewi ben labrāṭ ʿal rabbi saʿadiyah ga'on*. Edited by Robert Schroter. Breslau: Schletter'sche, 1866.

———. *Sefer teshuvot dūnash ben labrāṭ ʿim hakhraʿot rabbeinu yaʿaqov tam*. Edited by Leopold Dukes, Raphael Kirchheim, and Herschell Filipowski. London: Societatis Antiquitatum Hebraicarum, 1855.

———. *Poems* [Hebrew]. Edited by Nehemiah Allony. Jerusalem: Sifriyat Meqorot-Rav Kook Institute, 1947.

———. *Tešubot de Dūnash ben Labrāṭ*. Edited by Angel Sáenz-Badillos. Granada: Universidad de Granada, 1980.

———. *El Diván Poético de Dunash ben Labraṭ*. Edited by Carlos del Valle Rodríguez. Madrid: Consejo Superior de Investigaciones Científicas, Instituto de Filología, 1988.

Dūnash ben Tamim. *Le Commentaire sur le Livre de la Création de Dunash Ben Tamim de Kairouan (Xe siècle)*. New edition by Georges Vajda and Paul B. Fenton. Leuven: Peeters, 2002.

al-Fārābī. *Fuṣūl al-madanī*. Edited and translated by D. M. Dunlop. Cambridge: Cambridge University Press, 1961.

Fatḥ al-andalus. Edited by Emilio Molina López. Madrid: Consejo Superior de Investigaciones Científicas, 1994.

al-Ḥimyarī, Ibn ʿAbd al-Munʿim. *Al-Rawḍ al-miʿṭār fī khabar al-aqṭār* (*La péninsule Ibérique au moyen-âge d'après le Kitāb al-rawḍ al-miʿṭār fī khabar al-aqṭār d'Ibn ʿAbd al-Munʿim al-Ḥimyarī*). Edited by E. Lévi-Provençal. Leiden: E. J. Brill, 1938.

al-Ḥumaydī, Muḥammad ibn Abī Fattūḥ. *Jadhwat al-Muqtabis fī dhikr wulāt al-andalus*. Edited by Ṣalāḥ al-Dīn al-Hawārī. Beirut: Al-Maktaba al-ʿaṣriyya, 2004.

Ibn ʿAbd Rabbih. *al-ʿIqd al-farīd*. 9 volumes in 8. Edited by M. Muḥammad Qumayha and ʿAbd al-Majīd al-Tarḥīnī. Beirut: Dār al-Kutub al-ʿIlmiyya, 1997.

———. *Al-ʿIqd al-farīd*. 7 volumes. Edited by Muḥammad Tūnjī. Beirut: Dār Ṣādir, 2006.

Ibn Abī Uṣaybiʿa. *ʿUyūn al-anbā' fī ṭabaqāt al-aṭibbā'*. Edited by August Miller. Konigsberg: Selbstverlag, 1884; repr., Farnsborough: Gregg International, 1972.

Ibn Bājja. *Tadbīr al-mutawaḥḥid / El régimen del solitario*. Edited and translated by Miguel Asín Palacios. Madrid: Consejo Superior de Investigaciones Científicas, 1946.

Ibn Bassām al-Shantarīnī, Abū l-Ḥasan ʿAlī. *Al-Dhakhīra fī maḥāsin ahl al-jazīra*. 8 volumes. Edited by Iḥsān ʿAbbas. Beirut: Dār al-thaqāfa, 1975–1979.

Ibn Diḥya (al-Kalbī), Abū Khuṭṭāb ʿUmar ibn al-Ḥasan. *al-Muṭrib min ashʿār ahl al-maghrib*. Edited by Ṣalāḥ al-Dīn al-Hawārī. Sayda-Beirut: al-Maktaba al-ʿasriyya, 2008.

Ibn al-Faraḍī, Abū l-Walīd. *Taʾrīkh ʿulamāʾ l-andalus*. Cairo: Al-Dār al-miṣriyya li-l-taʾlīf wa-l-tarjama, 1966.

Ibn Ḥabīb, ʿAbd al-Malik. *Kitāb al-Taʾrīkh*. Edited by Jorge Aguadé. Madrid: Consejo Superior de Investigaciones Científicas, 1991.

Ibn Ḥamdīs, ʿAbd al-Jabbār ibn abī Bakr. *Dīwān ibn Ḥamdīs*. Edited by Iḥsān ʿAbbās. Beirut: Dār Ṣādir, 1960.

Ibn Ḥawqal, Abū l-Qāsim. *Kitāb ṣūrat al-arḍ*. 2nd edition. Edited by Johannes Hendrik Kramers. Leiden: Brill, 1967.

———. *Kitāb sūrat al-arḍ*. Edited by J. H. Kramers and G. Wiet. Leiden: E. J. Brill, 1938.

Ibn Ḥayyān, Abū Marwān. *Al-Muqtabis*. Edited by Pedro Chalmetta, Federico Corriente, and Maḥmūd Ṣubḥ. Madrid: Al-Maʿhad al-isbānī al-ʿarabī li-l-thaqāfa, 1979. Vol. 5.

Ibn Ḥazm, Abū Muḥammad ʿAlī. *Ṭawq al-ḥamāma fī l-ulfa wa-l-ullāf*. Edited by Ṣalāḥ al-Dīn al-Qāsimī. Baghdad: Dār al-shuʾūn al-thaqāfiyya al-ʿāmma, 1986.

———. *Al-Fiṣal wa-l-milal wa-l-ahwāʾ wa-l-niḥal*. 6 volumes. Edited by Muḥammad Ibrāhīm Naṣr and ʿAbd al-Raḥmān Ghumīra. Beirut: Dār al-jīl, 1982.

———. *Rasāʾil ibn ḥazm*. 4 volumes. Edited by Iḥsān ʿAbbās. Beirut: Al-Muʾassasa al-ʿarabiyya li-l-dirāsāt wa-l-nashr, 1981.

———. *Jamharat ansāb al-ʿarab*. Edited by ʿAbd al-Salām Muḥammad Hārūn. Cairo: Dār al-maʿārif, 1962.

Ibn ʿIdhārī [al-Marrākushī], Abū l-ʿAbbās Aḥmad. *Al-Bayān al-mughrib fī akhbār mulūk al-andalus wa-l-maghrib*. 4 volumes. Edited by J. S. Colin and E. Lévi-Provençal. Beirut: Dār al-thaqāfa, 1967.

———. *Kitāb al-bayān al-mughrib fī akhbār al-andalus wa-l-maghrib [qism al-muwaḥḥidīn]*. Edited by Muḥammad Ibrāhīm al-Katānī et al. Beirut: Dār al-gharb al-islāmī, 1985.

———. *Al-Muʿjib fī talkhīṣ akhbār ahl al-maghrib*. Edited by Saʿīd ʿIryān. Cairo: al-Majlis al-aʿlā li-l-shuʾūn al-islāmiyya, 1949.

Ibn Idrīs, Ṣafwān. *Zād al-musāfir wa-ghurrat muḥayyā l-adab al-sāfir*. Edited by Muḥammad b. Sharīfa. Casablanca: Maṭbaʿat al-Najāḥ al-Jadīdah, 2012.

Ibn Jubayr, Abū l-Ḥusayn Muḥammad b. Aḥmad. *Riḥlat bin jubayr*. Edited by Ḥusayn Nassar. Cairo: Maktabat Miṣr, 1992.

———. *Riḥlat ibn jubayr*. Edited by William Wright; 2nd revised edition edited by M. J. De Goeje. Cambridge: E. J. W. Gibb Memorial Trust, 1907; repr., 2007.

———. *The Travels of Ibn Jubayr*. Translated by R. J. C. Broadhurst. London: Jonathan Cape, 1952.

Ibn Khafāja, Abū Isḥāq. *Dīwān ibn khafāja*. Edited by Muṣṭafā Ghāzī. Alexandria: Al-Maʿārif, 1960.

Ibn Khaldūn, Abū Zayd ʿAbd al-Raḥmān ibn Muḥammad. *Al-Muqaddima*. 3 volumes. Edited by Abdesselam Cheddadi. Casablanca: Khizānat Ibn Khaldūn, Bayt al-funūn wa-l-ʿulūm wa-l-ādāb, 2005.

———. *The Muqaddimah: An Introduction to History*. 3 volumes. Translated by Franz Rosenthal. 2nd edition. Princeton, NJ: Princeton University Press, 1967.

Ibn Khāqān, Abū Naṣr al-Fatḥ ibn Muḥammad ibn ʿUbayd Allāh. *Kitāb ta'rīkh al-wuzarā' wa-l-kuttāb wa-l-shuʿarā' fī l-andalus = Maṭmaḥ al-anfus wa-masraḥ al-ta'annus fī mulaḥ ahl al-andalus*. Edited by Madīḥa Sharqāwī. Al-Ẓāhir: Maktabat al-thaqāfa al-dīniyya, 2001.

Ibn al-Khaṭīb, Lisān al-Dīn. "Mufākhara bayna mālaqa wa-salā," trans. García Gómez, "El 'Parangón entre Málaga y Saé' de Ibn al-Jaṭīb," *al-Andalus* 2 (1934): 183–96.

———. "Mufākhara bayna mālaqa wa-salā," in *Khaṭrat al-ṭayf: Raḥalāt fī l-maghrib wa-l-andalus*. Edited by Aḥmad Mukhtār al-ʿAbbādī. Beirut: Al-Mu'assasa al-ʿarabiyya li-l-dirāsāt wa-l-nashr, 2003.

———. *Jaysh al-tawshīḥ*. Edited by Alan Jones. Cambridge: E. J. W. Gibb Memorial Trust, 1997.

———. *Miʿyār al-ikhtiyār fī dhikr al-maʿāhid wa-l-diyār*. Edited by Muḥammad Kamāl Shabāna. Cairo: Maktabat al-thaqāfa al-dīniyya, 2002.

———. *Al-Iḥāṭa fī akhbār gharnāṭa*. 4 volumes. 2nd revised edition. Edited by Mohamed Abdulla Enan. Cairo: Al-Khangi Bookshop, 1973.

Ibn Manẓūr, Muḥammad ibn Mukarram. *Lisān al-ʿarab*. 6 volumes. Cairo: Dār al-Maʿārif, 1984–1986.

Ibn al-Qaṭṭāʿ, Abū l-Qāsim ʿAlī ibn Jaʿfar al-Saʿdī. *al-Durrah al-khaṭīra fī shuʿarā' l-jazīra*. Edited by Bashīr Bakkūsh. Beirut: Dār al-Gharb al-Islāmī, 1995.

Ibn Qutayba, Abū Muḥammad. *ʿUyūn al-Akhbār*. Edited by Yūsuf ʿAlī Ṭawīl. Beirut: Dār al-kutub al-ʿilmiyya, 1986.

Ibn al-Qūṭiyya [al-Qurṭubī], Muḥammad ibn ʿUmar. *Ta'rīkh iftitāḥ al-andalus*. Edited by Ibrāhīm al-Abyārī. Cairo: Dār al-kitāb al-maṣrī and Dār al-kitāb al-lubnānī, 1989.

———. *Ta'rīkh iftitāḥ al-andalus*. Edited by ʿAbd Allāh Anīs Tabbāʿ and ʿUmar Tabbā. Beirut: Mu'assasat al-Maʿārif, 1994.

———. *Early Islamic Spain: The History of Ibn al-Qūṭiyya*. Translated by David James. London: Routledge, 2009.

Ibn Rashīq al-Qayrawānī, Abū ʿAlī al-Ḥasan. *Dīwān ibn rashīq al-qayrawānī*. Edited by Muḥyā l-Dīn Dīb. Beirut: Al-Maktaba al-ʿarabiyya li-l-ṭibāʿa wa-l-nashr, 1998.

Ibn Rushd, Abū l-Walīd Muḥammad. *Talkhīṣ al-āthār al-ʿulwiyya*. Edited by Jamāl al-Dīn al-ʿAlawī. Beirut: Dār al-gharb al-islāmī, 1994.

Ibn Saʿīd al-Maghribī. *Rāyāt al-mubarrizīn wa-ghāyāt al-mumayyizīn*. Edited by Naʿman ʿAbd al-Matʿal al-Qāḍī. Cairo: al-Majlis al-aʿlā li-l-shu'ūn al-islāmiyya, 1973.

———. *The Banners of the Champions: An Anthology of Medieval Arabic Poetry from Andalusia and Beyond*. Translated by James A. Bellamy and Patricia Owen Steiner. Madison, WI: Hispanic Seminary of Medieval Studies, 1989.

Ibn Sanā' l-Mulk. *Dār al-ṭirāz fī ʿamal al-muwashshaḥāt*. Edited by Jawdat al-Rikābī. 2nd edition. Damascus: Dār al-fikr, 1977.

Ibn Shuhayd, Abū ʿĀmir Aḥmad. *Dīwān*. Edited by Charles Pellat. Beirut: Dār al-Makshūf, 1963.

Ibn Ṭufayl, Muḥammad ibn ʿAbd al-Malik. *Risālat ḥayy ibn yaqẓān*. Almānyā: Manshūrāt al-Jamal, 2007.

Ibn Zaydūn, Aḥmad ibn ʿAbd Allāh. *Dīwān*. Edited by Yūsuf Farḥāt. Beirut: Dār al-kitāb al-ʿarabī, 1991.

———. *Poesías*. Edited by Maḥmūd Sobḥ. Madrid: Instituto Hispano-Árabe de Cultura, 1985.

al-Idrīsī, al-Sharīf. *Waṣf al-masjid al-jāmi' bi-qurṭuba* [Description de la Grande Mosquée de Cordoue]. Texte arabe et traduction française par Alfred Dessus Lamare. Algiers: Éditions Carbonel, 1949.

Isaac Abravanel. *Commentary on the Later Prophets* [Hebrew]. Jerusalem: B^enei Arbal, 1979.

———. *Commentary on the Former Prophets* [Hebrew]. Jerusalem: Torah v^e-da'at, 1955–1956.

Isaac ibn Ghiyāth. *Poems* [Hebrew]. Edited by Yonah David. Jerusalem: Akhshav, 1987.

Isaac ibn Khalfūn, *Poems* [Hebrew]. Edited by Aharon Mirsky. Jerusalem: Bialik Institute, 1961.

Isidore of Seville. *History of the Goths, Vandals and Suevi*. 2nd ed. Translated by Guido Donini and Gordon B. Ford, Jr. Leiden: E. J. Brill, 1970.

Jonah al-Walīd Marwān ibn Janāḥ. *Kitāb al-uṣūl*. Edited by Adolf Neubauer, repr., Amsterdam: Philo, 1969.

———. *Sefer ha-riqmah*. 2 volumes. 2nd revised edition by Michael Wilensky and David Tene. Jerusalem: Hebrew Language Academy, 1964.

———. *Kitāb al-luma' = Le Livre des parterres fleuris*. Edited by Joseph Derenbourg and Hartwig Derenbourg. Paris: Vieweg, 1886.

Joseph ibn Ṣaddīq. *The Microcosm of Joseph ibn Ṣaddīq*. Edited and translated by Jacob Habermann and Saul Horovitz. Madison, NJ: Fairleigh Dickinson University Press, 2003.

Judah ben Barzillai al-Bargeloni. *Sefer ha-'Ittim*. Edited by Judah Avide-Zlotnik. New York: Menorah Institute, 1903.

———. *Peirush sefer y^eṣirah*. Edited by David Kaufman and Solomon Zalman Halberstam. Berlin: T. H. Iṭtsḳovsḳi, 1885.

Judah al-Ḥarizi. *Taḥk^emoni*. Edited by Joseph Yahalom and Naoya Katsumata. Jerusalem: Ben-Zvi Institute for the Study of the Jewish Communities in the East and the Hebrew University of Jerusalem, 2010.

———. *Kitāb al-durar* [A Book in Praise of God and the Israelite Community]. Edited by Joshua Blau, Joseph Yahalom, and Paul Fenton. Jerusalem: Ben-Zvi Institute, 2009.

———. *The Book of Taḥkemoni: Jewish Tales from Medieval Spain*. Translated by David Simha Segal. Portland, OR: Littman Library of Jewish Civilization, 1973.

———. *Taḥk^emoni*. Translated by Victor Emanuel Reichert. 2 volumes. Jerusalem: Raphael Haim Cohen's Press, 1965–1973.

———. *Taḥk^emoni*. Edited by Y. Toporowsky. Tel Aviv: Maḥbarot Lesifrut, 1952.

———. *Maḥb^erot iti'el*. Edited by Yitzhak Peretz. Tel Aviv: Maḥbarot Lesifrut, 1951.

Judah Ḥayyūj [Abū Zakariyya ibn Dāwūd of Fez]. *The Weak and Geminative Verbs in Hebrew* [Arabic]. Edited by Morris Jastrow. Leiden: Brill, 1897.

———. *Three Treatises on Hebrew Grammar by R. Judah Hayyuj: A New Critical Edition of the Arabic Text with a Modern Hebrew Translation* [Arabic and Hebrew]. Edited by Daniel Sivan and Ali Wated. Beersheva: Ben-Gurion University of the Negev and Bialik Publishing, 2012.

———. *Kitāb al-nutaf*. Edited by Nāsir Basal. Tel Aviv: Tel Aviv University Press, 2001.

———. (Yayyà Ibn Dāwūd). *El Libro de Hayyūy* [Versión original árabe del siglo x]. Edited by José Martinez Delgado. Granada: Universidad de Granada, 2004.

Judah Halevi. *Yehuda Halevi: Poemas*. Translated by Angel Sáenz-Badillos and Judit Targarona Borrás. Madrid: Clasicos Alfaguara, 1994.

———. *Liturgical Poetry of Rabbi Judah Halevi* [Hebrew]. Edited by Dov Yarden. 4 volumes. Jerusalem: Dov Yarden, 1978–1985.

———. *The Book of Refutation and Proof on the Despised Faith (The Khazarī Book)* [Arabic]. Edited by David H. Baneth and prepared for publication by Haggai Ben-Shammai. Jerusalem: Magnes, 1977.

Judah ibn Quraysh. *Risāla*. Edited by Dan Becker. Tel Aviv: Tel Aviv University Press, 1984.

al-Khushanī, Muḥammad ibn al-Ḥārith b. Asad. *Akhbār al-fuqahā' wa-l-muḥaddithīn*. Edited by María Luisa Ávila and Luis Molina. Madrid: Consejo Superior de Investigaciones Científicas and Instituto de Cooperación con el Mundo Árabe, 1992.

———. *Kitāb al-qudāt bi-qurṭuba*. Edited by Julian Ribera. Madrid: Imprenta Ibérica, 1914.

al-Marwazī, Nu'aym ibn Ḥammād. *Kitāb al-fitan*. Edited by Suhayl Zakkār. Beirut: Dār al-fikr, 1993.

al-Maqqarī, Shihāb al-Dīn Aḥmad ibn Muḥammad. *Nafḥ al-ṭīb min ghusn al-andalus al-raṭīb*. 8 volumes. Edited by Iḥsān 'Abbās. Beirut: Dār Ṣādir, 1968.

———. *Nafḥ al-ṭīb min ghusn al-andalus al-raṭīb*. 7 volumes. Edited by Muḥammad Muḥyī l-Dīn 'Abd al-Ḥamīd. Beirut: Dār al-kitāb al-'arabī, 1949.

Menaḥem Ben Sarūq. *Maḥberet*. Edited by Angel Sáenz-Badillos. Granada: Universidad de Granada and Universidad Pontificia de Salamanca, 1986.

Midrash 'eser galuyot in *Oṣar midrashim: A Library of Two Hundred Minor Midrashim*. 2 volumes. Edited by Judah David Eisenstein. New York: n.p., 1915.

Moses in Ezra. *Kitāb al-muḥāḍara wa-l-mudhākara*. Edited by Abraham S. Halkin. Jerusalem: Mekitze Nirdamim, 1975.

———. *Secular Poems* [Hebrew]. 3 volumes. Edited by Haim Brody and Dan Pagis. Berlin: Schocken Institute for Jewish Research, 1935–1977.

Moses Maimonides. *Teshuvot ha-rambam*. 4 volumes in 3. Edited by Joshua Blau. Jerusalem: Rubin Mass, and Kiryat Ono: Makhon le-ḥeqer mishnat ha-rambam, 2014.

———. *Moses Maimonides' Treatise on Resurrection*. Translated by Fred Rosner. New York: Ktav, 1982.

———. *The Guide of the Perplexed*. 2 volumes. Translated by Shlomo Pines. Chicago: University of Chicago Press, 1963.

———. *Maqāla fī teḥiyyat ha-meitim*. Edited by Joshua Finkel. New York: American Academy for Jewish Research, 1939.

Muḥammad ibn Muḥammad al-Ra'ī. *Intiṣār al-faqīr al-sālik li-tarjīḥ madhhab al-imām al-kabīr mālik*. Edited by Muḥammad Abū l-Ajfān. Beirut: Dār al-gharb al-islāmī, 1981.

al-Muqaddasī, Muḥammad ibn Aḥmad. *Kitāb aḥsan al-taqāsīm fī ma'rifat al-āqālīm*. 2nd edition. Edited by M. J. De Goeje. Leiden: Brill, 1906.

———. *The Best Divisions for Knowledge of the Regions*. Translated by Basil Anthony Collins. Reading: Garnett, 1994.

al-Muqammaṣ, Dāwūd ibn Marwān. *'Ishrūn maqāla* [Twenty Chapters]. Edited by Sarah Stroumsa. Leiden: E. J. Brill, 1989.

Nissim Gaon. *Rav Nissim Gaon: Five Books: Remnants from his Compositions* [Hebrew and Arabic]. Edited by Shraga Abramson. Jerusalem: Mekitze Nirdamim, 1965.

Oṣar midrashim: A Library of Two Hundred Minor Midrashim. 2 volumes. Edited by Judah David Eisenstein. New York: n.p., 1915.

al-Qurṭubī, 'Abd Allāh ibn Aḥmad. *Al-Tadhkīra fī ahwāl al-mawtā wa-umūr al-ākhira*. Beirut: Dār al-kutub al-'ilmiyya, 2002.

Sa'adya ben Joseph al-Fayyūmī Gaon. *Kitāb al-amānāt wa-l-i'tiqādāt*. Edited by Yosef Qāfaḥ. Qiryat Ono: Mahad, 1970.

———. *The Book of Beliefs and Opinions.* Translated by Samuel Rosenblatt, repr., New Haven, CT: Yale University Press, 1989.

———. *Sefer ha-Egron [Kitāb uṣūl al-shi'r al-'ibrānī].* Jerusalem: Academy of the Hebrew Language, 1969.

Ṣā'id ibn Aḥmad al-Andalusī, Abū l-Qāsim. *Kitāb ṭabaqāt al umam.* Edited by Louis Cheiko. Beirut: al-Maṭba'a al-Kāthūlīkiyya, 1912.

———. *Ṭabaqāt al-umam.* Edited by Hussein Mou'nes. Cairo: Dār al-ma'ārif, 1998.

Samuel ha-Nagid. *Dīwān: Ben T'hillim.* Edited by Dov Jarden. Jerusalem: Hebrew Union College, 1966.

———. *Poemas.* Edited by Angel Sáenz-Badillos and Judit Targarona Borrás. 2 volumes. Córdoba: Ediciones el Almendro, 1988.

al-Saraqusṭī ibn al-Ashtarkūnī, Abū l-Ṭāhir Muḥammad ibn Yūsuf al-Tamīmī. *Al-Maqāmāt al-luzūmiyya.* Translated by James T. Monroe. Leiden: Brill, 2002.

Seder 'olam zuṭa, in *Mediaeval Jewish Chronicles.* Edited by Adolph Neubauer. Oxford: Clarendon, 1888.

Sefer Eldad ha-Dani, in *The Literary Works of Abraham Epstein* [Hebrew]. 2 volumes. Edited by A. M. Habermann. Jerusalem: Rav Kook Institute, 1964.

Sh^erira' Gaon. *Iggeret sh^erira' ga'on* [Epistle of Sherira Gaon]. Edited by Benjamin M. Lewin. Haifa: n.p., 1921.

———. *Iggeret rav sh^erira' ga'on.* Edited by N. D. Rabinowich. Jerusalem: H. Vagshal, 1991.

Solomon ibn Gabirol. *Secular Poems of Ibn Gabirol* [Hebrew]. Edited by H. Brody and J. Schirmann. Jerusalem: Schocken Institute for Jewish Research, 1974.

———. *Liturgical Poems* [Hebrew]. 2 volumes. Edited by Dov Yarden. Jerusalem: Dov Yarden, 1971–1973.

al-Sumaysīr, Abū l-Qāsim Khalaf b. Faraj al-Ilbīrī. *Shi'r al-Sumaysīr.* Edited by Ismā'īl b. Ḥamad 'Abdallāh al-Sālimī. Cairo: Dār al-kitāb al-maṣrī and Dār al-kitāb al-lubnānī, 2016.

Tešubot de los discípulos de Menaḥem contra Dunaš Ben Labraṭ. Edited by Santiaga Benavente Robles. Granada: Universidad de Granada y Universidad Pontificia de Salamanca, 1986.

T'shuvot ha-g^e'onim. Edited by Albert E. Harkavy. Berlin: T. H. Iṭtsḳovsḳi, 1887; repr., New York: Menorah Institute, 1959.

al-Tha'ālibī, Abū Manṣūr 'Abd al-Malik ibn Muḥammad. *Yatīmat al-dahr fī shu'arā' ahl al-'aṣr.* 4 voulmes. Damascus, 1885.

Al-Wansharīsī, Abū 'Abbās Aḥmad. *Usnā l-mutājir.* Edited by Husayn Mu'nis in *Revista del Instituto de Estudios Islámicos en Madrid* 5 (1957): 129–91.

Yehudi Ben Sheshet. *Teshubot de Yehudi Ben Sheshet.* Edited by Encarnación Varela Moreno. Granada: Universidad de Granada and Universidad Pontificia de Salamanca, 1981.

SECONDARY SOURCES

Abou El Fadl, Khaled M. "Islamic Law and Muslim Minorities: The Juristic Discourse on Muslim Minorities from the Second/Eighth to the Eleventh/Seventeenth Centuries," *Islamic Law and Society* 1 (1994): 141–187.

Abu-Haidar, Jareer. "The Muwaššaḥāt in Light of the Literary Life That Produced Them," in *Studies in the Muwaššaḥ and the Kharja.* Edited by Alan Jones and Richard Hitchcock. Reading: Ithaca Press for Oxford University, 1991. 115–122.

Abulafia, David S. H. "The End of Muslim Sicily," in *Muslims Under Latin Rule 1100–1300*. Edited by James M. Powell. Princeton, NJ: Princeton University Press, 1990. 103–133.

Abun-Nasr, Jamil M. *A History of the Maghrib*. 2nd edition. Cambridge: Cambridge University Press, 1975.

Adler, Elkan N. *Jewish Travellers in the Middle Ages: 19 Firsthand Accounts*, repr., New York: Dover, 1987.

Afsaruddin, Asma. *Excellence & Precedence: Medieval Islamic Discourse on Legitimate Leadership*. Leiden: Brill, 2002.

Aguadé, Jorge. "Some Remarks About Sectarian Movements in al-Andalus," *Studia Islamica* 64 (1986): 54–77.

Ahmad, Aziz. *A History of Islamic Sicily*. Edinburgh: Edinburgh University Press, 1975.

Aidi, Hishaam D. "The Interference of al-Andalus: Spain, Islam, and the West," *Social Text* 87 (2006): 67–88.

———. "Let Us Be Moors: Islam, Race and Contested Histories," *Middle East Report* 87 (2003): 42–53.

Akasoy, Anna. "Al-Andalus in Exile: Identity and Diversity in Islamic Intellectual History," in *Christlicher Norde—Muslimischer Süden: Anspruche und Wirklichkeiten von Christen, Juden, und Muslimen auf der Iberischen Halbinsel im Hoch- und Spätmittelalter*. Edited by Matthias M. Tischler and Alexander Fidora. Münster: Aschendorff, 2011. 329–343.

———. "Convivencia and Its Discontents: Interfaith Life in al-Andalus," *International Journal of Middle Eastern Studies* 42 (2010): 489–499.

Akhtar, Ali Humayun. *Philosophers, Sufis, and Caliphs: Politics and Authority from Cordoba to Cairo and Baghdad*. Cambridge: Cambridge University Press, 2017.

Alcalay, Ammiel. *After Jews and Arabs: Remaking Levantine Culture*. Minneapolis: University of Minnesota Press, 1993.

Aleem, Abdul. "'Ijazu' l-Qur'an," *Islamic Culture* 7 (1933): 64–82, 215–233.

Alfonso, Esperanza. "Constructions of Exile in Medieval Hebrew Literature: Between Text and Context" [Hebrew], *Mikan* 1 (2000): 85–96.

———. "From al-Andalus to North Africa: The Lineage and Scholarly Genealogy of a Jewish Family (The Gavisons: A Foundational Story)," in *The Jew in Medieval Iberia, 1100–1500*. Edited by Jonathan Ray. Boston: Academic Studies Press, 2012. 395–425.

———. *Islamic Culture Through Jewish Eyes: Al-Andalus from the Tenth to Twelfth Century*. London: Routledge, 2008.

———. "The Uses of Exile in Poetic Discourse: Some Examples from Medieval Hebrew Literature," in *Renewing the Past, Reconfiguring Jewish Culture: From al-Andalus to the Haskalah*. Edited by Ross Brann and Adam Sutcliffe. Philadelphia: University of Pennsylvania Press, 2003. 31–49.

Ali, Samer M. *Arabic Literary Salons in the Islamic Middle Ages: Poetry, Public Performance, and the Presentation of the Past*. Notre Dame, IN: University of Notre Dame Press, 2010.

Allony, Nehemiah. "Karaite Views in 'Maḥberet' Mᵉnaḥem" [Hebrew], repr. in Nehemiah Allony, *Studies in Medieval Philology and Literature (Collected Papers III) Hebrew Linguistics in Middle Ages*. Prepared for publication by Yosef Tobi. Jerusalem: Ben-Zvi Institute for the Study of the Jewish Communities in the East, 1989. 25–58.

———. "Ha-kuzari: Sefer ha-milḥamah bᵉ-'arabiyya lᵉ-shiḥrur ha-yᵉhudi," *Eshel Be'er Sheva* 2 (1980): 119–143.

———. "Judah ben David and Judah Ḥayyūj" [Hebrew], in *Minḥah li-yehudah* [Judah Leib Zlotnik Jubilee Volume]. Edited by Simḥa Assaf, Yehudah Even-Shemu'el, and R. Benjamin. Jerusalem: Mosad Harav Kook, 1949–1950. 67–82.

———. "The Reaction of Moses ibn Ezra to 'Abrabiyya," *Bulletin of the Institute for Jewish Studies* 1 (1973): 19–40.

Altmann, Alexander, and Samuel M. Stern. *Isaac Israeli: A Neoplatonic Philosopher of the Early Tenth Century*. Oxford: Oxford University Press, 1958.

Álvarez Ramos, Miguel Ángel. "Gayangos and Politics in Spain," in *Pascual de Gayangos: A Nineteenth-Century Spanish Arabist*. Edited by Cristina Álvarez Millán and Claudia Heide. Edinburgh: Edinburgh University Press, 2008. 24–33.

Amichai, Yehuda. *Poems, 1948–1962* [Hebrew]. Jerusalem: Schocken, 1962.

Anderson, Glaire D. *The Early Islamic Villa in Early Medieval Spain*. Farnham: Ashgate, 2013.

Anidjar, Gil. "Medieval Spain and the Integration of Memory (On the Unfinished Project of Pre-Modernity)," in *Islam and Public Controversy in Europe*. Edited by Nilufer Gole. Farnham: Ashgate, 2013. 217–225.

———. *"Our Place in al-Andalus": Kabbalah, Philosophy, Literature in Arab Jewish Letters*. Stanford, CA: Stanford University Press, 2002.

———. "Postscript: Futures of al-Andalus," in *In the Light of Medieval Spain: Islam, the West and the Relevance of the Past*. Edited by Simon R. Doubleday and David Coleman. New York: Palgrave Macmillan, 2008. 189–208.

Antrim, Zayde. *Routes and Realms: The Power of Place in the Early Islamic World*. Oxford: Oxford University Press, 2012.

Arazi, Albert. "Al-ḥanīn ilā l-awṭān entre la Gāhiliyya et l-Islam: Le Bédouin et le citadin reconciliés," *Zeitschrift der Deutschen Morgenländischen Gesellschaft* 143 (1993): 287–327.

———. "Shi'r," *Encyclopaedia of Islam*. 2nd edition. 9:450.

Arigata, Elena. "Spain: The al-Andalus Legacy," in *The Borders of Islam: Exploring Samuel Huntington's Faultlines, from al-Andalus to the Virtual Ummah*. Edited by Stig Jarle Hansen, Atle Mesoy, and Tuncay Kardas. New York: Columbia University Press, 2009. 223–234.

Ashour, Radwa. *Granada*. Translated by William Granara. Syracuse, NY: Syracuse University Press, 2003.

Ashtor, Eliyahu. *History of the Jews in Muslim Spain* [Hebrew]. 2 volumes. Jerusalem: Qiryat Sefer, 1960–1966.

———. *The Jews of Moslem Spain*. 3 volumes. Translated by Aaron Klein and Jenny Machlowitz Klein; introduction by David J. Wasserstein. Philadelphia: Jewish Publication Society, 1992.

———. "Un Mouvement migratoire au haut Moyen Age: Migrations de l'Irak vers les pays méditerranéens," *Annales. Economies, Sociétés. Civilisations* 27 (1972): 185–214.

Asín Palacios, Miguel. *Abenhazam de Córdoba y su historia crítica de las ideas religiosas*. 5 volumes. Madrid: Real Academia de la Historia, 1927–1932; repr., Madrid: Turner, 1984.

Aslanov, Cyril. "*S*[e]*fārad* as an Alternative Name for *Hispania*: A Tentative Etymology," *Hispania Judaica Bulletin* 10 (2014): 241–249.

Assaf, Simḥa. *Texts and Studies in Jewish History* [Hebrew]. Jerusalem: Rav Kook Institute, 1946.

Assis, Yom Tov. "The Judeo-Arabic Tradition in Christian Spain," in *The Jews of Medieval Islam: Community, Society and Identity*. Edited by Daniel Frank. Leiden: E. J. Brill, 1995. 111–124.

———. "'Sefarad': A Definition in the Context of a Cultural Encounter," in *Encuentros and Desencuentros: Spanish Jewish Cultural Interaction Throughout History*. Edited by Carlos Carrete Parrondo et al. Tel Aviv: University Publishing Projects, 2000. 29–37.

———, and José Ramón Magdalena. *The Jews of Navarre in the Late Middle Ages* [Hebrew]. Jerusalem: Zalman Shazar Center for Jewish History, 1990.

Attar, Samar. "Beyond Family, History, Religion, and Language: The Construction of a Cosmopolitan Identity in a Twelfth-Century Arabic Philosophical Novel," in *Adventures of Identity: European Multicultural Experiences and Perspectives*. Edited by John Docker and Gerhard Fischer. Tübingen: Stauffenburg, 2001. 75–89.

Ávila, María Luisa. "The Search for Knowledge: Andalusi Scholars and Their Travels to the Islamic East," *Medieval Prosopography* 23 (2002): 125–139.

al-Azmeh, Aziz. "Mortal Enemies, Invisible Neighbours: Northerners in Andalusi Eyes," in *The Legacy of Muslim Spain*. Edited by Salma Khadra Jayyusi. Leiden: E. J. Brill, 1992. 259–272.

Bachrach, Bernard S. "A Reassessment of Visigothic Jewish Policy, 589–711," *American Historical Review* 78 (1973): 11–34.

Baer, Yitzhak. *A History of the Jews in Christian Spain*. 2 volumes. Translated by Louis Schoffman; introduction by Benjamin Gampel. Philadelphia: Jewish Publication Society, 1961–1966.

———. *History of the Jews in Christian Spain* [Hebrew]. 2 volumes. Tel Aviv: Am Oved, 1944–1945.

———. *Die Juden im christien Spanien*. Berlin: Akademie-Verlag, 1929–1936.

Balard, Michel. "A Christian Mediterranean: 1000–1500," in *The Mediterranean in History*. Edited by David Abulafia. Los Angeles: J. Paul Getty Museum, 2003. 183–217.

Baneth, David H. "R. Judah al-Ḥarizi and the Chain of Translations of Maimonides' Treatise on Resurrection" [Hebrew], *Tarbiẓ* 11 (1940): 260–270.

Barceló, Miquel. "The Manifest Caliph: Umayyad Ceremony in Cordoba, or the Staging of Power," in *The Formation of al-Andalus* [Part 1 History and Society]. Edited by Manuela Marín. Aldershot: Ashgate-Variorum, 1998. 425–455.

Bareket, Elinoar. *Eli Ben Amram and His Companions: Jewish Leadership in the Eleventh-Century Mediterranean Basin*. Brighton: Sussex Academic Press, 2017.

———. "*Head of the Jews* in Spain in Comparison with *Head of the Jews* in Egypt in the Eleventh Century: Methodological Remarks" [Hebrew], *Bein ʿever we-ʿarav* 7 (2014): 176–185.

Barkai, Ron. *Spanish Mythology* [Hebrew]. Tel Aviv: Mapa, 2003.

Barkan, Elazar, and Marie-Denise Shelton, eds. *Borders, Exiles, Diasporas*, Stanford, CA: Stanford University Press, 1998.

Baron, Salo Wittmayer. "Saadia's Communal Activities," in *Ancient and Medieval Jewish History*. Edited with a Foreword by Leon A. Feldman. New Brunswick, NJ: Rutgers University Press, 1972. 95–127.

Beaver, Adam G. "Nebuchadnezzar's Jewish Legions: Sephardic Legends' Journey from Biblical Polemic to Humanist History," in *After Conversion: Iberia and the Emergence of Modernity*. Edited by Mercedes García-Arenal. Leiden: Brill, 2016. 21–65.

Beeri, Tova. "Between Spain and the East: The Poetic Works of David Ben Ha-Nassi," in *Jewish Studies at the Turn of the 20th Century* [Volume 1: Biblical, Rabbinical and Medieval Studies]. Edited by Judit Targarona Borrás and Angel Sáenz-Badillos. Leiden: Brill, 1999. 370–383.

———. "ᶜEli he-Ḥaver ben ᶜAmram: A Hebrew Poet in Eleventh-Century Egypt" [Hebrew], *Sefunot* [n.s.] 8 (2003): 279–345.
———. "*Tochakha*: Un poème de remontrance de David Hanassi" [Hebrew], *Revue Européenne des Études Hébraïques* 9 (2003): 89–102.
Benbassa, Esther. *Suffering as Identity: The Jewish Paradigm*. Translated by G. M. Goshgarian. London: Verso, 2010.
Ben-Dor Benite, Zvi. *The Ten Lost Tribes: A World History*. Oxford: Oxford University Press, 2009.
Bennison, Amira K. *The Almoravid and Almohad Empires*. Edinburgh: Edinburgh University Press, 2016.
———. "Liminal States: Morocco and the Iberian Frontier Between the Twelfth and Nineteenth Centuries," in *North Africa, Islam and the Mediterranean World from the Almoravids to the Algerian War*. Edited by Julia Clancy-Smith. London: Frank Cass, 2001. 11–28.
Ben-Porat, Ziva. "'Golden Age' Poetry in Contemporary Israeli and Palestinian Poetry," *European Review* 16 (2008): 127–143.
Ben-Sasson, Menahem. "Al-Andalus: The So-Called 'Golden Age' of Spanish Jewry—A Critical View," in *The Jews of Europe in the Middle Ages (Tenth to Fifteenth Centuries)*. Edited by Christoph Cluse. Turnhout: Brepols, 2004. 123–136.
———. *Emergence of the Local Jewish Community in the Muslim World: Qayrawan, 800–1057* [Hebrew]. Jerusalem: Magnes, 1996.
———. "Religious Leadership in Islamic Lands: Forms of Leadership and Sources of Authority," in *Jewish Religious Leadership: Image and Reality*. 2 volumes. Edited by Jack Wertheimer. New York: Jewish Theological Seminary, 2004. 1:183–187.
———. "The Structure, Goals, and Content of the Story of Nathan ha-Babli" [Hebrew], in *Culture and Society in Medieval Jewry: Studies Dedicated to the Memory of Haim Hillel Ben-Sasson*. Edited by Menahem Ben-Sasson, Robert Bonfil, and Yosef Hacker. Jerusalem: Zalman Shazar Institute, 1989. 137–196.
———. "Varieties of Intercommunal Relations in the Geonic Period," in *The Jews of Medieval Islam: Community, Society, and Identity*. Edited by Daniel Frank. Leiden: E. J. Brill, 1995. 17–31.
Ben-Shammai, Haggai. "The Exegetical and Philosophical Writing of Sa'adya Gaon: A Leader's Endeavor" [Hebrew], *Pe'amim* 54 (1993): 63–81.
———. "The Karaites," in *The History of Jerusalem: The Early Islamic Period (638–1099)*. Edited by J. Prawer and H. Ben-Shammai. Jerusalem: Ben-Zvi Institute and New York University Press, 1996. 163–178.
———, and Bruno Chiesa. "Qᵉṭa'im mi-peirush rasa"g li-mgilat eikhah," *Ginzei Qedem* 3 (2007): 29–87 [Hebrew section].
Ben-Zaken, Avner. *Reading Ḥayy Ibn-Yaqẓān: A Cross-Cultural History of Autodidacticism*. Baltimore: Johns Hopkins University Press, 2011.
Black, Anthony. *The History of Islamic Political Thought: From the Prophet to the Present*. 2nd edition. Edinburgh: Edinburgh University Press, 2011.
Blau, Joshua. "'At Our Place in al-Andalus,' 'At Our Place in the Maghreb,'" in *Perspectives on Maimonides: Philosophical and Historical Studies*. Edited by Joel L. Kraemer. Oxford: Oxford University Press, 1991. 293–294.
———. "Maimonides, al-Andalus, and the Influence of the Spanish-Arabic Dialect on His Language," in *New Horizons in Sephardic Studies*. Edited by Yedida K. Stillman and George K. Zucker. Albany: State University of New York Press, 1993. 203–210.

———. "Maimonides' 'At Our Place in al-Andalus' Revisited," in *Maimónides y su época*. Edited by Carlos del Valle, Santiago García-Jalón, and Juan Pedro Monferrer. Córdoba: Sociedad Estatal de Conmemoraciones Culturales, 2007. 327–339.

Bonebakker, Seeger A. "*Adab* and the Concept of Belles-Lettres," in *The Cambridge History of Arabic Literature: Abbasid Belles-Lettres*. Edited by Julia Ashtiany et al. Cambridge: Cambridge University Press, 1990. 16–30.

Boone, James L. *Lost Civilization: The Contested Islamic Past in Spain and Portugal*. London: Duckworth, 2009.

Bossong, Georg. "Der Name *al-Andalus*: Neue Überlegungen zu einem alten Problem," in *Sounds and Systems: Studies in Structure and Change* [*A Festschrift for Theo Vennemann*]. Edited by David Restle and Dietmar Zaefferer. Berlin: Mouton de Gruyter, 2002. 150–164.

Boum, Aoumar. "The Performance of Convivencia: Communities of Tolerance and the Reification of Toleration," *Religion Compass* 6 (2012): 174–184.

Bourdieu, Pierre. *The Field of Cultural Production: Essays on Art and Literature*. New York: Columbia University Press, 1993.

———. "The Forms of Capital," in *Handbook of Theory and Research for the Sociology of Education*. Edited by John G. Richardson. New York: Greenwood, 1986. 241–258.

Boym, Svetlana. *The Future of Nostalgia*. New York: Basic Books, 2001.

Brann, Ross. *The Compunctious Poet: Cultural Ambiguity and Hebrew Poetry in Muslim Spain*. Baltimore: Johns Hopkins University Press, 1991.

———. "Constructions of Exile in Hispano-Hebrew and Hispano-Arabic Elegies" [Hebrew], in *Israel Levin Jubilee Volume: Studies in Hebrew Literature*. Edited by Reuven Tsur and Tova Rosen. Tel Aviv: Tel Aviv University, 1994. 1:45–61.

———. "Judah Halevi," in *The Literature of al-Andalus* [*The Cambridge History of Arabic Literature*]. Edited by María Rosa Menocal, Raymond P. Scheindlin, and Michael Sells. Cambridge: Cambridge University Press, 2000. 265–281.

———. "The Moors?," *Medieval Encounters* 15 (2009): 307–318.

———. *Power in the Portrayal: Representations of Jews and Muslims in Eleventh- and Twelfth-Century Islamic Spain*. Princeton, NJ: Princeton University Press, 2002.

Brener, Ann. *Isaac ibn Khalfun: A Wandering Hebrew Poet of the Eleventh Century*. Leiden: Brill, 2003.

Brody, Robert. The Enigma of *Seder Rav 'Amram*" [Hebrew], in *Knesset Ezra: Literature and Life in the Synagogue* [Studies Presented to Ezra Fleischer]. Edited by S. Elizur et al. Jerusalem: Ben-Zvi Institute, 1994. 21–34.

———. *The Geonim of Babylonia and the Shaping of Medieval Jewish Culture*. New Haven, CT: Yale University Press, 1998.

———. *Pirqoy ben Baboy and the History of Internal Polemics in Judaism* [Hebrew]. Tel Aviv: Tel Aviv University Press, 2003.

———. *Rabbi Saʿadia Gaon* [Hebrew]. Jerusalem: Zalman Shazar Center, 2006.

Browning, Robert. *The Complete Poetic Works*, repr., Boston: Houghton Mifflin, 1895.

Brubaker, Rogers, and Frederick Cooper. "Beyond 'Identity,'" *Theory and Society* 29 (2000): 1–47.

Brutzkus, J. "Sfarad un Ṣorfat," in *Yidn in frankrayx: Shṭudyes un maṭerialn*. 2 volumes. Edited by Eliyahu M. Cherikover. New York: Yivo Institute for Jewish Research, 1942. 1:9–15.

Bulliet, Richard W. "The Conversion Curve Revisited," in *Islamisation: Comparative Perspectives from History*. Edited by A. C. S. Peacock. Edinburgh: Edinburgh University Press, 2017. 69–79.

———. *Conversion to Islam in the Medieval Period: An Essay in Quantitative History*. Cambridge, MA: Harvard University Press, 1979.

Bynum, Caroline Walker. "Wonder," *American Historical Review* 102 (1997): 1–26.

Calderwood, Eric. *Colonial al-Andalus: Spain and the Making of Modern Moroccan Culture*. Cambridge, MA: Harvard University Press, 2018.

———. "The Invention of al-Andalus: Discovering the Past and Creating the Present in Granada's Islamic Tourism Sites," *Journal of North African Studies* 19 (2014): 31–55.

Campoy, M. Arcas, and D. Serrano Niza. "Ibn Ḥabīb al-Ilbīrī," in *Biblioteca de al-Andalus*. 7 volumes. Edited by Jorge Lirola Delgado and José Miguel Puerta Vilchez. Almería: Fundacíon Ibn Tufayl de Estudios Árabes, 2004–2012. 3:219–227.

Cano, María José. *Yishaq ibn Jalfun: Poeta cortesano cordobés*. Córdoba: Almendro, 1988.

Castro, Américo. *España en su historia: Cristianos, moros y judíos*. Buenos Aires: Editorial Losada, 1948.

———. *The Structure of Spanish History*. Translated by E. L. King. Princeton, NJ: Princeton University Press, 1954.

Catlos, Brian A. *Kingdoms of Faith: A New History of Islamic Spain*. New York: Basic Books, 2018.

Chejne, Anwar G. *Ibn Ḥazm*. Chicago: Kanzi, 1982.

Christys, Ann. *Christians in al-Andalus, 711–1000*. New York: Routledge, 2002.

Civantos, Christina. *The Afterlife of al-Andalus: Muslim Iberia in Contemporary Arab and Hispanic Narratives*. Albany: State University of New York Press, 2017.

Clarke, Nicola. *The Muslim Conquest of Iberia: Medieval Arabic Narratives*. New York: Routledge, 2012.

Cohen, Gerson D. *The Book of Tradition* [Abraham ibn Daud, *Sefer ha-qabbalah*]. Philadelphia: Jewish Publication Society, 1967.

———. "Messianic Postures of Ashkenazi and Sephardim (Prior to Shabbethai Zvi)," repr. in *Studies in the Variety of Rabbinic Cultures*. Philadelphia: Jewish Publication Society, 1991. 271–297.

———. "The Story of the Four Captives," repr. in *Studies in the Variety of Rabbinic Cultures*. Philadelphia: Jewish Publication Society, 1991.

Cohen, Julia Philips, and Sarah Abrevaya Stein. *Sephardi Lives: A Documentary History, 1700–1950*. Stanford, CA: Stanford University Press, 2014.

Cohen, Mark R. *Jewish Self-Government in Medieval Egypt: The Origins of the Office of Head of the Jews, ca. 1065–1126*. Princeton, NJ: Princeton University Press, 1980.

———. "The Origins of Sephardic Jewry in the Medieval Arab World," in *Sephardic and Mizrahi Jewry from the Golden Age of Spain to Modern Times*. Edited by Zion Zohar. New York: New York University Press, 2005. 23–39.

———. *Under Crescent and Cross: The Jews in the Middle Ages*. Reissued with a new introduction and afterword. Princeton, NJ: Princeton University Press, 2008.

Cohen, Martin A. "The Sephardic Phenomenon: A Reappraisal," *American Jewish Archives* 44 (1992): 1–79.

Cole, Peter. *The Dream of the Poem: Hebrew Poetry from Muslim and Christian Spain 950–1492*. Princeton, NJ: Princeton University Press, 2007.

———. *Selected Poems of Solomon Ibn Gabirol*. Princeton, NJ: Princeton University Press, 2001.

Collins, Roger. *The Arab Conquest of Spain, 710–797*. Oxford: Basil Blackwell, 1989.

Conrad, L. I. "The World of Ibn Tufayl," in *The World of Ibn Tufayl: Interdisciplinary Perspectives on Ḥayy ibn Yaqẓān*. Edited by L. I. Conrad. Leiden: E. J. Brill, 1996. 1–37.

Constable, Olivia Remie. *Medieval Iberia: Readings from Christian, Muslim, and Jewish Sources.* 2nd edition. Philadelphia: University of Pennsylvania Press, 2012.

———. "Muslim Merchants in Andalusi International Trade," in *The Legacy of Muslim Spain.* Edited by Salma Khadra Jayyusi. Leiden: E. J. Brill, 1992. 759–73.

———. *Trade and Traders in Muslim Spain: The Commercial Realignment of the Iberian Peninsula,* 900–1500. Cambridge: Cambridge University Press, 1996.

Cook, David. *Studies in Muslim Apocalyptic.* Princeton, NJ: Darwin, 2002.

Cook, Michael. "Ibn Saʿdī on Truth-Blindness," *Jerusalem Studies in Arabic and Islam* 33 (2007): 169–178.

Corriente, Federico. "Coptic Loanwords of Egyptian Arabic in Comparison with the Parallel Case of Romance Loanwords in Andalusi Arabic, with the True Egyptian Etymon of al-Andalus," *Collectanea Christiana Orientalia* 5 (2008): 59–123.

———. *Diccionario de arabismos y voces afines en iberorromance.* Madrid: Gredos, 1999.

Crone, Patricia. *God's Rule: Six Centuries of Medieval Islamic Political Thought.* New York: Columbia University Press, 2004.

Cruz Hernández, Miguel. "Islamic Thought in the Iberian Peninsula," in *The Legacy of Muslim Spain.* Edited by Salma Khadra Jayyusi. Leiden: E. J. Brill, 1992. 777–803.

Dana, Joseph. *Poetics of Medieval Hebrew Literature According to Moshe Ibn Ezra* [Hebrew]. Jerusalem: Dvir, 1982.

Dangler, Jean. "Edging Toward Iberia," *Diacritics* 36 (2006): 12–26.

———. *Edging Toward Iberia.* Toronto: Toronto University Press, 2017.

Davis, Ruth F. *Musical Exodus: Al-Andalus and Its Jewish Diasporas.* Lanham, MD: Rowman & Littlefield, 2015.

Decter, Jonathan. "Before Caliphs and Kings: Jewish Courtiers in Medieval Iberia," in *The Jew in Medieval Iberia, 1100–1500.* Edited by Jonathan Ray. Boston: Academic Studies Press, 2012. 1–32.

———. *Dominion Built of Praise: Panegyric and Legitimacy Among Jews in the Medieval Mediterranean.* Philadelphia: University of Pennsylvania Press, 2018.

———. *Iberian Jewish Literature: Between al-Andalus and Christian Europe.* Bloomington: Indiana University Press, 2007.

———. "A Myrtle in the Forest: Landscape and Nostalgia in Andalusian Hebrew Poetry," *Prooftexts* 24 (2004): 135–166.

Dejugnat, Yann. "La Méditerranée comme frontière dans le récit de voyage (*riḥla*) d'Ibn Gubayr: Modalités et enjeux d'une perception," *Mélanges de la Casa de Velázquez* 38 (2008): 237–257.

Delitzsch, Franz. *Zur Geschichte der jüdischen Poësie vom Abschluss der heiligen Schriften Alten Bundes bis auf die neueste Zeit.* Leipzig: K. Tauchnitz, 1836.

Delpech, François. "Du héros marqué au signe du Prophète: Esquisse pour l'archéologie d'un motif chevaleresque," *Bulletin Hispanique* 92 (1990): 237–257.

Dickie, James. "The Islamic Garden in Spain," in *The Islamic Garden.* Edited by Elisabeth MacDougall and Richard Ettinghausen. Washington, DC: Dumbarton Oaks, 1976. 89–105.

Dishon, Judith. "Medieval Panorama in the Book of Taḥkemoni," *Proceedings of the American Academy for Jewish Research* 56 (1989): 11–27.

Docker, John. *1492: The Poetics of Diaspora.* London: Continuum, 2001.

Dodds, Jerrilynn. *Architecture and Ideology in Early Medieval Spain.* University Park: Pennsylvania State University Press, 1990.

———. "The Great Mosque of Cordoba," in *Al-Andalus: The Art of Islamic Spain*. Edited by Jerrilynn D. Dodds. New York: Metropolitan Museum of Art, 1992. 11–25.

Dotan, Aron. *The Dawn of Hebrew Linguistics: The Book of Elegance of the Language of the Hebrews by Saadia Gaon* [Hebrew]. 2 volumes. Jerusalem: World Union of Jewish Studies, 1997.

———. "The Vicissitudes of Arabic Impact on Hebrew Language Study in the East and in Spain," in *Encuentros and Desencuentros: Spanish-Jewish Cultural Interaction Throughout History*. Edited by Carlos Carrete Parrondo et al. Tel Aviv: University Publishing Projects, 2000. 131–158.

Dozy, Reinhart. "Review of Ernest Renan, *Averroès et l'averroïsme, Journal asiatique* [5th s.] 2 (1853): 90–96.

———. *Spanish Islam: A History of the Moslems in Spain* [1861]. Translated by Francis Griffin Stokes. London: Frank Cass, 1972.

Draper, Hal. *The Complete Poems of Heinrich Heine: A Modern English Vers*ion. Translated by Hal Draper. Cambridge: Suhrkamp/Insel, 1982.

Drory, Rina. "The Maqama," in *The Literature of al-Andalus* [*The Cambridge History of Arabic Literature*]. Edited by María Rosa Menocal, Raymond P. Scheindlin, and Michael Sells. Cambridge: Cambridge University Press. 190–210.

———. *Models and Contacts: Arabic Literature and Its Impact on Medieval Jewish Culture*. Leiden: Brill, 2000.

Dunlop, D. M. *The History of the Jewish Khazars*. New York: Schocken, 1967.

Dutton, Yasin. *Original Islam: Mālik and the Madhhab of Madina*. London: Routledge, 2007.

Ebied, R. Y., and M. J. L. Young. "Abū 'l-Baqā' al-Rundī and His Elegy on Muslim Spain," *The Muslim World* 66 (1976): 31–34.

Edwards, Robert. "Exile, Self, and Society," in *Exile in Literature*. Edited by Maria-Ines Lagos-Pope. Lewisburg, PA: Bucknell University Press, 1988.

Efron, John M. *German Jewry and the Allure of the Sephardic*. Princeton, NJ: Princeton University Press, 2016.

Eisen, Arnold. *Modern Jewish Reflections on Homelessness and Homecoming*. Bloomington: Indiana University Press, 1986.

Elbogen, Ismar. *Jewish Liturgy: A Comprehensive History*. Translated by Raymond P. Scheindlin. Philadelphia: Jewish Publication Society and Jewish Theological Seminary, 1993.

Elinson, Alexander E. *Looking Back at al-Andalus: The Poetics of Loss and Nostalgia in Medieval Arabic and Hebrew Literature*. Leiden: Brill, 2009.

Elizur, Shulamit. "Ḥiddushim b^{e}-ḥeqer ha-shirah w^{e}-ha-piyyuṭ," in *The Cairo Geniza Collection in Geneva: Catalog and Studies* [Hebrew]. Edited by David Rosenthal. Jerusalem: Magnes, 2010. 200–207.

Ellenblum, Ronnie. *The Collapse of the Eastern Mediterranean: Climate Change and the Decline of the East*. Cambridge. Cambridge University Press, 2012.

Enderwitz, Susanne. "Homesickness and Love in Arabic Poetry," in *Myths, Historical Archetypes and Symbolic Figures in Arabic Literature: Towards a New Hermeneutic Approach*. Edited by Angelika Neuwirth et al. Beirut: Franz Steiner, 1999. 59–70.

Epstein, Abraham. *Eldad ha-Dani: Seine Berichte über die X Stämme und deren Ritus in verschiedenen Versionen nach Handschriften und alten Drucken*. Pressburg: Adolf Alkalay, 1891.

Euben, Roxanne L. *Journeys to Other Shores: Muslim and Western Travelers in Search of Knowledge*. Princeton, NJ: Princeton University Press, 2006.

Evri, Yuval. "Translating the Arab-Jewish Tradition: From al-Andalus to Palestine/ Land of Israel," *Essays of the Forum Transregionale Studien* 1 (2016): 5–39.

Ezrahi, Sidra DeKoven. *Booking Passage: Exile and Homecoming in the Modern Jewish Imagination*. Berkeley: University of California Press, 2000.

Fanjul, Serafín. "El mito de las tres culturas," *Revista de Occidente* 224 (2000): 9–30.

Faur, José. *Homo Mysticus: A Guide to Maimonides' Guide for the Perplexed*. Syracuse, NY: Syracuse University Press, 1998.

———. "Introducing the Materials of Sephardic Culture to Contemporary Jewish Studies," in *Sephardic Studies in the University*. Edited by Jane S. Gerber. Madison, NJ: Fairleigh Dickinson University Press, and London: Associated University Presses, 1995. 29–42.

Fernández-Morera, Darío. "The Myth of Andalusian Paradise," *Intercollegiate Review* 41 (2006): 23–31.

———. *The Myth of the Andalusian Paradise: Muslims, Christians, and Jews Under Islamic Rule in Medieval Spain*. Wilmington, DE: ISI, 2016.

Fernández Parrilla, Gonzalo. "Disoriented Postcolonialities: With Edward Said on (the Labyrinth of) al-Andalus," *Interventions* 20 (2018): 229–242.

Ferris, Paul Wayne, Jr. *The Genre of Communal Lament in the Bible and the Ancient Near East*. Atlanta: Scholars Press, 1992.

Fierro, Maribel. *'Abd al-Raḥmān III: The First Cordoban Caliph*. Oxford: One World Publications, 2005.

———. Anṣārīs in al-Andalus: 'Arabs' Without *Nasab*," *Jerusalem Studies in Arabic and Islam* 31 (2006): 232–247.

———. "Heresy and Political Legitimacy in al-Andalus," in *Heresy and the Making of European Culture: Medieval and Modern Perspectives*. Edited by Andrew P. Roach and James K. Simpson. Farnham: Ashgate, 2013. 51–76.

———. *La hetérodoxia en al-Andalus durante el período omeya*. Madrid: Instituto Hispano-Árabe de Cultura, 1987.

———. "The Introduction of Ḥadīth in al-Andalus," *Der Islam* 66 (1989): 68–93.

———. "The Islamisation of al-Andalus: Recent Studies and Debates," in *Islamisation: Comparative Perspectives from History*. Edited by A. C. S. Peacock. Edinburgh: Edinburgh University Press, 2017. 199–220.

———. "Madīnat al-Zahrā', Paradise and the Fatimids," in *Roads to Paradise: Eschatology and Concepts of the Hereafter in Islam*. 2 volumes. Edited by Sebastian Gunther and Todd Lawson. Leiden: Brill, 2017. 2:979–1009.

———. "The *Mahdī* Ibn Tumart and al-Andalus: The Construction of Almohad Legitimacy," in Maribel Fierro, *The Almohad Revolution: Politics and Religion in the Islamic West During the Twelfth–Thirteenth Centuries*. Farnham: Ashgate-Variorum, 2012. 3:1–20.

———. "Le mahdī Ibn Tūmart et al-Andalus: L'élaboration de le légitimit almohade," in *Millénarisme et Mahdisme*. Edited by Mercedes García-Arenal, *Revue des Mondes Musulmans et de la Mediteranée* 91–94 (2004): 107–124.

———. "Mawālī and Muwalladūn in al-Andalus (Second/Eighth–Fourth/Tenth Centuries)," in *Patronate and Patronage in Early and Classical Islam*. Edited by Monique Bernards and John Nawas. Leiden: Brill, 2005. 195–245.

———. "The Movable *Minbar* in Cordoba: How the Umayyads of al-Andalus Claimed the Inheritance of the Prophet," *Jerusalem Studies in Arabic and Islam* 33 (2007): 149–168.

———. "Mu'āwiya b. Ṣāliḥ al-Haḍramī al-Ḥimṣī: Historia y leyenda," in *Estudios onomástico-biográficos de al-Andalus*. Edited by Manuela Marín. Madrid: Consejo Superior de Investigaciones Científicas, 1988. 281–411.

———. "Opposition to Sufism in al-Andalus," in *Islamic Mysticism Contested: Thirteen Centuries of Controversies and Polemics*. Edited by F. de Jong and B. Radtke. Leiden: Brill, 1999. 174–206.

———. "Proto-Malikis, Malikis, and Reformed Malikis in al-Andalus," in *The Islamic School of Law: Evolution, Devolution, and Progress*. Edited by Peri Bearman, Rudolph Peters, and Frank E. Vogel. Cambridge, MA: Harvard University Press, 2005. 61–70.

———. "Red and Yellow: Colors and the Quest for Political Legitimacy in the Islamic West," in *And Diverse Are Their Hues: Color in Islamic Art and Culture*. Edited by Jonathan Bloom and Sheila Blair. New Haven, CT: Yale University Press, 2011. 79–97.

———. "Sobre la adopcíon del título califal por ʿAbd al-Raḥmān III," *Sharq al-Andalus* 6 (1989): 33–42.

———. "Spiritual Alienation and Political Activism: The *Ghurabāʾ* in al-Andalus During the Sixth/Twelfth Century," *Arabica* 47 (2000): 232–245.

———. "Ways of Connecting with the Past: Genealogies in Nasrid Granada," in *Genealogy and Knowledge in Muslim Societies: Understanding the Past*. Edited by Sarah Bowen Savant and Helena de Felipe. Edinburgh: Edinburgh University Press and Aga Khan University, 2014. 71–88.

———. "Why and How Do Religious Scholars Write About Themselves? The Case of the Islamic West in the Fourth/Tenth Century," *Mélanges de l'Université Saint-Joseph* 58 (2005): 403–408.

———, and Saadia Faghia. "Un nuevo texto de tradiciones escatológicas sobre al-Andalus," *Sharq al-Andalus* 7 (1990): 99–111.

Filios, Denise K. "Expulsion from Paradise: Exiled Intellectuals and Andalusian Tolerance," in *In the Light of Medieval Spain: Islam, the West and the Relevance of the Past*. Edited by Simon R. Doubleday and David Coleman. New York: Palgrave MacMillan, 2008. 91–113.

Fischel, Walter J. "'The Resh-Galuta' in Arabic Literature" [Hebrew], in *Magnes Anniversary Book*. Edited by F. I. Baer et al. Jerusalem: Hebrew University, 1938. 181–87.

Fishman, Talya. *Becoming the People of the Talmud: Oral Torah as Written Tradition in Medieval Jewish Culture*. Philadelphia: University of Pennsylvania Press, 2011.

Fleischer, Ezra. "The Culture of the Jews of Spain and Their Poetry According to the Findings of the Geniza" [Hebrew], *Peʿamim* 41 (1989): 5–20.

———. "Yehuda Halevi: Remarks Concerning His Life and Poetical Oeuvre" [Hebrew], in *Israel Levin Jubilee Volume*. Edited by Reuven Tsur and Tova Rosen. Tel Aviv: Tel Aviv University Press, 1994. 241–276.

Forcada, Miquel. "Books from Abroad: The Evolution of Science and Philosophy in Umayyad al-Andalus," *Intellectual History of the Islamicate World* 5 (2017): 55–85.

Fox, John W., Nada Mourtada-Sabbah, and Sulayman N. Khalaf. "Ethnography and the Culture of Tolerance in al-Andalus," *Harvard Middle Eastern and Islamic Review* 7 (2006): 146–171.

Franklin, Arnold E. *This Noble House: Jewish Descendants of King David in the Medieval Islamic East*. Philadelphia: University of Pennsylvania Press, 2013.

Frenkel, Miriam. "The Historiography of the Jews in Muslim Countries in the Middle Ages: Landmarks and Prospects" [Hebrew], *Peʿamim* 92 (2002): 23–62.

Friedlander, Israel. "The Arabic Original of the Report of R. Nathan Hababli," *Jewish Quarterly Review* [o.s.] 17 (1905): 747–761.

Fromherz, Allen. "Making 'Great Battles' Great: Christian and Muslim Views of las Navas de Tolosa," *Journal of Medieval Iberian Studies* 4 (2012): 33–38.

Fuchs, Barbara. *Exotic Nation: Maurophilia and the Construction of Early Modern Spain*. Philadelphia: University of Pennsylvania Press, 2009.

Gallois, William. "Andalusi Cosmopolitanism in World History," in *Cultural Contacts in Building a Universal Civilization: Islamic Contributions*. Istanbul: OIC Research Centre, 2005. 61–85.

Gampel, Benjamin R. "A Letter to a Wayward Teacher: The Transformations of Sephardic Culture in Christian Iberia," in *Cultures of the Jews: A New History*. Edited by David Biale. New York: Schocken, 2002. 389–447.

García Gómez, Emilio. *Andalucía contra Berbería: Reedición de Traducciones de Ben Ḥayyān, Shaqundī y Ben Al-Jaṭīb con un Prólogo*. Barcelona: Publicaciones del Departamento de Lengua y Literature Árabes, 1976.

García Sanjuán, Alejandro. "Al-Andalus, Etymology and Name," *Encyclopaedia of Islam*. 3rd edition. 1:18–25.

———. *La conquista islámica de la península ibérica y la tergiversación del pasado: Del catastrofismo al negacionismo*. Madrid: Marcial Pons Historia, 2013.

———. "Rejecting al-Andalus, Exalting the Reconquista: Historical Memory in Contemporary Spain," *Journal of Medieval Iberian Studies* (2016): 127–145.

Garulo, Teresa. *La literatura árabe de al-Andalus durante siglo XI*. Madrid: Hiperión, 1988.

———. "La Nostalgia de al-Andalus: Genesis de un Tema Literario," *Qurṭuba* 3 (1988): 47–63.

Gayangos, Pascual. *History of the Mohammedan Dynasties of Spain*. 2 volumes. London: Oriental Translation Fund, 1940.

Gellens, Sam I. "The Search for Knowledge in Medieval Muslim Societies: A Comparative Approach," in *Muslim Travellers: Pilgrimage, Migration and the Religious Imagination*. Edited by Dale F. Eickelman and James Piscatori. Berkeley: University of California Press, 1990. 50–65.

Gelston, Anthony. *The Peshiṭta of the Twelve Prophets*. Oxford: Clarendon, 1987.

Gerber, Jane S. *The Jews of Spain: A History of the Sephardic Experience*. New York: Free Press, 1992.

———. "Reconsiderations of Sephardic History: The Origins of the Image of the Golden Age of Muslim-Jewish Relations," *Solomon Goldman Lectures* 4 (1985): 85–93.

Gergen, Mary. "Narrative Structures in Social Explanation," in *Analysing Everyday Explanation: A Casebook of Methods*. Edited by Charles Antaki. London: Sage, 1988. 94–112.

Gil, Moshe. "The Babylonian Yeshivot and the Maghrib in the Early Middle Ages," *Proceedings of the American Academy for Jewish Research* 51 (1990): 69–120.

———. *In the Kingdom of Ishmael: Texts from the Cairo Genizah* [Hebrew and Arabic]. 3 volumes. Tel Aviv: Tel Aviv University, Bialik Institute, and Ministry of Defence Publishing, 1997.

———. *Jews in Islamic Countries in the Middle Ages*. Translated by David Strassler. Leiden: E. J. Brill, 2004.

———. *Palestine During the First Muslim Period (634–1099)* [Hebrew]. 3 volumes. Tel Aviv: Tel Aviv University Press, 1983.

———. *The Tustaris: Family and Sect* [Hebrew]. Tel Aviv: Diaspora Research Institute, Project Moreshet for the Research of Oriental Jewry, 1981.

Gilliot, Claude. "Prosopography in Islam: An Essay of Classification," *Medieval Prosopography* 23 (2002): 19–54.

Ginger, Andrew. "The Estranged Self of Spain: Oriental Obsession in the Time of Gayangos," in *Pascual de Gayangos: A Nineteenth-Century Spanish Arabist*. Edited by Cristina Álvarez Millán and Claudia Heide. Edinburgh: Edinburgh University Press, 2008. 49–67.

Ginzberg, Louis. *Geonica [Texts and Studies of the Jewish Theological Seminary of America, Volumes 1–2]*. New York: Jewish Theological Seminary, 1909; repr., New York: Hermon, 1968.

———. *Ginzei Schechter: Genizah Studies in Memory of Doctor Solomon Schechter*. 2 volumes. New York: Jewish Theological Seminary, 1929; repr., New York: Hermon, 1969.

Glasser, Jonathan. *The Lost Paradise: Andalusi Music in Urban North Africa*. Chicago: University of Chicago Press, 2016.

Glick, Thomas F. "Convivencia: An Introductory Note," in *Convivencia: Jews, Muslims and Christians in Medieval Spain*. Edited by Vivian B. Mann, Thomas F. Glick, and Jerrilynn D. Dodds. New York: George Braziller and the Jewish Museum, 1992. 1–9.

———. *From Muslim Fortress to Christian Castle: Social and Cultural Change in Medieval Spain*. Manchester: Manchester University Press, 1995.

———. *Islamic and Christian Spain in the Early Middle Ages*. 2nd revised edition. Leiden: Brill, 2005.

———. "Tribal Landscapes of Islamic Spain: History and Archeology," in *Inventing Medieval Landscapes: Senses of Place in Western Europe*. Edited by John Howe and Michael Wolfe. Gainesville: University Press of Florida, 2002. 113–135.

Goitein, S. D. "Judeo-Arabic Letters from Spain (Early Twelfth Century)," in *Orientalia hispanica: Sive studia F. M. Pareja octogenario dicata*. Edited by J. M. Barral. Leiden: E. J. Brill, 1974. 1:331–350.

———. "Al-Ḳuds." *Encyclopaedia of Islam*. 2nd edition. 5:327.

———. *A Mediterranean Society: The Jewish Communities of the Arab World as Portrayed in the Documents of the Cairo Geniza*. 6 volumes. Berkeley: University of California Press, 1967–1993.

———. "Three Letters from Qayrawān Addressed to Joseph ben Jacob ben ʿAwkal" [Hebrew], *Tarbiẓ* 34 (1965): 166–169.

———. "The Unity of the Mediterranean World in the 'Middle' Middle Ages," repr. in S. D. Goitein, *Studies in Islamic History and Institutions*. Leiden: E. J. Brill, 1968. 296–307.

———, and Mordechai A. Friedman. *India Traders of the Middle Ages: Documents from the Cairo Geniza [India Book]*. Jerusalem: Ben-Zvi Institute, 2008.

Golb, Norman. "Al-Rūjīi, Solomon and Menahem," *Encyclopedia of Jews in Islamic Lands*. 5 volumes. Edited by Norman A. Stillman et al. Leiden: 2010. 4:190–194.

———, and Omeljan Pritsak. *Khazarian Hebrew Documents of the Tenth Century*. Ithaca, NY: Cornell University Press, 1982.

Goldberg, Jessica L. *Trade and Institutions in the Medieval Mediterranean: The Geniza Merchants and Their Business World*. Cambridge: Cambridge University Press, 2012.

Golden, Peter B., Haggai Ben-Shammai, and András Róna-Tas, eds. *The World of the Khazars: New Perspectives*. Leiden: Brill, 2007.

Goldstein, Bluma. "A Politics and Poetics of Diaspora: Heine's *Hebräische Melodien*," in *Diasporas and Exile: Varieties of Jewish Identity*. Edited by Howard Wettstein. Berkeley: University of California Press, 2002. 60–77.

Goldziher, Ignáz. "The Spanish Arabs and Islam: The Place of the Spanish Arabs in the Evolution of Islam Compared with the Eastern Arabs," repr. in *Gesammelte Schriften*. 6 volumes. Edited by Joseph Desomogyi. Hildesheim: G. Olms, 1967. 1:370–423.

Gómez-Rivas, Camilo. "Las Navas de Tolosa, the Urban Transformation of the Maghrib, and the Territorial Decline of al-Andalus," *Journal of Medieval Iberian Studies* 4 (2012): 27–32.

González Alcantud, José Antonio. "The Beginning and End of the *Good* Myth of al-Andalus: 711 and 1609—Representations, Confrontations and Intellectual Interpretations of al-Andalus in Spanish Historical Narratives," *eHumanista* 38 (2018): 746–763.

Goodman, Lenn E. *Neoplatonism and Jewish Thought*. Albany: State University of New York Press, 1992.

Grabar, Oleg. "Islamic Spain, the First Four Centuries: An Introduction," in *Al-Andalus: The Art of Islamic Spain*. Edited by Jerrilynn D. Dodds. New York: Metropolitan Museum of Art, 1992. 3–8.

Graetz, Heinrich. *A History of the Jews* [Geschichte der Juden von den ältesten Zeiten bis auf die Gegenwart]. 6 volumes. Translated by Bella Löwy. Philadelphia: Jewish Publication Society, 1946.

Granara, William. "*Extensio Animae*: The Artful Ways of Remembering 'Al-Andalus,'" *Journal of Social Affairs* 19 (2002): 45–72.

Granat, Yehoshua. "Polémica, Equívico, o Ambivalencia? Nuevas Consideraciones Sobre el Primer Poema Báquico Hebreo Andalusí," in *Poesía Hebrea en al-Andalus*. Edited by Judit Targarona Borrás and Angel Sáenz-Badillos. Granada: Universidad de Granada, 2003. 27–38.

Gregory, Derek. *Geographical Imaginations*. Cambridge: Blackwell, 1994.

Grief, Avner. "Reputation and Coalitions in Medieval Trade: Evidence on the Maghribi Traders," *Journal of Economic History* 49 (1989): 857–882.

Grunebaum, G. E. von. "I'djāz," *Encyclopaedia of Islam*.· 2nd edition. 3:1018–1020.

Guichard, Pierre. *Al-Andalus: Estructura antropológica de una sociedad islámica en Occidente* Barcelona: Barral Editores, 1976.

Haarman, Ulrich. "Regional Sentiment in Medieval Egypt," *Bulletin of the School of Oriental and African Studies* 43 (1980): 55–66.

Hacohen, Aviad. "The Jerusalem Talmud in the Teachings of the Early Spanish Sages" [Hebrew], *Annual of the Institute for Research in Jewish Law* 18–19 (1992): 113–176.

Halevi-Wise, Yael. "Introduction: Through the Prism of Sepharad: Modern Nationalism, Literary History, and the Impact of the Sephardic Experience," in *Sephardism: Spanish Jewish History and the Modern Literary Imagination*. Edited by Yael Halevi-Wise. Stanford, CA: Stanford University Press, 2012. 1–32.

Halkin, Abraham S. "The Judeo-Islamic Age: Revolt and Revival in Judeo-Islamic Culture," in *Great Ages and Ideas of the Jewish People*. Edited by Leo W. Schwarz. New York: Modern Library, 1956. 234–263.

Halkin, Hillel. *Judah Halevi*. New York: Schocken-NextBooks, 2010.

———. "Out of Andalusia," *Commentary* (September 2003): 39–45.

Halm, Heinz. "Al-Andalus and Gothica Sors," in *The Formation of al-Andalus* [Part 1: History and Society]. Edited by Manuela Marín. Aldershot: Ashgate-Variorum, 1998. 39–50.

Hämeen-Antilla, Jaakko. "Adab, Arabic: Early Developments," *Encyclopaedia of Islam*. 3rd edition. Leiden: Brill, 2014. 3:4–14.

Harkavy, A. A. "Toldot r. shmu'el ha-nagid," in *Me'asef*. Edited by L. Rabinowitz. Saint Petersburg, 1902. 1–56.

Harrison, Alwayn. "Behind the Curve: Bulliet and Conversion to Islam in al-Andalus Revisited," *Al-Masāq* 24 (2012): 35–51.

Hartog, François. *The Mirror of Herodotus: The Representation of the Other in the Writing of History*. Translated by Janet Lloyd. Berkeley: University of California Press, 1988.

Harvey, L. P. *Islamic Spain, 1250–1500*. Chicago: University of Chicago Press, 1990.

———. "A Morisco Collection of Apocryphal *Ḥadīths* on the Virtues of al-Andalus," *Al-Masāq* 2 (1989): 25–39.

Hasson, Isaac. "Muslim Literature in Praise of Jerusalem: Faḍā'il Bayt al-Maqdis," *Jerusalem Cathedra* 1 (1981): 168–184.

Hayman, A. Peter. *Sefer yeṣira*. Tübingen: Mohr Siebeck, 2004.

Heath, Peter. "Knowledge," in *The Literature of al-Andalus* [*The Cambridge History of Arabic Literature*]. Edited by María Rosa Menocal, Raymond P. Scheindlin, and Michael Sells. Cambridge: Cambridge University Press, 2000. 96–125.

Heinrichs, Wolfhart. "Rose Versus Narcissus: Observations of Arabic Literary Debate," in *Dispute Poems and Dialogues in the Ancient and Mediaeval Near East: Forms and Types of Literary Debate in Semitic and Related Literatures*. Edited by G. J. Reinink and H. L. J. Vanstiphout. Leuven: Peeters, 1991. 179–188.

Helm, Heinz. "Al-Andalus und Gotica Sors," *Der Islam* 66 (1989): 252–263.

———. "L'Origine du nom *al-Andalus*," *Proceedings of the Fourteenth Congress of the Union Européenne des Arabisants et Islamisants* [*Budapest Studies in Arabic* 15–16] (1999): 49–55.

Henderson, John B. *The Construction of Orthodoxy and Heresy: Neo-Confucian, Islamic, Jewish and Early Christian Patters*. Albany: State University of New York Press, 1988.

Hendrickson, Jocelyn. "Is al-Andalus Different? Continuity as Contested, Constructed, and Performed Across Three Mālikī *Fatwās*," *Islamic Law and Society* 20 (2013): 371–424.

Herman, Marc. "Situating Maimonides' Approach to the Oral Torah in Its Andalusian Context," *Jewish History* (2017): 31–46.

Hermes, Nizar F. "Nostalgia for al-Andalus in Early Modern Moroccan *Voyages en Espagne*: Al-Ghassānī's *Riḥlat al-Wazīr fī Iftikāk al-Asīr* (1690–91) as a Case Study," *Journal of North African Studies* 21 (2016): 433–452.

Hillenbrand, Robert. "'The Ornament of the World': Medieval Cordoba as a Cultural Centre," in *The Legacy of Muslim Spain*. Edited by Salma Khadra Jayyusi. Leiden: E. J. Brill, 1992. 112–135.

———. "Zīnat al-dunyā: Qurṭuba al-qarūṣṭiyya markaz^{an} thaqāfiy^{an} 'ālimiy^{an}," in al-Ḥaḍāra al-'arabiyya al-islāmiyya fi-l-andalus. 2 volumes. Edited by Salma Khadra Jayyusi. Beirut: Markaz dirāsāt al-waḥda al-'arabiyya. 1:183–209.

Hirschberg, H. Z. *A History of the Jews in North Africa*. 2 volumes. Leiden: E. J. Brill, 1974.

Hirschkind, Charles. "The Contemporary Afterlife of Moorish Spain," in *Islam and Public Controversy in Europe*. Edited by Nilufer Gole. Farnham: Ashgate, 2013. 227–240.

Hitti, Philip K. *A History of the Arabs from the Earliest Times to the Present*. 7th edition. London: MacMillan, 1960.

Hollander, Robert. "Typology and Secular Literature: Some Medieval Problems and Examples," in *Literary Uses of Typology*. Edited by Earl Miner. Princeton, NJ: Princeton University Press, 1977. 3–19.

Holmberg, Bo. "*Adab* and Arabic Literature," in *Literary History: Towards a Global Perspective*. 4 volumes. Edited by Anders Petersson et al. Berlin: De Gruyter, 2006. 1:180–205.

Holod, Renata. "Luxury Arts of the Caliphal Period," in Jerrilynn R. Dodds, *Al-Andalus: The Art of Islamic Spain*. New York: Metropolitan Museum of Art, 1992. 40–47.

Hopkins, J. F. P. "Geographical and Navigational Literature," in *Religion, Learning, and Science in the ᶜAbbasid Period*. Edited by M. L. J. Young, John D. Latham, and Robert B. Serjeant. Cambridge: Cambridge University Press, 1990. 301–327.

———. *Medieval Muslim Government in Barbary Until the Sixth Century of the Hijra*. London: Luzac, 1958.

Horovitz, Josef. "Ibn Q̱uteiba's 'Uyūn al-Akhbār," *Islamic Culture* 4 (1930): 171–198, 331–361; *Islamic Culture* 5 (1931): 1–27.

Hourani, Albert. *A History of the Arab Peoples*. New York: Time Warner Books, 1992.

Hughes, Aaron H. "The 'Golden Age' of Muslim Spain: Religious Identity and the Invention of a Tradition in Modern Jewish Studies," in *Historicizing Tradition in the Study of Religion*. Edited by Steven Engler and Gregory Price Grieve. Berlin: De Gruyter, 2005. 51–74.

Huss, Matti. "'It Never Happened, Nor Did It Ever Exist': The Status of Fiction in the Hebrew *Maqāma*" [Hebrew], *Jerusalem Studies in Hebrew Literature* 18 (2001): 57–104.

Idris, Roger. "Reflections on Mālikism Under the Umayyads of Spain," in *The Formation of al-Andalus* [Part 2: Language, Religion, Culture and the Sciences]. Edited by Maribel Fierro and Julio Samso. Aldershot: Ashgate-Variorum, 1998. 85–101.

Iglesias, L. García. *Los judíos en la España antigua*. Madrid: Ediciones Cristiandad, 1978.

al-Jabiri, Mohammad 'Abid. *Arab-Islamic Philosophy: A Contemporary Critique*. Austin: Center for Middle Eastern Studies, University of Texas at Austin, 1999.

Jabert, Voir K. "The Birthmark in Folk-Belief, Language, Literature and Fashion," *Romance Philology* 10 (1956–1957): 307–342.

Jacobs, Martin. "'A Day's Journey': Spatial Perception and Geographic Imagination in Benjamin of Tudela's *Book of Travels*," *Jewish Quarterly Review* 109 (2019): 203–232.

———. *Reorienting the East: Jewish Travelers to the Medieval Muslim World*. Philadelphia: University of Pennsylvania Press, 2014.

Jacoby, David. "Benjamin of Tudela and His 'Book of Travels,'" in *Venezia incrocio di culture: Percezioni di viaggiatori europei e non europei a confronto*. Edited by Klaus Herbers and Felicitas Schmieder. Rome: Centro Tedesco di Studi Veneziani [Ricerche 4], 2008. 135–164.

Juberías, Julia Hernández. *La península imaginaria: Mitos y leyendas sobre al-Andalus*. Madrid: Consejo Superior de Investigaciones Científicas, 1966.

Kaminsky, Amy K. *After Exile: Writing the Latin American Diaspora*. Minneapolis: University of Minnesota Press, 1999.

Kammen, Henry. *Imagining Spain: Historical Myth and National Identity*. New Haven, CT: Yale University Press, 2008.

Kanarfogel, Ephraim. *The Intellectual History and Rabbinic Culture of Medieval Ashkenaz*. Detroit: Wayne State University Press, 2013.

Kassis, Hanna E. *A Concordance of the Qur'an*. Berkeley: University of California Press, 1983.

———. "Roots of Conflict: Aspects of Christian-Muslim Conflict in Eleventh-Century Spain," in *Conversion and Continuity: Indigenous Christian Communities in Islamic Lands Eighth to Eighteenth Centuries*. Edited by Michael Gevers and Ramzi Jibran Bikhazi. Toronto: Pontifical Institute of Mediaeval Studies, 1990. 151–160.

Katz, Solomon. *The Jews in the Visigothic and Frankish Kingdoms of Spain and Gaul*. Cambridge: Mediaeval Academy of America, 1937.

Kedar, Benjamin Z. "The Jews of Jerusalem, 1187–1267, and the Role of Naḥmanides in the Reestablishment of Their Community" [Hebrew]. In *Jerusalem in the Middle Ages: Selected Papers*. Edited by Benjamin Z. Kedar, repr., Jerusalem: Ben-Zvi Institute, 1986. 122–136.

Kennedy, Hugh. "From Oral Tradition to Written Record in Arabic Genealogy," *Arabica* 44 (1997): 531–544.

———. *Muslim Spain and Portugal: A Political History*. London: Routledge, 1996.

Khan, Geoffrey. "The Early Karaite Grammatical Tradition," in *Jewish Studies at the Turn of the 20th Century* [Volume 1: Biblical, Rabbinical and Medieval Studies]. Edited by Judit Targarona Borrás and Angel Sáenz-Badillos. Leiden: Brill, 1991. 72–80.

———. *The Early Karaite Tradition of Hebrew Grammatical Thought Including a Critical Edition, Translation and Analysis of the Diqduq of Abū Yaʿqūb Yūsuf ibn Nūḥ on the Hagiographa*. Leiden: Brill, 2000.

Khoury, Nuha N. N. "The Meaning of the Great Mosque of Cordoba in the Tenth Century," *Muqarnas* 13 (1996): 80–98.

Kimmel, Seth. *Parables of Coercion: Conversion and Knowledge at the End of Islamic Spain*. Chicago: University of Chicago Press, 2015.

Kobler, Franz. *Letters of Jews Through the Ages*. 2 volumes. New York: East and West Library, 1953.

Ḳoḳovtsov, Pavel Konstantinovich. *Evreisko-khazarskaia perepiska v X veke*. Leningrad: Izd-vo Akademii nauk SSSR, 1932.

Kraemer, Joel, L. *Humanism in the Renaissance of Islam: The Cultural Revival During the Buyid Age*. Leiden: E. J. Brill, 1986.

———. *Maimonides: The Life and World of One of Civilization's Greatest Minds*. New York: Doubleday, 2008.

———. "Maimonides and the Spanish Aristotelian School," in *Christians, Muslims and Jews in Medieval and Early Modern Spain: Interaction and Cultural Change*. Edited by Mark D. Meyerson and Edward D. English. Notre Dame: Notre Dame University Press, 2000. 40–68.

Krauss, Samuel. "The Names Ashkenaz and Sepharad" [Hebrew], *Tarbiẓ* 3 (1931–1932): 423–435.

Krinis, Ehud. *God's Chosen People: Judah Halevi's Kuzari and the Shīʿī Imām Doctrine*. Turnhout: Brepols, 2014.

Kuhn, William. *The Politics of Pleasure: A Portrait of Benjamin Disraeli*. London: Free Press, 2006.

Langermann, Tzvi. "Another Andalusian Revolt? Ibn Rushd's Critique of al-Kindī's Pharmacological Computus," in *The Enterprise of Science in Islam: New Perspectives*. Edited by Jan Pieter Hogendijk and Abdelhamid I. Sabra. Cambridge, MA: Harvard University Press, 2003. 351–372.

Lapidus, Ira M. *A History of Islamic Societies*. Cambridge: Cambridge University Press, 1988.

Laredo, A. I., and David Gonzalo Maeso. "El nombre de 'Sefarad,'" *Sefarad* 4 (1944): 349–363.

Lassner, Jacob. *Jews, Christians, and the Abode of Islam*. Chicago: University of Chicago Press, 2012.

Lazarus-Yafeh, Hava, ed. *The Majlis: Interreligious Encounters in Medieval Islam*. Wiesbaden: Harrassowitz, 1999.

Leaman, Oliver. *Moses Maimonides*. London: Routledge, 1990.

Leed, Eric J. *The Mind of the Traveler: From Gilgamesh to Global Tourism*. New York: Basic Books, 1991.

Lefebvre, Henri. *The Production of Space.* Translated by Donald Nicholson-Smith. Oxford: Blackwell, 1991.

Leibes, Yehudah. "The Book of Creation in R. Shelomoh Ibn Gabirol and a Commentary of His Poem 'I Love You'" [Hebrew], *Proceedings of the Second International Congress on the History of Jewish Mysticism* (1987): 73–123.

Leroy, Beatrice. *The Jews of Navarre in the Late Middle Ages.* Translated by Jeffrey Green. Jerusalem: Magnes, 1985.

Levanoni, Amalia. "'Aṣabiyya," *Encyclopaedia of Islam.* 3rd edition. http://dx.doi.org/10.1163/1573-3912_ei3_COM_24241.

Levin, Israel. *Abraham ibn ʿEzra: His Life and Poetry* [Hebrew]. Tel Aviv: Hakibbutz Hameuchad, 1969.

———. *The Embroidered Coat: The Genres of Secular Hebrew Poetry in Spain* [Hebrew]. 3 volumes. Tel Aviv: Tel Aviv University Katz Research Institute for Hebrew Literature and Hakibbutz Hameuchad, 1994.

———. *Mystical Trends in the Poetry of Ibn Gabirol* [Hebrew]. Lod: Habermann Institute for Literary Research, 1986.

———. *Tannim w*ᵉ*-khinnor: Ḥurban galut, naqam u-g'ulah ba-shirah ha-'ivrit ha-l*ᵉ*umit.* Tel Aviv: Hakibbutz Hameuchad, 1998.

Lévi-Provençal, E. (Évariste). "La description de l'Espagne d'Aḥmad al-Razi," *Al-Andalus* 18 (1953): 51–108.

———. *Histoire de l'Espagne musulmane.* 3 volumes. Paris: G. P. Maisonneuve, 1950–1953.

Lewin, Benjamin M. "Geniza Fragments" [Hebrew], *Tarbiẓ* 2 (1931): 383–410.

Lewis, Bernard. "The Cult of Spain and the Turkish Romantics," repr. in Bernard Lewis, *Islam in History: Ideas People, and Events in the Middle East.* New edition. Chicago: Open Court, 1993. 129–133.

———. *History Remembered, Recovered, Invented.* Princeton, NJ: Princeton University Press, 1975.

———. *The Jews of Islam.* Princeton, NJ: Princeton University Press, 1984.

———. "The Pro-Islamic Jews," repr. in *Islam in History: Ideas People, and Events in the Middle East.* New edition. Chicago: Open Court, 993. 137–151.

Lewis, Rose. "Maimonides and the Muslims," *Midstream* (November 1979): 16–22.

———. "Muslim Glamour and the Spanish Jews," *Midstream* (February 1977): 26–37.

Linhard, Tabea Alexa. *Jewish Spain: A Mediterranean Memory.* Stanford, CA: Stanford University Press, 2014.

Lipinski, E. "Obadiah 20," *Vetus Testamentum* 23 (1973): 368–370.

Lobel, Diana. *A Sufi-Jewish Dialogue: Philosophy and Mysticism in Baḥya ibn Paqūda's Duties of the Heart.* Philadelphia: University of Pennsylvania Press, 2007.

Lombard, Maurice. *The Golden Age of Islam.* Translated by Joan Spencer. Amsterdam: North-Holland, 1975.

López Lázaro, Fabio. "The Rise and Global Significance of the First 'West': The Medieval Islamic Maghrib," *Journal of World History* 24 (2013): 259–308.

Majid, Anouar. *Freedom and Orthodoxy: Islam and Difference in the Post-Andalusian Age.* Stanford, CA: Stanford University Press, 2004.

Makkī, Maḥmūd Ali. "Egypt and the Origins of Spanish Arabic Historiography: A Contribution to the Study of the Earliest Sources for the History of Islamic Spain," *The Formation of al-Andalus* [Part 2: Language, Religion, Culture, and the Sciences]. Edited by Maribel Fierro and Julio Samso. Aldershot: Ashgate-Variorum, 1998. 173–233.

Mallette, Karla. *The Kingdom of Sicily, 1100–1250: A Literary History*. Philadelphia: University of Pennsylvania Press, 2005.

Maman, Aharon. *Comparative Semitic Philology in the Middle Ages: From Saʿadiah Gaon to Ibn Barun (10th–12th C.)*. Translated by David Lyons. Leiden: E. J. Brill, 2004.

Mann, Jacob. *Texts and Studies in Jewish History and Literature*. 2 volumes. Cincinnati: Hebrew Union College Press, 1931–1935; repr., introduction by Gerson D. Cohen. New York: Ktav, 1972.

———. "A Tract by an Early Karaite Settler in Jerusalem," *Jewish Quarterly Review* 12 (1922): 257–298.

Manzano-Moreno, Eduardo. "Oriental 'Topoi' in Andalusian Historical Sources," *Arabica* 39 (1992): 42–58.

Marcus, Ivan G. "Beyond the Sephardic Mystique," *Orim* 1 (1985): 35–53.

———. "Medieval Jewish Studies: Toward an Anthropological History of the Jews," in *The State of Jewish Studies*. Edited by Shaye J. D. Cohen and Edward L. Greenstein. Detroit: Wayne State University Press, 1990. 113–127.

Margaliot, Mordechai. *Sefer hilkhot ha-nagid*. Jerusalem: Judah Leib and Mini Epstein Fund, American Academy for Jewish Research, 1962.

———(Mordecai Margulies). "The Differences Between Babylonian and Palestinian Jews" [Hebrew]. Ph.D. diss., Hebrew University, 1938.

Marías Aguilera, Julián. *Understanding Spain*. Translated by Frances M. López-Morillas. Ann Arbor: University of Michigan Press, 1992.

Marín, Manuela. "La actividad intelectual," in *Historia de España VIII. Parte 1. Los reinos de Taifas. Al-Andalus en el siglo XI*. Madrid: Espasa-Calpe, 1994. 502–564.

———. "Dos calas en la visión sobre al-Andalus del orientalismo europeo: A propósito de I. Goldziher y A. R. Nykl," in *Al-Andalus/España: Historiografías en Contraste siglos xvii–xxi* [Estudios Reunidos y Presentados por Manuela Marín]. Madrid: Casa de Velázquez, 2009. 195–212.

———. "Historical Images of al-Andalus and Andalusians," in *Myths, Historical Archetypes and Symbolic Figures in Arabic Literature: Towards a New Hermeneutic Approach*. Edited by Angelika Neuwirth et al. Stuttgart: Franz Steiner, 1999. 409–421.

———. "Legends on Alexander the Great in Moslem Spain," *Graeco-Arabica* 4 (1991): 71–89.

———. "Ṣahāba et Tābiʿūn dans al-Andalus: Histoire et legend," *Studia Islamica* 54 (1981): 5–49.

———. "Scholarship and Criticism: The Letters of Reinhart Dozy to Pascual Gayangos 1841–1852), in *Pascual de Gayangos: A Nineteenth-Century Spanish Arabist*. Edited by Cristina Álvarez Millán and Claudia Heide. Edinburgh: Edinburgh University Press, 2008. 68–85.

Martín, Adrienne L., and Cristina Martínez-Carazo, eds. *Spain's Multicultural Legacies: Studies in Honor of Samuel G. Armistead*. Newark, DE: Juan de la Cuesta, 2008.

Martínez-Gros, Gabriel. "L'Ecriture et la 'Umma': La 'Risāla fī Faḍl al-Andalus' d'Ibn Ḥazm," *Mélanges de la Casa de Velázquez* 21 (1985): 99–113.

———. *Identité andalouse*. Arles: Sindbad, 1997.

———. *L'idéologie omeyyade: La construction de la légitimité du califat de Cordoue (xe–xie siècles)*. Madrid: Casa de Velázquez, 1992.

Marx, Alexander. "The Expulsion of the Jews from Spain," *Jewish Quarterly Review* [o.s.] 20 (1908): 240–271.

Masarwah, Nader, and Abdallah Tarabieh. "Longing for Granada in Medieval Arabic and Hebrew Poetry," *Al-Masāq* 26 (2014): 299–318.

Matthews, John A., and David T. Herbert. *Geography: A Very Short Introduction*. Oxford: Oxford University Press, 2008.

Melammed, Ezra Zion. *Bible Commentators* [Hebrew]. 2 volumes. Jerusalem: Magnes, 1978.

Melville, Charles, and Ahmad Ubaydli. *Christians and Moors in Spain* [Volume 3: Arabic Sources]. Warminster: Aris & Phillips, 1992.

Menocal, María Rosa. *The Arabic Role in Medieval Literary History: A Forgotten Heritage*, repr., Philadelphia: University of Pennsylvania Press, 2004.

———. "'The Finest Flowering': Poetry, History, and Medieval Spain in the Twenty-First Century," in *A Sea of Languages. Rethinking the Arabic Role in Medieval Literary History*. Edited by Suzanne Conklin Akbari and Karla Mallette. Toronto: University of Toronto Press, 2013. 342–353.

———. *Ornament of the World: How Muslims, Christians and Jews Created a Culture of Tolerance in Medieval Spain*. Boston: Little, Brown, 2002.

———. "Visions of al-Andalus," in *The Literature of al-Andalus* [*The Cambridge History of Arabic Literature*]. Edited by María Rosa Menocal, Raymond P. Scheindlin, and Michael Sells. Cambridge: Cambridge University Press, 2002. 1–24.

———, Jerrilynn D. Dodds, and Abigail Krasner Balbale. *The Arts of Intimacy: Christians, Jews and Muslims in the Making of Castilian Culture*. New Haven, CT: Yale University Press, 2009.

du Mensil, Emmanuelle Tixier. *Géographes d'al-Andalus: De l'inventaire d'un territoire à la construction d'une mémoire*. Paris: Publications de la Sorbonne, 2014.

Meri, Josef W. *The Cult of Saints Among Muslims and Jews in Medieval Syria*. Oxford: Oxford University Press, 2002.

Michalowski, Piotr. "Mental Maps and Ideology: Reflections on Subartu," in *Origins of Cities in Dry-Farming Syria and Mesopotamia in the Third Millennium B.C.* Edited by Harvey Weiss. Guilford, CT: Four Quarters, 1986. 129–156.

Miles, George Carpenter. *The Coinage of the Umayyads of Spain*. 2 volumes. New York: American Numismatic Society, 1950.

Miquel, André. "Al-Iṣṭakhrī," *Encyclopaedia of Islam*. 2nd edition. 4:222–23.

Monroe, James T. "Hispano-Arabic Poetry During the Caliphate of Cordoba," in *Arabic Poetry: Theory and Development*. Edited by G. E. von Grunebaum. Wiesbaden: Otto Harrassowitz, 1973. 125–154.

———. *Hispano-Arabic Poetry: A Student Anthology*, repr., Piscataway, NJ: Gorgias, 2004.

———. "The Hispano-Arabic World," in *Américo Castro and the Meaning of Spanish Civilization*. Edited by José Rubia Barciahas. Berkeley: University of California Press, 1976. 69–90.

———. "The Historical Arjūza of ibn 'Abd Rabbihi: A Tenth-Century Hispano-Arabic Epic Poem," *Journal of the American Oriental Society* 91 (1971): 67–95.

———. *Islam and the Arabs in Spanish Scholarship* (Sixteenth Century to the Present). Leiden: E. J. Brill, 1970.

———. *The Shu'ūbiyya in al-Andalus: The Risāla of Ibn Garcia and Five Refutations*. Berkeley: University of California Press, 1970.

Morris, Cyril Brian. *Son of Andalusia: The Lyrical Landscapes of Federico García Lorca*. Nashville, TN: Vanderbilt University Press, 1997.

al-Munajjad, Ṣalāḥ al-Dīn. *Faḍā'il al-andalus wa-ahlihā*. Beirut: Dār al-jadīd, 1968.

Nasr, Seyyed Hossein, and Oliver Leaman, eds. *The History of Islamic Philosophy*. 2 volumes. London: Routledge, 1996. 1:275–364.

Nemoy, Leon. *Karaite Anthology*. New Haven, CT: Yale University Press, 1952.
———. "The Pseudo-Qumisian Sermon to the Karaites," *Proceedings of the American Academy for Jewish Research* 43 (1976): 49–105.
Netton, Ian Richard. *Al-Fārābī and His School*. London: Routledge, 1992.
———. *Seek Knowledge: Thought and Travel in the House of Islam*. Surrey: Curzon, 1966.
Neubauer, Adolf D., ed. *Mediaeval Jewish Chronicles*. Oxford: Clarendon, 1887.
———. "Where Are the Ten Tribes? Eldad the Danite," *Jewish Quarterly Review* 1 (1889): 104–108.
Nicholson, Reynold A. *Translations of Eastern Poetry and Prose*, repr., London: Curzon, 1987.
Noorani, Yaseen. "The Lost Garden of al-Andalus: Islamic Spain and the Poetic Inversion of Colonialism," *International Journal of Middle Eastern Studies* 31 (1999): 237–254.
Nora, Pierre. "Between Memory and History: *Les Lieux de Mémoire*," *Representations* 26 (1989): 7–24.
Novikoff, Alex. "Between Tolerance and Intolerance in Medieval Spain: An Historiographic Enigma," *Medieval Encounters* 11 (2005): 7–36.
Nykl, A. R. *Hispano-Arabic Poetry and Its Relations with the Old Provençal Troubadours*. Baltimore: J. H. Furst, 1946.
O'Callaghan, Joseph. *A History of Medieval Spain*. Ithaca, NY: Cornell University Press, 1975.
Oettinger, Ayelet. "The Characteristics of Satire on Jewish Communities in Yehudah al-Ḥarizi's 'Book of Taḥkᵉmoni'" [Hebrew], in *Maḥbarot li-Yehudit: Studies Presented to Professor Judith Dishon* [Hebrew]. Edited by Ephraim Hazan and Shmuel Refael. Ramat-Gan: Bar-Ilan University Press, 2012. 59–87.
Olagüe, Ignacio. *Les Arabes n'ont jamais envahi l'Espagne*. Paris: Flammarion, 1969.
Oppenheimer, Aharon. "From Qurtava to Aspamya" [Hebrew], in *Exile and Diaspora* [Studies in the History of the Jewish People Presented to Professor Haim Beinart on the Occasion of his Seventieth Birthday]. Edited by Aharon Mirsky, Avraham Grossman, and Yosef Kaplan. Jerusalem: Ben-Zvi Institute, 1988. 57–63.
Ormsby, Eric. "Ibn Ḥazm," in *The Literature of al-Andalus* [*The Cambridge History of Arabic Literature*]. Edited by María Rosa Menocal, Raymond P. Scheindlin, and Michael Sells. Cambridge: Cambridge University Press, 2000. 237–251.
Pagis, Dan. *Secular Poetry and Poetic Theory: Moses Ibn Ezra and His Contemporaries* [Hebrew]. Jerusalem: Bialik Institute, 1970.
Pearce, Sarah J. *The Andalusi Literary and Intellectual Tradition: The Role of Arabic in Judah ibn Tibbon's Ethical Will*. Bloomington: Indiana University Press, 2017.
———. "'His (Jewish) Nation . . . and His Muslim King': Poetics and Nationalism in Medieval and Modern Hebrew Literature," in *His Pen and Ink Are a Powerful Mirror*. Edited by Adam Bursi, S. J. Pearce, and Hamza Zafer. Leiden: Brill, 2020. 140–162.
Pellat, Charles. "Ibn Djubayr." *Encyclopaedia of Islam*. 2nd edition. Leiden: Brill, 1971. 3:755.
———. "Ibn Ḥazm, bibliographe et apologiste de l'Espagne musulmane," *Al-Andalus* 19 (1954): 3–102.
———. "The Origin and Development of Historiography in Muslim Spain," in *Historians of the Middle East*. Edited by Bernard Lewis and P. M. Holt. London: Oxford University Press, 1962. 118–125.
———. "Variations sur le thème de l'adab," *Correspondence d'Orient: Etudes* 5–6 (1964): 19–37.
Penelas, Mayte. "Some Remarks on Conversion to Islam in al-Andalus," *Al-Qanṭara* 23 (2002): 193–200.

Pérès, Henri. *Esplendor de al-Andalus: La poesía andaluza en árabe clásico en el siglo XI: Sus aspectos generales, sus principales temas y su valor documental*. Translated by Mercedes García-Arenal. Madrid: Hiperión, 1990.

———. *La poésie andalouse en arabe classique au onzième siècle: Ses aspects généraux, ses principaux thèmes et sa valeur documentaire*. 2nd edition. Paris: Adrien-Maisonneuve, 1953.

Peters, Edward, trans. "Charter of Expulsion," in *Medieval Iberia: Readings from Christian Muslims, and Jewish Sources*. 2nd edition. Edited by Olivia Remie Constable. Philadelphia: University of Pennsylvania Press, 2012. 508–513.

Peters, F. E. *Jerusalem: The Holy City in the Eyes of Chroniclers, Visitors, Pilgrims, and Prophets from the Days of Abraham to the Beginnings of Modern Times*. Princeton, NJ: Princeton University Press, 1985.

Pinto, Karen C. *Medieval Islamic Maps: An Exploration*. Chicago: University of Chicago Press, 2004.

Polliak, Meira. *The Karaite Tradition of Arabic Bible Translation*. Leiden: Brill, 1997.

Pons, Mariona Vernet. "The Origin of the Name Sepharad: A New Interpretation," *Journal of Semitic Studies* 59 (2014): 297–313.

Poznański, Samuel. "The Arabic Commentary of Abu Zakariya Yaḥya (Judah ben Samuel) ibn Balʿam on the Twelve Minor Prophets," *Jewish Quarterly Review* 15 (1924): 1–53.

Prado-Vilar, Francisco. "Circular Visions of Fertility and Punishment: Caliphal Ivory Caskets from al-Andalus," *Muqarnas* 17 (1997): 19–41.

Puerta Vilchez, José Miguel. "Abū Muḥammad 'Alī Ibn Ḥazm: A Biographical Sketch," in *Ibn Ḥazm of Cordoba: The Life and Works of a Controversial Thinker*. Edited by Camilla Adang, Maribel Fierro, and Sabine Schmidtke. Leiden: 2013. 3–24.

Rabinowitz, Isaac. "Sefarad," *Enṣiqlopedya miqra'it*. 9 volumes. Jerusalem: Bialik Institute, 1950–1988. 5:1100–1103.

Ramírez del Río, José. "Acerca del origen del topónimo al-Andalus," *eHumanista/IVITRA* 12 (2017): 124–161.

———. "Acerca del origen del topónimo al-Andalus (II): Hesperia, al-Andalus, Sefarad y Madīnat al-Zahrā'," *eHumanista/IVITRA* 14 (2018): 707–731.

———. "Al-Ḏajīra al-saniyya: Una fuente relevante para el siglo XII en la Península Ibérica," *Al-Qanṭara* 33 (2012): 7–44.

Rand, Michael. *The Evolution of al-Ḥarizi's Taḥkemoni*. Leiden: Brill, 2018.

Ray, Jonathan. *After Expulsion: 1492 and the Making of Sephardic Jewry*. New York: New York University Press, 2013.

———. "Between Tolerance and Persecution: Reassessing our Approach to Medieval *Convivencia*," *Jewish Social Studies* 11 (2005): 1–18.

———. "Images of the Jewish Community in Medieval Iberia," *Journal of Medieval Iberian Studies* 1 (2009): 195–211.

———. "The Jews of al-Andalus: Factionalism in the Golden Age," in *Jews and Muslims in the Islamic World*. Edited by Bernard Dov Cooperman and Zvi Zohar. Bethesda: University Press of Maryland, 2013. 253–263.

Reedon, Michael. *Ideology: A Very Short Introduction*. Oxford: Oxford University Press, 2003.

Rejwan, Nissim. *Israel's Place in the Middle East: A Pluralist Perspective*. Gainesville: University Press of Florida, 1998.

Robinson, Cynthia. "*Ubi Sunt*: Memory and Nostalgia in Taifa Courtly Culture," *Muqarnas* 15 (1998): 20–31.

Rogozen-Soltar, Mikael. "Al-Andalus in Andalusia: Negotiating Moorish History and Regional Identity in Southern Spain," *Anthropological Quarterly* 80 (2007): 863–886.

Romm, James. "Continents, Climates, and Cultures: Greek Theories of Global Structure," in *Geography and Ethnography: Perceptions of the World in Pre-Modern Societies*. Edited by Kurt A. Raaflaub and Richard J. A. Talbert. Chichester: Wiley-Blackwell, 2010. 215–235.

Rosen, Tova. "'As in a Poem by Shmuel Ha-Nagid': Between Shmuel Ha-Nagid and Yehuda Amichai" [Hebrew], *Jerusalem Studies in Hebrew Literature* 15 (1995): 83–106.

Rosenthal, David. "Rav Paltoi Gaon and His Place in the Halakhic Tradition" [Hebrew], *Annual of the Institute for the Research in Jewish Law* 11–12 (1984–1986): 589–683.

Rosenthal, Franz. *A History of Muslim Historiography*. Leiden: E. J. Brill, 1968.

———. *Knowledge Triumphant*. Leiden: E. J. Brill, 1970.

Roth, Norman. "A Note on the Meaning of Sefarad," *Iberia Judaica* 10 (2018): 245–251.

Roughi, Ramzi. "The Andalusi Origin of the Berbers," *Journal of Medieval Iberian Studies* 2 (2010): 93–108.

Rozen, Minna. "Pedigree Remembered, Reconstructed, Invented": Benjamin Disraeli Between East and West," in *The Jewish Discovery of Islam: Studies in Honor of Bernard Lewis*. Edited by Martin Kramer. Tel Aviv: Tel Aviv University Press, 1999. 49–75.

Ruderman, David. B. "The Impact of Early Modern Jewish Thought on the Eighteenth Century: A Challenge to the Notion of the Sephardi Mystic," in *Sepharad in Ashkenaz: Medieval Knowledge and Eighteenth-Century Enlightened Discourse*. Edited by Resianne Fontaine, Andrea Schatz, and Irene Zwiep. Amsterdam: Royal Netherlands Academy of Arts and Sciences, 2007. 11–22.

Ruggles, D. Fairchild. "Arabic Poetry and Architectural Memory in al-Andalus," *Ars Orientalis* 23 (1993): 171–178.

———. *Gardens, Landscape, and Vision in the Palaces of Islamic Spain*. University Park: Pennsylvania State University Press, 2000.

Rustow, Marina. *Heresy and the Politics of the Community: The Jews of the Fatimid Caliphate*. Ithaca, NY: Cornell University Press, 2008.

Sabra, Abdelhamid I. "The Andalusian Revolt Against Ptolemaic Astronomy," in *Transformation and Tradition in the Sciences: Essays in Honor of I. Bernard Cohen*. Edited by Everett Irwin Mendelsohn. Cambridge: Cambridge University Press, 1984. 233–253.

Sachar, Howard M. *Farewell España: The World of the Sephardim Remembered*. New York: Vintage, 1995.

Sadan, Joseph. "Identity and Inimitability: Contexts of Inter-Religious Polemics and Solidarity in Light of Two Passages by Moshe Ibn 'Ezra and Ya'aqov ben El'azar," *Israel Oriental Studies* 14 (1994): 325–347.

———. "R. Judah al-Ḥarizi as a Cultural Junction: An Arabic Biography of a Jewish Writer as Perceived by an Orientalist" [Hebrew], *Pe'amim* 68 (1996): 16–67.

Sáenz-Badillos, Angel. "Los discípulos de Menahem sobre métrica hebrea," *Sefarad* 46 (1986): 421–431.

———. "Menahem and Dunaš in Search of the Foundations of the Hebrew Language," *Studia Orientalia* 95 (2003): 177–190.

———. "Sobre el autor de las *Tešubot 'al Se'adyah*," in *Exile and Diaspora: Studies in the History of the Jewish People Presented to Professor Haim Beinart*. Edited by Aaron Mirsky, Avraham Grossman, and Yosef Kaplan. Jerusalem: Ben-Zvi Institute, and Madrid: Consejo Superior de Investigaciones Científicas, 1991. 26–43.

Safran, Bezalel. "Baḥya ibn Paquda's Attitude Toward the Courtier Class," in *Studies in Medieval Jewish History and Literature*. Edited by Isadore Twersky. Cambridge, MA: Harvard University Press, 1979. 154–196.

Safran, Janina M. *Defining Boundaries in al-Andalus: Muslim, Christians and Jews in Islamic Iberia*. Ithaca, NY: Cornell University Press, 2013.

———. *The Second Umayyad Caliphate: The Articulation of Legitimacy in al-Andalus*. Cambridge, MA: Harvard University Press, 2000.

Said, Edward. *Orientalism*. New York: Vintage, 2004.

Saleh, Walid A. "Paradise in an Islamic *'Ajā'ib* Work: *The Delight of Onlookers and the Signs for Investigators* of Marʿī b. Yūsuf al-Karmī (d. 1003/1624)," in *Roads to Paradise: Eschatology and Concepts of the Hereafter in Islam*. 2 volumes. Edited by Sebastian Gunther and Todd Lawson. Leiden: Brill, 2017. 2:931–952.

Sardar, Ziauddin, and Robin Yassin-Kassab, eds. *Critical Muslim* 06 (2013).

Schapkow, Carsten. *Role Model and Countermodel: The Golden Age of Iberian Jewry and German Jewish Culture During the Era of Emancipation*. Lanham, MD: Lexington, 2016.

Scheiber, Alexander, and Zvi Malachi. "Letter from Sicily to Ḥasdai ibn Shaprut," *Proceedings of the American Academy for Jewish Research* 41–42 (1973–1974): 207–218.

Scheindlin, Raymond P. "'The Battle of Alfuente,' by Samuel the Nagid," in *History as Prelude: Muslims and Jews in the Medieval Mediterranean*. Edited by Joseph V. Montville. Lanham, MD: Lexington, 2011. 61–69.

———. *Form and Structure in the Poetry of al-Muʿtamid ibn ʿAbbād*. Leiden: E. J. Brill, 1974.

———. *The Gazelle: Medieval Hebrew Poems on God, Israel, and the Soul*. Philadelphia: Jewish Publication Society, 1991.

———. "Ibn Gabirol's Religious Poetry and Arabic *Zuhd* Poetry," *Edebiyat* [n.s.] 4 (1993): 229–242.

———. "The Jews in Muslim Spain," in *The Legacy of Muslim Spain*. Edited by Salma Khadra Jayyusi. Leiden: E. J. Brill, 1992. 188–200.

———. "Merchants and Intellectuals, Rabbis and Poets: Judeo-Arabic Culture in the Golden Age of Islam," in *Cultures of the Jews*. Edited by David Biale. New York: Schocken, 2002. 313–386.

———. "Rabbi Moshe Ibn Ezra on the Legitimacy of Poetry," *Medievalia et Humanistica* 7 (1976): 101–115.

———. *The Song of the Distant Dove: Judah Halevi's Pilgrimage*. Oxford: Oxford University Press, 2008.

———. *Wine, Women, and Death: Medieval Hebrew Poems on the Good Life*. Philadelphia: Jewish Publication Society, 1986.

Schippers, Arie. "Literacy, Munificence and Legitimation of Power During the Reign of the Party Kings in Muslim Spain," in *Tradition, and Modernity in Arabic Language and Literature*. Edited by J. R. Smart. Richmond: Curzon, 1996. 75–86.

———. "Two Andalusian Poets on Exile: Reflections on the Poetry of Ibn 'Ammār (1031–1086) and Moses Ibn 'Ezra (1055–1138)," in *The Challenge of the Middle East: Middle Eastern Studies at the University of Amsterdam*. Edited by Ibrahim A. El-Sheikh, C. Aart van de Koppel, and Rudolph Peters. Amsterdam: University of Amsterdam, 1982. 113–121.

Schirmann, Jefim. *Hebrew Poetry in Spain and Provence* [Hebrew]. 4 volumes, repr., Jerusalem: Bialik Institute, 2006.

———. *The History of Hebrew Poetry in Christian Spain and South France* [Hebrew]. Edited by Ezra Fleischer. Jerusalem: Magnes, 1997.

———. *The History of Hebrew Poetry in Muslim Spain* [Hebrew]. Edited by Ezra Fleischer. Jerusalem: Magnes, 1995.

———. *New Hebrew Poems from the Genizah* [Hebrew]. Jerusalem: Israel Academy of Sciences and Humanities, 1965.

———. "Samuel Hanagid: The Man, The Soldier, the Politician," *Jewish Social Studies* 13 (1951): 99–126.

———. "The Wars of Samuel ha-Nagid" [Hebrew], *Zion* 1 (1936): 261–283, 359–376.

Schlanger, Jacques. *La Philosophie de Salomon Ibn Gabirol: Étude d'un néoplatonisme.* Leiden: E. J. Brill, 1968.

Schonfield, Ernest. "Heine and Convivencia: Coexistence in Muslim Spain," *Oxford German Studies* 47 (2018): 35–50.

Schorsch, Ismar. "The Myth of Sephardic Supremacy," *Leo Baeck Institute Yearbook* 34 (1989): 47–66.

Schroeter, Daniel J. "The Shifting Boundaries of Moroccan Jewish Identities," *Jewish Social Studies* 15 (2008): 145–164.

Selheim, R. "Faḍīla," *Encyclopaedia of Islam.* 2nd edition. 2:728–29.

Septimus, Bernard. *Hispano-Jewish Culture in Transition: The Career and Controversies of Ramah.* Cambridge, MA: Harvard University Press, 1992.

Shabbas, Audrey. *Cultural Symbiosis in al-Andalus: A Metaphor for Peace.* Edited by Sanaa Osserian. Beirut: UNESCO Regional Office for Education in the Arab State, 2004.

———. *A Medieval Banquet in the Alhambra Palace.* Berkeley: Arab World and Islamic Resources and School Services, 1994.

Shamsie, Munezza, ed. "Al-Andalus," *Journal of Postcolonial Writing* 52 (2016): 127–231.

Shannon, Jonathan H. *Performing al-Andalus: Music and Nostalgia Across the Mediterranean.* Bloomington: Indiana University Press, 2015.

———. "There and Back Again: Rhetorics of al-Andalus in Modern Syrian Popular Culture," *International Journal of Middle East Studies* 48 (2016): 5–24.

Shatzmiller, Maya. *The Berbers and the Islamic State: The Marinid Experience in Pre-Protectorate Morocco.* Princeton, NJ: Markus Wiener, 2000.

Silver, Daniel Jeremy. *Maimonidean Criticism and the Maimonidean Controversy, 1180–1240.* Leiden: E. J. Brill, 1965.

Silverstein, Adam J. "The Medieval Islamic Worldview: Arabic Geography in Its Historical Context," in *Geography and Ethnography: Perceptions of the World in Pre-Modern Societies.* Edited by Kurt A. Raaflaub and Richard J. A. Talbert. Chichester: Wiley-Blackwell, 2010. 273–250.

Simon, Uriel. *Four Approaches to the Book of Psalms: From Saadia Gaon to Abraham ibn Ezra.* Translated by Lenn J. Schramm. Albany: State University of New York Press, 1991.

Simonsohn, Shlomo. "Sicily: A Millennium of *Convivenzia* (or Almost)," in *The Jews of Europe in the Middle Ages (Tenth to Fifteenth Centuries).* Edited by Christoph Cluse. Turnhout: Brepols, 2004. 105–121.

Sivan, Emmanuel. "The Beginnings of the Faḍā'il al-Quds Literature," *Israel Oriental Studies* 1 (1971): 263–271.

———. "Le caractère sacré de Jérusalem dans l'Islam aux 12–13th siècles," *Studia Islamica* 27 (1967): 149–182.

Snir, Reuven "'Al-Andalus Rising from Damascus': Al-Andalus in Modern Arabic Poetry," in *Charting Memory: Recalling Medieval Spain.* Edited by Stacey N. Beckwith. New York: Garland, 2000. 63–93.

Soifer, Maya. "Beyond Convivencia: Critical Reflections on the Historiography of Interfaith Relations in Christian Spain," *Journal of Medieval Iberian Studies* 1 (2009): 19–35.

Solà-Solé, Josep M. "Semitic Elements in Ancient Hispania," *Catholic Biblical Quarterly* 29 (1967): 487–494.

Soravia, Bruna. "Al-Andalus au Miroir du Multiculturalisme: Le Mythe de la *Convivencia* dans Quelques Essais Nord-Américains Récents," in *Al-Andalus/España: Historiografías en Contraste Siglos XVII–XXXI* [Estudios Reunidos Presentados por Manuela Marín]. Madrid: Casa de Velázquez, 2009. 351–365.

———. "A Portrait of the 'Ālim as a Young Man: The Formative Years of Ibn Ḥazm, 404/1013–420/1029," in *Ibn Ḥazm of Cordoba: The Life and Works of a Controversial Thinker.* Edited by Camilla Adang, Maribel Fierro, and Sabine Schmidtke. Leiden: Brill, 2013. 27–37.

Spiegel, Shalom. "On the Polemic of Pirqoy ben Baboy: From the New Series of the Geniza in Cambridge" [Hebrew], in *Harry Austryn Wolfson Jubilee Volume.* 3 volumes. Jerusalem: American Academy for Jewish Research, 1965. 243–275 [Hebrew section].

Stearns, Justin. "Representing and Remembering al-Andalus: Some Historical Considerations Regarding the End of Time and the Making of Nostalgia," *Medieval Encounters* 15 (2009): 355–374.

Steiner, Richard C. *A Biblical Translation in the Making: The Evolution and Impact of Saadia Gaon's Tafsir.* Cambridge, MA: Harvard University Press, 2010.

Steinschneider, Moritz. *Jewish Literature from the Eighth to the Eighteenth Century with an Introduction on Talmud and Midrash.* New York: Hermon, 1965 (repr. of a translation by William Spottiswoode, first published in London, 1857; translated, with alterations, from the author's "Jüdische Literatur" in Ersch & Gruber's *Allgemeine Encyklopädie der Wissenschaften und Künste.* Leipzig, 1850. 2nd section, v. 27, 357–471).

Stern, Samuel Miklos. *Hispano-Arabic Strophic Poetry: Studies Selected and Edited by L. P. Harvey.* Oxford: Oxford University Press, 1974.

Stetkevych, Jaroslav. "Spaces of Delight: A Symbolic Topoanalysis of the Classical Arabic Nasīb," *Literature East and West* 25 [*Critical Pilgrimages: Studies in the Arabic Literary Tradition*, edited by Fedwa Malti-Douglas] (1989): 5–28.

Stetkevych, Suzanne Pinckney. *The Mute Immortals Speak: Pre-Islamic Poetry and the Poetics of Ritual.* Ithaca, NY: Cornell University Press, 1993.

———. "The Poetics of Ceremony and the Competition for Legitimacy: Al-Muhannad al-Baghdādī, Muḥammad ibn Shukhayṣ, Ibn Darrāj al-Qasṭallī, and the Andalusian Ode," in Suzanne Pinckney Stetkevych, *The Poetics of Islamic Legitimacy: Myth, Gender and Ceremony in the Classical Arabic Ode.* Bloomington: Indiana University Press, 2002. 241–282.

Stillman, Norman A. "Al-Andalus," *Encyclopedia of Jews in the Islamic World.* 5 volumes. Edited by Norman A. Stillman et al. Leiden: Brill, 2010. 1:100–115.

———. "Aspects of Jewish Life in Islamic Spain," in *Aspects of Jewish Culture in the Middle Ages.* Edited by Paul E. Szarmach. Albany: State University of New York Press, 1979. 51–84.

———. "The Judeo-Islamic Historical Encounter: Visions and Revisions," in *Israel and Ishmael: Studies in Muslim-Jewish Relations.* Edited by Tudor Parfitt. New York: St. Martin's, 2000. 1–12.

Stoetzer, Willem. "Floral Poetry in Muslim Spain," in *The Authentic Garden: A Symposium on Gardens.* Edited by L. Tjon Sie Far and E. A. de Jong. Leiden: Clusius Foundation, 1991. 177–186.

Stroumsa, Sarah. "Between Acculturation and Conversion in Islamic Spain: The Case of the Banū Ḥasday," *Mediterranea* 1 (2016): 9–36.

———. *Maimonides in His World: Portrait of a Mediterranean Thinker.* Princeton, NJ: Princeton University Press, 2009.

———. *Saadia Gaon: A Jewish Thinker in a Mediterranean Society* [Hebrew]. Tel Aviv: Tel Aviv University Press, 2001.

———. "Thinkers of 'This Peninsula': Toward an Integrative Approach to the Study of Philosophy in al-Andalus," in *Beyond Religious Border: Interaction and Intellectual Exchange in the Medieval Islamic World.* Edited by David M. Freidenreich and Miriam Goldstein. Philadelphia: University of Pennsylvania Press, 2012. 44–53.

———, and Sara Sviri. "The Beginnings of Mystical Philosophy in al-Andalus: Ibn Masarra and His *Epistle on Contemplation,*" *Jerusalem Studies in Arabic and Islam* 36 (2009): 201–253.

Sumner, Graham Vincent. "The Chronology of the Early Governors of al-Andalus to the Accession of 'Abd al-Raḥmān I," *Mediaeval Studies* 48 (1986): 422–469.

Szpiech, Ryan. "The Convivencia Wars: Decoding History's Polemic with Philology," in *A Sea of Languages: Rethinking the Arabic Role in Medieval Literary History.* Edited by Suzanne Conklin Akbari and Karla Mallette. Toronto: Toronto University Press, 2013. 135–161.

Ṭāhā, 'Abd al-Wāḥid Dhannūn. *The Muslim Conquest and Settlement of North Africa and Spain.* London: Routledge, 1989.

Taḥṭaḥ, Fāṭimah. *Al-ghurba wa-l-ḥanīn fī l-shi'r al-andalusī.* Rabat: al-Mamlaka al-Maghribiyya, Jāmi'at Muḥammad al-Khāmis, Kullīyat al-ādāb wa-l-'ulūm al-insāniyya, 1993.

Tanenbaum, Adena. *The Contemplative Soul: Hebrew Poetry and Philosophical Theory in Medieval Spain.* Leiden: E. J. Brill, 2002.

Tarbieh, Abdallah Ibrahim. *Nostalgia and Elegy for Cities in the Andalusian Arabic and Hebrew Poetry* [Hebrew]. Bāqah al-Gharbiyya: Center for the Study of Comparative Literature, Al-Qasemi College of Education, 2015.

Ta-Shma, Israel M. *Talmudic Commentary in Europe and North Africa: Literary History, Part One: 1000–1200* [Hebrew]. Jerusalem: Magnes, 1999.

Terés, Elias. "Linajes árabes de al-Andalus según la 'Yamhara' de Ibn Ḥazm," *Al-Andalus* 22 (1957): 55–111, 337–376.

———. "Textos poéticos árabes sobre Valencia," *Al-Andalus* 30 (1965): 291–307.

Tibbetts, Gerald R. "The Balkhi School," in *The History of Cartography* [Volume 2, Book 1]. Edited by J. B. Hartley and David Woodward. Chicago: University of Chicago Press, 1992. 108–129.

Tirosh-Rothschild, Hava. "Response [to Ivan Marcus]," in *The State of Jewish Studies.* Edited by Shaye J. D. Cohen and Edward L. Greenstein. Detroit: Wayne State University Press, 1990. 128–142.

Tobi, Yosef. "Sa'adia Gaon, Poet-*Paytan*: The Connecting Link Between the Ancient *Piyyut* and Hebrew Arabicised Poetry in Spain," in *Israel and Ishmael: Studies in Muslim-Jewish Relations.* Edited by Tudor Parfitt. New York: St. Martin's, 2000. 59–85.

Todorov, Tzvetan. *The Fantastic: A Structural Approach to a Literary Genre.* Translated by Richard Howard. Ithaca, NY: Cornell University Press, 1975.

Torres Balbás, L. "Al-Andalus," *Encyclopaedia of Islam.* 2nd edition. Leiden: E. J. Brill, 1960. 1:486–503.

Touati, Houari *Islam and Travel in the Middle Ages.* Translated by Lydia G. Cochrane. Chicago: University of Chicago Press, 2010.

Trilling, Renée R. *The Aesthetics of Nostalgia: Historical Representation in Old English Verse.* Toronto: University of Toronto Press, 2009.

Twersky, Isadore. *Introduction to the Code of Maimonides* (*Mishneh Torah*). New Haven, CT: Yale University Press, 1980.

Turki, Abdel Magid. "La vénération pour Malik et la physionomie du malikisme andalou," *Studia Islamica* 33 (1971): 41–66.

Urvoy, Dominique. "Sur l'evolution de la notion de gihād dans l'Espagne musulman," *Mélanges de la Casa de Velázquez* 9 (1973): 335–371.

———. "*The 'Ulamā'* of al-Andalus," in *The Legacy of Muslim Spain.* Edited by Salma Khadra Jayyusi. Leiden: E. J. Brill, 1992. 849–877.

Vallejo Triano, Antonio. "Madīnat al-Zahrā': Transformation of a Caliphal City," in *Revisiting al-Andalus: Perspectives on the Material Culture of Islamic Iberia and Beyond.* Edited by Glaire D. Anderson and Mariam Rosser-Owen. Leiden: Brill, 2007. 3–26.

———. "Madinat al-Zahra': The Triumph of the Islamic State," in *Al-Andalus: The Art of Islamic Spain.* Edited by Jerrilynn D. Dodds. New York: Metropolitan Museum of Art, 1992. 26–39.

Vallvé Bermejo, Joaquín. "Mater Spania (siglos VIII–XIII)," in *Homenaje académico a D. Emilio García Gómez.* Madrid: La Academia, 1993. 329–341.

———. "El Nombre de al-Andalus," *Al-Qanṭara* 4 (1983): 301–355.

Van Gelder, Geert. "Arabic Debates of Earnest and Jest," in *Dispute Poems and Dialogues in the Ancient and Mediaeval Near East: Forms and Types of Literary Debate in Semitic and Related Literatures.* Edited by G. J. Reinink and H. L. J. Vanstiphout. Leuven: Peeters, 1991. 199–211.

Vesser, H. Aram, ed. *The New Historicism.* New York: Routledge, 1989.

Viguera Molíns, María Jesús. "The Muslim Settlement of Spania/al-Andalus," in *The Formation of al-Andalus.* Edited by Manuela Marín. Aldershot: Ashgate-Variorum, 1998. 13–38.

———. "Al-Andalus como interferencia," in *Comunidades islámicas en Europa.* Edited by Montserrat Abumalham. Madrid: Editorial Trotta, 1995. 61–70.

Vycichl, Werner. "Al-Andalus (sobre la historia de un nombre)," *Al-Andalus* 17 (1952): 449–450.

Wachs, David A. *Double Diaspora in Sephardic Literature: Jewish Cultural Production Before and After 1492.* Bloomington: Indiana University Press, 2015.

Wasserstein, David. "Byzantium and al-Andalus," *Mediterranean Historical Review* 2 (1987): 76–101.

———. *The Caliphate in the West: An Islamic Political Institution in the Iberian Peninsula.* Oxford: Clarendon, 1993.

———. "Does Benjamin Mention Portugal?," *Journal of Semitic Studies* 24 (1979): 193–200.

———. "A Family Story: Ambiguities of Identity in Medieval Islam," in *Islamic Cultures, Islamic Contexts: Essays in Honor of Professor Patricia Crone.* Edited by Behnam Sadeghi et al. Leiden: Brill, 2015. 498–532.

———. "Ibn Ḥazm and al-Andalus," in *Ibn Ḥazm of Cordoba: The Life and Work of a Controversial Thinker.* Edited by Camila Adang, M. Isabel Fierro, and Sabine Schmidtke. Leiden: Brill, 2013. 69–86.

———. "Ibn Jaw, Jacob," *Encyclopedia of Jews in the Islamic World.* 5 volumes. Edited by Norman A. Stillman et al. Leiden: Brill, 2010. 2:504.

———. "Jewish Elites in al-Andalus," in *The Jews of Medieval Islam: Community, Society, and Identity.* Edited by Daniel Frank. Leiden: E. J. Brill, 1995. 101–110.

———. "The Khazars and the World of Islam," in *The World of the Khazars: New Perspectives*. Edited by Peter B. Golden, Haggai Ben-Shammai, and Andrá Róna-Tas. Leiden: Brill, 2007. 373–386.

———. "The Library of al-Ḥakam II al-Mustanṣir and the Culture of Islamic Spain," *Manuscripts of the Middle East* 5 (1990–1991): 99–105.

———. "The Muslims and the Golden Age of the Jews in in al-Andalus," *Israel Oriental Studies* 17 (1997): 179–196.

———. *The Rise and Fall of the Party-Kings: Politics and Society in Islamic Spain*, 1002–1086. Princeton, NJ: Princeton University Press, 1985.

———. "Where Have All the Converts Gone? Difficulties in the Study of Conversion to Islam in al-Andalus," *Al-Qanṭara* 33 (2012): 325–342.

Wasserstrom, Steven M. "Jewish-Muslim Relations in the Context of Andalusian Emigration," in *Christians, Muslims, and Jews in Medieval and Early Modern Spain*. Edited by Mark D. Meyerson and Edward D. English. Notre Dame: Notre Dame University Press, 2000. 69–87.

Weber, Elka. "Construction of Identity in Twelfth-Century Andalusi: The Case of Travel Writing," *Journal of North African Studies* 5 (2000): 1–8.

Weber, Max. *Economy and Society: An Outline of Interpretive Sociology*. Edited by Guenther Roth and Claus Wittich. Berkeley: University of California Press, 1978.

Wexler, Paul. *The Non-Jewish Origins of the Sephardic Jews*. Albany: State University of New York Press, 1996.

Wolf, Kenneth Baxter. *Christian Martyrs in Muslim Spain*. Cambridge: Cambridge University Press, 1988.

———. *Conquerors and Chroniclers of Early Medieval Spain*. Liverpool: Liverpool University Press, 1990.

———. "La conquista islámica: Negacionar negacionismo," *Revista de Libros* (June 2014), http://www.revistadelibros.com/articulos/la-conquista-islamica.

———. "Convivencia in Medieval Spain: Brief History of an Idea," *Religion Compass* 3 (2009): 72–85.

Xavier, François. *Mahmoud Darwich et la nouvelle Andalousie*. Paris: I. D. Livre, 2002.

Yahalom, Joseph. "The Immigration of Rabbi Judah Halevi to Eretz Israel in Vision and Riddle" [Hebrew], *Shalem* 7 (2001–2002): 33–45.

———. "The Temple and the City in Liturgical Hebrew Poetry," in *The History of Jerusalem: The Early Islamic Period (638–1099)*. Edited by J. Prawer and H. Ben-Shammai. Jerusalem: Ben-Zvi Institute, 1996. 215–235.

———, and Joshua Blau. *The Wanderings of Judah al-Ḥarizi: Five Accounts of His Travels* [Hebrew]. Jerusalem: Ben-Zvi Institute, 2002.

Yerushalmi, Yosef Hayyim. "Exile and Expulsion in Jewish History," in *Crisis and Creativity in the Sephardic World, 1391–1648*. Edited by Benjamin R. Gampel. New York: Columbia University Press, 1997. 3–22.

———. "Medieval Jewry: From Within and from Without," in *Aspects of Jewish Culture in the Middle Ages*. Edited by Paul E. Szarmach. Albany: State University of New York Press, 1979. 1–26.

Yuval, Jacob. "Yitzhak Baer and the Search for Authentic Judaism," in *The Jewish Past Revisited: Reflections on Modern Jewish Historians*. Edited by David N. Myers and David R. Ruderman. New Haven, CT: Yale University Press, 1998. 77–87.

Zadeh, Travis. "From Drops of Blood: Charisma and Political Legitimacy in the Translation of the 'Uthmānic Codex of al-Andalus," *Journal of Arabic Literature* 39 (2008): 321–346.

Zafrani, Haïm. *Juifs d'Andalousie et du Maghreb.* Paris: Maisonneuve et Larose, 1996.
al-Zayyāt, 'Abd Allāh Muḥammad. *Rithā' l-mudun fī l-shi'r al-andalusī.* Benghazi: Manshūrāt jāmi'at qaryūns, 1990.
Zeitler, Jessica. "Legacy of Muslim Spain: The Construction of Networks, Knowledge, and *Convivencia*," in *Revisiting Convivencia in Medieval and Early Modern Iberia.* Edited by Connie L. Scarborough. Newark, DE: Juan de la Cuesta Hispanic Monographs, 2014. 61–76.
Zimmels, Hirsch Jacob. *Ashkenazim and Sephardim: Their Relations, Differences, and Problems as Reflected in the Rabbinical Responsa.* 3rd revised edition. Hoboken, NJ: Ktav, 1996.
Zohori, Menahem. *The Khazars, Their Conversion to Judaism and History in Hebrew Historiography* [Hebrew]. Jerusalem: Carmel, 2002.
Zulay, Menahem. "The Poem of Adonim Halevi of Fez" [Hebrew], *Sinai* 29 (1951): 24–37.
Zwiep, Irene E. *Mother of Reason and Revelation: A Short History of Medieval Jewish Linguistic Thought.* Amsterdam: J. C. Gieben, 1997.

Index

www.ingramcontent.com/pod-product-compliance
Lightning Source LLC
Chambersburg PA
CBHW030922150426
42812CB00046B/489
9780812252880